New perspectives on teaching and working with languages in the digital era

Edited by Antonio Pareja-Lora,
Cristina Calle-Martínez,
and Pilar Rodríguez-Arancón

Published by Research-publishing.net, not-for-profit association
Dublin, Ireland; Voillans, France, info@research-publishing.net

© 2016 by Antonio Pareja-Lora, Cristina Calle-Martínez, and Pilar Rodríguez-Arancón (collective work)
© 2016 by Authors (individual work)

New perspectives on teaching and working with languages in the digital era
Edited by Antonio Pareja-Lora, Cristina Calle-Martínez, Pilar Rodríguez-Arancón

Rights: All articles in this collection are published under the Attribution-NonCommercial -NoDerivatives 4.0 International (CC BY-NC-ND 4.0) licence. Under this licence, the contents are freely available online as PDF files (http://dx.doi.org/10.14705/rpnet.2016.tislid2014.9781908416353) for anybody to read, download, copy, and redistribute provided that the author(s), editorial team, and publisher are properly cited. Commercial use and derivative works are, however, not permitted.

Disclaimer: Research-publishing.net does not take any responsibility for the content of the pages written by the authors of this book. The authors have recognised that the work described was not published before, or that it was not under consideration for publication elsewhere. While the information in this book are believed to be true and accurate on the date of its going to press, neither the editorial team, nor the publisher can accept any legal responsibility for any errors or omissions that may be made. The publisher makes no warranty, expressed or implied, with respect to the material contained herein. While Research-publishing.net is committed to publishing works of integrity, the words are the authors' alone.

Trademark notice: product or corporate names may be trademarks or registered trademarks, and are used only for identification and explanation without intent to infringe.

Copyrighted material: every effort has been made by the editorial team to trace copyright holders and to obtain their permission for the use of copyrighted material in this book. In the event of errors or omissions, please notify the publisher of any corrections that will need to be incorporated in future editions of this book.

Typeset by Research-publishing.net
Cover design and frog picture by © Raphaël Savina (raphael@savina.net)

ISBN13: 978-1-908416-34-6 (Paperback - Print on demand, black and white)
Print on demand technology is a high-quality, innovative and ecological printing method, with which the book is never 'out of stock' or 'out of print'.

ISBN13: 978-1-908416-35-3 (Ebook, PDF, colour)
ISBN13: 978-1-908416-36-0 (Ebook, EPUB, colour)

Legal deposit, Ireland: The National Library of Ireland, The Library of Trinity College, The Library of the University of Limerick, The Library of Dublin City University, The Library of NUI Cork, The Library of NUI Maynooth, The Library of University College Dublin, The Library of NUI Galway.

Legal deposit, United Kingdom: The British Library.
British Library Cataloguing-in-Publication Data.
A cataloguing record for this book is available from the British Library.

Legal deposit, France: Bibliothèque Nationale de France - Dépôt légal: mai 2016.

Table of contents

viii   Acknowledgements

1   Applying information and communication technologies to language teaching and research: an overview
Antonio Pareja-Lora, Pilar Rodríguez-Arancón, and Cristina Calle-Martínez

Section 1.
General applications of ICTs to language teaching and learning

Section 1.1.
E-learning and languages in primary/secondary/tertiary education

27   Technology use in nursery and primary education in two different settings
Mª Camino Bueno Alastuey and Jesús García Laborda

39   How working collaboratively with technology can foster a creative learning environment
Susana Gómez

51   The e-generation: the use of technology for foreign language learning
Pilar Gonzalez-Vera

63   Evaluation of reading achievement of the program school 2.0 in Spain using PISA 2012
Cristina Vilaplana Prieto

73   Language learning actions in two 1x1 secondary schools in Catalonia: the case of online language resources
Boris Vázquez Calvo and Daniel Cassany

83   Innovative resources based on ICTs and authentic materials to improve EFL students' communicative needs
Rebeca González Otero

95 Teaching the use of WebQuests to master students
in Pablo de Olavide University
Regina Gutiérrez Pérez

105 ICTs, ESPs and ZPD through microlessons in teacher education
*Soraya García Esteban, Jesús García Laborda,
and Manuel Rábano Llamas*

Section 1.2.
Language distance, lifelong teaching and learning, and massive open online courses

117 Learning specialised vocabulary through Facebook
in a massive open online course
Patricia Ventura and Elena Martín-Monje

129 Identifying collaborative behaviours online: training teachers in wikis
Margarita Vinagre Laranjeira

141 The community as a source of pragmatic input for learners of Italian:
the multimedia repository LIRA
Greta Zanoni

153 Grammar processing through English L2 e-books:
distance vs. face-to-face learning
Mª Ángeles Escobar-Álvarez

Section 1.3.
Interaction design, usability and accessibility

163 A study of multimodal discourse in the design of interactive digital
material for language learning
Silvia Burset, Emma Bosch, and Joan-Tomàs Pujolà

173 Audiovisual translation and assistive technology:
towards a universal design approach for online education
Emmanouela Patiniotaki

Section 2.
New trends in the application of ICTs to language learning

Section 2.1.
Mobile-assisted language learning

189   Mobile learning: a powerful tool for ubiquitous language learning
Nelson Gomes, Sérgio Lopes, and Sílvia Araújo

201   Critical visual literacy: the new phase of applied linguistics in the era of mobile technology
Giselda Dos Santos Costa and Antonio Carlos Xavier

213   Virtual learning environments on the go: CALL meets MALL
Jorge Arús Hita

223   Exploring the application of a conceptual framework in a social MALL app
Timothy Read, Elena Bárcena, and Agnes Kukulska-Hulme

233   Design and implementation of BusinessApp, a MALL application to make successful business presentations
Cristina Calle-Martínez, Lourdes Pomposo Yanes, and Antonio Pareja-Lora

245   Using audio description to improve FLL students' oral competence in MALL: methodological preliminaries
Ana Ibáñez Moreno, Anna Vermeulen, and Maria Jordano

Section 2.2.
ICTs for content and language integrated learning

259   ICT in EMI programmes at tertiary level in Spain: a holistic model
Nuria Hernandez-Nanclares and Antonio Jimenez-Munoz

269   Vocabulary Notebook: a digital solution to general and specific vocabulary learning problems in a CLIL context
Plácido Bazo, Romén Rodríguez, and Dácil Fumero

Table of contents

Section 2.3.
Computerised language testing and assessment

283   Using tablet PC's for the final test of Baccalaureate
Jesús García Laborda and Teresa Magal Royo

293   The implications of business English mock exams
on language progress at higher education
Rocío González Romero

303   Assessing pragmatics: DCTs and retrospective verbal reports
Vicente Beltrán-Palanques

Section 3.
Applying computational linguistics and language resources to language teaching and learning

315   An updated account of the WISELAV project:
a visual construction of the English verb system
Andrés Palacios Pablos

327   Generating a Spanish affective dictionary
with supervised learning techniques
*Daniel Bermudez-Gonzalez, Sabino Miranda-Jiménez,
Raúl-Ulises García-Moreno, and Dora Calderón-Nepamuceno*

339   Transcription and annotation of a Japanese accented spoken corpus
of L2 Spanish for the development of CAPT applications
Mario Carranza

351   Using ontologies to interlink linguistic annotations
and improve their accuracy
Antonio Pareja-Lora

363   The importance of corpora in translation studies: a practical case
Montserrat Bermúdez Bausela

375 Using corpus management tools in public service translator training: an example of its application in the translation of judgments
María Del Mar Sánchez Ramos and Francisco J. Vigier Moreno

385 Integrating computer-assisted translation tools into language learning
María Fernández-Parra

397 Author index

Acknowledgements

The publication of this volume has been partly funded by the following grants and/or projects:

- the SO-CALL-ME project, Social Ontology-based Cognitively Augmented Language Learning Mobile Environment, financed by the Spanish Ministry of Science and Innovation (grant ref. FFI2011-29829);

- the eLITE-CM project, Edición Literaria Electrónica (Literary Electronic Publishing – grant ref. H2015/HUM-3426), evenly co-financed by

    (a) the R&D Task Programme for Social Sciences' and Humanities' research groups of the Comunidad de Madrid (Programa de Actividades de I+D entre grupos de investigación de la Comunidad de Madrid en Ciencias Sociales y Humanidades), and

    (b) the European Social Funds (European Commission) for the current programming period (2014-2020).

We would like to thank the ATLAS (UNED) research group as well, for their constant inspiration, encouragement and support, and also all the authors of the volume, for their wonderful contributions, their comprehension and their patience.

Antonio Pareja-Lora,
Cristina Calle-Martínez,
and Pilar Rodríguez-Arancón

1 Applying information and communication technologies to language teaching and research: an overview

Antonio Pareja-Lora[1], Pilar Rodríguez-Arancón[2], and Cristina Calle-Martínez[3]

Abstract

Currently, there is an international change in education that includes the development of new learning programmes and policies, such as (a) bilingual education programmes, (b) the Bologna process, with an emphasis on a more autonomous way of learning, or (c) the systematic evaluation and assessment of students and educational results. These changes in the educational situation require changing the way we learn, think and behave. Thus have emerged several new scenarios and environments for teaching and learning, such as blended learning, e-learning, ubiquitous learning or incidental learning. All these new approaches put the focus on learners and are intended to adapt to their needs and limitations. It seems that the easiest way to implement these new approaches is to apply Information and Communication Technologies (ICTs) to teaching and/or learning. This is the main assumption underlying the research in important language teaching and learning areas, such as Computer-Assisted Language Learning (CALL) and Mobile-Assisted Language Learning (MALL). This chapter (as well as this whole volume) tries to show how this goal is currently being achieved.

Keywords: language learning, language teaching, distance learning, autonomous learning, blended learning, ubiquitous learning, MALL, CLIL, LMOOCs.

1. Universidad Complutense de Madrid / ATLAS (UNED), Madrid, Spain; apareja@sip.ucm.es

2. ATLAS (UNED), Madrid, Spain; prodriguez@flog.uned.es

3. Universidad Complutense de Madrid / ATLAS (UNED), Madrid, Spain; cristinacalle@filol.ucm.es

How to cite this chapter: Pareja-Lora, A., Rodríguez-Arancón, P., & Calle-Martínez, C. (2016). Applying information and communication technologies to language teaching and research: an overview. In A. Pareja-Lora, C. Calle-Martínez, & P. Rodríguez-Arancón (Eds) *New perspectives on teaching and working with languages in the digital era* (pp. 1-22). Dublin: Research-publishing.net. http://dx.doi.org/10.14705/rpnet.2016.tislid2014.418

Chapter 1

1. Introduction and motivation

As shown by most theories and studies about evolution and adaptation, changes in habitat (or environment) entail mutations and other types of adaptations in nature and all its beings. This is also true for science, education, the human mind and behaviour: changes in our environment require modifying the way we learn, think and behave (Barkow, Cosmides, & Tooby, 1992).

Currently, there is an international change in education that includes the development of new learning programmes and policies, such as (a) bilingual education programmes (Thomas & Collier, 2012), including courses taught in a second language (usually English); (b) University programmes resulting from the implementation of the Bologna process and the European Higher Education Area, with an emphasis on a more autonomous way of learning (EHEA, 2010); (c) the systematic evaluation and assessment of students and educational results, such as PISA (Programme for International Student Assessment, OECD, 2014); and (d) the application of guidelines and recommendations in order to correct the problems in education identified by means of these evaluations and assessments.

This international shift in education has recently motivated the emergence of several new scenarios and environments for teaching and learning. Thus, we are witnesses to the transition from the traditional, pure (and opposed) face-to-face and distance approaches to teaching and learning to a whole new range of (mixed) ways of learning, such as blended learning, e-learning, ubiquitous learning, social learning, incidental learning, contextual learning, autonomous learning or lifelong learning. All these new approaches (discussed in the next chapters) put the focus on learners and are intended to adapt to their needs and limitations. In our days, for example, people do not have much time for learning, and it is often difficult for us to allocate a fixed moment in our schedules to attend courses (be they virtual or not).

This is the new scenario for education, and the way we teach and learn is adapting in accordance. Indeed, this new global education context requires some adaptations not only in the way we learn, but also in the way we teach and in the way we do educational research. An easy way to move ahead and adapt to this new education scenario is applying ICTs to teaching and/or learning. This is one of the main assumptions underlying many recent research advances in language teaching and learning, in particular in the areas of CALL, MALL, Content and Language Integrated Learning (CLIL), or Language Massive Open Online Courses (LMOOCs).

However, what are the real benefits of applying new technologies to teaching and/or learning? Are they actually also applicable to language teaching and learning? Are CALL, MALL, CLIL, LMOOCs, etc., as effective as traditional models of language teaching and/or learning? Do they really help language learners? Will language teachers and researchers (or learners) who fail to adapt and apply ICTs to language teaching and/or research (or use ICTs for language learning) be neglected and left aside?

The present volume tries to shed a light on these issues. For this reason, it has been divided into three different but fairly interrelated sections. The first aims at describing how information and language technologies are generally applied to language teaching and learning. Its different sections provide detailed information, for instance, about how ICTs are being used in the different levels of face-to-face language learning or in distance language learning and/or e-learning. The second section introduces some new trends in the application of ICTs to language learning, such as MALL or CLIL. Finally, the third section presents how language technologies, i.e. computational linguistics and language resources, are being applied to language teaching and learning.

2. General applications of ICTs to language teaching and learning

This section contains three different subsections, namely (a) E-learning and languages in primary/secondary/tertiary education, (b) Language distance, lifelong teaching and learning, and Massive Open Online Courses (MOOCs), and (c) Interaction design, usability and accessibility.

Chapter 1

The first subsection shows how ICTs are being used to enhance both face-to-face and distance language learning within the different levels of formal education. The second one explores how ICTS are being used in other contexts of language learning, mainly entailing autonomous and collaborative teaching or learning. In particular, this subsection shows how social networks and online collaboration are being used in order to learn languages. The third subsection discusses the importance of correctly designing and implementing the human-machine interfaces of language learning applications, so that they are user-friendly and/or accessible enough and, thus, do not diminish the motivation of language learners if they decide to use them.

2.1. E-learning and languages in primary/secondary/tertiary education

This subsection focuses on the new approaches to teaching that overcome barriers of distance, time and age. These new approaches provide broad opportunities for learning beyond the classroom, and also for more varied and deeper learning. These opportunities (a) include online interaction between the learner and their teacher or peers, and (b) show that e-learning is no longer associated just with distance learning, but is also about using relevant technologies. Thus, e-learning is an important part of a suite of approaches that aim at providing the best and most appropriate ways of supporting learners' engagement and achievement.

E-learning demands a deep change both in the teacher's role and the student's. The role of the teachers moves from transmitter of knowledge to guide or tutor of the learning process. Likewise, they acquire an elementary importance as designers of learning strategies and materials, creating conducive conditions for this purpose. On the other hand, students move to channel their own process of learning, relying on the teacher and classmates to achieve their objectives.

One of the most important disadvantages of e-learning is a major abandonment of the students. Carrying out a successful learning process requires fulfilling a series of conditions. The motivation of the students, their level of responsibility and autonomy are key factors. Moreover, the importance of quality digital materials and the design of contexts and appropriate methodologies to accomplish learning, as well as a proper and efficient tutoring of students, are essential elements. There are a wide variety of e-learning activities, which range, for instance, from using short digital videos in the classroom to programming an online course via the Internet.

In this regard, **Mª Camino Bueno Alastuey** and **Jesús García Laborda** in their article *"Technology use in nursery and primary education in two different settings"*, explore the use of ICTs in several schools of two provinces in Spain: Madrid and Navarre. The authors describe the applications and programs used in nursery and primary education and compare the frequency of use in both provinces. In line with other similar works in the area, the results show a lower than expected use of ICTs in education.

Susana Gómez, in *"How working collaboratively with technology can foster a creative learning environment"*, details the results of an experience funded by the European Union within the project PopuLLar. In this experience, music and ICTs are combined; schoolchildren worked autonomously and collaboratively in order to create lyrics for songs of their choice in their L2. They sang their songs, recorded them and uploaded their creations to a wiki. Children from other countries later translated those songs from the L2 to their L1. The conclusions of the piloting (both local and large-scale) were very positive and went beyond the expectations of the researchers involved. Excellent feedback was received from all participants in the project, due to its humanistic approach to teamwork and creativity.

In the next article, *"The e-generation: the use of technology for foreign language learning"*, **Pilar Gonzalez-Vera** explores how e-learning platforms and new technologies have contributed to the process of learning languages in first year students of primary education. The research has been carried out through some questionnaires, at the beginning and at the end of the course, to assess the role of ICTs and the improvement of the students' skills and competences. The results demonstrate the positive effects of the use of new technologies in education as well as a positive reaction among students towards technology.

Then, **Cristina Vilaplana Prieto**, in her article "*Evaluation of reading achievement of the program school 2.0 in Spain using PISA 2012*", analyses which part of the variation in reading scores is due to the Program School 2.0 implemented in some Spanish regions, which has the aim of introducing digital methodologies at schools. To this end, the author used data from PISA (2009 and 2012) for 15-year old students attending public schools. The results show that the increase in the provision of computers has different effects over reading scores based on the teaching methodology applied.

Boris Vázquez Calvo and **Daniel Cassany**, in their article "*Language learning actions in two 1x1 secondary schools in Catalonia: the case of online language resources*", provide details on the prevailing project Educat1x1, focusing on practices carried out by six language teachers of Catalan, Spanish and English and twelve students from two schools. They seek to provide information about (a) the attitudes of teachers and students towards classroom digitisation, (b) language learning practices led by teachers and students when in a digitised classroom, and (c) the online language resources used and their purpose. Three preliminary conclusions can be extracted from this research: first, School 2.0 and OLPC (one-laptop-per-child) programs are not a guarantee for success; second, individual teachers make change happen, and not technology in itself; and finally, Online Language Resources (OLRs) remain unknown and poorly taught.

Rebeca González Otero, in her article "*Innovative resources based on ICTs and authentic materials to improve EFL students' communicative needs*", reflects on English as a Foreign Language (EFL) students' communicative needs and the development of their oral skills through the use of authentic materials and ICTs in the classroom. She carried out her study on three secondary schools in Madrid, focusing specifically on students who attend a subject whose aim is to improve their oral skills. To this end, the author developed a set of innovative resources designed to check whether these materials promote students' oral skills. Her research has shown that innovative materials based on ICTs provide great results in Teaching English to Speakers of Other Languages (TESOL).

Regina Gutiérrez Pérez, in her article "*Teaching the use of WebQuests to master students in Pablo de Olavide University*", shows the aims and results of the implementation of the use of WebQuest in the module of foreign languages into the "*Máster de enseñanza de profesorado de educación secundaria obligatoria y bachillerato, formación profesional y enseñanza de idiomas*" (Teacher Training and Language Teaching Degree). In so doing, she proposes blended and cooperative learning through the use of this educational resource in order to support autonomous learning. The result of the study is positive, as this tool can help teachers include the Internet into their programs in addition to creating motivating activities.

The first part ends with the study "*ICTs, ESPs and ZPD through microlessons in teacher education*", from **Soraya García Esteban, Jesús García Laborda** and **Manuel Rábano Llamas**, which seeks to enhance English for Specific Purposes (ESP) learning as well as a Zone of Proximal Development (ZPD) interaction with technology through microteaching in teacher education. In this light, the authors explore how ICTs can be used in these frameworks in three different educational ways: (a) as a support (video) for analysis through teacher-instructor interaction, (b) as means of social interaction and use of language for education between teacher and students, and (c) for the creation of their own designed materials for language training. The results obtained show that the use of technology through microlessons is positive not only as a training technique, but also to introduce new content.

2.2. Language distance, lifelong teaching and learning, and MOOCs

Distance learning offers flexibility, as the student determines when and how much time to dedicate to a course. It fosters learner autonomy and can cater for multiple intelligences. Thus, it is a very useful setting in lifelong learning and teaching, as the students can have other work or family commitments to fulfill during the day, and spend their free time learning or improving other skills without the need for total dedication.

One of the most recent formats of distance and/or lifelong learning and teaching are MOOCs. MOOCs are a new model of online education that appeared and immediately spread in 2011 (Conole, 2013; Yuan & Powell, 2013). They are a natural evolution of social network based learning and, thus, also constitute a new type of Open Educational Resources (OERs, cf. Read & Rodrigo, 2014).

Hence, MOOCs are closely related to distance learning education, technology and innovation. They are centered on a topic, and its language-related variant (i.e. LMOOCs) are an ideal setting for language learning. Learners benefit from practicing the L2 and having immediate feedback from the many students enrolled. The open nature of an LMOOC means that the contents can be very varied and adapted to the specific needs of any particular program. They are also suitable for Lifelong Learning, as they provide open access to content in many fields of study. LMOOCs are a very 'democratic' way to learn languages, as anyone can create a topic of discussion.

However, any of these types of education suffers from similar disadvantages: a high dropout rate, the feeling of isolation on the part of the students, the difficulties they encounter to keep their motivation levels up, etc. Social networks are starting to be present in these courses and seem to provide a more 'human touch' to the use of technologies to learn. This topic is present in several articles of this section of the volume, and is specifically researched in the first one within a MOOC course.

There are also three other papers describing research in distance education. The second addresses the need to foster collaborative behaviour in a group of in-service teachers and, although the outcome of the experience was not totally positive, it highlighted the features that make good collaborative practice. If the students feel isolated from the group, they stop taking part, as social interaction was the driving force behind the tasks. The third paper again points out the enriching motivational qualities of the social dimension of a course.

The last paper presents an investigation into the features that make an electronic textbook more useful for learners. It is clear that if a textbook is designed bearing in mind its future audience it can provide activities that can make the student feel in control of the learning process, such as by adding the possibility of including learner generated examples.

Thus, **Patricia Ventura** and **Elena Martín-Monje** author "*Learning specialised vocabulary through Facebook in a massive open online course*". Their paper explores the inclusion of social networks in MOOCs in order to improve the learning experience of Professional English-related vocabulary. The results of the experience are rather positive, as participants believe that they learnt more by benefitting from the added presence of Facebook in their course. Moreover, although this is part of ongoing research, it seems clear that this inclusion partially solves the problems associated with this type of course, with a lower than average dropout rate among Facebook participants.

Margarita Vinagre Laranjeira offers in "*Identifying collaborative behaviours online: training teachers in wikis*" the results of a training program of in-service teachers in collaborative tasks. The conclusions of the experience were not very positive; however, the author pinpoints the features that were relevant to those teachers who were successful collaborators: (a) they gave priority to social interaction over finishing the tasks; and (b) collaborative groups regularly discussed topics, made relevant contributions and were prompt in their communication.

Greta Zanoni points out, in her paper called "*The community as a source of pragmatic input for learners of Italian: the multimedia repository LIRA*", the usefulness of a repository of multimedia materials to help Italian speakers living abroad develop or recover their linguistic and pragmatic competences. The paper highlights the motivation that can be fostered by the social dimension of e-learning in deepening socio-cultural knowledge.

Mª Ángeles Escobar-Álvarez highlights in "*Grammar processing through English L2 e-books: distance vs. face-to-face learning*" the choice between the use of printed and e-textbooks, depending on the type of educational setting (whether distance or face-to-face). As most students seem to prefer the printed version of textbooks, the author concludes the paper with some interesting points to take into account when designing materials for electronic dissemination.

2.3. Interaction design, usability and accessibility

As shown all throughout this volume, lately, many language learning activities are taking place on different types of computers (PCs, laptops, etc.) and more recently on mobile devices (tablet PCs, smartphones, etc.). Thus, devices that had not been originally designed for educational purposes are being used in an educational setting. In addition, the new MALL apps that are being launched for smartphones present some problems for certain target groups, such as people with complex communication needs or even some disabled users. As a result, the level of usability and/or accessibility (i.e. usability from a disabled person's perspective) of these devices is often lower than desired. This is a clear setback if they are to be used at a greater scale for inclusive learning (Jordano de la Torre, Pareja-Lora, Read, & Rodrigo San Juan, 2013).

As also pointed out by these authors, one of the problems of usability and accessibility is that they are frequently defined in overly brief and ambiguous terms (see, for example, ISO/IEC, 2011). Accordingly, more comprehensive and precise definitions of usability, accessibility and their basic attributes and indicators are needed. This is particularly true when dealing more specifically with mobile device usability in education, where it is not possible to characterise the whole range of user experiences that comprises many different technologies, contexts of use, study modes and learning objectives (Jordano de la Torre et al., 2013).

Silvia Burset, **Emma Bosch**, and **Joan-Tomàs Pujolà** partly fulfil this need in their article "*A study of multimodal discourse in the design of interactive digital material for language learning*". They provide some interesting criteria that can be used to analyse and assess the usability and the 'clarity of contents' of language learning applications. These criteria focus on the screen design of learning applications, such as (a) the shape, colour, size, resolution, or significance of their graphic elements; and (b) their screen typography or composition. They also discuss the way in which these features of multimodal discourse can influence the language learning processes.

Then, **Emmanouela Patiniotaki** explains in *"Audiovisual translation and assistive technology: towards a universal design approach for online education"* how the fields of audiovisual translation and assistive technology are rarely studied together, although they share many common features. The paper concludes that the future of online education is bright and, therefore, there is a need for universally accessible materials and whole educational contexts on the web.

3. New trends in the application of ICTs to language learning

This section includes three subsections, namely (a) MALL, (b) ICTs for CLIL, and (c) Computerised language testing and assessment. All these subsections present some examples of application of ICTs to some new purposes or within a recently created scenario or teaching/learning modality. The first one describes how language learning can be enhanced by the use of mobile devices and/ or specific language learning mobile apps, within both distance learning and blended learning. The second one deals with a setting of language learning that is becoming more and more frequent, CLIL, in particular in Spain, with the advent of bilingual learning programmes. The articles of the third one explore how ICTs can be applied to automatically evaluate the results of language learning and/or teaching.

3.1. MALL

MALL is a new learning modality that uses mobile devices as a medium to teach and/or to learn languages. As described in Calle-Martínez, Pomposo Yanes, and Pareja-Lora (2016, this volume), mobile devices allow for an almost ubiquitous web access and, hence, make MALL most suitable for today's language learners, who usually combine their learning tasks with other multiple activities, such as work or child care. These new learners usually learn 'anytime, anywhere'. This is yet another learning modality, referred to as ubiquitous learning (Kukulska-Hulme, 2012; Peng, Su, Chou, & Tsai, 2009), and usually implied by MALL.

Mobile apps for language learning probably are the main outcome of MALL. MALL apps are, together with LMOOCs, the main elements that enable not only ubiquitous, but also blended learning (Bueno-Alastuey & López Pérez, 2013) nowadays.

However, as also shown by Calle-Martínez et al. (2016, this volume), whereas (L)MOOCs are more adequate to present theoretical content, apps are more suitable not only for this, but also to practice what has been or is being learnt, since they are usually more interactive and less restricted than LMOOCs.

Accordingly, we present in this section a selection of MALL apps, which provide altogether a nice survey on the state of the art in MALL app development and its related technologies. This MALL section begins with an article by **Nelson Gomes**, **Sérgio Lopes**, and **Sílvia Araújo**, who write in "*Mobile learning: a powerful tool for ubiquitous language learning*" about ongoing research on the use of mobile devices as tools for language learning. The authors, together with other IT experts, have created an app for Portuguese language teachers and learners. This app can be used for the creation of content to teach and test all the different skills by using the templates provided. Although the project is still in process, the authors hope to foster standardisation in online teaching and to encourage teachers to work together and share materials.

Next, **Giselda Dos Santos Costa** and **Antonio Carlos Xavier** show in "*Critical visual literacy: the new phase of applied linguistics in the era of mobile technology*" that, although our society lives surrounded by visual information, there is still a significant lack of visual literacy. They describe a classroom activity to foster this skill and conclude that their critical approach helped the students to decode visual meanings. The authors consider critical visual literacy as a fifth linguistic skill in L2 learning.

The following four articles describe four pieces of research (and/or MALL apps) that belong in the SO-CALL-ME project, whose final aim is to design and create EFL mobile apps by applying a solid pedagogy to teaching technical and language skills.

First, **Jorge Arús Hita**, in his article *"Virtual learning environments on the go: CALL meets MALL"*, presents *Eating out*, a tool that he and other authors have developed for EFL teaching. *Eating out* is a Moodle-based digital learning resource that can be run both on computers and mobile devices. This is one of its main advantages. However, its main contribution to the area may possibly be that it has been developed using "a carefully planned methodology and a well-grounded theoretical basis for the explanation of lexicogrammatical issues" (this volume, p. 213). As the author shows in his paper, *Eating out* has already been tested by University students with quite outstanding results.

Second, the use of a sound theoretical framework and/or basis in the development of MALL apps is further discussed in the article *"Exploring the application of a conceptual framework in a social MALL app"*, written by **Timothy Read, Elena Bárcena**, and **Agnes Kukulska-Hulme**. This article presents Audio News Trainer (ANT), a first prototype of a social MALL app, based on Kukulska-Hulme's (2012) conceptual framework. This framework postulates that time, place and activity type are the three axes around which the development of MALL apps should revolve. Thus, the article (a) describes how this framework has been used to create ANT, which aims at developing oral and written competences in a mixed individual-social modality; and (b) presents the formal features and functionality of this app.

Third, *"Design and implementation of BusinessApp, a MALL application to make successful business presentations"* also provides insight into the methodological aspects of app development; however, in this case, **Cristina Calle-Martínez, Lourdes Pomposo Yanes**, and **Antonio Pareja-Lora** focus not only on the pedagogical and/or linguistic aspect, but also on a Software Engineering perspective. They present *BusinessApp*, a MALL app that they have developed following this hybrid methodological approach, (a) to help its users create and perform successful business presentations in English; and, in general, (b) to improve their oral and communication skills in this language. Another main contribution of *BusinessApp* is that it enables autonomous learning by means of self-evaluation (automatically-corrected) exercises.

Finally, the article "*Using audio description to improve EFL students' oral competence in MALL: methodological preliminaries*", whose authors are **Ana Ibáñez Moreno**, **Anna Vermeulen** and **Maria Jordano**, presents the methodological steps taken to develop a MALL app prototype (VISP v1), which aims to help B1 English language learners to use their oral skills, especially speaking. This app uses audio description (which is normally used to describe orally visual information in the gaps between dialogues for accessibility reasons) as a tool to promote oral production skills by means of mobile devices (Android smart phones).

3.2. ICTs for CLIL

CLIL is a learning environment that aims at teaching subjects of the curriculum by using an L2 as the vehicular language. It promotes intercultural communicative competence, computer literacy and lifelong learning skills, as well as multidisciplinary learning and positive attitudes and acceptance towards other languages and other ways of life.

This holistic approach to teaching is not without its problems, as its fast development requires materials designed for this purpose and not simply translated from the L1 to the L2. Unfortunately, this is not always the case, and teachers find themselves with the extra task of adapting and creating activities for their classes.

The papers presented in this section of the volume address some of the needs in the field: students entering tertiary CLIL education without the necessary previous foundations in the L2, and the difficulties related to specific area vocabulary acquisition. Students can greatly improve their level of L2 at university level through a combination of ICT methods used in and out of the classroom. Vocabulary acquisition can be made easier through the use of software specially designed for this task, which (a) can replace the old hand-written notebooks, and (b) free some of the time that area teachers used to devote to teaching words and expressions and dedicate it to putting them into practice.

Nuria Hernandez-Nanclares and **Antonio Jimenez-Munoz** address in *"ICT in EMI programmes at tertiary level in Spain: a holistic model"* the problems that are experienced when universities offer degrees taught through English to students whose secondary education has not prepared them for such events. They present a holistic model for ICT-supported learning, which combines CLIL blended learning (i.e. a combination of distance and face-to-face learning), social networks and micro-blogging, among other tools, in order to help students to improve their performance. Their conclusions are that the use of one single element of the previous ICT forms does not result in better learning outcomes, and that only an integrated holistic method combining several in-class practices improves students' performance.

Plácido Bazo, Romén Rodríguez and **Dácil Fumero** highlight in *"Vocabulary Notebook: a digital solution to general and specific vocabulary learning problems in a CLIL context"* the advantages of the use of this digital tool and its features. They conclude that Vocabulary Notebook helps the teacher to devote more time to practicing the vocabulary as it frees the time taken by teaching it. This tool (a) stores the information compiled by the student in the cloud, (b) can organise words and expressions according to different criteria, and (c) has specific functionalities for teachers.

3.3. Computerised language testing and assessment

The success of most of the approaches to language learning mentioned above (e.g. distance learning, lifelong learning, autonomous learning, blended learning and ubiquitous learning) requires defining convenient and effective

Chapter 1

ways to test and assess language learners' knowledge improvement and skill development advances. On the one hand, this entails including self-evaluation (and automatically-corrected) activities in distance learning modules and MALL apps, as pointed out by Calle-Martínez et al. (2016, this volume). These self-evaluation activities should help (a) keep learners motivated, and (b) provide the learning system with information to further guide and/or tutor the learning process by proposing some additional scaffolding activities. On the other hand, as pointed out by García Laborda and Magal Royo (2016, this volume), the use of computerised language testing is becoming urgent in massive education scenarios, where "[o]nline testing is becoming a popular way to deliver language tests, partly because of its reduced cost, partly because of the high quality of test data collection" (p. 283).

Accordingly, in this subsection, we have included three articles dealing with computerised approaches to language testing and assessment. These articles (together with Pareja-Lora (2016, this volume), who presents an extreme computational linguistic approach to this issue) also provide an overview of the different problems that these approaches have to face and how to (partially) solve them.

The first article is entitled "*Using tablet PC's for the final test of Baccalaureate*", and has been authored by **Jesús García Laborda** and **Teresa Magal Royo**. This piece of writing introduces OPENPAU, a tablet PC app developed by the authors for assessing both productive and receptive skills in foreign languages for its prospective use in the final test of the Baccalaureate. The main contribution of this article is that it offers reliable, simple and effective solutions at a low cost for the needs of a nationally delivered online test, which can serve to assess all the traditional language skills.

The second one, namely "*The implications of business English mock exams on language progress at higher education*" **by Rocío González Romero**, provides an application of computerised language testing within a particular language teaching and learning area, namely Business English. The goal of the research presented in this article was to evaluate and describe the impact of taking mock exams on learners' foreign language progress. Thus, an experiment was conducted with adult participants taking online Business English as a compulsory subject of their degree in Economics. The results of this experiment (a) verify the benefits of mock exams as scaffolding activities to foster language learning, and (b) indicate that "these types of activities promote outstanding final grades as well as prove to be an effective way of engaging students in learning tasks" (this volume, p. 301).

Finally, **Vicente Beltrán-Palanques**, in the third article of this section, "*Assessing pragmatics: DCTs and retrospective verbal reports*", discusses the use of a communication tool, namely *Skype*, in conjunction with two different research methodologies (DCTs, i.e. discourse completion tests/tasks, and verbal reports) in order to investigate the cognitive processes undertaken by a group of English language learners as regards their pragmatic performance. This study shows that retrospective verbal reports are instrumental in providing further information concerning participants' speech act production.

4. Applying computational linguistics and language resources to language teaching and learning

Computational linguistics can be roughly defined as the particular area of linguistics in which languages and/or language resources are created, generated, enriched, analysed, processed and/or managed digitally and/or automatically. A language resource, in turn, can be defined as a component that models, processes and/or manages some language(s) or some language or linguistic metadata and/or phenomena. Typical and well-known examples of language resources are corpora, digital dictionaries and computational lexicons, as well as the tools to manage and process languages in general or these other language resources (e.g. applications for linguistic annotation or computer aided translation tools). Computational linguistics is already a consolidated research and development area, with well known applications, like machine translation, speech recognition and generation, or information retrieval and extraction.

Chapter 1

This section includes seven different articles that provide seven quite particular examples of the applications of computational linguistics to language learning and teaching. Whereas some of them aim at developing a particular language resource (for instance, an application to store and display English verb graphical representations or an affective dictionary for Spanish), some others apply language resources and/or computational linguistics techniques (such as machine learning or Part-Of-Speech (POS) taggers) to (a) solve a particular problem in language teaching and/or learning applications, or (b) to create new useful resources for this area.

In the first article, *"An updated account of the WISELAV project: a visual construction of the English verb system"*, **Andrés Palacios Pablos** provides a summary of the work carried out in the WISELAV ongoing project. WISELAV offers a visual interpretation of English verbs through colours and shapes. This software is becoming more user-friendly and illustrates operational aspects of verbs in order to produce grammatical forms and meanings. The computer program has been designed as a support with the aim of helping students to improve their grammar by detecting and showing the mistakes made.

The second one, *"Generating a Spanish affective dictionary with supervised learning techniques"*, written by **Daniel Bermudez-Gonzalez**, **Sabino Miranda-Jiménez**, **Raúl-Ulises García-Moreno**, and **Dora Calderón-Nepamuceno**, shows some research on combining several machine learning techniques (decision trees, naive Bayes, and a support vector machine) to develop a particular language resource for Spanish, namely an affective dictionary for this language. This affective dictionary will be used later on to analyse and determine the affective orientation of texts, that is, for opinion mining and sentiment analysis. The resulting lexicon has 30,773 words, classified as positive or negative words, and has an acceptable quality (precision=67.0%), especially when compared with the quality of other similar lexicons.

The third one, *"Transcription and annotation of a Japanese accented spoken corpus of L2 Spanish for the development of CAPT applications"*, by **Mario**

Carranza, describes some research aiming at compiling a training corpus for the development of Computer Assisted Pronunciation Training (CAPT) applications. Towards this end, a longitudinal non-native spoken corpus of L2 Spanish by Japanese speakers was (a) collected, (b) fully transcribed at both phonological and phonetic levels, and (c) annotated at error level. This error annotation was statistically analysed in order to evaluate the influence of oral proficiency, speaking style and L2 exposition in pronunciation accuracy. The results of this analysis show that (a) only the starting oral proficiency level of the student has an attested positive impact on Spanish pronunciation acquisition, and (b) in general, exposure to the target language is not enough to expect pronunciation accuracy improvement in foreign language learners.

The fourth one, "*Using ontologies to interlink linguistic annotations and improve their accuracy*", whose author is **Antonio Pareja-Lora**, proposes to reuse natural language annotation and/or analysis tools in order to include mistake and exercise automatic correction in language learning applications. The main problems that prevent these tools from being reused for these purposes are that (a) they usually provide annotations with a much too high error rate, and (b) they are hardly interoperable. Thus, this work also proposes to use a structured software architecture to combine the annotation of several tools, both ontology and standards-based, in order to solve these problems. The article concludes with showing the impressive results obtained in an experiment that implemented this architecture to reduce the POS tagging error rate for Spanish by combining the annotations of three different POS taggers for this language. These results should allow the inclusion of these technologies before long in learning applications for the purposes aforementioned.

The fifth, sixth and seventh articles show the close relation between (a) computational linguistics and/or language resources, (b) translation, and (c) language teaching and/or learning. On the one hand, the fifth and sixth papers feature two applications of language resources (namely corpora and corpora management tools) to Translation Studies; on the other hand, the seventh article shows how Computer-Assisted Translation (CAT) tools can be reused and retargeted for language learning purposes.

Chapter 1

Thus, in the fifth article, "*The importance of corpora in translation studies: a practical case*", **Montserrat Bermúdez Bausela** presents how another type of language resource, so-called 'ad hoc corpora' or 'translator's corpora' can be used in Translation Studies as a working tool both in the classroom and for the professional translator. Indeed, corpora can be "an inestimable source [...] for terminology and phraseology extraction" (this volume, p. 363). The main challenge and contribution of this work is showing how this other type of corpora can be applied to help students acquire and develop their own competence in translation.

The sixth article in this section is "*Using corpus management tools in public service translator training: an example of its application in the translation of judgments*", by **María Del Mar Sánchez Ramos** and **Francisco J. Vigier Moreno**. This article presents how monolingual virtual corpora and corpus management tools (e.g. concordance software) are being used for teaching within a particular domain of Translation Studies, commonly referred to as Public Service Interpreting and Translation (PSIT). PSIT deals mainly with the legal translation of the documents most commonly used in criminal proceedings and, accordingly, is intended to help trainees to develop their legal translation competence and, fundamentally, on the rendering of a text which is both valid in legal terms and comprehensible to the final reader. As shown in the article, these language technologies really help translation students acquire both subject field knowledge and linguistic knowledge, such as terminology, collocations, phraseology, style and register.

The last article, written by **María Fernández-Parra**, "*Integrating computer-assisted translation tools into language learning*", describes how to use CAT tools not only within the translation curriculum, but also within the foreign language learning curriculum, as additional language learning tools, especially in universities or schools where CAT tools are already part of the curriculum. The article shows that, in effect, CAT tools can co-exist with other methods already used in language learning, and contribute to enhance the language learning experience.

5. Conclusions

To sum up, this volume tries to show how new and emerging approaches to teaching and learning (such as blended learning, e-learning, ubiquitous learning or incidental learning) can be successfully implemented within language teaching and/or learning by means of the application of ICTs. In fact, this is the main assumption underlying the research in important language teaching and learning areas, such as CALL, MALL, CLIL or LMOOCs.

We also (a) show how information and language technologies are generally applied to language teaching and learning, (b) introduce some new trends in the application of ICTs to language learning (MALL, CLIL, etc.), and (c) present how language technologies (i.e. computational linguistics and language resources) are being applied to language teaching and learning.

References

Barkow, J. H., Cosmides, L., & Tooby, J. (Eds.). (1992). *The adapted mind: evolutionary psychology and the generation of culture*. New York, NY: Oxford University Press.

Bueno-Alastuey, M. C., & López Pérez, M. V. (2013). Evaluation of a blended learning language course: students' perceptions of appropriateness for the development of skills and language areas. *Computer Assisted Language Learning, 2013(1)*, 1-19.

Calle-Martínez, C., Pomposo Yanes, L., & Pareja-Lora, A. (2016). Design and implementation of BusinessApp, a MALL application to make successful business presentations. In A. Pareja-Lora, C. Calle-Martínez, & P. Rodríguez-Arancón (Eds), *New perspectives on teaching and working with languages in the digital era* (pp. 233-243). Dublin: Research-publishing.net. Retrieved from http://dx.doi.org/10.14705/rpnet.2016.tislid2014.437

Conole, G. (2013). Los MOOCs como tecnologías disuptivas: estrategias para mejorar la experiencia de aprendizaje y la calidad de los MOOCs. In *Campus Virtuales 2, v. II*.

EHEA. (2010). *Bologna process – European higher education area*. Retrieved from the Romanian Bologna Secretariat website: http://www.ehea.info/article-details.aspx?ArticleId=73

García Laborda, J., & Magal Royo, T. (2016). Using tablet PC's for the final test of Baccalaureate. In A. Pareja-Lora, C. Calle-Martínez, & P. Rodríguez-Arancón (Eds), *New perspectives on teaching and working with languages in the digital era* (pp. 283-292). Dublin: Research-publishing.net. Retrieved from http://dx.doi.org/10.14705/rpnet.2016.tislid2014.441

ISO/IEC. (2011). ISO/IEC 25010:2011: Systems and software engineering – Systems and software Quality Requirements and Evaluation (SQuaRE) – System and software quality models. *International Organization for Standardization*. Retrieved from http://www.iso.org/iso/catalogue_detail.htm?csnumber=35733

Jordano de la Torre, M., Pareja-Lora, A., Read, T., & Rodrigo San Juan, C. (2013). The design of accessible mobile and ontology-based applications for ubiquitous foreign language learning. In *Proceedings of the UNED – ICDE International Conference* (pp. 1-14). Madrid, Spain.

Kukulska-Hulme, A. (2012). Language learning defined by time and place: a framework for next generation designs. In J. E. Díaz-Vera (Ed.), *Left to my own devices: learner autonomy and mobile assisted language learning. Innovation and leadership in English language teaching, 6* (pp. 1–13). Bingley, UK: Emerald Group Publishing Limited. Retrieved from http://dx.doi.org/10.1163/9781780526478_002

OECD. (2014). Key findings – PISA 2012 results. *Organisation for Economic Co-operation and Development*. Retrieved from http://www.oecd.org/pisa/keyfindings/pisa-2012-results.htm

Pareja-Lora, A. (2016). Using ontologies to interlink linguistic annotations and improve their accuracy. In A. Pareja-Lora, C. Calle-Martínez, & P. Rodríguez-Arancón (Eds), *New perspectives on teaching and working with languages in the digital era* (pp. 351-362). Dublin: Research-publishing.net. Retrieved from http://dx.doi.org/10.14705/rpnet.2016.tislid2014.447

Peng, H., Su, Y. J., Chou, C., & Tsai, C. (2009). Ubiquitous knowledge construction: mobile learning re-defined and a conceptual framework. *Innovations in Education Technology, 46*(2), 171-183. Retrieved from http://dx.doi.org/10.1080/14703290902843828

Read, T., & Rodrigo, C. (2014). Towards a quality model for UNED MOOCs. In *Proceedings of the European MOOC Stakeholder Summit 2014* (pp. 282-287). Retrieved from http://emoocs2014.eu/sites/default/files/Proceedings-Moocs-Summit-2014.pdf

Thomas, W. P., & Collier, V. P. (2012). *Dual language education for a transformed world*. Albuquerque, NM: Dual Language Education of New Mexico – Fuente Press.

Yuan, L., & Powell, S. (2013). MOOCs and disruptive innovation: implications for higher education. *eLearning Papers, In-depth 33*(2), 1-7.

Section 1.
General applications of ICTs to language teaching and learning

Section 1.1.

E-learning and languages
in primary/secondary/tertiary education

# Technology use in nursery and primary education in two different settings

Mª Camino Bueno Alastuey[1] and Jesús García Laborda[2]

Abstract

This article studies which and how Information and Communications Technologies (ICTs) are used by nursery and primary education in-service teachers as reported by their pre-service teacher trainees after observations in their practicum in two provinces in Spain, Alcalá de Henares-Guadalajara and Navarre. Results indicate that in-service teachers tend to use traditional technological tools (audio files, video files, multimedia, games, Microsoft Word, interactive whiteboards) more than social networking (Facebook, blogs or wikis) both for teaching and for organisational purposes. Thus, more training in recent applications seems necessary to get ICT social applications into education.

Keywords: ICT, teachers, pre-service, pre-school, social networking.

1. Introduction

The great investment carried out to introduce ICTs in schools and the fact that young people seem to be technologically savvy has resulted in the assumption that the use of computers and technological tools has increased in education. However, research has started to point out that ICTs are not used as extensively as assumed (Almerich, Suárez, Jornet, & Orellana, 2011), and this lack of usage

---

1. Universidad Pública de Navarra, Pamplona, Spain; camino.bueno@unavarra.es

2. Universidad de Alcalá, Alcalá de Henares, Madrid, Spain; jesus.garcialaborda@uah.es

How to cite this chapter: Bueno Alastuey, M. C, & García Laborda, J. (2016). Technology use in nursery and primary education in two different settings. In A. Pareja-Lora, C. Calle-Martínez, & P. Rodríguez-Arancón (Eds), *New perspectives on teaching and working with languages in the digital era* (pp. 27-37). Dublin: Research-publishing.net. http://dx.doi.org/10.14705/rpnet.2016.tislid2014.419

should be further explored as technological tools can improve students' learning experience, and pre-service teachers need to be provided in their training period with knowledge on how to use technology effectively.

In order to do so, this paper compares the use of ICT in the schools of two provinces in Spain (Navarre and Madrid) to describe which applications and programmes are used in nursery and primary education and their frequency of use, and to report any divergence in usage between these two provinces.

2. Literature review

The use of ICT tools has been shown to have many educational benefits (García-Valcárcel, Basilotta, & López, 2014), and thus research has investigated students' and teachers' ICT use in different contexts and settings to report frequency of use and perceived advantages and disadvantages associated to such usage.

Students' preferences and perceived benefits regarding the use of computers and ICT tools have been documented at university (Conole, 2008; Steel & Levy, 2013) and secondary levels (Purcell, Heaps, Buchanan, & Friedrich, 2013). Students' perceptions of ICT integration and use have also been compared to their teachers' showing some divergence between what teachers think is effective and what learners consider to be so (Wiebe & Kabata, 2010).

Teachers' usage of ICT has also been reported both at university and secondary school levels, but mostly based on self-reports (Georgina & Olson, 2008) and case studies (Romero, Cervera, & Farran, 2009). This research may offer a limited view as the former may be biased by what is considered appropriate and thus report subjectively on perceived usage, and the latter are mostly based on observations of voluntaries with a good knowledge base and attitude towards ICT, which may not be representative of the general population of in-service teachers.

Research on ICT use and level of integration into the curriculum has stressed the importance of pre-service training in Computer-Assisted Language Learning (CALL) (Yunus, 2007) to increase trainees' awareness of the affordances and constraints of technological tools, and to raise teachers' self-confidence to improve and increase technological tools usage (Dooly, 2009; Georgina & Olson, 2008).

Despite all the research regarding the technological tools currently used in education, there is a lack of studies about ICT usage in nursery and primary education, and no report based on third party observations of in-service teachers' actual use in the classroom. Our project tries to fill this gap in research by exploring the technological tools used in these levels in two different settings in Spain. The usage reported is based on pre-service teacher trainees' observations of their tutors' (in-service teachers) ICT use for teaching and for managerial purposes.

3. Method

Our research project was carried out in two provinces in Spain: Madrid and Navarre. The schools where the participants did their practicum provided immersion programs in two languages (44.6% of the schools in Madrid; 51% in Navarre), or monolingual Spanish programs with English as a foreign language (44.6% in Madrid; 21% in Navarre). Most schools were state schools (79.6 % in Madrid; 87.8% in Navarre) located both in the city and suburbs around the city (38.8%), or outside the city (42.7%) in the first setting, and in the city and in the suburbs around the city (90%) in the second setting.

The participants were 142 pre-service primary and nursery teachers (103 from Madrid; 39 from Navarre), who answered a survey after their practicum period (ranging from seven to eight weeks) in the afore-mentioned schools. The students in Madrid answered the survey in a paper-based format in class, while the students in Navarre answered the survey on-line in a class equipped with computers.

Chapter 2

The survey consisted of 9 questions:

- Three closed questions to select the type of programme (bilingual, English as a subject only, etc.), the type of school (state vs. semi-private or private), and location of the school they had done their internship in.

- Two Likert-scale questions about their schools tutors' frequency of use, in a scale from 1 ('never') to 4 ('often'), of some technological tools for teaching and for managerial duties during their internship.

And four open questions asking about the following:

- other technological tools which had been used at the school for teaching and/or managerial purposes;

- whether they had taught their tutor to use any technological tool and a report about their experience teaching the usage of it;

- whether ICTs had been used enough; and

- how teaching or management could be improved in those schools by using more technological tools.

Data were collected from the answers to the survey. Quantitative data were collected from the three closed questions, the two Likert-scale questions and the open questions. Percentages were obtained for all the students and for each cohort to analyse both general trends and possible divergences. Second, means of use were calculated and technologies were ordered from highest to lowest use. Finally, both cohorts' reported usage was compared.

Qualitative data were obtained from the open questions of the survey and organised into groups of common themes.

4. Results and discussion

4.1. Frequency of use of technologies for teaching purposes

Table 1. Mean Frequency for teaching: often > 2, rarely < 2

Technology	Mean >2	Technology	Mean < 2
Audio Files	3.52	Blogs	1.96
Video Files	3.33	Virtual Learning Platforms	1.92
Multimedia	3.24	Microsoft Excel	1.60
Games	2.99	Wiki	1.39
Browsers for Internet Search	2.72	Forum	1.39
Microsoft Word	2.52	Dropbox	1.38
Interactive Whiteboards	2.38	Surveys	1.30
Microsoft PPT	2.26	Facebook	1.28
		Skype	1.27
		Tuenti	1.13

As shown in Table 1, only three technological tools (audio files, video files and multimedia) had a mean higher than 3 and, thus, were used quite frequently for teaching purposes. Five other types of technology had means higher than 2 and thus, were usually employed: two affordances of Internet (games and browsers for Internet search), two software programmes (Microsoft Word and Power Point), and interactive whiteboards. The rest of the technologies had means lower than 2 and, consequently, were used rarely.

Our results point out to the limited use of many technological tools in the school context. Although the use of technologies related to improved ways of presenting information by providing dual-channel input (audio and video) can show an improvement in teaching methodologies and some of the tools may be used by students to create knowledge (Power Point), most of the technological tools used frequently seem to be related to the transmission of information. Consequently, technological tools could be perpetuating traditional teacher-centred methodologies in which students are mere recipients of the knowledge transmitted by the teacher. This seems to be confirmed by the fact that no collaborating technological tools are used.

The tutors in both settings used most ICTs with similar frequency rates. The first five most frequently used technological tools were the same as in the general classification in both settings. However, browsers for searching the web had a mean lower than 3 in Madrid, and both games and browsers had a mean lower than 3 in Navarre.

Microsoft Word, Power Point and interactive whiteboards had means higher than 2 in both settings, though virtual learning platforms only for Madrid. Interactive whiteboards were used more frequently in Navarre (2.89 vs. 2.18) and Virtual learning platforms in Madrid (2.09 vs. 1.45). The rest of technological tools were used rarely or never in both settings and means were lower in Navarre than in Madrid. Social networks (Facebook and Tuenty, M=1.02), which are popular for students out of school, were almost 'never' used.

4.2. Frequency of use for organisational purposes

Table 2. Mean Frequency for organisational purposes: often > 2, rarely < 2

Technology	Mean > 2	Technology	Mean < 2
Microsoft Word	3.21	Dropbox	1.84
Browsers for Internet Search	2.95	Wiki	1.60
Audio Files	2.89	Forum	1.59
Multimedia	2.90	Surveys	1.42
Video Files	2.87	Facebook	1.29
Microsoft PPT	2.59	Skype	1.24
Microsoft Excel	2.51		
Games	2.30		
Interactive Whiteboards	2.20		
Virtual Learning Platforms	2.18		
Blogs	2.08		

As can be seen in Table 2, the only type of technological tool used very often (M=3.21) for organisational purposes was the software program Microsoft Word. However, ten more technological tools were usually employed for organisational purposes and thus, more technology seems to have been used frequently for organisational than for teaching purposes in the schools in both settings.

Comparing both groups of trainees reported frequency of use for organisational purposes; it was observed that there were more differences than for teaching. More tools had a mean higher than 2 in Madrid than in Navarre (three tool means higher than 3 and eight higher than 2 vs. one tool mean higher than 3 and eight higher than 2). The divergences were mostly due to the fact that technological tools typically used for teaching purposes, such as audio files (3.09 Madrid vs. 2.27 Navarre), video files (2.98 vs. 2.52), multimedia (3.08 vs. 2.39), Microsoft Power Point (2.68 vs. 2.29), and games (2.55 vs. 1.58) had higher means, and thus, seemed to have been used more frequently in Madrid than in Navarre for organisational/managerial purposes. On the contrary, technological tools typically used for managerial duties such as Microsoft Word (3.04 Madrid vs. 3. 71 Navarre), Microsoft Excel (2. 43 vs. 2.76) and Virtual Learning Platforms (2.15 vs. 2.27) were reported as having been used more frequently in Navarre.

4.3. Use of ICT and ways ICT could improve teaching

Regarding whether students considered the use of technological tools as sufficient during their internship, only 40 students (28.1%) considered ICT use as enough, while 99 trainees (69.7%) judged it as not enough, although some of these students (5) recognised it was being introduced little by little in schools. However, it must be pointed out that these research results confirm previous findings regarding a lower than expected use of technological tools in education (Almerich et al., 2011).

Suggested ways of improving teaching in the school where they had carried out their practicum by using ICTs more included:

Chapter 2

- better learning, better activities and interactivity by more use of interactive whiteboards (28 students);

- more playful learning with interactive games and activities (19);

- more multimedia for content introduction (12);

- using blogs (7) and wikis (3) for collaborative learning;

- using more videos for listening (6);

- using Survey monkey as an evaluation tool (4);

- using Skype to interact with other speakers (6); and

- using virtual learning platforms for real material, and for homework (4).

The answers of students to how to improve teaching with technological tools indicated that first, some students are quite conscious of the benefits of using technology as they signalled more interactivity, more playful learning, collaborative learning, etc. as possible improvements.

Second, it showed that few students seem conscious of some of the possible usages of certain tools, for example, real interaction with other speakers by using Skype was only mentioned by six students and, thus, more teacher training in CALL seems to be a priority to extend techno-pedagogical knowledge of the possible affordances of ICT.

5. Conclusions

ICT mostly used for teaching purposes are audio files, video files, multimedia, games, browsers to search the web, Microsoft Word, interactive whiteboards and

Microsoft Power Point, and only the first four are utilised very often with slight differences between both settings analysed.

Technological tools used frequently are mostly traditional programmes and audio and video files downloaded from the Internet. This usage of CALL for teaching seems to be related to traditional transmission of knowledge teaching-centred methodologies. Interactive whiteboards are becoming popular and their use is increasing in both settings.

Technologies mostly used for organisational purposes are Microsoft Word, Internet browsers for searching the web, audio files, video files, multimedia, Microsoft Power Point and Excel, games, interactive whiteboards, virtual learning platforms and blogs, but only the first five very often. Differences are greater between both settings in ICT use for organisational purposes than for teaching purposes.

Most trainees considered the use of ICT as quite limited in the schools where they had been doing the practicum. This finding has also been reported in secondary education contexts (García Laborda, Bejarano, & Simons, 2012), and is probably a more accurate perspective of real usage than the one previously reported by the teachers themselves, who might try to justify what they consider their expected use of technological tools and not their real usage. Given the considerable investment that has been carried out to equip schools with technological tools, this low usage should be further researched to try and find its cause and possible solutions.

Training pre-service teachers in ICT affordances will probably increase ICT use in primary and nursery schools as these students will train their tutors and give them first-hand experience (Dooly, 2009). Furthermore, even though younger students seem to be more technologically savvy and thus should be more conscious of the affordances of technological tools to improve knowledge, personal usage is not apparently so easy to transpose into academic or educative contexts, and CALL training appears to be necessary to make students aware of the affordances and constraints of technological tools (Bueno Alastuey & Kleban, 2016).

References

Almerich, G., Suárez, J. M., Jornet, J. M., & Orellana, M. N. (2011). Las competencias y el uso de las Tecnologías de Información y Comunicación (TIC) por el profesorado: estructura dimensional. *Revista electrónica de investigación educativa, 13*(1), 28-42.

Bueno Alastuey, M. C., & Kleban, M. (2016). Matching linguistic and pedagogical objectives in a telecollaboration project: a case study. *Computer Assisted Language Learning, 29*(1), 148-166. Retrieved from http://dx.doi.org/10.1080/09588221.2014.904360

Conole, G. (2008). Listening to the learner voice: the ever changing landscape of technology use for language students. *ReCALL, 20*(2), 124-140. Retrieved from http://dx.doi.org/10.1017/S0958344008000220

Dooly, M. (2009). New competencies in a new era? Examining the impact of a teacher training project. *ReCALL, 21*(3), 352-369. Retrieved from http://dx.doi.org/10.1017/S0958344009990085

García Laborda, J., Bejarano, L. G., & Simons, M. (2012). ¿Cuánto aprendí en la secundaria? Las actitudes de los estudiantes universitarios de primer año respecto a la relación enseñanza-aprendizaje de su segunda lengua en la escuela secundaria en tres contextos internacionales. *Educación XXI, 15*(2), 159-184. Retrieved from http://dx.doi.org/10.5944/educxx1.15.2.131

García-Valcárcel, A., Basilotta, V., & López, C. (2014). Las TIC en el aprendizaje colaborativo en el aula de Primaria y Secundaria. *Comunicar, 42*, 65-74.

Georgina, D. A., & Olson, M. R. (2008). Integration of technology in higher education: a review of faculty self-perceptions. *The Internet and Higher Education, 11*(1), 1-8. Retrieved from http://dx.doi.org/10.1016/j.iheduc.2007.11.002

Purcell, K., Heaps, A., Buchanan, J., & Friedrich, L. (2013). *How teachers are using technology at home and in their classrooms*. Retrieved from http://www.pewinternet.org/Reports/2013/Teachers-and-technology.aspx

Romero, M., Cervera, M. G., & Farran, F. X. C. (2009). Centro virtual de recursos de tecnología educativa: una herramienta para la formación inicial de maestros en TIC. *RUSC. Universities and Knowledge Society Journal, 6*(2), 5.

Steel, C., & Levy, M. (2013). Language students and their technologies: charting the evolution 2006–2011. *ReCALL, 25*(3), 306-320. Retrieved from http://dx.doi.org/10.1017/S0958344013000128

Wiebe, G., & Kabata, K. (2010). Students' and instructors' attitudes toward the use of CALL in foreign language teaching and learning. *Computer Assisted Language Learning, 23*(3), 221-234. Retrieved from http://dx.doi.org/10.1080/09588221.2010.486577

Yunus, M. (2007). Malaysian ESL teachers' use of ICT in their classrooms: expectations and realities. *ReCALL, 19*(1), 79-95. Retrieved from http://dx.doi.org/10.1017/S0958344007000614

3 How working collaboratively with technology can foster a creative learning environment

Susana Gómez[1]

Abstract

Research has shown that collaborative learning is a very powerful methodology as it ensures interaction among students, humanises the learning process and has positive effects on academic achievement. An activity based on this approach can also benefit from the use of technology, making this task more appealing to our students today. The aim of this paper is to present a project which combines both ingredients so as to develop a successful creative learning environment. The project we are talking about is called PopuLLar[2], a European Union funded innovative educational project designed to harness music and Information and Communications Technology (ICT), the primary social interests of youngsters, into their language learning. The paper will describe the project goals together with the methodology and results obtained in the initial piloting of the project carried out in Spain before being launched around Europe.

Keywords: ICT, music, language learning, writing lyrics, videos, cooperative work, creativity.

---

1. Universidad de Valladolid, Soria, Spain; susanag@fing.uva.es

How to cite this chapter: Gómez, S. (2016). How working collaboratively with technology can foster a creative learning environment. In A. Pareja-Lora, C. Calle-Martínez, & P. Rodríguez-Arancón (Eds), *New perspectives on teaching and working with languages in the digital era* (pp. 39-50). Dublin: Research-publishing.net. http://dx.doi.org/10.14705/rpnet.2016.tislid2014.420

2. Parts of this article were used in a written report written by the author and sent to the European Commission at the end of the PopuLLar project. Although the report was intended for internal use and never published, it can be found online at the following address: http://popullar.eu/files/DLV-25_Annex-a--6-Best-Practice-Case-Study-Report.pdf?&session-id=51fa21504bb360e2cbadd7b186ef260e

Chapter 3

1. Introduction and background to the project

New research findings show that students are motivated when they feel in control of their learning, that they are learning something which is relevant to their lives, connected with others and that the activities they are doing are interesting and fun (Biggs, 1995; McCombs, 1994). Thus, as Deci and Ryan (1991) noted, knowing how to meet the individual needs of each student for control, competence, and belonging in the classroom is the key to unlocking students' motivation to learn.

PopuLLar: Motivating Secondary School Students to Learn Language with Relevant Media (Ref. EU Project PopuLLar 518346-LLP-1-2011-1-UK-COMENIUS-CMP) is a European Union funded project in which seven educational institutions – The Mosaic Art And Sound (UK), Pelikan Language School (Czeck Republic), Cukurova University (Turkey), Kulturring in Berlin (Germany), Kindersite (UK), Opera Bazar (Italy) and University of Valladolid (Spain) – have been working together in an innovative educational project designed to harness music and ICT into language learning.

The idea and methodology behind the PopuLLar project is simple, but it has proved to be very powerful and motivating at the same time. Thus, students work autonomously and collaboratively on the melody of the song of their choice and create new lyrics both in their mother tongue (L1) and in a foreign language (L2). Then they record their final products as a video and/or as audio files and upload their productions in the project Wiki[3] so that students from all around Europe can see their work and interact with each other on the forum available or the Facebook group[4].

A step further, students from other countries take these songs and translate them into their L1, so that the same song can have different language versions sung in different European languages, therefore making the project a multilingual and multicultural experience.

---

3. http://popullar.wikispaces.com/

4. https://www.facebook.com/PopuLLar.Music.and.Languages

Working with popular songs and ICT, especially Web 2.0 tools, fulfils all of the above mentioned requirements for engaging students and foster their motivation: they are interested in songs and technologies and they work independently of the teacher in groups. This fosters collaboration and autonomy, builds wholesome social connections, and helps students to use an L2 in a real context. As they work in groups, they are responsible for their own project and they are fully in control of the shape of the final outcomes, being the ones who 'own' the project from the very beginning; they can work on their own by using the materials and guidelines available online.

Considering all these issues, we can say that the project supports research done so far which accounts for the positive effects of using music (cf. Sposet, 2008; Taglialatela, 2012), ICT (cf. Prensky, 2001; Wang, 2005), and new technologies to foster cooperative work for language learning (cf. Carrió, 2007). But the project goes beyond this; the most important goals of the PopuLLar project are: (i) to help students to combine their love of music with creativity, literacy, digital competencies, group collaboration and use of foreign languages through creative writing in an L2; (ii) to enhance the ability of young European students to apply creative thinking, curiosity and enquiry, social and communications skills, and achieve a positive change through innovative approaches to teaching; and (iii) to ultimately promote language learning together with linguistic and cultural diversity.

The project partners have created a set of materials, to be used by both teachers and students, which are available for free in six languages on the project website www.popullar.eu. These include printable, interactive and video guides that explain how to develop the project step by step:

- Teachers' materials: http://www.popullar.eu/teacher-materials.html

- Students' materials: http://www.popullar.eu/student-materials.html

- Video guide (set of 12 how to videos describing the different steps and activities for the project): http://www.popullar.eu/video-guide.html

Chapter 3

Before the project was launched around Europe, it went through an initial piloting phase in six different countries, and Spain played a key role in this phase and the development of the large-scale piloting, as we will analyse in detail in the following sections.

2. The piloting of the project: research methods

The partners from the project – experts in the fields of language education, music, ICT and video production – have been working on the development of the materials for the project for over a year, after which time, these materials were piloted. The piloting phase was crucial as it is a way to test the sustainability of the project materials for the target groups, to receive feedback for improving the materials and to gain experience for the long-term implementation of the project.

Figure 1. Pictures from Spanish students participating in the initial piloting

This initial piloting (also called small-scale piloting) was carried out in the school Nuestra Señora del Pilar in Soria (Spain) and in five other schools around Europe which correspond to the partners' countries.

The piloting period started in October 2012 and finished in May 2013. It was a complex and long piloting as this phase was crucial for the success of the project, but the methodology used gave light to improve some aspects of the project and was the first chance we had to confirm our hypothesis, i.e. that the use of music, ICT and cooperative work can definitely foster a creative learning environment and therefore has positive effects on language learning.

The methodology used to carry out the observations for our piloting process was varied, as will be explained below, and it was implemented in the same way in the six different European schools.

2.1. Questionnaires for students and teachers

Students' and teachers' questionnaires, prepared within the PopuLLar set of pedagogical materials, reflect the students and teachers perspective towards the project, the materials and the implementation in their classes.

The questionnaires were divided into a pre-questionnaire (before the beginning of the experience), including information on the expectations of the students and teachers about the proposed new approach to learning, and a post-questionnaire (after the end of the activitie), where they could reflect on the process, results and compare them with their expectations. Google Forms was used for this task and the links are the following:

- Students' pre-questionnaire: http://tinyurl.com/d3hkpo7

- Students' post-questionnaire: http://tinyurl.com/cd75fm3

- Teachers' pre-questionnaire: http://tinyurl.com/cw2h8kz

- Teachers' post-questionnaire: http://tinyurl.com/cwcqf39

After all the participants filled the questionnaires, a summary of the answers was created using the application available on Google Forms to this effect, and results (statistics, opinions, graphs) were analysed accordingly. Both closed and open questions gave the project team very useful information to reflect on possible changes for the large-scale piloting.

2.2. Observations

Before meeting the students and the teachers, we had prepared a series of questions and descriptions of situations to observe during the initial piloting. Moreover, a logbook was created on Google Drive, so as to gather all the information and coordinate the work, tasks to do, meetings, visits, comments, etc. with the participants. This document was very useful as it allowed us to work very effectively, do a closer and more efficient follow up and have everything centralised in one single document. On top of that, several visits were paid to the schools in order to feel and be immersed in the process of this initial piloting phase.

2.3. Interviews

Informal interviews were arranged with students and teachers to clarify and illustrate some answers from the questionnaires, get a deeper knowledge of specific points which needed further explanation, etc. Questions to be asked were sent to the respondents beforehand so that they could prepare them in advance, and the information obtained here was very useful, especially to understand the implementation of the project in a real situation.

2.4. Filming

We filmed part of the experience carried out during our visits to highlight important aspects of the students' performances. We recorded the students working in groups and some of the interviews in which participating students and teachers share their experience in working in the project[5].

---

5. http://www.youtube.com/watch?v=XfmaX_v_H20

Figure 2. Filming in the piloting school

2.5. Review of students' video clips

The important milestones for students regarding the development of the project are their final productions: video clips showing the performance of the song with their own lyrics.

The project team used the following criteria to analyse the students' video clips: (i) do students get to match their lyrics with the rhythm, melodies and timing of the instrumental part?; (ii) do students work collaboratively as a team?; (iii) do the L1 and the L2 version of the lyrics show a similar level of quality?; (iv) do students show motivation and enthusiasm while working in the project?; (v) are students familiar with ICT, especially with the use of Web 2.0 tools?; and (vi) does the final project (lyrics writing, video/audio recording/editing) show a high level of creativity?

3. Findings

The initial piloting proved that the PopuLLar project is an excellent way to motivate students to learn and practice languages in a real context, develop their

Chapter 3

IT skills, trigger their creativity and promote teamwork, something which has also been supported later on in the large-scale piloting.

During the initial piloting in Spain, there were eleven students – 8 girls and 3 boys – aged between 12 and 17, and three teachers – English teacher plus two Content and Language Integrated Learning (CLIL) teachers – on board. Results from the questionnaires, interviews and observations showed that they liked languages and they also loved music, as most of them either played instruments or sang in the school chorus. Regarding the use of ICT, they felt confident when using the Internet and new technologies, especially Web 2.0 tools. They had positive expectations for the project and thought it would be fun, but there were different opinions as to whether it would be difficult or not.

On top of practising foreign languages, working with new technologies and using their music skills, they thought from the very beginning that the PopuLLar project would give them the chance to work with their peers, get in contact with other countries, meet new people and have fun, overall accomplished by the end.

After the piloting[6] was finished, they realised all their expectations had been fully and successfully achieved, both from the students' and teachers' perspectives:

- Teachers invited students in the school to participate in the piloting and a team was created with volunteers.

- Instead of choosing a song, they created their own musical theme and played instruments, a new challenge they dared face, which was their own initiative.

- They wrote the lyrics for their song in Spanish (L1).

---

6. The Spanish school participating in the initial piloting carried out all the different steps from the project, which are described below, and can be viewed in the PopuLLar project wiki at http://popullar.wikispaces.com/Nuestra_Se%C3%B1ora_del_Pilar

- They recorded themselves singing their song and edited two different videos: (i) http://www.youtube.com/watch?v=vhP8P34GIMA; and (ii) http://www.youtube.com/watch?v=vv4vPAQmFxc.

- They translated their song into English, the main L2 they were learning.

- They video recorded themselves singing their song in English: http://www.youtube.com/watch?v=n65a9djuA6U.

- They shared their recording through the project wiki and got very active in the forum, sharing multiple messages with students and teachers from all over Europe (this information can be checked at http://tinyurl.com/n5b6sru).

- They chose a song created by the Italian school -the partner school for the piloting- and translated the song from English into Spanish.

- They used their instruments to play this new song, did the recording in Spanish, and created a video clip with the new song: http://www.youtube.com/watch?v=Jyai3os4rbc.

Images and videos are very illustrative and are worth a thousand words, so in the following videos we can see (i) an interview with students participating in the piloting process talking about their positive experience while working on the project[7]; (ii) students being interviewed by journalists on the news[8]; and (iii) official launch of the PopuLLar Project in Spain – after the piloting was over – with interviews of teachers and students participating in the project[9].

As well as the powerful and illustrative messages we get from the previous videos, we can also say that through the pre- and post-questionnaires, plus

---

7. http://www.youtube.com/watch?v=XfmaX_v_H20
8. http://www.youtube.com/watch?v=UaxrTfKo1kk
9. http://www.youtube.com/watch?v=frk1jhsNCNs

Chapter 3

several interviews carried out during different visits we did at the school during the piloting phase, we could see and feel how enthusiastic the students were with this project from the very beginning to the very end, and how they encouraged other students to take part. They loved the project: creating the lyrics, playing their instruments for an original song, and especially watching other students singing the song they had created in other EU languages, which made them feel really special:

- Italian (http://www.youtube.com/watch?v=8vhcU3bzYd4);

- Norwegian (http://popullar.wikispaces.com/Tromso);

- Basque (http://www.youtube.com/watch?v=gtxyni4HtQ8); and

- Arabic (http://popullar.wikispaces.com/Redzek).

Figure 3. Feedback videos

The initial piloting in Spain got a big coverage in the press, with many pieces of news on the printed and digital press, TV and radio about the project and also about the excellent results from the piloting. All the different publications have been collected in the following online document: http://tinyurl.com/n9sxjuv.

4. Conclusions

The initial piloting phase has been very beneficial for the project, as we could test the materials with different schools around Europe and get very useful feedback to improve it before the large-scale piloting.

Students and teachers participating in the piloting process in Spain were really involved and pleased to know that they were the first group participating in their country and that they would be role models for other European students. That is why they put a lot of enthusiasm and hard work on this process, did their best and the final products they created were very good for the project, for dissemination purposes and for reference. This school was chosen as an example of good practice, as it can be seen at https://www.youtube.com/watch?v=ZnyOxSJ-F9g and http://www.youtube.com/watch?v=7u120FsYnGI.

The results obtained went beyond our expectations, first because they created their own melody and played their own music (something which was not a requirement and implied harder work), and also because they created several very interesting feedback videos where they share their experiences and tips with students from all around Europe.

The success of the initial piloting was even bigger for the large-scale piloting, as Spain has been the country with the most schools participating in the project – up to 65 –, and the quality, variety and creativity of the videos created have surpassed the partners' expectations.

After a close follow up of the whole process, not only through the initial piloting phase but also through the large-scale piloting which started after May 2013, my experience as a project coordinator in Spain is that the best way to approach students to become involved in the project is to show them that the goal is not to become an expert in music or languages, but to be creative and have fun. After this, language learning and language practice will flow automatically. It is also very important to show students that they play a crucial role in the project, that they own it, that they can work on their own, and that they can challenge themselves to create something new and original with freedom in their choices, showing them the powerful meaning behind the word TEAM (together each achieves more).

As a final conclusion, and after the huge success and excellent feedback from all the European students participating in it, we can conclude that the idea behind the PopuLLar project is very simple but extremely powerful. It is full of energy, enthusiasm and group work, so it goes beyond language learning and offers students a very humanistic approach to teamwork and creativity, therefore something definitely worth considering for any teacher who is after a successful new learning experience.

References

Biggs, J. (1995). Assessing for learning: some dimensions underlying new approaches to educational assessment. *The Alberta Journal of Educational Research, 41*(1), 1-17.

Carrió, M. L. (2007). Ventajas del uso de la tecnología en el aprendizaje colaborativo. *Revista Iberoamericana de Educación, 41*(4), 1-10.

Deci, E. L., & Ryan, R. M. (1991). A motivational approach to self: integration in personality. In R. Dienstbier (Ed.), *Nebraska Symposium on Motivation: Vol. 38, Perspectives on motivation* (pp. 237-288). Lincoln: University of Nebraska Press.

McCombs, B. L. (1994). Strategies for assessing and enhancing motivation: keys to promoting self-regulated learning and performance. In H. F. O'Neil, Jr., & M. Drillings (Eds.), *Motivation: theory and research* (pp. 49-69). Hillsdale, NJ: Erlbaum.

Prensky, M. E. (2001). Digital natives, digital immigrants part 1. *On the Horizon, 9*(5), 1-6. Retrieved from http://dx.doi.org/10.1108/10748120110424816

Sposet, B. A. (2008). *The role of music in second language acquisition: a bibliographical review of seventy years of research, 1937-2007*. Lewiston, NY: E. Mellen Press.

Taglialatela, A. (2012). Exploiting sound and music for foreign/second language acquisition. *Englishes, 46,* 125-140.

Wang, L. (2005). The advantages of using technology in second language education: technology integration in foreign language teaching demonstrates the shift from a behavioral to a constructivist learning approach. *T.h.e. Journal, 32*(10), 38-42.

4 The e-generation: the use of technology for foreign language learning

Pilar Gonzalez-Vera[1]

Abstract

After the Bologna Process, European Higher Education was reformulated as a response to a change of roles in higher education in a globalised society. The implementation of a new system of credits, the European Credit Transfer System (ECTS), implied an enormous increase of autonomous learning hours. The high percentage of student workload reflected the new active role of students in the learning process and it was bound to the philosophy of learner-centeredness. In addition, the rise of autonomous hours led teachers to look for new media that fulfill the requirements of non-presential hours of education and that allow teachers to monitor the students' learning. One of the most useful tools has been e-learning platforms. This paper aims to explore how e-learning platforms and new technologies, in general, have contributed to the process of learning foreign languages. The point of departure of this research is a questionnaire about the use of new technologies in the English class and about their competence in English, which was designed for first-year students studying the primary education degree. After the analysis of the results of the questionnaires, the study presents a post-questionnaire presented at the end of the year in which the role of Information and Communications Technologies (ICTs) is assessed together with the improvement of the students' skills and competences.

Keywords: autonomous learning, ICTs, e-learning platforms, skills, competencies.

1. Universidad de Zaragoza, Zaragoza, Spain; pilargv@unizar.es

How to cite this chapter: Gonzalez-Vera, P. (2016). The e-generation: the use of technology for foreign language learning. In A. Pareja-Lora, C. Calle-Martínez, & P. Rodríguez-Arancón (Eds), *New perspectives on teaching and working with languages in the digital era* (pp. 51-61). Dublin: Research-publishing.net. http://dx.doi.org/10.14705/rpnet.2016.tislid2014.421

Chapter 4

1. Introduction

Over the last few decades, the use of technology and multimedia for foreign language teaching has expanded rapidly. Recent developments in the worlds of technology and the Internet have offered new and numerous opportunities for teaching and learning. One of the main advantages of the Internet is that the time teachers require in order to gather authentic material is considerably reduced (Dudeney, 2000, p. 1). In the early stages, the introduction of the Internet meant the possibility of creating online courses by uploading files as class-materials and sending emails in an attempt to achieve a similar teacher-student interaction as in face-to-face classes. However, nowadays the part that technology plays in education is not limited to this.

The evolution in the role of technology in education is related to the development from distance learning to online learning. As Colpaert (2004) pointed out, "online learning or e-learning has gradually replaced the older 'distance learning' paradigm" (p. 43). While distance learning was an attempt to solve time and space limitations of traditional face-to-face teaching, online learning was the result of the complete adoption of technology as part of our lives. Teachers rely on technology as a medium to deliver courses, either fully online or as a complementary resource used with the aim of adapting learning to the needs of a new generation, the e-generation.

The e-generation is defined as a new group of students that has "spent their entire lives surrounded by and using computers, videogames, digital music players, video cams, cell phones, and all the other toys and tools of the digital age" (Prensky, 2001, p. 1). Living surrounded by a digital culture has had an effect on the way these young people learn. Firstly, the Internet and then, the mobile phone have contributed to a profound change in the modes of interaction and expression among the youth. This new generation of students prefers receiving information quickly, relying on communication technologies as well as performing multiple tasks (Oblinger & Oblinger, 2005). These students have a low tolerance for lectures and prefer active rather than passive learning, which leads to a change in the model of pedagogy, "from a teacher focused approach based on instruction to a student-focused model based on collaboration" (Tapscott, 2009, p. 11).

This transition from teacher-centred models of education to student-centred models is reflected in the model of education proposed in the European Higher Education Area that alludes to ECTS. In this system, the way in which teaching is understood is modified together with the type of relationship between the learning outcomes and the time students need to achieve them (workload). Thus, a 6 ECTS subject amounts to 150 hours for the student, 50 hours of which are class hours, distributed between lectures and seminars, and 100 hours of autonomous learning. The high percentage (75%) of student workload reflects the new active role of students in the learning process, which is bound to the philosophy of learner-centredness where learners and teachers are involved in a process of give-and-take. Autonomous learners are those who explicitly accept responsibility for their own learning (Little, 1991) and who show initiative regarding learning, and participate in monitoring progress and evaluating the extent to which learning is achieved (Schunk, 2005). Students take control of their learning; however, teachers have a major impact on their progress towards autonomy (Reinders & Balciakanli, 2011, p. 15), which leads them to create activities that foster fruitful learning and that monitor the students' progress.

2. Case study

In order to study the impact of new technologies on the English class in higher education, we analysed a total of 200 Spanish students in their freshman year from the university degree in primary education. All the students, whose ages ranged from 18 to 22, belonged to the 'e-generation'.

An initial questionnaire developed specifically for this study asked students about four main sections: 1) access to and use of technologies, 2) their competence in linguistic communication, 3) the way in which they learn English, and 4) their autonomy and personal initiative when learning. This questionnaire was complemented with a second questionnaire designed for the last sessions

Chapter 4

of the course. Its aim is to observe whether there was an improvement in the students' general level of English and in the different skills assessed in the initial questionnaire. This last survey includes questions about 1) the use of technologies in their learning process, and 2) their current competence in linguistic communication.

3. Results

In the first section, students were asked about their access to a range of technology hardware as well as about their membership to social networks. They were also asked if they had previously used any e-learning platforms (Table 1).

Table 1. Pre-questionnaire: access to and use of technologies

Do you have…	%	Do you belong to any social networks?	%
Computers (desktop and/or laptop)	100	Tuenti	89
Tablets	35	Twitter	75
Smart phones	100	Have you ever used e-learning platforms (Moodle, Blackboard, etc.)?	
Internet access	100	No	-
Do you belong to any social networks?		Yes	100
No	8	School	15
Yes	92	University	100
Facebook	83		

As would be expected, all our students have a computer and a smart-phone as well as access to the Internet. Although some of them also had a tablet, the majority of them (65%) did not. The questionnaire confirmed the initial hypothesis that a high percentage of students (92%) belonged to social networks, Tuenti (89%) being the most popular, followed by Facebook (83%) and Twitter (75%). It was very enlightening that students expressed their concern about the fact that Tuenti was in Spanish, whereas Facebook and Twitter were associated with the English language and a more international profile. In spite of the use of e-learning platforms being relatively new, 100% of the students said that they had already used them. However, the percentage was considerably lower in the case of schools, where some reticence regarding their use can still be observed.

In the second section, competence in linguistic communication, students were asked to state whether they had an official certificate and if so the level obtained, and if not, to self-assess their general level of English (Table 2). In both cases students had to indicate their level of English in different skills (oral/interaction, listening, writing and reading), using a five-option scale: basic, lower intermediate, intermediate, upper intermediate and advanced. This nomenclature substituted the Common European Framework of Reference (CEFR) for Languages: Learning, teaching, assessment levels A1, A2, B1, B2 and C1. This was done in order for it to be easier for participants to make a selection and so that the analysis of the results would be more accurate. The C2 level was dismissed in this questionnaire due to the fact that they are freshman students.

Table 2. Pre-questionnaire: competence in linguistic communication

2.1 Have you got any English level certification	%	2.4 my listening skills	%
PET	2	Basic	48
FCE	-	Lower intermediate	32
CAE	-	Intermediate	18
Trinity. Level	-	Upper intermediate	2
Others (specify and level)	8	Advanced	-
I consider…			
2.2 my general level of English to be		**2.5 my writing skills**	
Basic	46	Basic	36
Lower intermediate	23	Lower intermediate	25
Intermediate	30	Intermediate	35
Upper intermediate	1	Upper intermediate	4
Advanced	-	Advanced	-
2.3 oral/interaction skills		**2.6 my reading skills**	
Basic	60	Basic	25
Lower intermediate	22	Lower intermediate	25
Intermediate	16	Intermediate	38
Upper intermediate	2	Upper intermediate	12
Advanced	-	Advanced	-

Chapter 4

The high percentage (90%) of students who did not have any certificate stood out. Only 10% stated that they had a certificate and the level of their certificates was A2. Of this 10%, 8% had got their certificate in the Official Language Schools and only 2% had a Cambridge certificate. Official Language Schools have a good reputation in Spain due to their long tradition which explains why their certificates are preferred to other certificates that remain unknown to the parents, who are the ones that encourage their children to get them.

Considering the questions 2.3-2.6 as a whole, one can observe that there is an increase in level as we progress from 2.3 to 2.6 and that none of our students considers their language skills to be advanced despite the considerable number of years they have been learning English. A similarly high percentage of the participants consider their oral/interaction skills (60%) and their listening skills (48%) to be basic; whereas there is a significant change in the tendency if one refers to writing and reading skills. Thus, Spanish students seem to feel more self-confident when dealing with writing and reading skills than with those which involve some type of oral interaction.

The third section included questions related to the way in which they learn and improve their English (Table 3).

Table 3. Pre-questionnaire: way in which students learn English

What type of materials do you use to learn English?	%	What type of materials do you use to learn English?	%
Printed…		Internet resources	
Books	95	English activities on websites	64
Newspapers	-	English courses on e-learning platforms	-
Magazines	-	E-books	16
Audiovisual materials		Journals	3
Films on digital television	10	Magazines	-
Tv series on digital television	2	YouTube (tutorials, clips)	48
DVDs	15	Films	70
		Series (subtitled)	80
Indicate if you prefer to do…			
Individual work	81		
Group work	19		

On the one hand, it included questions about their use of traditional formats such as printed materials and more up-to-date materials like audiovisual materials and Internet resources. On the other hand, students were also asked, in this section, to show their preference either for activities that involve individual work or alternatively activities which involve group work.

The study reveals that although the students belong to the e-generation, they mainly use materials that are in traditional formats. However, the wide variety of Internet resources employed by the students is noteworthy. Among these activities, a preference for those on websites and of audiovisual materials on the Net such as YouTube videos, films, and series stands out. The highest percentage is found in the use of downloaded series subtitled in English. This is in line with the interests of the students who see it as a leisure activity. Their interest in seeing the latest episodes of their favourite series together with the time required, 40 minutes in comparison with the 120 minutes of films, make this activity one of the most attractive ones.

In addition, the students' answer in relation to the way they prefer to work in class shows that the traditional learning model was used in their first learning stages.

The fourth section was designed to assess the level of motivation of our students. In terms of education, it is particularly relevant to know this since a students' lack of interest can make the learning process difficult (Table 4). One of the best ways to motivate students in the English class is the use of technology and the Internet, which provide the students with a great deal of information and innovative resources that contribute to making the learning process more attractive. The questionnaire showed the students' preference (75%) for using technology. We cannot forget the fact that the life of the e-generation is marked by digital communication that becomes as natural as face-to-face communication. Their affinity for the integration of technological devices in their lives seems to lead them to show a certain attraction to integrate them into their learning and "encouraging involvement is the key to its success and we should stress it is sometimes not easy to get the ball rolling" (Hannam & Constantinides, 2011, p. 63).

Chapter 4

Table 4. Pre-questionnaire: autonomy and personal initiative when learning

Mark the type of activities that you prefer doing	%
Classroom exercises and tasks	25
New technology and/or computer-based exercises and tasks	75

The following table (Table 5) presents the questionnaire proposed at the end of the year to students and their results.

Table 5. Post-questionnaire: role of technology in the learning process and students' competence in English

Was Moodle useful?	%	-oral/interaction skills	
No. It does not contribute to my learning at all	-	Basic	45
No. Too much effort for little improvement	30	Lower intermediate	35
Yes. Definitely, it has contributed to my learning	60	Intermediate	17
Yes. It has been an additional tool	10	Upper intermediate	2
Possible disadvantages:		Advanced	1
Difficult to use	15	**- listening skills**	
Time-consuming	30	Basic	30
Others	-	Lower intermediate	44
Possible advantages:		Intermediate	20
Source of additional information	40	Upper intermediate	4
Power point presentations	40	Advanced	2
Self-assessment quizzes	90	**- writing skills**	
Others	-	Basic	20
Would you recommend using Moodle next year?		Lower intermediate	29
No	30	Intermediate	45
Yes	70	Upper intermediate	5
Competence in English. I consider my		Advanced	1
-general level of English to be		**- reading skills**	
Basic	20	Basic	15
Lower intermediate	32	Lower intermediate	36
Intermediate	41	Intermediate	27
Upper intermediate	6	Upper intermediate	20
Advanced	1	Advanced	2

Students were asked to express their concerns regarding the e-platform used, their usefulness and the difficulties found as a consequence of their introduction when learning. In this respect, most of them (70%) considered that Moodle had contributed to a great extent (60%) or to some extent (10%) to their learning, whereas 30% thought that although it contributed it was hardly worth using. According to the students, the main disadvantage was that it was time-consuming and in a few cases students found their use complicated. However, 90% of the students found the quizzes in Moodle especially useful for self-assessment, and a reasonable percentage (40%) used this e-platform to enhance their learning.

Students were also asked to assess their progress as we consider that the students' perception of improvement is intrinsically linked to a motivation for continuing working in the same way. Finally, the use of Moodle and new technologies played a significant role in the improvement of the students' English competence. All their skills were improved, according to their personal opinions and to the results obtained in the tests and quizzes done throughout the year.

4. Conclusion

This study has attempted to prove and demonstrate the positive effects of the use of new technologies in education. We are conscious that large classes like ours of 70 students limit the interaction between students and lecturers and make it more difficult to provide students with immediate feedback. However, the results of this study reveal that the use of Moodle has contributed to assisting students and making them feel that they receive instant and individual feedback.

A positive reaction among students has also been observed. Firstly, students showed their enthusiasm for technology as they associated it with fun and, secondly, they were familiar with its use, which provided them with confidence. A consequence of the acceptance of technology is the students' request to continue using new technologies in the coming years.

ICTs are adapted in novel ways to enrich the learning environment (Stevens & Dudeney, 2009) and their use can foster independent learning. The results have proved their potential value. Students developed transversal skills working on linguistic, autonomous and digital competences. The quizzes done on Moodle revealed a significant improvement in all skills. Although these preliminary quizzes show a notable development in English, we will have to wait until the final and official assessment to confirm the actual improvement of our students.

5. Acknowledgements

This study was possible thanks to the research projects Swift H46 financed by Diputación General de Aragón (DGA) and 2014 SGR 27 financed by AGAUR.

References

Colpaert, J. (2004). Design of online interactive language courseware: conceptualization, specification and prototyping. *Research into the impact of linguistic-didactic functionality on software architecture*. Doctoral thesis. University of Antwerp.

Dudeney, G. (2000). *The internet and the language classroom*. Cambridge: Cambridge University Press.

Hannam, S., & Constantinides, M. (2011). Using technology to improve your English language teachers' association. In S. Gómez (Ed.), *Running an association for language teachers: directions and opportunities* (pp. 63-68). Canterbury: IATEFL and British Council.

Little, D. (1991). *Learner autonomy: definitions, issues and problems*. Dublin: Authentik.

Oblinger, D. G., & Oblinger, J. (2005). *Educating the Net neneration*. EDUCAUSE Online book. Retrieved from http://www.educause.edu/ir/library/pdf/pub7101.pdf

Prensky, M. (2001). Digital natives, digital immigrants part 1. On the Horizon, 9(5), 1-6. Retrieved from http://dx.doi.org/10.1108/10748120110424816

Reinders, H., & Balcikanli, C. (2011). Learning to foster autonomy: the role of teacher education materials. *Studies in Self-Access Learning Journal, 2*(1), 15-25.

Schunk, D. (2005). Self-regulated learning: the educational legacy of Paul R. Pintrich. *Educational Psychologist, 40*(2), 85-94. Retrieved from http://dx.doi.org/10.1207/s15326985ep4002_3

Stevens, V., & Dudeney, G. (2009). Online conferences and teacher professional development: SLanguages and WiAOC 2009. *TESL-EJ Teaching English as a Second or Foreign language, 13*(1). Retrieved from http://tesl-ej.org/ej49/int.html

Tapscott, D. (2009). *Grown up digital: how the Net generation is changing your world*. New York: McGraw-Hill.

5 Evaluation of reading achievement of the program school 2.0 in Spain using PISA 2012

Cristina Vilaplana Prieto[1]

Abstract

In 2009, some Spanish regions implemented the Program School 2.0 with the purpose of introducing digital methodologies at schools. The aim of this paper is to analyse which part of the variation in reading scores is due to this program. For this purpose, we use data from the Program for International Student Assessment (PISA 2009 and 2012) for 15-year old students attending public schools. We estimate a difference-in-difference model and observe that the net effect derived from an increase in the provision of Information and Communications Technology (ICT) at schools has been positive, although small, in participant regions. However, elapsed time since the onset of the program has not equally affected repeater and non-repeater students. Finally, only a moderate use (1-2 times/week) of ICT for doing homework has a positive effect over reading scores.

Keywords: reading, PISA, ICT, Spain.

1. Introduction

The analysis of the implementation of ICT in schools and high schools has sparked debate during the last decade. Some studies have appreciated a substantial improvement of students' achievement as a result of the introduction

---

1. Universidad de Murcia, Murcia, Spain; cvilaplana@um.es

How to cite this chapter: Vilaplana Prieto, C. (2016). Evaluation of reading achievement of the program school 2.0 in Spain using PISA 2012. In A. Pareja-Lora, C. Calle-Martínez, & P. Rodríguez-Arancón (Eds), *New perspectives on teaching and working with languages in the digital era* (pp. 63-72). Dublin: Research-publishing.net. http://dx.doi.org/10.14705/rpnet.2016.tislid2014.422

of ICT. Machin, McNally, and Silva (2007) used an instrumental variables approach to control for a potential endogeneity problem of the use of ICT, and concluded that the increase in computer investment had improved academic results in Elementary education. In the same line, Banerjee, Cole, Duflo, and Linden (2004) for India, Barrow, Nmarkman, and Rouse (2009) for the United States and Carrillo, Onofa, and Ponce (2010) for Canada, ascertained a positive influence of ICT over academic results.

However, other analyses have found an insignificant or even negative relationship between both variables. Golsbee and Guryan (2002) concluded that a program implemented in the United States aimed at increasing the computer-to-student ratio had not had any significant effect over students' achievement. For Israel, Angrist and Lavy (2002) observed a negative effect of ICT over Mathematics scores for 4th grade students. Similarly, Leuven, Lindahl, Oosterbeek, and Webbink (2004) concluded that the increase of computer-to-student ratio in Dutch schools had led to worse Language and Mathematics results.

2. The program school 2.0

In July 2009, the Spanish Ministry of Education approved the development of the Program School 2.0, whose objectives were: provide each student with a notebook or digital pad, transform all classrooms into digital classrooms, offer instruction to teachers and prepare new digital contents.

The program was implemented in 5th and 6th grade of Elementary Education and 1st and 2nd grade of High School, but only in public centers. Participation in the Program was not homogeneous across Communities, and the following classification can be established (see CEAPA, 2010):

- Communities that applied the Program in all centers, denoted 'Total Participants' (TP): Andalucía, Aragón, Cantabria, Castilla La Mancha, Castilla-León, Cataluña, Extremadura, Galicia, Navarra, País Vasco, Rioja, Ceuta and Melilla.

- Communities that applied the Program in a fraction of centers denoted as 'Partial Participants' (PP) Asturias, Baleares and Canarias.

- Communities that did not implemented the Program, denoted as 'Non-Participants' (NP): Madrid, Murcia and Comunidad Valenciana.

3. Data

Data come from PISA survey carried out by the Organisation for Economic Cooperation and Development (OECD) every three years to assess the competencies of 15-year-old students in reading, mathematics and science. This paper is focused on students with level ISCED-2A[2] attending public centers. We have a sample of 15,375 observations for the general module and 5,579 observations for the Computer Based Assessment (CBA) module.

To assess the success degree of the Program School 2.0, it is necessary to compare reading scores in 2012 with pre-implementation scores. We incorporate 11,049 observations from PISA 2009 and 1,897 from PISA-Electronic Reading Assessment (ERA).

Table 1 shows reading scores in 2009 and 2012 by type of participation. For non-repeater students, there is no significant difference among the three types of Communities, neither in 2009 nor in 2012. In the modules ERA (2009) and CBA (2012), we appreciate that NP and TP attain higher scores than PP. For 1-year repeaters, mean score for TP was higher than for NP in 2009, but quite the opposite happens in the module CBA (2012).

For 2-year repeater students, the mean score for NP was higher than for PP according to PISA-ERA (2009), but no significant differences are observed in electronic reading achievement in 2012.

---

2. International Standard Classification of Education; 2A: Secondary School Intermediate Level

Table 1. Descriptive statistics for reading scores

	Has participated in School 2.0?			Test for equal means		
	No (1)	Totally (2)	Partially (3)	(1) vs (2)	(1) vs (3)	(2) vs (3)
PISA (2009). General Module						
Total	436.80	446.59	450.79	0.0613	0.0071	0.1266
No rep	490.94	489.83	495.94	0.6274	0.5828	0.1888
1-year rep.	397.22	410.66	416.00	0.0055	0.0082	0.6360
2-year rep.	347.26	342.49	353.60	0.1835	0.1762	0.8312
PISA (2009). ERA						
Total	488.82	481.82	438.28	0.7392	0.0000	0.0000
No rep	522.84	514.80	487.51	0.7627	0.0000	0.0000
1-year rep.	447.51	441.83	409.91	0.2631	0.1692	0.0310
2-year rep.	416.88	410.65	383.09	0.7372	0.0064	0.0157
PISA (2012). General Module						
Total	477.14	480.21	457.54	0.0116	0.6465	0.0596
No rep	515.26	513.98	502.00	0.4394	0.1898	0.3533
1-year rep.	440.54	431.44	421.68	0.2044	0.3079	0.1736
2-year rep.	390.63	381.16	375.27	0.9505	0.6076	0.5060
PISA (2012). CBA						
Total	470.77	477.89	457.48	0.1478	0.1107	0.0066
No rep	507.35	512.51	490.67	0.8205	0.0373	0.0252
1-year rep.	437.98	423.59	420.74	0.0001	0.0861	0.5544
2-year rep.	379.57	380.60	378.91	0.8595	0.6036	0.8675

Table 2 shows the degree of use of ICT at schools and students' households according to the type of participation in the Program School 2.0. In 2009, all Communities exhibited similar levels of technological equipment at schools (0.15-0.16). In 2012, the highest ratio of computer-per-student corresponds to TP Communities (0.65). Regarding the provision of technological equipment, there has been a higher investment in PCs in PP Communities (69%) in comparison with notebooks in TP Communities (31%).

Nearly 20% of students belonging to TP or PP Communities have reported that they use ICT for 'looking for information' at school 'almost every day' or 'every day', as opposed to only 12% in NP Communities. In the context of using ICT for 'practice/drilling' or 'doing homework at school', the percentage is higher in PP Communities (14% and 11%) as opposed to TP Communities (9%).

Finally, around 12% of students of TP or PP have reported to use ICT to do their homework (at home) 'almost every day' or 'every day'.

Table 2. Implementation of ICT at schools and students' households; PISA (2012)

	Autonomous Communities		
	Total participants	Partial participants	No participants
Ratio computers-per-student 2009	0.15	0.15	0.16
Ratio computers-per-student 2012	0.65	0.63	0.57
At classroom, the student has PC (%)	56.6	69.14	61.43
At classroom, the student has Notebook (%)	30.99	20.90	6.97
ICT for looking for information at school (%)			
1-2 times/week	28.74	28.50	27.95
Almost every day/every day	19.95	19.20	12.72
ICT for practice/drilling at school (%)			
1-2 times/week	15.11	19.41	14.8
Almost every day/every day	8.69	14.18	7.08
ICT for doing homework at school (%)			
1-2 times/week	13.27	11.76	10.52
Almost every day/every day	8.94	11.13	5.66
At home, the student uses ICT for doing homework (%)			
1-2 times/week	20.35	23.70	19.46
Almost every day	10.86	12.75	7.51
Every day	4.99	4.18	3.28

4. Econometric model

Due to space limitations, the econometric analysis is restricted the comparison between NP and TP. To disentangle which part of the score variation is due to the participation in the Program, we propose to estimate a difference-in-difference model. The dependent variable is the reading score of student i belonging to school j ($Read_{ij}$):

$$Read_{ij} = {}_0 + {}_1X_i + {}_2X_j + {}_3Year_{2012} + {}_4Part_j + {}_3Year_{2012} \cdot Part_j + \varepsilon_i + \mu_j + \upsilon_{ij}$$

Where X_i refers to characteristics of the student and his/her family (nationality, age when arrived at Spain, language spoken at home, immigrant mother/father, lives with only one parent, minutes per week devoted to reading at home, having more than 100 books at home, level of education of father/mother, relation with economic activity of father/mother); X_j refers to school characteristics (size of municipality, class size, proportion of girls at class, proportion of immigrants students); $Part_j$ takes the value 1 if the Community has participated in School 2.0; $Year_{2012}$ takes the value 1 in 2012; $Year_{2012} \cdot Part_j$ denotes the interaction between participation in School 2.0 and year 2012; ε_i and μ_j denote student and school unobservable characteristics, and v_{ij} is a random error term. For the estimation of the model, the methodology proposed by OECD (2009) has been followed.

4.1. Results for PISA (2009) and PISA (2012)

A higher ratio of computers-per-student, as illustrated in Table 3, has a negative effect over reading score for non-repeaters (-75.93 points) and 2-year repeaters (-141.35 points). However, for the case of TP this negative effect is offset by a positive one (86.04 for non-repeaters, 154.87 for 2-year repeaters).

The starting year of the Program has meaningfully influenced reading scores. It is negative for non-repeaters and 1-year repeaters, although smaller in absolute value for those who started in 2009 as compared to 2010. This could indicate that there is a learning curve and students need some time to come to terms with the new teaching methodology. On the other hand, the difference in the estimated coefficients between non-repeaters and 1-year repeaters is thought-provoking. It could be that new teaching methodologies have involved a step backward for 1-year repeater students.

GDP[3] per capita has been introduced as a proxy of regional purchasing power. The interaction with participation in the Program is positive and significant, although with a very small magnitude. Therefore, the results of the Program School 2.0 have not been conditioned by regional economic differences.

---

3. Gross Domestic Product

Table 3. Difference-in-difference regression for reading scores

	No repeater		1-year repeater		2-year repeater	
	Coef	t	Coef	t	Coef	t
Computers-per-student	-75.93	-3.40	-63.98	-1.24	-141.35	-4.03
Growth rate of computers-per-student 2007-2012	0.99	2.23	1.04	1.35	1.74	2.62
Has notebook/digital pad in school	-5.28	-2.55	-11.12	-3.41	-13.40	-3.01
Participation in School 2.0	9.35	1.36	0.53	0.03	15.05	1.27
Year 2012	17.64	2.49	32.68	3.28	63.62	5.54
Interaction with participation in School 2.0:						
Computers-per-student	86.04	3.52	81.55	1.52	154.87	4.46
Notebook at school	-2.85	-0.95	4.90	1.13	4.05	0.56
Year 2012	-14.35	-1.36	-15.46	-0.92	-54.51	-2.23
Growth rate computers-per-student 2009-2012	-1.18	-2.48	-1.24	-1.53	-1.78	-2.53
Program started in 2009	-14.90	-3.33	8.84	0.60	-59.68	-3.30
Program started in 2010	-19.56	-5.07	-2.65	-0.17	-29.67	-2.41
Constant	428.22	56.56	383.59	30.11	280.06	19.69
N	14,200		6,102		1,762	
R²	0.1558		0.1306		0.2140	

4.2. Results for PISA-ERA (2009) and PISA-CBA (2012)

Using the special modules of ERA (PISA, 2009) and CBA (PISA, 2012), the difference-in-difference model has been estimated to determine the influence of the Program School 2.0 over the development of digital competences (see Table 4). Explanatory variables are the same as in Table 3.

The variable year 2012 is significant and negative for non-repeaters (-90.23 points) and for 2-year repeaters (-151.41 points). This variable affects both PP and NP, and may gather a group of sociological determinants that have damaged the intrinsic value of education and learning. For the same group of students, the participation in the Program School 2.0 has implied an additional decrease of reading scores (-58.76 and -124.82 points, respectively).

Table 4. Difference-in-difference regression for electronic reading scores

	No repeater		1-year repeater		2-year repeater	
	Coef	t	Coef	t	Coef	t
Computers-per-student	0.00	-0.04	0.01	0.60	-0.01	-0.05
Growth rate of computers	-0.33	-0.96	-0.96	-2.74	-0.01	-0.13
Notebook at school	-23.36	-1.72	3.59	0.18	-27.77	-1.24
Uses ICT for homework						
1-2 times/month	7.20	0.48	21.83	1.35	-12.91	-0.88
1-2 times/week	55.62	4.66	-0.19	-0.01	-54.68	-3.39
Almost all days	5.67	0.36	0.15	0.01	-20.41	-1.08
Participation in School 2.0	-58.76	-2.45	-15.45	-0.59	-124.82	-4.14
Year 2012	-90.23	-4.51	24.37	-1.06	-151.41	-3.19
Interaction with School 2.0						
Computers-per-student	21.55	1.02	1.54	0.12	13.42	0.72
Notebook at school	33.78	1.78	-30.54	-1.63	35.77	1.58
Year 2012	81.00	1.72	-6.67	-0.20	136.23	1.57
Growth rate computers	0.36	0.67	0.86	2.12	0.27	0.26
ICT for homework						
1-2 times/month	33.74	2.48	24.65	1.37	31.512	1.43
1-2 times/week	-14.20	-1.19	7.79	0.37	104.77	5.14
Almost all days	34.84	1.65	19.14	0.85	56.33	1.71
Constant	505.76	13.66	414.98	10.23	535.49	9.68
N	**4,933**		**1,609**		**499**	
R²	**0.2700**		**0.3092**		**0.6334**	

Using ICT for doing homework is only significant for the category 1-2 times/week for non-repeaters (55.62 points) and 2-year repeaters (-54.68 points). The interaction between participation in School 2.0 and ICT for homework 1-2 times/week is positive and significant for 2-year repeater students (+104.77). This result implies that, for this specific group, there has been a remarkable difference in the benefit derived from the use of ICT at home between NP and PP.

5. Conclusions

Our results show that the increase in the provision of computers has different effects over reading scores based on the teaching methodology applied. The increase in the provision of computers in total participant Communities leads to positive (although small) effects over academic performance. For TP and NP, the negative effect of the variable year 2012 is quite alarming. We should analyse which combination of factors has damaged reading scores (i.e. implication of families in children's education, influence of depressive economic contexts...).

Regarding the use of ICT at home, a moderate use (1-2 times/week) has positive effects for non-repeater students, although a negative one for 2-year repeater students. However, the interaction of participation and ICT for homework 1-2 times/week shows a positive and significant effect for 2-year repeater students, which offsets the previous negative one. The implications of these results are twofold: (1) intensive use of ICT at home (almost every day or every day) does not affect academic results, but positive results emerge when they are used as a complement tool; and (2) the appropriate use of ICT (guided by specific teaching contents) may be stimulating for repeater students and help them to improve their academic performance.

Regarding previous literature that ascertained a positive impact of ICT over student assessment, two different explanations are offered to explain the divergence of results. On one hand, ICT should be considered as an additional 'input' in the student's learning function, because the student can obtain more information and access more easily to learning resources at school and at home (and at any moment). On the other hand, the benefits derived of ICT are conditioned by the ability of the centers to modify their teaching methods, so that teachers and ICT become complementary. The availability of data including future cohorts of students participating in School 2.0 will dig into the relationship of ICT and student performance in Spain.

References

Angrist, J., & Lavy, V. (2002). New evidence on classroom computers and pupil learning. *Economic Journal, 112*(482), 735-765. Retrieved from http://dx.doi.org/10.1111/1468-0297.00068

Chapter 5

Banerjee, A., Cole, S., Duflo, E., & Linden, L. (2004). Remedying education: evidence from two randomized experiments in India. *Quarterly Journal of Economics 122(*3), 1235-1264. Retrieved from http://dx.doi.org/10.1162/qjec.122.3.1235

Barrow, L., Nmarkman, L., & Rouse, C. (2009). Technology's edge: the educational benefits of computer-aided instruction. *American Economic Journal: Economic Policy, 1(*1), 52-74. Retrieved from http://dx.doi.org/10.1257/pol.1.1.52

Carrillo, P., Onofa, M., & Ponce, J. (2010). Information technology and student achievement: evidence from a randomized experiment in Ecuador. *Inter-American Development Bank Working Paper Series No. 223.*

CEAPA. (2010). *Incidencias y recortes presupuestarios. Inicio de curso 2010-2011. Confederación Española de Asociaciones de Padres y Madres de Alumnos.* Retrieved from http://www.ceapa.es/

Golsbee, A., & Guryan, J. (2002). The impact of internet subsidies on public schools. *NBER Working Paper No. 9090.*

Leuven E., Lindahl, M., Oosterbeek, H., & Webbink, D. (2004). The effect of extra funding for disadvantaged pupils on achievement. *IZA Discussion Paper No. 1122.*

Machin, S., McNally, S., & Silva, O. (2007). New technology in schools: is there a payoff? *Economic Journal 117*(522), 1145-1167. Retrieved from http://dx.doi.org/10.1111/j.1468-0297.2007.02070.x

OECD. (2009). *PISA Data analysis manual: SPSS* (2nd ed.). Organization for Economic Cooperation and Development.

6 Language learning actions in two 1x1 secondary schools in Catalonia: the case of online language resources

Boris Vázquez Calvo[1] and Daniel Cassany[2]

Abstract

This paper identifies and describes current attitudes towards classroom digitization and digital language learning practices under the umbrella of EduCAT 1x1, the One-Laptop-Per-Child (OLPC or 1x1) initiative in place in Catalonia. We thoroughly analyze practices worked out by six language teachers and twelve Compulsory Secondary Education (CSE) students from two schools participating in a competitive research project analyzing digital literacies. Preliminary results show that at a project-based level, committed teachers find ways to innovate, use technologies efficiently and foster language learning in all skills. However, at an activity-based level, Online Language Resources (OLR) such as dictionaries, automated translation software, spelling and grammar checkers and others remain underused, if not unexplored.

Keywords: classroom digitization, 1x1 initiatives, digital language learning, online language resources.

---

1. Universitat Pompeu Fabra, Barcelona, Spain; boris.vazquez@upf.edu

2. Universitat Pompeu Fabra, Barcelona, Spain; daniel.cassany@upf.edu

How to cite this chapter: Vázquez Calvo, B., & Cassany, D. (2016). Language learning actions in two 1x1 secondary schools in Catalonia: the case of online language resources. In A. Pareja-Lora, C. Calle-Martínez, & P. Rodríguez-Arancón (Eds), *New perspectives on teaching and working with languages in the digital era* (pp. 73-82). Dublin: Research-publishing.net. http://dx.doi.org/10.14705/rpnet.2016.tislid2014.423

Chapter 6

1. Introduction

In the context of the digital culture (Deuze, 2006), the digitized classroom may be like the same old wine in a brand-new bottle. Emerging technologies still cause technophobic or techno-deterministic attitudes (Bax, 2003). Some argue that the technological component must be normalized (Chambers & Bax, 2006) through, for instance, the integration of online language resources into language learning (Levy, 2009; Warschauer, 2009).

The competitive research project *IES2.0: Digital literacy practices: materials, classroom activities and online language resource* analyzes whether and how digitization has changed literacy as well as language teaching and learning practices across the curriculum (Cassany, 2013). Current lines of research a) describe technophobic and technophilic attitudes by teachers (Aliagas & Castellà, 2014), b) characterize the discourse by families against 1x1, c) analyze the norms set up by every school on how laptops must be used in the classrooms, d) explore how social networking can be used for educational purposes, and e) analyze specific aspects on how laptops can enhance language learning by means of effective informational searches or online language resources. In this sense, this paper focuses on technology-enhanced practices led by teachers of Catalan, Spanish and English in two selected schools, with special regard to how OLR, such as dictionaries, automated translation software and spelling and grammar checkers, are used in all three languages.

Research questions

- What are attitudes of teachers and students towards classroom digitization?

- Which are language learning practices led by teachers and students when in a digitized classroom?

- Which are the OLR used? How and for what purposes are they used?

2. E-learning

A report by Sangrà, Vlachopoulos, Cabrera, and Bravo (2011, p. 35) concludes that the most inclusive definition of e-learning would be a modality of teaching and learning, which may represent the whole or a part of the educational model in which it is implemented, which uses electronic means and appliances to ease the access, the evolution and the improvement of the quality of education and training.

With this definition in mind, we can easily agree that initiatives like OLPC programs are to be included into e-learning, yet with their own idiosyncratic features in front of other types of e-learning (such as long-distance e-learning), considering as well the variety of implementation formats of OLPC programs.

2.1. OLPC initiatives in Spain and Catalonia

In Spain, *Escuela 2.0* (School 2.0) was launched in 2009 and actualized under different tags depending on the region (*EduCAT 1x1* and *EduCAT 2.0* in Catalonia). From 2009 to 2012 many schools were able to set up power grids and Wi-Fi networks, and started using digital books, and, mainly, to provide every student with their own laptop. The Departments of Education of the different regions in Spain applied the program in slightly different ways. Common and divergent features are as follows (see Table 1 and Table 2).

Table 1. Common features of 1x1 programs in Spain

Technology/User	Every student has one low-performance laptop.
Network	Access to the Internet is universal.
Teaching materials	Teachers and students normally use digital books.
Information storage	Information delivery and production normally occurs through a Virtual Learning Environment (VLE), frequently Moodle.

Table 2. Common differences of 1x1 programs in Spain

Ownership	Students own the laptop, or the school owns the laptop.

Extension	The program can be implemented across the curriculum or in some selected subjects.
Level/Age	The program can be implemented in Primary (10-12 years old) or Secondary (12-16 years old) Education (CSE).
Teacher training	There is (no) specific training and/or support.

In the case of Catalonia, every student owns their laptop. The program has been implemented in CSE, but only in schools which asked submitted a specific request for it. Schools are also free to implement the program in some subjects or in all of them. And teachers report the training available to date is not enough.

2.2. Technology-enhanced language learning

In the sub-context of language e-learning, the current trend is Technology Enhanced Language Learning (TELL), successor of Computer Assisted Language Learning (CALL), and representative of what Bax (2003) named integrative CALL, where the computer is a means for learning and not the end in itself, allowing for open, creative, collaborative practices with and through computers.

Now, technologies comprise all sorts of devices includable into language learning, both in and out of the classroom. This goes contrary to a conceptualization of technologies in the language classroom, or whatever the subject, as an aid for the automatization of certain activities such as assessment, as in the case of self-corrective grids.

3. Methodology and corpus of data

The methodology we adopted is the case study (Cresswell, 2012). We center our research on two schools as representative cases, because a) both schools are 1x1 schools, b) both schools self-portrait themselves as highly technological, and c) both schools are immersed in a different reality of Catalonia; urban, middle-class, cosmopolitan area against a peri-urban, low-class area.

In-depth semi-structured interviews were conducted with teachers and students to elucidate their attitudes towards the teaching methodology adopted with technologies, the learning practices attached, and to check whether, which, and how online language resources are used in the long run.

In Table 3 and Table 4 below there is the number of informants. To read the tables, '3 (5)' would be read as three informants and five interviews conducted with those three informants. Schools and informants have been given nicknames for confidentiality reasons.

Table 3. Number of informant teachers and interviews by role or subject

Role/Subject School	Principal	Catalan	Spanish	English	Social Sciences	Math	Natural Sciences	TOTAL
Hope	2 (2)	3 (5)	2 (2)	1 (1)	2 (2)	1 (1)	1 (1)	**12 (14)**
Torrent	1 (1)	-	2 (2)	2 (3)	-	-	-	**5 (6)**
TOTAL	**3 (3)**	**3 (5)**	**2 (2)**	**3 (4)**	**2 (2)**	**2 (2)**	**1 (1)**	**17 (19)**

Table 4. Number of informant students and interviews by level

Students						
Year School	1y CSE	3y CSE	4y CSE	1y BAC	TOTAL
Hope	4 (2)	-	4 (2)	-	**8 (4)**
Torrent	-	2 (7)	2 (7)	2 (7)	**6 (28)**
TOTAL	**18 (12)**	**2 (7)**	**12 (12)**	**10 (10)**	**(41)**

4. Preliminary results and discussion

The analysis of results is at a preliminary stage. Nevertheless, some attitudes and teaching practices were identified to be representative of the teachers involved in the study.

4.1. Attitudes towards classroom digitization

Reticent attitudes were identified as derived from problems in the implementation of the program, as seen in the quote below:

> "The first problem is to study on the screen. One thing is to search for information on the computer, and another is to study. The other problem […] is that the screen conditions the contents and not otherwise, so that the lectures need to be adapted to the screens" (Rosa, teacher of Catalan) [Translated from Catalan].

Teachers and students complain largely over the quality of the digital books and manuals at their disposal. In her words, Rosa suggests that screen size limits the quality of the content of the digital books made for the purpose of e-learning and School 2.0. This impacts on a number of linguistic aspects, such as the study of text genres, as she holds that "on screens a description is rarely longer than a paragraph".

They also say that the characteristics of the computers limit the quality and outcome of learning, as simple tasks such as watching a video can cause major slowdown in the computer. Apart from digital material limitations, scarcely funded schools with some or no technical support struggle to keep up with broadband demands.

4.2. TELL practices

We have identified a number of practices which were representative as they used computers actively and beyond the mere automatization of certain features of teaching a language. In the case below, Eliseo comments on how Spanish as a first language should be taught: "to communicate and to learn to love to read and write". He explains a creative writing project:

> "In pairs [the students] had to compose a story to read during the holidays. All of the stories made by each pair were published on a blog, where

we voted which of them should be continued. [On the blog] we edited the selected text and each pair had to continue the story in a limited amount of time under a number of parameters concerning time unit, space, characters, and so on. They used Google Docs at home; they self-organized to compose their part of the story. They sent the final draft back to me and I published it on the blog for the whole classroom. The pair of students who would write the end of the story were the ones who started it, and they had to title it. […] In the end, we held a debate over the text, if we had respected the initial plot or not, who had introduced new characters, who had driven away from the plot, who had abandoned some character, who had created troubling components which added nothing to the text" (Eliseo, teacher of Spanish) [Translated from Spanish].

Other cases of innovative and leading projects in language learning were also identified, namely projects concerning augmented reality in English as a foreign language, or the use of social networking as a means for language learning. However, we have not seen school-wide innovative learning projects, as they tend to be teacher-driven, even if School 2.0 is conceived as a learning philosophy for the whole academic institution implementing it.

4.3. Online language resources

In contrast with larger projects led by innovative teachers, daily classroom activities seem to be less imaginative and productive. Teachers are aware of the need students have to know how to use OLR, yet they tend to give little or no instruction. This instruction is usually rather intuitive, and the range of OLR known by them and taught to the students is rather limited. Eliseo's quote is an example of how OLR are seen:

"I never correct students' spelling mistakes by giving the correct answer. I merely underline it and they are responsible for correcting it. […] They need to make use of the resources [he refers to dictionaries such as DRAE and WordReference, to Wikipedia and spelling and grammar checkers] to find out and correct it. [Have you ever taught these resources in some way?] Of course, I taught them all in the 1st year of CSE. All of the students can use them. [...] For instance, the grammatical aspect of whether "pálido" [pale in Spanish] is an adjective. What do I do? [I tell them:] "the DRAE has it and besides that, please read the meaning" (Eliseo, teacher of Spanish) [Translated from Spanish].

He assures he teaches OLR, yet the example he gives as to how he teaches them is poor and leaves the students with a number of unknown features present in the dictionary. No teacher in the cases studied has reported any OLR-oriented activity. So, besides further training, other resources could be added for specific linguistic needs. A whole set of types of dictionaries (by language, by search functions, etc.), a range of useful spell and grammar checkers, basic automated machine translation software, and possibly parsers, conjugation software and text corpora in higher levels. Depending on the linguistic context and purpose, different text-based activities should be designed for each set of OLR.

5. Concluding remarks

A number of preliminary conclusions can be extracted from this ongoing research:

- School 2.0 and OLPC programs are not guaranteed for success

Digitization is inherent to the 21st century society. Schools cannot and should not be kept aside, but school digitization should happen in a way that allows teachers and students to take maximum profit of technology both in technical aspects and, mostly, as regards teacher training.

- Individual teachers make change happen, and not technology in itself

If technology leads the way of teaching in a digitized classroom, teachers tend to constrain themselves to the limitations of computers and digital materials, rather than make the computer their ally in order to motivate students and liberate themselves from books and manuals. Teachers who create their own material and search for new sources of information and materials beyond the digital textbook normally come up with engaging projects where students learn what the curriculum expects them to learn, but using the affordances technologies put at their disposal. Collaboration is of the essence for innovation to be contagious, otherwise innovative projects die within the boundaries of specific classrooms and teachers lose their momentum to connect with the school and community as a whole. In this sense, teacher training and motivation is what the administration should take into consideration.

- OLRs remain unknown, underused, and poorly taught

The same lack of training has an impact on daily activities with language resources. The learning of OLR is taken for granted as they are easily accessible, yet few teachers teach or use them in their teaching. The examples identified in this regard make a poor use of OLR and leave their learning to rustic methods of rehearse-error and intuition, whereas formal instruction through OLR-oriented, text-based activities could arguably help students get familiar with a whole range of OLR, use them when appropriate for specific linguistic purposes in online or offline communicative situations, in the most effective and autonomous manner as possible.

6. Acknowledgements

Boris Vázquez Calvo holds a competitive grant from the Spanish Ministry of Economy with reference number BES-2012-052622.

The data in this article are based on the research project *IES2.0: Digital literacy practices. Materials, classroom activities and online language resources* (EDU2011-28381; 2012-14), funded by the 2011 National Program for Scientific Research, Development and Technological Innovation from the Spanish government.

References

Aliagas, C., & Castellà, J. M. (2014). Enthusiast, reluctant and resistant teachers towards the one-to-one laptop program: a multi-site ethnographic case study in Catalonia. In M. Stochetti (Ed.), *Media and education in the digital age. Concepts, assessments, subversions* (pp. 237-258). Frankfurt am Main: Peter Lang Publishers.

Bax, S. (2003). CALL – past, present and future. *System, 31*(1), 13-28. Retrieved from http://dx.doi.org/10.1016/s0346-251x(02)00071-4

Chambers, A., & Bax, S. (2006). Making CALL work: towards normalization. *System, 34*(4), 465-479. Retrieved from http://dx.doi.org/10.1016/j.system.2006.08.001

Cassany, D. (2013). ¿Cómo se lee y escribe en línea?. *RELED: Revista electrónica: leer, escribir y descubrir*. International Reading Association. Retrieved from https://repositori.upf.edu/bitstream/handle/10230/21235/Cassany_RELED_1.pdf?sequence=1

Cresswell, J. W. (2012). *Qualitative inquiry and research design*. New York: SAGE publications.

Deuze, M. (2006). Participation, remediation, bricolage: considering principal components of a digital culture. *The Information Society, 22*(2), 63-75. Retrieved from http://dx.doi.org/10.1080/01972240600567170

Levy, M. (2009). Technologies in use for second language learning. *Modern Language Journal, 93*(s1), 769-782. Retrieved from http://dx.doi.org/10.1111/j.1540-4781.2009.00972.x

Sangrà, A., Vlachopoulos, D., Cabrera, N., & Bravo, S. (2011). Hacia una definición inclusiva del e-learning. Barcelona: eLearn Center UOC.

Warschauer, M. (2009). Learning to write in the laptop classroom. *Writing and Pedagogy, 1*(1), 101-112.

7 Innovative resources based on ICTs and authentic materials to improve EFL students' communicative needs

Rebeca González Otero[1]

Abstract

Our global society and our current communication needs have put a strain on English as a Foreign Language (EFL) teaching, since common resources such as textbooks may fail to adapt to the needs and interests of our students. The present action research study aims at identifying EFL students' communicative needs and developing their oral skills through the use of authentic materials and Information and Communications Technologies (ICTs) in the classroom. For that purpose, a set of innovative resources was designed in order to decide whether these activities promote students' oral skills – namely oral production, pronunciation and fluency and listening comprehension – and whether they foster motivation among them.

Keywords: ICTs, authentic materials, innovation, oral skills, motivation.

1. Introduction

We live in a global world where communication demands have dramatically changed in the past decades and where EFL has acquired a central position. The Spanish educational system has tried to adapt to this new reality following the steps of other European countries that pioneered in this field. However, the effort

---

1. Universidad Autónoma de Madrid, Madrid, Spain; rebeca.gonzalez.otero@gmail.com

How to cite this chapter: González Otero, R. (2016). Innovative resources based on ICTs and authentic materials to improve EFL students' communicative needs. In A. Pareja-Lora, C. Calle-Martínez, & P. Rodríguez-Arancón (Eds), *New perspectives on teaching and working with languages in the digital era* (pp. 83-93). Dublin: Research-publishing.net. http://dx.doi.org/10.14705/rpnet.2016.tislid2014.424

seems inadequate as it can be inferred from our results in external evaluations, which show less satisfying results than those of other neighbouring countries, even if our students have been studying the language for longer.

Having analysed the situation, we can easily remark that the approach and the materials which are being used have not evolved at the same pace as the reality of our students. Therefore, we would like to propose a set of innovative resources based on ICTs and authentic materials to test whether they foster better results among our EFL students.

2. Literature review

English, the world lingua franca, is nowadays the first foreign language taught in most European countries. It seems that our current communicative needs in this global society and the efforts that are been made to construct a cohesive Europe have reached the education institutions and have been translated into a great concern for foreign languages – especially English.

According to Morales et al. (2000, pp. 214-215), even if all countries have different traditions in the field of language teaching, most of them share some common objectives – such as developing a social and cultural identity by studying a foreign language or using the language for communication purposes – and promote a wider use of authentic and motivating materials, ICTs and a student-centred approach. However, it seems that these objectives and recommendations do not translate the same way in all countries.

This can be inferred from the results of several studies and evaluations carried out all across Europe regarding the students' level and the teachers' performance (Bonnet, 1998; Gil & Alaban, 1997; OFSTED, 1996, quoted in Morales et al., 2000, p. 220), where we can see that many teachers do not enforce such objectives and recommendations in the actual classroom and where we can see how different students' performances are when comparing different countries, i.e. Spain and Sweden.

Taking into account that the key elements that interact in the language classroom are the teacher, the students and the materials used (Allwright, 1981 quoted in Hutchinson & Torres, 1994, p. 318), an analysis of the materials used is one of the easiest and most objective ways to assess the current state of language teaching in a given country.

After reading Spanish school plans and having the chance to observe English lessons in several schools, we came to the conclusion that the textbook was still a central resource in most Spanish EFL classrooms. The use of textbooks is not something negative per se; in fact, textbooks are helpful guides and sources of inspiration for the teacher (Hutchinson & Torres, 1994). However, an exclusive or excessive use of textbooks or any other ready-made materials can have negative effects in the EFL classroom, as they may foster a teacher-centred model and they may not always fit the classroom context, i.e. they present unreal language (Gilmore, 2007) and unreal contexts (Hwang, 2005) that will not help students to use the language in real life, and thus, will not motivate them.

On the other hand, we also realised that the development of students' communicative skills was generally disregarded in the language classroom, especially in what respects listening comprehension, oral production and pronunciation and fluency. There may be a clear explanation for that, since oral skills have been neglected in ELT literature/methodology for a long time, they were thought to be developed "through exposure of the language and practice of grammar" (Hedge, 2000, p. 228). However, times have changed and scholars have realised that oral skills are central in communication and that their study and development must be considered as a separate field in its own right.

In order to tackle this situation, some researchers have studied the potential of authentic materials and ICTs to develop more effective and motivating activities and thus EFL students' oral skills.

In what respects motivating alternatives in language learning, we have revised authors who highlighted the close relationship between authentic materials and

ICTs and motivation. Peacock (1997), for example, revised the work of several scholars who connected authentic materials and motivation in different ways, i.e. they bring learners closer to the target culture (Little, Devitt, & Singleton, 1989 quoted in Peacock, 1997, p. 144) and they offer rewarding challenges for students (Cross, 1984 quoted in Peacock, 1997, p. 144). On the other hand, authors like Warschauer (1996) show that ICTs can influence language learning motivation because they foster communication, they enhance students' personal power, they help students learn better and more independently and they make it easier to perceive achievement.

In what respects the development of oral skills, we have mainly analysed the effects of three of the most popular resources within the area of authentic materials and ICTs: the video format, eTandems and the combined use of blogs and podcasts.

Videos are believed to be one of the best authentic materials available for the EFL teacher when trying to cope with the students' communicative needs because, among other things, a) they "allow learners not only to listen to native speakers, but also to observe the gestures, facial expressions and other aspects of body language that accompany speech" (Hayati & Mohmedi, 2011, p. 181), b) they are great contextualisation tools (Tuffs & Tudor, 1990), and c) they are suitable for all levels as long as materials and tasks are carefully selected (Gilmore, 2007). The study on how to use different aid options – subtitles, transcripts, and so on – should also be taken in consideration, as they help students in the viewing process and show a great learning potential (Grgurovic & Hegelheimer, 2007; Hayati & Mohmedi, 2011).

Regarding eTandems, we have paid close attention to authors who studied conversation exchanges through ICTs. Most literature focuses on the use of chats or emails to give EFL students the chance to communicate with native speakers and thus improve their communicative skills (Lee, 2004; Tudini, 2003). These exchanges proved very positive, as they engaged students in cooperative learning and they had a positive effect on face-to-face oral production – they enhanced negotiation of meaning and corrective feedback. However, we must be aware of the superiority of audio-conferencing for such purposes. If we revise the studies of authors like Tsukamoto, Nuspliger, and Senzaki (2009), or Skinner and Austin (1999), we can see how audio-conferencing provides not only the same positive outcomes of chats, but also some other specific benefits of face-to-face communication.

Finally, the use of blogs and podcasts shows once again the potential of the web 2.0 for the education of the 21st century. In what respects blogs, they are presented as a simplified model of a website with many educational possibilities: they can host all kinds of resources and they can be easily created and easily accessible for the students and the teacher. Podcasts, on the other hand, can be used by the EFL student in two main ways: a) an authentic source of input, which the teacher/student can easily edit for learning purposes (Fox, 2008; Kavaliauskiene & Anusiene, 2009), and b) a tool for students who want to record themselves and upload it on the Internet (Ducate & Lomicka, 2009). As a result, using both resources combined can provide us with a lot of ideas for designing meaningful projects where students may access different materials and create finished products (Ducate & Lomicka, 2009).

3. Action research: a proposal

3.1. Participants

The study is being carried out with three groups of seventeen-year-old students attending 1st year of Bachillerato in three different secondary schools within the region of Madrid (IES Juan de Mairena, San Sebastián de los Reyes; IES Giner de los Ríos, Alcobendas; and IES Atenea, San Sebastián de los Reyes).

These three groups are not similar in number (26, 23 and 15 students respectively), but they all attend the same optional subject: *Ampliación de Lengua Extranjera I*. This subject, which is aims at students who want to improve their oral skills in English, was believed to be the perfect place for our study – not only because students were already working on their oral skills specifically, but also because students and teachers were expected to be more willing to participate in a study like this one due to the type of subject that we were dealing with.

3.2. Materials and procedures

This action research project is based on a preliminary research study where we were able to observe the current EFL teaching practices in Spain and to identify the students' communicative needs, which were usually not addressed in the EFL classroom (González, 2013). This study, which measured the potential of a set of innovative activities in terms of the motivation gains it enforced on students, provided very positive outcomes. For that reason, we decided to further explore this field in a more comprehensive fashion.

Our current study is structured in three different parts: (1) a pre-study analysis in which the proficiency and the motivation of students was measured, (2) the development of a series of innovative activities based on authentic materials and ICTs (the treatment), and (3) a post-study analysis to measure the proficiency and motivation of students after the treatment.

The pre-study analysis, as we have already mentioned, is divided in two steps. First of all, students will complete a motivation questionnaire based on Dörnyei's (1994) list of strategies to motivate language learners. This questionnaire contains two parts: one where students decide to what degree Dörnyei's (1994) strategies are relevant for them and another one where students state to what degree those strategies have been carried out in this course. Afterwards, students' proficiency level in the areas of listening and speaking will be tested with samples of the Preliminary English Test (PET).

The activities included in the treatment are based on the resources we mentioned above (the video format, eTandems and blogs and podcasts). These resources, mainly selected due to their tested potential, inspired three teaching units where activities were carefully designed and selected to match the students' interests and needs. The teaching unit with videos contains the following activities: (1) special days and celebration (listening comprehension questions), (2) opinion about cultural issues (opinion about topics that appear on a video), (3) cross-cultural references (follow-up to a sequence), and (4) audiovisual translation workshop (subtitling some videos). As for the teaching unit with eTandems, a four-session tandem with a British school via Skype is planned so that EFL Spanish students and Spanish as a foreign language British students work cooperatively in several tasks: an introductory speech, a presentation, a discussion and a joint project. Finally, the teaching unit with blogs and podcasts revolves around the creation of an online radio station where students have to create a series of radio broadcasts – namely a news broadcast, a debate, a storytelling broadcast and a commercial.

The post-study analysis is structured in a very similar way to the pre-study analysis. Students' proficiency level will be measured again using the PET Cambridge Test (Listening and Speaking Tests) and then students will have to complete a motivation post-questionnaire. This questionnaire is based on Dörnyei's (1994) strategies as well, but this time it will measure to what degree the activities proposed in the treatment fit these strategies. Moreover, this questionnaire contains two additional parts where students will be asked to assess activities proposed.

3.3. Hypothesis, planning, and expected results

The common axes of our action research project are the following hypotheses:

> **H1** – If we foster a more real and exhaustive use of the foreign language among our students, they will achieve better results in what respects their oral skills.

> **H2** – If we use ICTs and authentic materials, students will make improvements in their oral skills and will be more motivated in the learning process.

This quasi-experimental research is thus similar to our previous study. However, our previous research relied on subjective results and this time we want to make sure that results are more objective. For that reason, we will measure motivation

Chapter 7

and improvement on the language in quantitative terms to carry out a statistical analysis.

As we have previously explained, the motivation questionnaires are all based on Dörnyei's (1994) strategies and have a very similar structure in order to carry out a t-test regarding (1) what students are interested in and what students actually do in their classes, (2) what students are interested in and what students will actually achieve after this treatment, and (3) what students actually do in their classes and what students will achieve after this treatment. Statistical analysis is expected to show that there is a significant difference between what students actually do in their classes and what students are interested in and what students will achieve with this treatment. On the other hand, results should show that after the treatment, there is no significant difference between what students are interested in and what students will achieve with this treatment.

Regarding the improvement on the foreign language, results between the pre- and post-tests will be easily compared, since both tests are samples of the PET test, and thus have been extensively tested to entail the same level of difficulty. In this case, we will use a t-test again to see whether results in the pre-test and in the post-test are significantly different – a result that would show that the treatment is effective regarding the improvement of the students' oral skills.

Apart from this quantitative data, we plan on collecting some other kinds of qualitative data. The motivation post-questionnaire, for instance, includes an open question in which students will have to give their opinion on the activities proposed. Furthermore, all sessions of this action research project will be filmed in order to extract as much information as possible, i.e. involvement of students in the activities, oral performance of students, and so on.

In order to foster the use of these kinds of activities and manage to share their benefits with other professionals of the area, a final proposal will entail the creation of an online tool where members of the teaching community are able to share their ideas and materials, something that would enrich this field while turning the experience of creating innovative resources into an easier task.

4. Conclusions

The key to improvement in EFL teaching is nowadays more accessible than ever. If we consider Allwright's (1981) framework again, we may realise that making changes in what respects the role of the teacher and the role of the student in the classroom is rather complicated. However, changing the role of the materials used and implementing innovation through them is, as it has been shown in this study, something easily attainable and achievable.

Research in this field has previously showed that innovative materials based on authentic materials and ICTs provide great outcomes in teaching English to speakers of other languages, so the aim of this study is to contribute to this area of research with more optimistic results and reinforce this idea. Perhaps we can eventually prove that the materials and resources used in the language classroom can actually become a driving force in the renovation of the EFL teaching system in Spanish schools.

References

Allwright, R. L. (1981). What do we want teaching materials for? *ELT Journal, 36*(1), 5-18. Retrieved from http://dx.doi.org/10.1093/elt/36.1.5

Bonnet, G. (1998). *The assessment of pupils' skills in English in eight European countries 2002: a European project*. European network of policy makers for the evaluation of education systems.

Cross, N. (1984). *Developments in design methodology*. Chichester: Wiley.

Dörnyei, Z. (1994). Motivation and motivating in the foreing language classroom. *The Modern Language Journal, 78*(3), 273-284. Retrieved from http://dx.doi.org/10.1111/j.1540-4781.1994.tb02042.x

Ducate, L., & Lomicka, L. (2009). Podcasting: an effective tool for honing language students' pronunciation? *Language Learning & Technology, 13*(3), 66-86.

Fox, A. (2008). Using podcasts in the EFL classroom. *TESL-EJ Teaching English as a Second or Foreign Language, 11*(4), 1-12.

Gil, G., & Alaban, I. (1997). Evaluación comparada de la enseñanza y aprendizaje de la lengua extranjera. España, Francia, Suecia. Madrid, INCE.

Gilmore, A. (2007). Authentic materials and authenticity in foreign language learning. *Language Teaching*, *40*(2), 97-118. Retrieved from http://dx.doi.org/10.1017/S0261444807004144

González, R. (2013). An innovative proposal for the subject of Ampliación de Lengua Extranjera. *Mejores trabajos fin de Máster de la UAM 2010-2011*. Madrid: Servicio de publicaciones de la UAM.

Grgurovic, M., & Hegelheimer, V. (2007). Help options and multimedia listening: students' use of subtitles and the transcript. *Language Learning & Technology*, *11*(1), 45-66.

Hayati, A., & Mohmedi, F. (2011). The effect of films with and without subtitles on listening comprehension of EFL learners. *British Journal of Educational Technology*, *42*(1), 181-192. Retrieved from http://dx.doi.org/10.1111/j.1467-8535.2009.01004.x

Hedge, T. (2000). *Teaching and learning in the language classroom*. Oxford: Oxford University Press.

Hutchinson, T., & Torres, E. (1994). The textbook as an agent of change. *ELT Journal*, *48*(4), 315-328. Retrieved from http://dx.doi.org/10.1093/elt/48.4.315

Hwang, C. C. (2005). Effective EFL education through popular authentic materials. *Asian EFL Journal – The EFL Professionals' Written Forum*, *7*(1), Article 7.

Kavaliauskiene, G., & Anusiene, L. (2009). English for specific purposes: podcasts for listening skills. *Santalka: Filologija, Edukologija*, *17*(2), 28-37. Retrieved from http://dx.doi.org/10.3846/1822-430X.2009.17.2.28-37

Lee, L. (2004). Learners' perspectives on networked collaborative interaction with native speakers of Spanish in the US. *Language Learning & Technology*, *8*(1), 83-100.

Little, D., Devitt, S., & Singleton, D. (1989). *Learning foreign languages from authentic texts: theory and practice*. Dublin: Authentik.

Morales, C. et al. (2000). *La enseñanza de lenguas extranjeras en España*. Ministerio de Educación, Cultura y Deporte. Madrid: Subdirección General de Información y Publicaciones.

OFSTED. (1996). *Subjects and standards: issue for school development. Arising from OFSTED Inspection Findings 1994-5: Key Stages 3 & 4 and Post 16*. London: HMSO.

Peacock, M. (1997). The effect of authentic materials on the motivation of EFL learners. *ELT Journal*, *51*(2), 144-156. Retrieved from http://dx.doi.org/10.1093/elt/51.2.144

Skinner, B., & Austin, R. (1999). Computer conferencing – does it motive EFL students? *ELT Journal*, *53*(4), 270-279. Retrieved from http://dx.doi.org/10.1093/elt/53.4.270

Tsukamoto, M., Nuspliger, B., & Senzaki, Y. (2009). Using Skype to connect a classroom to the world: providing students an authentic language experience within the classroom. *CamTESOL Conference on English Language Teaching: Selected Papers, Volume 5.*

Tudini, V. (2003). Using native speakers in chat. *Language Learning & Technology, 7*(3), 141-159.

Tuffs, R., & Tudor, I. (1990). What the eye does not see: cross cultural problems in the comprehension of video material. *Relc Journal, 21*(2), 29-43. Retrieved from http://dx.doi.org/10.1177/003368829002100203

Warschauer, M. (1996). Motivational aspects of using computers for writing and communication. In M. Warschauer (Ed.), *Telecollaboration in foreign language learning* (pp. 29-46). Honolulu, HI: University of Hawai'i Second Language Teaching and Curriculum Center.

8 Teaching the use of WebQuests to master students in Pablo de Olavide University

Regina Gutiérrez Pérez[1]

Abstract

This paper deals with the new pedagogical approaches that the European Space of Higher Education (ESHE) demands in the university system. More specifically, it describes the experience of teaching the use of WebQuest to future educators in the module of foreign languages belonging to the 'Máster de enseñanza de profesorado de educación secundaria obligatoria y bachillerato, formación profesional y enseñanza de idiomas'. In the module of English, a unit is dedicated to new ways of teaching and learning. Blended learning, e-learning, tandem learning and cooperative learning are dealt with in detail. The WebQuest activity is provided as an example of blended learning and cooperative learning. This paper shows the objectives and outcomes of the implementation of this teaching experience.

Keywords: WebQuest, European Space of Higher Education, ESHE, blended learning, cooperative learning.

1. Introduction

Our proposal is based on the experience of teaching the use of WebQuest to future educators in the module of foreign languages belonging to the 'Máster de enseñanza de profesorado de educación secundaria obligatoria y bachillerato, formación profesional y enseñanza de idiomas'.

1. Universidad Pablo de Olavide, Sevilla, Spain; rgutper@upo.es

How to cite this chapter: Gutiérrez Pérez, R. (2016). Teaching the use of WebQuests to master students in Pablo de Olavide University. In A. Pareja-Lora, C. Calle-Martínez, & P. Rodríguez-Arancón (Eds), *New perspectives on teaching and working with languages in the digital era* (pp. 95-104). Dublin: Research-publishing.net. http://dx.doi.org/10.14705/rpnet.2016.tislid2014.425

Chapter 8

The subject taught, for five academic years since 2009, is 'Innovation and Research'. The main aim of this subject is to help students become familiar with the use of new technologies which have recently been introduced in secondary school centers in Andalucía. Information and Communication Technologies (ICT) have a number of widely recognised advantages for the new teaching methodology demanded by ESHE. We agree with Pennock-Speck (2009) who states that "if our university and state universities are to remain at the forefront in teaching and research in the future, we have to make sure that we implement ICT as effectively as possible in the new degree" (p. 183).

Special attention is also paid to the evaluation of languages according to the Common European Framework of Reference for Languages (CEFR). Finally, new ways of teaching and learning are taught and practised thoroughly. Blended learning "designates the range of possibilities presented by combining Internet and digital media with established classroom forms that require the physical co-presence of teacher and students" (Friesen, 2012, p. 1). Cooperative learning encourages students to work with and learn from each other (Johnson & Johnson, 1998). This method can help them develop leadership skills and the ability to work with others as a team.

It is in this last unit where we teach the use of WebQuests, given that it is an ideal activity to combine face-to-face learning with autonomous and cooperative work. March (2003) defines it in the following way:

> "[a] WebQuest is a scaffolded learning structure that uses links to essential resources on the World Wide Web and an authentic task to motivate students' investigation of a central, open-ended question, development of individual expertise and participation in a final group process that attempts to transform newly acquired information into a more sophisticated understanding. The best WebQuests do this in a way that inspires students to see richer thematic relationships, facilitate a contribution to the real world of learning and reflect on their own metacognitive processes" (p. 43).

It is a didactic resource based on the constructivist learning and on the cooperative methodology that is very successful at the moment in pre-School, primary and secondary level.

Our main aim is to show them that WebQuests are different from other web-based lessons in that they go beyond simply answering questions. The focus is on using information rather than looking for it. They require higher thinking skills such as problem solving, analysis, synthesis, and creativity. The task can be almost anything. For instance, students can be asked to design a collage, make a powerpoint presentation, write an essay, perform a play, etc.

2. Methodology

In the subject taught, 'Innovation and Research', students carry out several tasks, such as devising an activity according to the new methods of teaching and learning (blended learning, e-learning, tandem learning and cooperative learning). Besides, we decided to introduce WebQuests, since they had never heard of them. For that purpose, classes in an IT classroom take place. We also make them design their own WebQuest in groups of two (three maximum in some cases).

Students are shown the WebQuest generator chosen (http://aula21.net/ Wqfacil/intro.htm), which facilitates the task, since it is quite intuitive. The template shows that the WebQuest is comprised of six components:

- Introduction: the intent of the introduction is twofold: first, to orient the learner by setting the stage and explaining the main goals. Second, it should capture their attention.

- Task: it is a description of what the learner will accomplish during the exercise.

Chapter 8

- Process: the process identifies the steps the students should go through to achieve the task. It also includes the online resources they will need.

- Resources: this is "a list of [websites] which the instructor has located that will help the learner accomplish the task. The resources are pre-selected so that learners can focus their attention on the topic rather than surfing aimlessly" (Lambert, n.d).

- Evaluation: it describes how their performance will be evaluated, and it is often in the form of a scoring rubric.

- Conclusion: the conclusion brings closure to the quest. It summarises what the learners will have achieved by completing the WebQuest and often encourages reflection about what was learned.

After investigating and learning how to implement this activity, students design WebQuests with diverse up-to-date topics that catch their pupils' attention and interest (see Figure 1 and Figure 2 below) and make the tasks authentic: carnival, portraits, trips, tsunamis, inventions, multiculturalism, sports, mobile phones, etc., some of them interdisciplinary, and applied to two different levels, primary and secondary education.

Figure 1.   Mobile phones, friends or enemies?

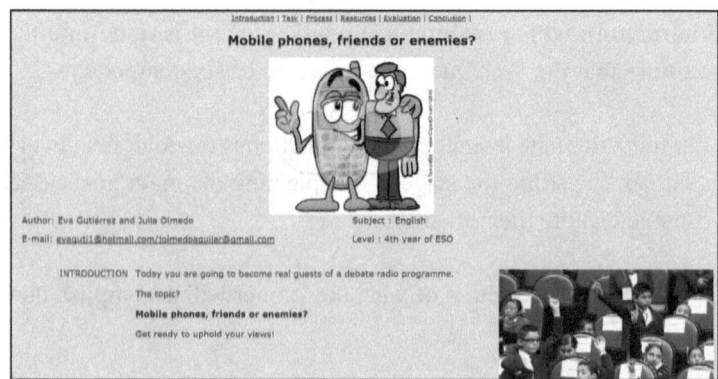

Figure 2. English is multicultural

Most of them are short-term WebQuests designed to be completed in one to three classes. They are highly visual; they include lots of pictures, animations, maps and even sounds, tools which hold students' interest. Once they have finished, each group makes a presentation of their WebQuests and their classmates evaluate it according to Dodge's (2001) rubric for evaluating WebQuests, so that a cooperative way of evaluation is also fulfilled. The rubric[2] (evaluates the following:

	Beginning	Developing	Accomplished	Score
Overall Visual Appeal	0 points	2 points	4 points	
	There are few or no graphic elements. No variation in layout or typography. Color is garish and/or typographic variations are overused and legibility suffers. Background interferes with the readability.	Graphic elements sometimes, but not always, contribute to the understanding of concepts, ideas and relationships. There is some variation in type size, color, and layout.	Appropriate and thematic graphic elements are used to make visual connections that contribute to the understanding of concepts, ideas and relationships. Differences in type size and/or color are used well and consistently.	

2. Modified by Bellofatto, Bohl, Casey, Krill, and Dodge; http://webquest.org/sdsu/webquestrubric.html.

Chapter 8

Navigation & Flow	0 points Getting through the lesson is confusing and unconventional. Pages can't be found easily and/or the way back isn't clear.	2 points There are a few places where the learner can get lost and not know where to go next.	4 points Navigation is seamless. It is always clear to the learner what all the pieces are and how to get to them.
Mechanical Aspects	0 points There are more than 5 broken links, misplaced or missing images, badly sized tables, misspellings and/or grammatical errors.	1 point There are some broken links, misplaced or missing images, badly sized tables, misspellings and/or grammatical errors.	2 points No mechanical problems noted.
Introduction			
Motivational Effectiveness of Introduction	0 points The introduction is purely factual, with no appeal to relevance or social importance The scenario posed is transparently bogus and doesn't respect the media literacy of today's learners.	1 point The introduction relates somewhat to the learner's interests and/or describes a compelling question or problem.	2 points The introduction draws the reader into the lesson by relating to the learner's interests or goals and/or engagingly describing a compelling question or problem.
Cognitive Effectiveness of the Introduction	0 points The introduction doesn't prepare the reader for what is to come, or build on what the learner already knows.	1 point The introduction makes some reference to the learner's prior knowledge and previews to some extent what the lesson is about.	2 points The introduction builds on the learner's prior knowledge and effectively prepares the learner by foreshadowing what the lesson is about.
Task			

Connection of Task to Standards	0 points The task is not related to standards.	2 point The task is referenced to standards but is not clearly connected to what learners must know and be able to do to achieve proficiency of those standards.	4 points The task is referenced to standards and is clearly connected to what learners must know and be able to do to achieve proficiency of those standards.	
Cognitive Level of the Task	0 points Task requires simply comprehending or retelling of information found on web pages and answering factual questions.	3 points Doable but is limited in its significance to learners' lives. The task requires analysis of information and/ or putting together information from several sources.	6 points Task is doable and engaging, and elicits thinking that goes beyond rote comprehension. The task requires synthesis of multiple sources of information, and/ or taking a position, and/or going beyond the data given and making a generalisation or creative product.	
Process				
Clarity of Process	0 points Process is not clearly stated. Learners would not know exactly what they were supposed to do just from reading this.	2 points Some directions are given, but there is missing information. Learners might be confused.	4 points Every step is clearly stated. Most learners would know exactly where they are at each step of the process and know what to do next.	
Richness of Process	0 points Few steps, no separate roles assigned.	1 points Some separate tasks or roles assigned. More complex activities required.	2 points Different roles are assigned to help learners understand different perspectives and/or share responsibility in accomplishing the task.	

Chapter 8

Scaffolding of Process	0 points	3 points	6 points	
	The process lacks strategies and organisational tools needed for learners to gain the knowledge needed to complete the task. Activities are of little significance to one another and/or to the accomplishment of the task.	Strategies and organisational tools embedded in the process are insufficient to ensure that all learners will gain the knowledge needed to complete the task. Some of the activities do not relate specifically to the accomplishment of the task.	The process provides learners coming in at different entry levels with strategies and organisational tools to access and gain the knowledge needed to complete the task. Activities are clearly related and designed to take the learners from basic knowledge to higher level thinking.	
Resources				
Relevance & Quantity of Resources	0 points	2 point	4 points	
	Resources provided are not sufficient for learners to accomplish the task. There are too many resources for learners to look at in a reasonable time.	There is some connection between the resources and the information needed for learners to accomplish the task. Some resources don't add anything new.	There is a clear and meaningful connection between all the resources and the information needed for learners to accomplish the task. Every resource carries its weight.	
Quality of Resources	0 points	2 points	4 points	
	Links are mundane. They lead to information that could be found in a classroom encyclopedia.	Some links carry information not ordinarily found in a classroom.	Links make excellent use of the Web's timeliness and colorfulness. Varied resources provide enough meaningful information for learners to think deeply.	

Evaluation				
Clarity of Evaluation Criteria	0 points Criteria for success are not described.	3 points Criteria for success are at least partially described.	6 points Criteria for success are clearly stated in the form of a rubric. Criteria include qualitative as well as quantitative descriptors. The evaluation instrument clearly measures what learners must know and be able to do to accomplish the task.	
Total Score				/50

Each student selects the three WebQuests they had granted the highest scores. At the end of the class there is a counting of the votes and the best WebQuests get the highest grades.

3. Results

The use of the Internet provides a good exposure to the target language and makes students more independent. The WebQuests generated in groups achieve the following objectives:

- Learning to design a WebQuest through a constructivist based approach to education and inquiry-based instruction.

- Developing the task through blended and cooperative methodologies.

- Designing WebQuests to be implemented in their specialty as future educators.

- Evaluation through a specific rubric for evaluating WebQuests.

- Cooperative evaluation.

The results of this practice in the last years have been very positive. Many of the students are able to carry out their WebQuests in schools in the final period of the master. They find the experience and results extremely satisfactory, since, by implementing ICT in the teaching process, students´ autonomy and motivation are fostered, they assure.

4. Conclusion

The ESHE is bringing about structural changes and new pedagogical approaches. In this paper we have proposed blended and cooperative learnings through the use of WebQuests, a student-oriented teaching approach, in order to foster autonomous learning. The positive results achieved shows that teaching tools such as this one can help teachers integrate the Internet into the curriculum while creating fun instructional activities that motivate students.

References

Dodge, B. (2001). *Rubric for evaluating WebQuests*. Retrieved from http://webquest.org/sdsu/webquestrubric.html

Friesen, N. (2012). Report: defining blended learning. Retrieved from http://learningspaces.org/papers/Defining_Blended_Learning_NF.pdf

Johnson, D. W., & Johnson, R. T. (1998). *Learning together and alone: cooperative, competitive, and individualistic learning* (5th ed.). Needham Heights, MA: Allyn & Bacon.

March, T. (2003). The learning power of WebQuests. *Educational Leadership, 61*(4), 42-47.

Lambert, J. (n.d). *Steps to creating a WebQuest*. Retrieved from https://www.ncsu.edu/project/middletech/lambert/TIME/webquests/create.html

Pennock-Speck, B. (2009). European convergence and the role of ICT in English studies at the Universitat de València: lessons learned and prospects for the future. *English Language Teaching in the European Credit Transfer System: Facing the Challenge*. Frankfurt am Main: Peter Lang.

9 ICTs, ESPs and ZPD through microlessons in teacher education

Soraya García Esteban[1], Jesús García Laborda[2], and Manuel Rábano Llamas[3]

Abstract

This paper presents the initial results of the use of dialogic interaction enhanced by the use of technology in teaching English in different settings and subjects of teacher education. Technology is used in three different ways: as a support (video) for analysis through teacher-instructor interaction, as a means of social interaction and use of language for education between teacher and students (use of the computer for instruction), and as the creation of own designed materials for language training (through the use of technology). Data is obtained from video-recordings related to teaching and learning English as a foreign language by three different teachers in three subjects from Primary and Infant Education at Universidad de Alcalá. Results indicate that microteaching is not only valid as a training method but also to introduce new content and concepts that have not been previously introduced in the classes. The interaction in the Zone of Proximal Development (ZPD) between the teacher-instructor and the teacher-students also proves to have a powerful effect in motivation, teaching improvement and language for education skills development through self-reflection.

Keywords: ICT, microteaching, pre-service teachers, pre-school, dialogic interaction.

---

1. Universidad de Alcalá, Alcalá de Henares, Madrid, Spain; soraya.garciae@uah.es

2. Universidad de Alcalá, Alcalá de Henares, Madrid, Spain; jesus.garcialaborda@uah.es

3. Universidad de Alcalá, Alcalá de Henares, Madrid, Spain; manuel.rabano@uah.es

How to cite this chapter: García Esteban, S., García Laborda, J., & Rábano Llamas, M. (2016). ICTs, ESPs and ZPD through microlessons in teacher education. In A. Pareja-Lora, C. Calle-Martínez, & P. Rodríguez-Arancón (Eds), *New perspectives on teaching and working with languages in the digital era* (pp. 105-113). Dublin: Research-publishing.net. http://dx.doi.org/10.14705/rpnet.2016.tislid2014.426

Chapter 9

1. Introduction

Microteaching goes back to the early and mid-1960s where it was designed at the University of Stanford (Allen & Wang, 1996) and has been considered as one of the most successful techniques in teacher training. The main purpose was that future professionals were conscious of what we call 'educational ac' and that they acquire the pedagogic 'know how' (skill) defined in terms of observable behaviour. This project is based on the main features of these practices, which are: restricted and concise aims formulated in terms of teaching behaviour, independent of the lesson content; symbolic modelling (written and verbal instructions, description of teaching behaviour, verbal interaction) and/or perception (recording sequence, visual and audible in which a 'teacher' shows the behaviours to acquire); teacher-student performance in a simplified teaching situation (with 4 or 5 students; 5 minute lesson) and results analysis with a positive reinforcement of the reached aims.

2. Literature review

Trying to define the concept, we find terms called 'training model', which came from microteaching sessions conceived (Ferry, 1983) as a transference model between a real and a simulated session. Sometimes, it is related with the teaching basic abilities (Turney & Col, 1973), with the stream of action-investigation (Smith & Lovat, 1991), with reflective teaching (Schon, 1983), or with the experiential-reflective learning (Kolb, 1984). Although these concepts will be reviewed in the next section, we picked Wallace's (1991) definition, which indicates, first, three basic conceptual aspects for the 'putting into practice'; to set the teacher's role, the length of the lesson, and the distribution of the students, and second, the several phases of the project, of which the first three stand out; the first stage entails preparation (*the Briefing*) in small groups before the second stage, the lesson production or performance (*the Teaching*). The third stage (*the Critique*) is maybe the most important one because authentic space for the reflective-experiential learning is developed. Therefore, we will pay special attention to this stage, not just in theory but also in practice.

The pedagogical model called 'reflexive-experiential learning' holds that the knowledge acquisition cycle is based on the reflection of facts previously experienced which, once conceptualised, become the backbone of the 'feedback' or 'active experimentation' (Kolb, 1984). In professional competence terms, we understand the main way for the improvement of teaching in general, and the teaching of foreign languages in particular. It is not only to establish a link between theory and practice, but is defined as a 'cognitive learning process' (Kelly, 1997) in which critical reflection reaches a special role.

Critical reflection entails and includes, among other considerations, the implementation of analysis and synthetic processes, the interaction between students and teachers, and search and information management. Some experiences with learning theory emphasise the importance of involving the students in projects which, based on meaningful learning, enhance critical reflection by the proposed activities, highlighting that the learning process itself takes on particular importance in the success. Virtual platforms become, therefore, very useful tools for interaction, analysis and synthesis, and evaluate information to build and share knowledge of the group as motivating and enriching elements in the teaching and learning process. Here, technology becomes, once again, prime location to meet and interact.

The use of technology in English for Specific Purposes (ESP) for teacher education through microlessons also implies operations such as "revision of time, planning and facilities for the practicing of subject skills" (Pool, Reitsma, & Mentz, 2013, p. 455) along with the provision of opportunities for interaction between the language teacher tutor and the teacher-apprentices. This interaction should lead to adequate opportunities to practice, analyse and reflect on the specific language as well as the methods and skills to teach foreign languages.

The use of technology in this approach to teacher education, however, changes the importance of traditional individual use of the specific language (Frye, 1971) by the teacher-learners into a more dialogic relation in which the interaction between the language teacher-instructor and the teacher-candidates is clearly marked by the mediation of technology to facilitate a dialogic ESP discourse in the teacher-learners performance (Johnson, 2007) within the ZPD (Vygotsky, 1978).

Technology favours the possibility to reshape lesson planning and engage into collaborative working partnerships, which is mediated by the instructor either in face to face interaction (Casey, 2011) or in distance learning (Sarigoz, 2013) and is developed in the verbal interaction between the pre-service teacher(s) and the instructor. In this way, the microlesson is potentially enriched by the dialogic interaction. This development is clearly supported by the use of recording techniques as well as the audiovisual techniques used to include visual information that serves to construct the potential students' knowledge (Macleod, 1987). This interaction is also valid to develop new contents and concepts that may have formal and informal origins. Since many of these issues have not been put into test yet, it was necessary to observe whether students also engage in this dialogic context and how it is perceived by them.

3. Procedure

Since the major goal of this study was to enhance ESP learning and ZPD interaction with technology through microteaching in teacher education, researchers considered to identify how Information and Communications Technology (ICT) can be used in these settings in three different instructive ways: as a support (video) for analysis through teacher-instructor interaction, as a means of social interaction and use of language for education between teacher and students (use of technology for instruction), and as a way to create their own designed materials for language training (through the use of technology).

The most frequent and efficient method for identifying learning acquisition, dialogic interaction and critical thinking is through self-reported data questionnaires and interviews (Kavaliauskienè, Kaminskienè, & Anusiene, 2007, p. 161), which are the means for data collection in the current study. The questionnaire, based on Johnson (2007) and Pool et al. (2013, p. 455), placed reliance on quantitative data and contained twelve Likert-scale questions related to the use of interaction, ICTs and ESPs in microlessons where students selected in a scale from 1 ('agree') to 2 ('disagree'). Qualitative data were obtained from an open question concerning rationalisation of their experience and proposals for improvement. Succeeding data analysis, interviews were held in order to foster student's critical thinking about their own teaching-learning experience. This reflection was discussed in a dialogic relation between the language teacher-instructor and the teacher-candidates, therefore enhancing the ZPD.

This study used a microteaching practise to study learner's training, analysis and reflection on the specific language, as well as the methods and skills needed to teach foreign languages. The participants were thirty-four second-year full time students of English as a foreign language in BA (Hons.) Primary Education. The case study has been carried out outside class time in groups of three students along the twelve European Credit Transfer and Accumulation System (ECTS) contact hours assigned to the course. The action, designed to reinforce the contents of the subject, is divided in three different sections after Wallace (1991) and Seidel's (1998) model of qualitative data analysis: noticing, collecting and thinking.

The main project consisted of the preparation, presentation and video recording in class of a microteaching that developed activities, methods and strategies for teaching English in early childhood education. The most relevant topics were recapitulated in a glossary to be reviewed and considered during the action. The microlesson involved noticing language development, appropriate use of terms and concepts related to ESP in pre-school, interaction between group members to plan and time the lesson (e.g. face to face meetings, technological communication using different resources like Google Drive, Dropbox, etc.), co-construction and collaborative working, and creation of own designed (technological) materials for language training.

The evaluation process is an important part of any training program; therefore the second assignment required data collection and analysis. After watching their own microteaching video-recordings in YouTube or Dropbox, students were required to work autonomously through a closed questionnaire about self-performance based on the four rubrics mentioned above.

Kvale (1983) defines the qualitative research interview as an "interview, whose purpose is to gather descriptions of the life-world of the interviewee with respect to interpretation of the meaning of the described phenomena" (p. 174). In the final phase, learners contribute their own thinking and proposals for improving interaction in the ZPD in a reflective individual discussion face to face with the tutor about their video recording presentation.

4. Results and discussion

The results of the learners' responses and reflections on their own teaching after watching their video performance show that the developed process meets the objectives, as shown in Table 1.

The findings revealed that most respondents (97%) contemplate using ESP vocabulary and concepts related to teaching English in pre-school, whereas 88% used it if from the Glossary "Materials, methods & resources in Early Childhood Education", hence broadening their specific knowledge in the area.

All participants have indicated that in order to achieve teaching goals, lessons were correctly planned and timed (85%) in face to face meetings (84%), and using technology (85%) like e-mails, mobile telephone text messages and Dropbox in collaborative and partnership work (95%). Students have mainly considered that interaction and co-construction of learning deepens relationships (94%) and understanding between partners, leading, therefore, to improvement (91%).

Results have shown, however, that most students (94%) prefer to use traditional resources (flashcards, songs and realia) with the help of technology (YouTube, TEFL websites, etc.) rather than creating their own designed technological materials or programs for language training (6%). Analysis and specification of these data, both written and in personal interviews, indicates that students rated highly the experience, exceeding our expectations in terms of commitment and interest in the project. Technology (videos) is used for microteaching evaluation and as a means of language and social interaction (students and instructors) not only through the computer, but also with mobile resources (telephone texting). An unexpected outcome showed that ICT was not used for the creation of own designed materials for language training through the use of technical programs due to the considerable amount of time that it involves.

Table 1. Reflection on microteaching video recording

ESP content and concepts	Agree%	Disagree %
Use of specific vocabulary and concepts related to teaching English in primary education	97	3
Development of (new) concepts from the Glossary "Materials, methods & resources in Early Childhood Education"	88	12
Interaction (lesson planning & timing)	**Agree%**	**Disagree %**
Lesson was correctly planned to achieve teaching goals	100	0
Lesson was planned in face to face meetings	84	16
Lesson was planned using technology (e-mail, dropbox telephone texting…)	85	15
Correct timing to achieve teaching goals	94	6
Co-construction & Collaborative working	**Agree%**	**Disagree %**
Collaborative & partnership working	94	6
Co-construction of learning' deepens relationships	94	6
Understanding between partners leads to improvement	91	9
Creation of own designed (technological?) activities/materials for language training	**Agree%**	**Disagree %**
Use of technological programs (Hot potatoes, Quia…)	6	94
Use of technological resources (YouTube, TEFL websites…)	100	0
Use of traditional resources	100	0

5. Conclusions

From the statistical data obtained, the use of technology through microlessons is favourably valued not only as a training technique, but also to practice and introduce new content. Analysis of the different learning-teaching strategies used in the videos led to self-reflection in a dialogic interaction between the language teacher and the teacher-candidates by means of technology (videos and internet) within the ZPD, according to the idea that development is defined both by what a learner can do independently and by what he/she can do when assisted by a more competent adult.

The present paper just showed that teachers can use information about Vygotsky's (1978) ZPD to organise classroom activities, providing planned instruction, scaffolding and cooperative learning with technology. These preliminary findings recommend further research on two additional phases; microteaching re-planning and re-teaching, to study how reflection and dialogic interaction within the ZPD can lead to improvement in the desired direction.

References

Allen, D., & Wang, W. (1996). *Microteaching*. Beijing: Xinhua Press.
Casey, K. (2011). Modeling lessons. *Educational Leadership, 69*(2), 24-29.
Ferry, G. (1983). *Le trajet de la formation*. Paris: Dunot.
Frye, B. J. (1971). *An analysis of teacher education innovations with recommendations for their utilization in the professional preparation of prospective industrial arts teachers*. University Microfilms: Michigan.
Johnson, K. E. (2007). Tracing teacher and student learning in teacher-authored narratives. *Teacher Development, 11*(2), 1-14. Retrieved from http://dx.doi.org/10.1080/13664530701442879
Kavaliauskienè, G., Kaminskienè, L., & Anusiene, L. (2007). Reflective practice: assessment of assignments in English for specific purposes. *Ibérica, 14*, 149-166.
Kelly, C. (1997). David Kolb, the theory of experiential learning and ESL. *The Internet TESL Journal, 3*(9). Retrieved from http://iteslj.org/Articles/Kelly-Experiential/
Kolb, D. A. (1984). *Experiential learning: experience as the source of learning and development.* Englewood Cliffs, New Jersey: PrenticeHall.
Kvale, S. (1983). The qualitative research interview: a phenomenological and a hermeneutical mode of understanding. *Journal of Phenomenological Psychology, 14*, 171-196. Retrieved from http://dx.doi.org/10.1163/156916283X00090

Macleod, G. (1987). Microteaching: end of a research era? *International Journal of Educational Research, 11*(5), 531-542. Retrieved from http://dx.doi.org/10.1016/0883-0355(87)90013-9

Pool, J., Reitsma, G., & Mentz, E. (2013). An evaluation of technology teacher training. *International Journal of Technology and Design Education, 23*(2), 455-472.

Sarigoz, I. H. (2013). Adjusting language level in teacher-talk in ELT microteachings with specific reference to distance education teacher. *Turkish Online Journal of Distance Education, 14*(2), 165-184.

Schon, D. (1983). *The reflective practitioner: how professionals think in action.* New York: Basic Books.

Seidel, J. V. (1998). *Qualitative data analysis.* Colorado Springs, CO: Qualis Research.

Smith, D., & Lovat, T. (1991). *Curriculum: action on reflection* (2nd ed.). Wentworth Falls: Social Science Press.

Turney, N., & Col, R. (1973). *Microteaching: research theory and practice*, Sidney: Sidney University Press.

Vygotsky, L. S. (1978). *Mind in society.* Cambridge, MA: Harvard University Press.

Wallace, J. (1991). *Training foreign language teachers. A reflective approach.* Melbourne: Cambridge University Press.

Section 1.2.

Language distance, lifelong teaching and learning, and massive open online courses

10 Learning specialised vocabulary through Facebook in a massive open online course

Patricia Ventura[1] and Elena Martín-Monje[2]

Abstract

This paper explores how the incorporation of a social network such as Facebook can enhance the acquisition of specialised vocabulary in the context of a Massive Open Online Course (MOOC). Such initiative took place in the second edition of the MOOC Professional English, the first ever English for Specific Purposes (ESP) MOOC to be launched in Spain as one of the courses offered by Aprendo, the UNED online platform. The main aim of the experiment was to ascertain how this social network, which has proved to foster motivation and engagement in language learning contexts (Blattner & Lomicka, 2012; Zourou, 2012), could enhance the students' learning experience and promote vocabulary acquisition in an ESP MOOC context. Following an action-research methodology (Lewin, 1946) a Facebook group was created by the MOOC curator and ran for eight weeks out of the twelve that the course was comprised of (11 November 2013-31 January 2014). A mixed-method approach was adopted for the data collection, using both quantitative techniques, such as student tracking in the MOOC, and also qualitative ones (e.g. questionnaires). The results point towards a positive impact of the Facebook network in the motivation of students to learn specialised vocabulary and an improvement in their progress in the MOOC, likewise fighting the main two problems that MOOCs currently are said to have: high drop-out rates and lack of student engagement.

Keywords: ESP, social networks, massive open online courses, vocabulary.

1. Universidad Nacional de Educación a Distancia (UNED), Madrid, Spain; patricia.vex@gmail.com

2. Universidad Nacional de Educación a Distancia (UNED), Madrid, Spain; emartin@flog.uned.es

How to cite this chapter: Ventura, P., & Martín-Monje, E. (2016). Learning specialised vocabulary through Facebook in a massive open online course. In A. Pareja-Lora, C. Calle-Martínez, & P. Rodríguez-Arancón (Eds), *New perspectives on teaching and working with languages in the digital era* (pp. 117-128). Dublin: Research-publishing.net. http://dx.doi.org/10.14705/rpnet.2016.tislid2014.427

1. Introduction

Today, informal learning offers teachers and students a variety of resources that can be combined to create personal and adapted learning experiences. MOOCs, the latest trend in education, are being enriched by the incorporation of different social media tools, such as blogs and social networks (Facebook, Google+), with the aim of increasing students' participation and engagement.

As stated in Ventura Expósito (2014),

> "the motivation of this research was precisely to provide students in a Professional English MOOC with a new enhanced language-learning experience by integrating a Facebook Group (henceforth FG) that focused on the acquisition of specialised vocabulary. The research hypothesis put forward was that [...] social networks such as Facebook in a foreign language learning MOOC [can foster] motivation and engagement, thus enhancing the students' educational experience" (n.p.).

Also, in the context of ESP, it can promote the acquisition of specialised vocabulary in Professional English. In line with this, the authors posed the following research questions:

- What was the participants' knowledge of specialised vocabulary in Professional English before joining the FG?

- Did the FG have any positive impact on their knowledge of specialised vocabulary in Professional English?

- Was the implementation of the FG perceived as useful for language learning by the course participants?

- Did the FG help reduce dropout rates keeping students motivated and engaged enough to complete the whole course?

2. Literature review

MOOCs are one of the most recent models of online education and in fact an increasingly popular one (Dhawal, 2013). Although there is still no consensus regarding its definition and despite some criticism raised by experts (Jackson, 2013), the reality is that they have been very well received, as data in terms of student numbers, course statistics and teacher satisfaction seem to demonstrate (Martín-Monje, Bárcena, & Read, 2013). Probably one of their main strengths is the way in which they place the emphasis on social interaction, and the flexible learning materials which allow students to make progress at their own pace, while at the same time feeling part of a community.

As far as foreign Language MOOCs (LMOOCs henceforth) are concerned, there have been quite a few solid initiatives, although it must be said that language learning is not one of the most prolific disciplines in MOOC development, and it has also faced controversy, such as Romeo's (2012) forcefully negative view on MOOCs on English as a Second Language (ESL): "[i]f you think about it, ESL is all about exactly what the MOOCs specifically, and self-study in general, cannot do" (p. 2). Nevertheless, there are some excellent examples of successful LMOOCs: Bryant (2013) developed two parallel online courses using his language exchange website, The Mixxer (http://www.language-exchanges.org/); one in Spanish, "MOOC de Español" and one in English, "English MOOC", which were selected as one of six "Big Ideas" for the Emerging Leaders Competition to be presented at the New Media Consortium Summer Conference in the UK; and another award-winning LMOOC "Alemán para Hispanohablantes", from UNED, Spain, which obtained the first prize for the Best MOOC in the MiríadaX platform (Castrillo, 2013).

This paper focuses on the implementation of Facebook, a social networking tool, into an LMOOC with the aim of enhancing social interaction and specialised vocabulary acquisition. Although social networking has been used for a number of years in language learning, it has mainly focused on the build-up of identity in online communities (Harrison & Thomas, 2009), and has not been properly investigated (Wang & Vásquez, 2012). One of the few instances of insightful research is provided by Blattner and Lomicka (2012), who aim at developing a better understanding of the role that Facebook can play in foreign language education. They also admit that more research is needed in order to ascertain its effectiveness.

As far as the acquisition of specialised vocabulary is concerned, there is conversely abundant literature already published, highlighting the types of vocabulary, underlying pedagogy and current trends in lexis teaching and learning (see for example Carter & McCarthy, 1988; or Nation, 2001). Since the LMOOC focus of this research deals with ESP, it was important to draw the distinction between core and non-core vocabulary (McCarthy, 1990) and make clear to the participants the significant role of vocabulary in ESP teaching and learning.

3.   Methodology

This experiment falls under the fourth stage of a wider action-research investigation (Lewin, 1946) on students' motivation and engagement in ESP MOOCs. On our first stage, coincident with the first edition of the Professional English MOOC (January-April 2013), the authors' aim was to foster interaction and collaborative learning through the social component of the course: the forums. After the first edition, data were gathered and analysed, their results showing a very low participation rate in the forums (Martín-Monje, Bárcena, & Ventura, 2013). Following a reflection period previous to the second edition of the course, the authors devised a new strategy to enhance the students' learning experience in the MOOC and promote vocabulary acquisition through a social network.

It was the authors' belief that the integration of a social network in the MOOC, such as Facebook, would provide students with a different, more familiar approach to the course and facilitate engagement, given the fact that social networks have become an integral part of our daily lives (Elogia, 2013). Thus, the MOOC curator and member of the teaching team, created an FG as a complement to the Professional English MOOC on its second edition, focusing on the acquisition of specialised vocabulary.

3.1. Context

The Professional English MOOC was the first ever ESP MOOC to be launched in Spain, offered by Aprendo (https://unedcoma.es/), UNED online platform and MiríadaX (https://miriadax.net/home), Telefónica Learning Services and the Universia platform, with more than 50,000 students between them at the highest peak of the course, on its first edition.

The second edition of the course, launched in Aprendo, comprised 12 weeks (11 November 2013 – 31 January 2104) and was followed by more than 8,000 students. Over the fourth week, a massive email announcing the opening of an FG as a complement to the MOOC was sent to all the students. The email explained the purpose of the FG and contained a list of frequently asked questions with their answers, and a series of recommendations to take full advantage of students' participation in the FG.

3.2. Instruments and procedure

A mixed-method approach was adopted for the data collection during this experiment, using quantitative techniques (student tracking in the MOOC and Facebook) and qualitative techniques (questionnaires and observation), with the aim of considering multiple perspectives and developing a complete understanding of the problem (Bryman, 2006). FG participants were asked to fill in two questionnaires during the experiment, one previous to the beginning of the experiment (pre-course) and one at the end (post-course). The pre-course questionnaire aimed at gathering information about how Professional English MOOC students used technology and social networks in language learning. The post-course questionnaire's objective was getting to know more on the MOOC students' experience in Facebook. For the purposes of this paper, we will analyse the qualitative data obtained from the post-course questionnaire.

4. Data analysis

Similar to Ventura Expósito (2014), the eight-week experiment on Facebook focused on learning specialised vocabulary related to the MOOC subject, Professional English, and was divided into different topics, following the MOOC syllabus but also expanding its scope. There were 657 participants – 8% of the total amount of Professional English MOOC students – who voluntarily requested to join the FG. The FG administrator provided vocabulary input on a regular basis and if necessary elicited participants' responses, as well as their exchanging of feedback in order to keep the conversations flowing.

Sixty-one participants answered the post-course questionnaire, which amounts to less than 10% of the FG members, which may seem low but is actually a good number if only actual participants – students who actively participated during the course – are taken into account. In this questionnaire, participants were asked about their expectations before taking part of this new learning experience, their opinion on the course contents and dynamics and their vocabulary learning techniques among other questions. For this paper, we will focus on participants' perception of their learning experience and their professional English vocabulary knowledge before and after joining the FG.

To the question "How would you rate your vocabulary knowledge on the subject (Professional English) before joining the FG?" more than half of participants (58%) answered they had a "basic" vocabulary knowledge, whereas 38% rated their vocabulary knowledge as "wide" and only 3% as "weak", as we can see in Figure 1.

Figure 2 shows participants' perception of their improvement after the FG experience. Only 5% of them considered that their vocabulary knowledge on the subject had not been affected by their participation on the course. Thirty-nine per cent of participants stated that their vocabulary knowledge had really improved and 56% considered it had slightly improved after joining the FG.

Figure 1. Participants' vocabulary knowledge perception

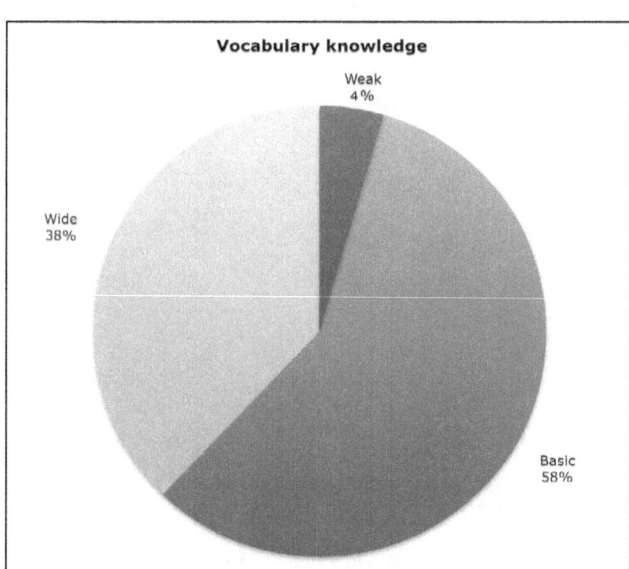

Figure 2. Participant's perception on improvement

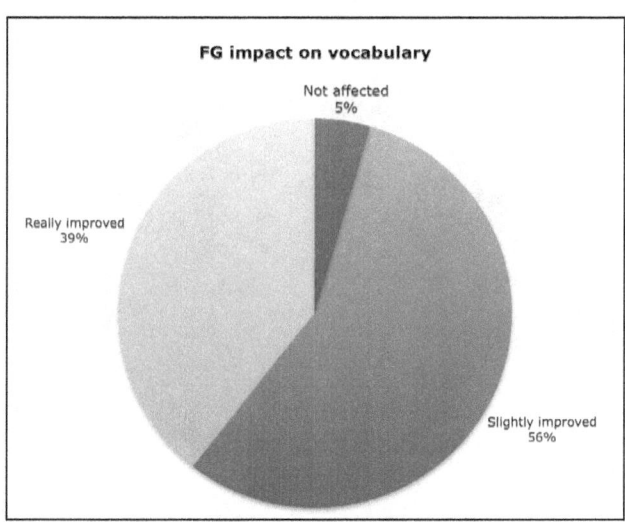

Figure 3. FG participants' MOOC results

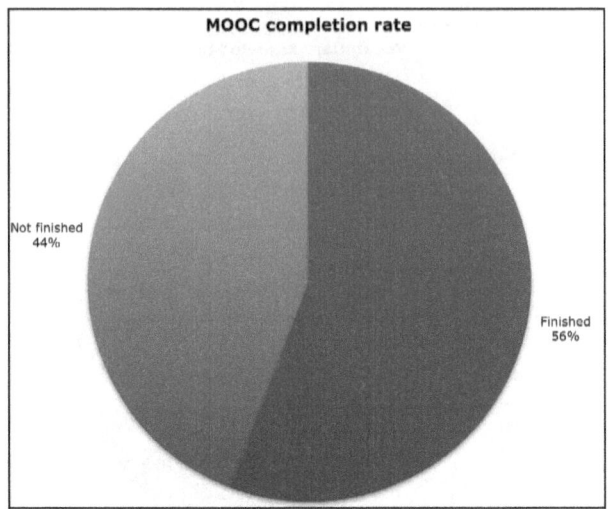

Figure 4. Participants' views on MOOCs + FG

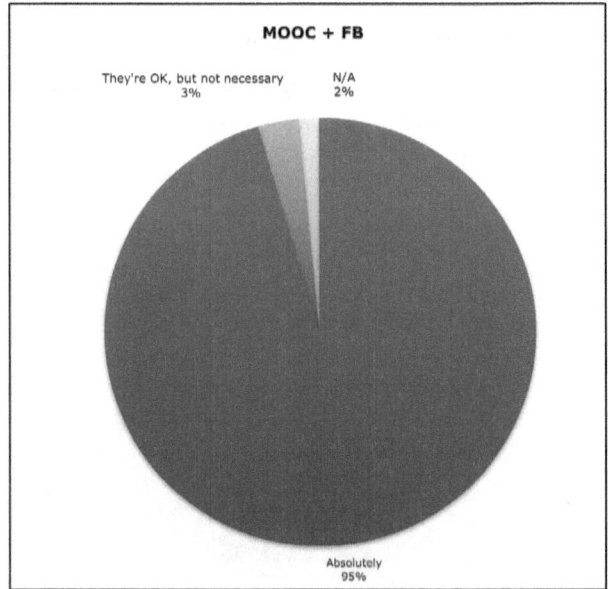

Participants' perceptions of their improvement are in line with their opinions about the overall experience in Facebook, since more than half of them (58%) rated it as "good" and 13% as "excellent". Twenty per cent of participants rated their overall experience as "OK" and only 1% as "poor". The rest (2%) indicated that they had not participated enough and could not rate their experience.

Tracking the progress and results of Professional English MOOC students who participated in the FG will be analysed and compared with their activity on Facebook, in order to reach a conclusion on the effectiveness of using a social network as a complement to language learning MOOCs. For the time being, completion rates of students who participated and answered the post-course questionnaire have been analysed and the results obtained point towards a positive impact of Facebook on students' engagement in the MOOC, since 58% of them finished the MOOC (Figure 3). Almost the totality of FG participants (95%) thinks that Facebook groups are a good complement to MOOCs, as Figure 4 shows, and only 5% either thinks "they are OK, but they are not necessary", or did not provide a concrete answer.

5. Discussion and conclusion

This section of the paper is structured following the four research questions stated in the introductory part. The first research question dealt with the participant's previous knowledge of specialised vocabulary. The majority of students perceived it as basic, which is probably caused by the sort of language courses that students have previously taken. It is not common for Spanish students to join ESP courses, they tend to be general ones; consequently, the amount of Professional English lexis they have been exposed to beforehand is rather limited.

With regard to the second research question, whether their participation in the FG had favoured their acquisition of specialised vocabulary, the students' perception was generally quite optimistic, since the vast majority felt that they had widened their knowledge of Professional English terminology. However, when asked to rate it, just over one third of the participants (39%) deemed it as significant.

As for the third research question, the students' overall opinion about the usefulness of a FG for language learning, the general response was rather positive – it must be taken into account the fact that this was a voluntary, optional part in the course, which would give them no extra credit towards course completion. Not only that, when asked specifically about the appropriateness of such a complement for an online course, virtually all of them regarded it as essential (cf. Figure 4).

Finally, the fourth research question dealt with the long debated issue of dropout rates in MOOCs. Although, as stated previously, the quantitative analysis has not been finalised yet and is not included in this paper, the analysis and tracking of those students who joined the FG has already been done and results confirm the data shared by the qualitative analysis: the participation in the FG has had a very encouraging impact on students' completion rate, since more than half of those belonging to the FG continued to finish the whole course (56%), which is over 20% more than the percentage considered to be satisfactory in terms of MOOC completion, that is, around 30% (see for example Martín-Monje, Bárcena, & Ventura, 2013).

After discussing the four research questions, the initial hypothesis is confirmed, which leads the authors to sustain that social networking, and in particular Facebook, can be a powerful tool to reinforce online interaction and engagement in MOOCs. It will be interesting now to look into ways of increasing that positive impact of the use of FG in ESP in such a way that it caters for learners' needs more accurately, identifying their specific requirements in terms of core and non-core vocabulary and consolidating their engagement in these new types of online courses.

References

Blattner, G., & Lomicka, L. (2012). Facebook-ing and the social generation: a new era of language learning. *Alsic, 15*(1). Retrieved from http://dx.doi.org/10.4000/alsic.2413

Bryant, T. (2013). *MOOCs + Learning Networks = The Mixxer*. Retrieved from https://blog.coerll.utexas.edu/moocs-and-learning-networks-equals-mixxer/

Bryman, A. (2006). Integrating quantitative and qualitative research: how is it done? *Qualitative Research, 6*(1), 97-113. Retrieved from http://dx.doi.org/10.1177/1468794106058877

Carter, R., & McCarthy, M. (1988). *Vocabulary and language teaching*. London: Longman.

Castrillo, M. D. (2013). *¡Enhorabuena! ¡Hemos conseguido el primer premio!* Retrieved from http://aleesp.hypotheses.org/262

Dhawal, S. (2013). *MOOCs in 2013: breaking down the numbers*. Retrieved from https://www.edsurge.com/n/2013-12-22-moocs-in-2013-breaking-down-the-numbers

Elogia. (2013). *IV Estudio sobre redes sociales de IAB Spain y Elogia* [Blog post]. Retrieved from http://elogia.net/blog/cuarto-estudio-redes-sociales-iab-2012/

Harrison, R., & Thomas, M. (2009). Identity in online communities: social networking sites and language learning. *International Journal of Emerging Technologies & Society, 7*(2), 109-124.

Jackson, N. (2013). *On MOOCs and some possible futures for higher ed*. Retrieved from http://noelbjackson.wordpress.com/2013/06/01/on-moocs-and-some-possible-futures-for-higher-ed/

Lewin, K. (1946). Action research and minority problems. *Journal of Social Issues, 2*(4), 34-46. Retrieved from http://dx.doi.org/10.1111/j.1540-4560.1946.tb02295.x

Martín-Monje, E., Bárcena, E., & Read, T. (2013). Exploring the affordances of massive open online courses on second languages. *Proceedings of UNED-ICDE (International Council for Open and Distance Education*. Madrid: UNED.

Martín-Monje, E., Bárcena, E., & Ventura, P. (2013). The effects of peer-to-peer sociolinguistics interaction and linguistic feedback in a Professional English MOOC. *Proceedings of ECLL: European Conference on Language Learning* (pp. 350-364). Nagoya, Japan: IAFOR.

Nation, I. S. P. (2001). *Learning vocabulary in another language*. Cambridge: Cambridge University Press. Retrieved from http://dx.doi.org/10.1017/CBO9781139524759

McCarthy, M. (1990). *Vocabulary*. Oxford: Oxford University Press.

Romeo, K. (2012). *Language learning MOOCs?* Retrieved from https://www.stanford.edu/group/ats/cgi-bin/hivetalkin/?p=3011

Ventura Expósito, P. (2014). The role of motivation and engagement in English language learning through facebook and MOOCs. *ACTAS del II Congreso Internacional Nebrija en Lingüística Aplicada a la Enseñanza de Lenguas*. Nebrija Universidad. Retrieved from http://www.nebrija.com/la_universidad/servicios/pdf-publicaciones/ActasNebrija_SegundoCongreso.pdf?

Wang, S., & Vásquez, C. (2012). Web 2.0 and second language learning: What does the research tell us? *CALICO Journal, 29*(3), 412-430. Retrieved from http://dx.doi.org/10.11139/cj.29.3.412-430

Zourou, K. (2012). On the attractiveness of social media for language learning: a look at the state of the art. *Alsic, 15*(1). Retrieved from http://dx.doi.org/10.4000/alsic.2436

11 Identifying collaborative behaviours online: training teachers in wikis

Margarita Vinagre Laranjeira[1]

Abstract

In this paper we explore the data gathered from a group of nine in-service teachers who were trained online to become future telecollaborative teachers. Participants from different countries worked in two small groups in a wiki designed specially to facilitate discussion and collaboration. Tasks included reading and reviewing articles on telecollaboration, critically analysing examples from authentic exchanges, organising a hypothetical exchange and designing a tool for its assessment. Analyses of the pattern, scope and nature of user contributions as reliable measures of collaborative behaviours by wiki-users were carried out on the data gathered from six wiki pages and corresponding discussion pages. Findings and discussion elaborate on the collaborative behaviour (or lack thereof) observed among participants.

Keywords: distance learning, teacher training, telecollaboration, wikis.

1. Introduction

In recent years, the use of wikis in the classroom has become very popular due to their pedagogical benefits as "participatory technologies" (Ajjan & Hartshorne, 2008, p. 71). Most authors agree on the collaborative nature of wikis and their suitability to foster interaction. Thus, a number of studies have emphasised that wikis facilitate reflection and collaboration (Lund, 2008).

1. Universidad Autónoma de Madrid, Madrid, Spain; margarita.vinagre@uam.es

How to cite this chapter: Vinagre Laranjeira, M. (2016). Identifying collaborative behaviours online: training teachers in wikis. In A. Pareja-Lora, C. Calle-Martínez, & P. Rodríguez-Arancón (Eds), *New perspectives on teaching and working with languages in the digital era* (pp. 129-140). Dublin: Research-publishing.net. http://dx.doi.org/10.14705/rpnet.2016.tislid2014.428

Other authors have described them as enhancers of peer interaction, group work and collaboration, as opposed to competition (Li, 2012). According to Boulos, Maramba, and Wheeler (2006) they are excellent resources for the learners' own construction of knowledge and Weeler, Yeomans, and Wheeler (2008) mention that wikis have the ability to keep learners connected, so that they feel closer to one another and more engaged in the learning task. Wikis are also considered highly democratic by authors such as Lee (2010), since they disperse individual power and all participants have an equal status and the right to contribute or edit entries. They are unique in that they serve as a platform for scaffolding and fostering student-centred learning and allow for the incorporation of multiple perspectives.

In contrast to the benefits mentioned above, other studies have reported less encouraging findings. Thus, authors such as Forte and Bruckman (2006) have mentioned how their students did not work consistently in the wiki and tended to post the largest edits close to the assessment deadline, while "smaller contributions like sharing resources and giving evaluations were more consistently spaced out over many days preceding due dates" (p. 184). Along the same lines, authors such as Cole (2009) reported that their students did not contribute to the wiki at all over an entire semester, despite the fact that it was integrated as an activity on their courses.

Finally, other authors have mentioned how, even "even when participation is relatively high, much of the work [is down] to a relatively small proportion of contributors (Carr, Morrison, Cox, & Deacon, 2007). These and other findings suggest that wikis [may not be] inherently collaborative" (Judd, Kennedy, & Cropper, 2010, p. 343), and, therefore, more research needs to be carried out on the nature of collaboration in wikis. In order to contribute to current research, we decided to use a wiki as an online tool to train nine in-service teachers from different countries in order to become future telecollaborative teachers. Telecollaboration is a complex activity that requires teachers to work in collaboration with one or more teachers who belong to a different culture and are in distant locations. Therefore, fostering collaboration among participants was of primary concern, and this study attempts to find answers to the following research question: did the teachers who worked online in small groups in a wiki engage (or not) in collaborative behaviours?

Although most studies on educational wiki implementations tend to be perception-based, a growing number of studies have drawn on the data generated by wikis to support their research on student participation (Cole, 2009). In order to provide answers for our research question, we decided to follow this trend and analyse participation and interaction as reliable measures of collaborative behaviour by wiki-users (Judd et al., 2010; Trentin, 2009).

2. Project outline

2.1. Context and participants

The participants in this study were nine in-service teachers who enrolled for a semester on the course *Intercultural Collaborative Exchanges in Virtual Environments*, which was delivered online as part of their Master's Degree on Information and Communications Technology (ICT). Five were teachers of Spanish as a foreign language; two were based in Colombia, two others in Cyprus and one in Spain. Three other participants were teachers of English as a foreign language, all based in Spain. The last student was a teacher of French as a foreign language, also based in Spain. As regards gender, six participants were female and three were male. They were all native Spanish speakers, with the exception of one student who had Greek as her mother tongue. As mentioned elsewhere, "[t]he level of experience with the use of the technology was very similar and they had [little or] no previous experience in telecollaboration, although they were familiar with the use of some ICT tools (blogs, wikis, Skype, hangouts and Google+)" (Vinagre, 2015, n.p.).

2.2. Activities and tools

The teachers had to work collaboratively in two small groups in a wiki. They had to carry out a series of activities that included reading and reviewing articles on telecollaborative learning and then exchanging views on different aspects of telecollaboration (i.e. theoretical and pedagogical principles, models of telecollaboration, critical analysis of examples from authentic exchanges, guidelines for implementation of projects, task design and assessment).

Participants also had to organise a hypothetical exchange and design a tool for its assessment. These tasks were designed to foster collaboration among participants so that they gained a deeper understanding of what collaboration entailed through hands-on experience. A summary of the tasks is provided below in Table 1.

Table 1. Tasks to be carried out in the wiki[2]

	Unit	Activity
1	Experiencing telecollaboration	Working in groups: select, read, upload, summarise and review one article about CSCL on your wiki page. Comment and discuss articles with your group members and decide jointly on possible applications to your FL classroom.
2	Organising a telecollaborative project	Decide with your group members how to organise your own exchange. You will need to include guidelines, activities and tools you would use, and justify your decisions.
3	Developing tools for the assessment of telecollaboration	Design a tool that allows you to assess different aspects of telecollaboration (e.g. portfolio, learning diary, questionnaire, etc.).

Each group, as detailed in Vinagre (2015), was "provided with three blank wiki pages on which to develop their entries, and they were encouraged to use the discussion facility to interact with other group members" (n.p.). All teachers also had access to the wiki pages of the other group and the tasks were the same for both groups.

---

2. Published in Vinagre (2015), and reproduced with kind permissions from © British Educational Research Association.

3. Method

The study was exploratory and attempted to identify whether those behaviours that characterise collaboration and that the teachers had read about, studied and critically analysed during the first task were reflected in their own interaction in the wiki. Data was gathered from the contributions on the six (three per group) wiki pages and their corresponding discussion pages. Then, quantitative and qualitative analyses of the pattern, scope and nature (participation and interaction) of user contributions were carried out in order to identify (in)effective collaborative behaviours.

3.1. Level of contribution

In the wiki, the student-teachers carried out a total of 99 page revisions and contributed a total of 700 lines (sentences) to the wiki pages, with a total word count of 17,213. When analysed individually, we found that almost 11.6% of all edits were superficial, resulting in no change to the textual content of the page, whilst a further 5.2% involved changes to a single line (sentence) of text. As discussed in Vinagre (2015) and in line with Judd (2010, p. 346), we believe that this may be due to the fact that participants were saving the pages a number of times during longer editing sessions (they made an average of 3.6 edits per session). Finally, 83.2% of all edits involved changes to three or more sentences of text. Table 2 and Table 3 show a summary of the contributions per group and member to the total activity in the wiki (all participants' names have been changed).

Table 2. Summary of contributions to the wiki by Group 1

Name	Page revisions in wiki	Text lines	Contribution to total text in wiki	Discussion posts in wiki	Contribution to total discussion comments in wiki
Gloria	22	149	16.9%	29	20.2%
Emma	11	125	16.4%	28	19.5%
María	23	53	10%	39	27%
Pablo	5	40	8.1%	7	4.8%
Total	61	367	51.4%	103	71.5%

Table 3. Summary of contributions to the wiki by Group 2

Name	Page revisions in wiki	Text lines	Contribution to total text in wiki	Discussion posts in wiki	Contribution to total discussion comments in wiki
Rosa	12	93	15.6%	11	7.7%
Ángela	8	103	11.1%	8	5.5%
Óscar	7	39	9%	8	5.5%
David	4	44	7.4%	5	3.5%
Penélope	7	54	5.5%	9	6.3%
Total	**38**	**333**	**48.6%**	**41**	**28.5%**

As can be seen above, there was not a great difference between both groups regarding their contribution to the total text in the wiki. However, Group 1 contributed 51.4% of the total text despite having one member less than Group 2. More noticeable differences refer to the discussion comments written by each of the groups. Thus, Group 1 wrote 103 comments (71.5% of the total), whereas participants in Group 2 wrote 41 (28.5%). On average, participants in Group 1 made one comment per page edit, whereas participants in Group 2 did not comment that often. In Group 1, the number of comments per wiki page varied from 19 to 52, whereas in Group 2 it varied from 0 to 21. In Group 1, all comments were sent within the task deadline, whereas 10 comments were sent after the deadline in Group 2.

3.2. Timing of contributions

The comparative analysis between both groups (Figure 1) show that participants in Group 1 started working on their tasks during the first week and worked regularly (although not very productively at the beginning) throughout the entire time allocated to the tasks, with only one edit being made after the deadline. Group 2 started to work in Week 4 and had two productive weeks, Weeks 7 and 11. The week after the deadline was also quite productive for Group 2, although page edits were carried out only by two students who had personal problems and could not finish the tasks on time, so an extension to the deadline was granted. The majority of the teachers' contributions were made during the last few days before the deadline, with 18 page edits (26%) being made during the last week of the activity, 14 (20%) during the previous week and seven (10%) of the edits being made after the deadline.

Figure 1. Group comparative of temporal distribution of page revisions over the time allocated for tasks[3]

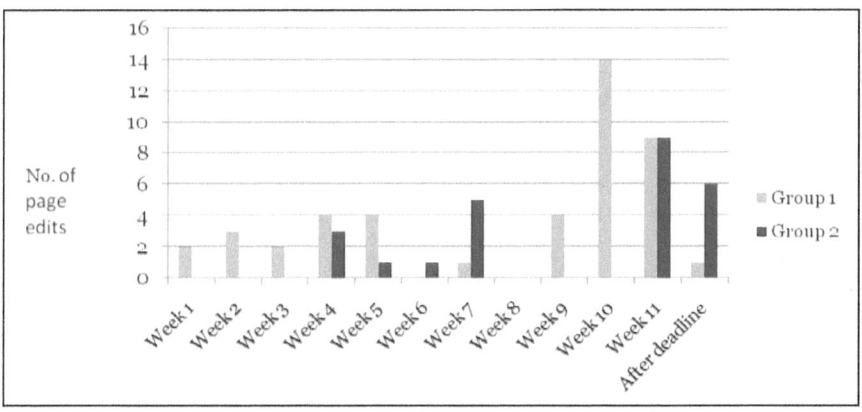

All nine students contributed to the wiki on three days and six students contributed to the wiki on five days. Some students (4) contributed to the wiki on six days and three contributed on seven days. Two students contributed on nine days and one contributed on ten days or more. No student contributed more than 13 days.

3.3. Nature of contributions

A content analysis was carried out in order to code the teachers' contributions following a modified version of Judd et al.'s (2010) coding scheme (Table 4). A comment was coded into a category if part or all of it matched the description. Each utterance was independently coded by two researchers and the results were then combined in order to ascertain number and scope of messages a) within the wiki (all users), b) within the groups, and c) from individual students.

---

3. Published in Vinagre (2015), and reproduced with kind permissions from © British Educational Research Association.

Table 4. Categories of comments from content analysis (modified from Judd et al., 2010)[4]

Category	Description
Reply	A comment in response to an existing comment.
Collaboration	A comment that showed that the author was attempting to develop a shared understanding of some aspect of the page content. Explaining and elaborating. Seeking input and feedback. Reflecting and monitoring. Looking for consensus.
Organisation	A comment that showed that the author was attempting to organise the task or workload among his/her peers. Initiating activities, setting shared tasks and deadlines.
Content	A comment concerned with factual content on or relevant to the target page. Providing information and feedback. Sharing knowledge.
Editing	A comment that concerned some aspect of page editing or relevant to the target page.
Individual	A comment directed at an individual.
Group	A comment directed at the group generally.

All comments were scored in at least one of the categories (group or individual and others as applicable). Although findings in the editing and individual categories were very similar or identical in both groups, the findings relating to the rest of the categories were significantly different (Figure 2).

Teachers in Group 1 posted 52 (36.1%) comments related to content, 93 (64.5%) to collaboration and 46 (31.9%) to task organisation. They addressed most comments to the whole group (86, 59.7%) and replied to other members often (44, 30.5%). Teachers in Group 2 posted 27 (18.7%) comments related to content, a similar number (33, 22.9%) were comments related to collaboration and nine (6.2%) to task organisation. They did not address most comments to the whole group (25, 18%) and only sent 15 comments (10.4%) to reply to other members' comments.

---

4. Published in Vinagre (2015), and reproduced with kind permissions from © British Educational Research Association.

Figure 2. Percentages of comments in each of the seven contextual categories per group (mean of two coders)[5]

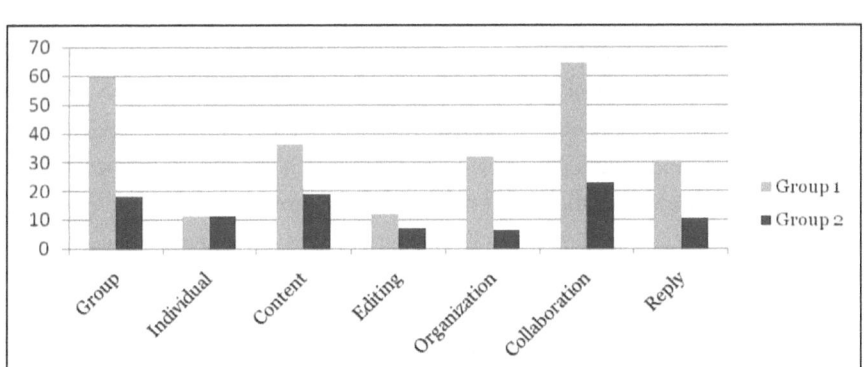

4. Discussion

The research question in this study led us to examine the pattern, scope and nature of contributions of nine teachers as reliable measures of collaborative behaviour by wiki-users (Trentin, 2009). Although, as mentioned by Arnold, Ducate, Lomicka, and Lord (2009), these are only quantitative surface indicators which are "not necessarily indicative of a group's success, [...] they provide a glimpse into the inner workings of a group and can reflect heterogeneity of participation, roles, social loafing and free riding" (p. 126).

Similar to findings in a previous study (Vinagre, 2015), three members in Group 1 showed collaborative behaviours: they worked regularly and constantly over the time allocated to the task, and engaged in discussion most of the time (looking for feedback, input and consensus) whilst also engaging in fair amounts of contributing (content). Members in this group commented often and they spent a lot of time replying to other members' suggestions, which reflects the participants' efforts at engaging in group discussion and building consensual knowledge.

---

5. Published in Vinagre (2015), and reproduced with kind permissions from © British Educational Research Association.

Members in Group 2 did not display the same effective dynamics. Their contributions were made late in the activity and very close to the deadline, which means that participants would have had limited opportunities to interact with other members of their group. Two teachers in Group 2 did make a serious effort to contribute regularly, extensively and within the deadlines. Unfortunately, lack of (timely) response from the other group members meant that these participants went ahead and made individual decisions in order to finish the task. Comments were few and far between and there was no activity for three weeks. The majority of teachers in this group, as pointed out by Vinagre (2015), "were happy to contribute from time to time in order to meet the task requirements rather than develop a more equitable, consensual and comprehensive group submission that would require more [regular and consistent] collaboration with the other group members" (n.p.).

5. Conclusion

The findings in this study suggest that an analysis of the pattern, scope and nature of user contributions can signal (in)effective collaborative behaviour by wiki-users as suggested by Judd et al. (2010). In this case, those teachers who engaged in successful collaboration gave priority to fostering social interaction (process) over finishing the task (final product) and collaborative group behaviors were characterised by prompt communication, regular group discussion, timely and relevant contributions, commitment to the task (task organisation, joint responsibility) and consistent participation (Vinagre, 2015).

These findings, although encouraging, are not conclusive due to the small sample size. Therefore, further research needs to be undertaken with larger data sets in order to obtain more significant results. Moreover, data analysis has been restricted to participation and interaction as measures of collaborative behaviour. In order for this study to be complete, an in-depth content analysis is necessary to determine the quality of contributions.

These findings also suggest that designing activities or using technologies that are collaborative does not guarantee that the participants will be successful at collaboration. Therefore, special attention should be paid to those indicators that allow practitioners to identify and assess collaborative behaviours in group interaction during the learning process.

References

Ajjan, H., & Hartshorne, R. (2008). Investigating faculty decisions to adopt Web 2.0 technologies: theory and empirical tests. *Internet and Higher Education*, *11*(2), 71-80. Retrieved from http://dx.doi.org/10.1016/j.iheduc.2008.05.002

Arnold, N., Ducate, L., Lomicka, L., & Lord, G. (2009). Assessing online collaboration among language teachers: a cross-institutional case study. *Journal of Interactive Online Learning*, *8*(2), 121-139.

Boulos, M. N. K., Maramba, I., & Wheeler, S. (2006). Wikis, blogs and podcasts: a new generation of web-based tools for virtual collaborative clinical practice and education. *BMC Medical Education*, *6*(41). Retrieved from http://dx.doi.org/10.1186/1472-6920-6-41

Carr, T., Morrison, A., Cox, G., & Deacon, A. (2007). Weathering wikis: net-based learning meets political science in a South African university. *Computers and Composition*, *24*(3), 266-284. Retrieved from http://dx.doi.org/10.1016/j.compcom.2007.06.001

Cole, M. (2009). Using wiki technology to support student engagement: lessons from the trenches. *Computers & Education*, *52*(1), 141-146. Retrieved from http://dx.doi.org/10.1016/j.compedu.2008.07.003

Forte, A., & Bruckman, A. (2006). From Wikipedia to the classroom: exploring online publication and learning. *Proceedings of the International Conference of the Learning Sciences, Bloomington* (pp. 182-188).

Judd, T., Kennedy, G., & Cropper, S. (2010). Using wikis for collaborative learning: assessing collaboration through contribution. *Australasian Journal of Educational Technology*, *26*(3), 341-354.

Lee, L. (2010). Exploring wiki-mediated collaborative writing: a case study in an elementary Spanish course. *CALICO Journal*, *27*(2), 260-276. Retrieved from http://dx.doi.org/10.11139/cj.27.2.260-276

Li, M. (2012). Politeness strategies in wiki-mediated communication on EFL collaborative writing tasks. *The IALLT Journal of Language Learning Technologies*, *42*(2), 1-26.

Lund, A. (2008). Wikis: a collective approach to language production. *ReCALL*, *20*(1), 35-54. Retrieved from http://dx.doi.org/10.1017/s0958344008000414

Trentin, G. (2009). Using a wiki to evaluate individual contribution to a collaborative learning project. *Journal of Computer Assisted Learning, 25*, 43-55.

Vinagre, M. (2015). Training teachers for virtual collaboration: a case study. *British Journal of Educational Technology, Early View*. Retrieved from http://dx.doi.org/10.1111/bjet.12363

Wheeler, S., Yeomans, P., & Wheeler, D. (2008). The good, the bad and the wiki: evaluating student-generated content for collaborative learning. *British Journal of Educational Technology, 39*(6), 987-995. Retrieved from http://dx.doi.org/10.1111/j.1467-8535.2007.00799.x

12. The community as a source of pragmatic input for learners of Italian: the multimedia repository LIRA

Greta Zanoni[1]

Abstract

This paper focuses on community participation within the LIRA project – Lingua/Cultura Italiana in Rete per l'Apprendimento (Italian language and culture for online learning). LIRA is a multimedia repository of e-learning materials aiming at recovering, preserving and developing the linguistic, pragmatic and cultural competences of second and third generation Italians living abroad. The paper addresses a crucial issue in teaching pragmatics, namely, how to combine the intrinsic variability of this area with the need to employ a standard reference system and to provide clear corrective feedback to learners. Can user experience, interaction, and active participation in the community foster collaborative knowledge and develop pragmatic competence?

Keywords: Web 2.0, community, informal learning, pragmatics, Italian as a second language.

1. E-learning web 2.0

Over the past decade, mass access to the internet, with the development of new tools and platforms and the spread of social networking, has come to enable language learners to be globally connected. The term Web 2.0 (O'Reilly, 2005)

---

1. University of Bologna, Bologna, Italy; greta.zanoni2@unibo.it

How to cite this chapter: Zanoni, G. (2016). The community as a source of pragmatic input for learners of Italian: the multimedia repository LIRA. In A. Pareja-Lora, C. Calle-Martínez, & P. Rodríguez-Arancón (Eds), *New perspectives on teaching and working with languages in the digital era* (pp. 141-151). Dublin: Research-publishing.net. http://dx.doi.org/10.14705/rpnet.2016.tislid2014.429

has increasingly become used to represent a different use of the web where users have an active role in the production and sharing of content. Web 2.0 is composed of applications that facilitate communication, and promote interaction and cooperation among users, allowing the creation of web communities where each individual is user and author at the same time. This transformation has also changed e-learning models and environments: the term e-learning 2.0 (Downes, 2005) is now used with regards to the modes and the practices related to the use of the web for e-learning. E-learning 2.0 aspires to recover and promote the potential within the spontaneous and informal modes of web use (Bonaiuti, 2006), both by individual learning and by building networks of experts and communities of interests, which aggregate and interact spontaneously to find solutions for specific issues.

The rise of Web 2.0 platforms, tools and communities has meant that learners and users can not only access a wealth of language material online, but can also take part in online communities which produce their own content and share their experiences, hence emphasising learner autonomy and creating further learning opportunities.

In this paper, we analyse some of the informal modalities of interaction and participation developed by the user community in LIRA, in particular, the extent to which, in learning environments characterised by Web 2.0 technologies, the sharing of resources, experiences and knowledge amongst individuals effectively promotes a socially built learning experience.

2. The LIRA repository

The main goal of LIRA[2], an inter-university project funded by the Italian Ministry of Higher Education and Research, is to create a multimedia repository which can assist Italian speakers born and/or living abroad to develop/recover

---

2. lira.unistrapg.it

their linguistic and pragmatic competences in the language. The repository aims to:

- satisfy the interests of those individuals who are motivated to maintain and recover their linguistic and cultural roots, or to achieve specific social and/or professional goals that involve (re)approaching the Italian language/culture;

- support the work of teachers of Italian as a second language and of Italian culture abroad;

- establish a centre of aggregation, albeit virtual, for Italians and learners of Italian abroad, promoting the development of communities of interest and practice.

In defining the structure of the repository, we drew up a list of key characteristics for a learning environment of this type, which should:

- encourage knowledge construction relating linguistic and cultural content to context;

- avoid oversimplifying the complexity of real situations;

- present language use in specific real contexts, avoiding generalisation and abstraction;

- provide multiple representations of reality;

- promote knowledge construction through cooperation and exchange with others.

The digital content in the repository is characteristic of contemporary Italian. We have selected authentic materials which show language being used within real interactions, and allow a large number of variables to be taken into account.

The content is grouped into 13 macro-areas: seven aimed at the development of pragmatic-linguistic competence (e.g. the capacity to make linguistic choices that are consistent with the context); and six aimed at strengthening social and cultural competence (showing how social and cultural factors are reflected in communicative practices). Each macro area contains a series of units focusing on a particular pragmatic and/or cultural issue.

The structure of the repository provides the user with a controlled linear modality, following a sequence recommended by the authors, and a free modality, passing from one unit to another or from one macro area to another at will. Each unit contains a flexible number of activities which are designed to make the user aware of the variety and variation of language uses illustrated in that unit. Through the correction of these activities and the feedback received, it is hoped that users will better understand the relationships between communicative forms and functions in different contexts. This is why LIRA provides various types of materials for various types of users, and allows various types of interaction and comparison.

Thanks to the framework made available, each user can become an actor and author of content which is exchanged and shared with the rest of the community in a collaborative participatory process. LIRA is based on the constant interaction between the different participants in the virtual community (including native and non-native speakers) to create content and share their language experience and knowledge. At any time, users can enter the repository, and in addition to using the materials and carrying out the activities, they can exchange views and information; through their contributions, participants make available to other users their knowledge and skills which contribute to the process of collaborative construction of knowledge (Manca & Sarti, 2002) which "directly affects the actors involved in the interaction and, indirectly, the whole community" (Mazzoni, 2005, p. 54; my translation).

In implementing LIRA, we referred to the model of the 'community of learners' theorised by Brown and Campione (1990), with the aim of going beyond the idea of the school/classroom as a place where knowledge is merely transmitted, to develop a learning environment based on communities of practice and on knowledge construction, where the community acts as a group working together and joining forces to produce new knowledge. In the field of language learning, this means that knowledge is not simply assimilated but constructed thanks to deeply contextualised resources and activities, and dialogue exchange (Scardamalia & Bereiter, 1993): problem solving (e.g. agreeing, negotiating, resolving conflicts, making suggestions, apologising), explaining points of view, reporting personal experiences, and understanding other users' opinions.

In such communities, learning is active and collaborative, and diversity (sociolinguistic variables such as age, gender, geographical origin, etc.) becomes a resource to be valued and shared. It enables the community to increase through mutual exchange: each user acts in the zone of proximal development (Vygotsky, 1978) of others. In the context of a community of practice (see inter alia, Lave & Wenger, 1991), any participation of the individual, even if marginal or peripheral, is legitimate. In a group of learners, where communication is horizontal and among peers, even those with less experience are eligible to participate and to access the resources of the group.

The technological evolution of communications media has greatly expanded the possibilities for aggregation and comparison among people. Socialising, collaborating, and cooperating on the web projects the individual into a new dimension where the normally defined boundaries of physical environments become increasingly vague, revealing new opportunities for learning. With the use of computer technologies, the concept of community, i.e. a group of people who "have a common interest, that is to say they share a common destiny, and communicate with each other on a regular basis" (Rheingold, 2001, p. 212; my translation), becomes open to a virtual dimension. Preece (2001) lists the following elements as characteristic of such communities:

- the presence of individuals who interact socially to meet their personal needs;

- a common purpose (an interest or need to exchange information);

- a policy that governs behaviour, in the form of tacit assumptions and rules that guide the interactions between individuals;

- online systems which can support and negotiate social interaction, encouraging the development of a sense of membership.

From this perspective, LIRA has been used to support communities of learners operating at different levels: among learners of Italian in order to develop or improve their linguistic-pragmatic competences, among teachers of Italian as a second language to provide materials and elements of reflection for use in classes, among native speakers of Italian to meditate on less typical uses of their language, and as a means for exchange and discussion amongst the international community of learners and native speakers of Italian.

3. An example

To the user, LIRA takes the form of a social network rather than a simple repository, presenting users with an environment where they can take full advantage of the potential of the web. The following example illustrates some of the modes of cooperation that can support the expression, representation, processing, and sharing of knowledge in LIRA communities.

All the didactic units in LIRA are integrated into discussion areas (forums) where learners are stimulated to talk about their linguistic and cultural experiences, and to ask questions and offer opinions on the materials and the activities proposed. Numerous studies document how the interaction in online forums can support the process of collaborative knowledge construction (Muukkonen, Hakkarainen, & Lakkala, 1999; Scardamalia & Bereiter, 1994), and involve users in three dimensions (cognitive, social, motivational) that are crucial to the success of the learning process (Wilson & Whitelock, 1997). Every participant tries to respond by expressing personal ideas, assumptions and interpretations in a kind of theoretical elaboration where the idea of one individual is evaluated by others. Through discussion, requests for clarification, and negotiation of the proposals of other users, suggested hypotheses can be refined and shared knowledge improved. These trends are evident in various LIRA discussion forums: for example, Zanoni (2014) describes a community debate on the use of the formal and informal Italian personal pronouns *tu, voi* and *Lei*, in particular on the use of *voi* and *Lei* from a regional and generational perspective. The forum we shall examine here concerns the Italian exclamation *Complimenti!*. According to the authoritative Treccani (2014) online dictionary, it's most common use is to express "admiration and praise for the addressee, positively assessing their physical appearance, character, skill, possessions, or also expressing appreciation" (n.p.; my translation). In the forum entitled "A compliment to tell you …", users first relate to this meaning of the exclamation:

> "Compliments are made primarily on physical appearance, on a sports or professional performance etc., achievements, and births".

However, in everyday use the exclamation can take on other meanings. It can be used ironically, for example, to express opposition or reproach. This second meaning is reported and integrated into the discussion on the forum, thereby allowing the community to reconsider and expand their knowledge (cited contributions from the forum are my translations from the original Italian):

> "I also think that in Italian you say 'Complimenti!' when you do a nice thing or an important event occurs. However, once I got to work late and my boss told me 'Complimenti! I asked you to arrive early today'… Well, probably I did not understand. Your boss did not want to congratulate you, but to tell you off (for being late). We often use the same expression 'Complimenti!!', but with a different tone, to be more or less ironic depending on the occasion or the context. Yes. Exactly… it was a telling off not a compliment!!! It is like saying 'congratulations' or 'thank you so much' in an ironic way to a person who promised to do something for you, but has then changed their mind and not done it. I was thinking that, in addition to the ironic meaning, sometimes when we say 'complimenti!' we express our disappointment with someone's behaviour or actions".

Chapter 12

Through such discussions, the user, driven by their own interests (e.g. understanding the variation in the meaning of *Complimenti!* according to the circumstances) can actively build up a personal idea of reality by integrating the perspectives offered by the rest of the community. Here we can see how a problem is overcome through the 'person presents problem – community offers solution' procedure. But at the same time, we can see how new lines of discussion develop, new doubts develop, and the processes of investigation and knowledge construction continue.

In addition to using the LIRA forums, members of the community can also turn to social networks (Facebook, Twitter, Google+) to stimulate re-elaboration of the learning process (see e.g. Deng & Yuen, 2009). These allow them to return to previously treated issues in a critical manner, further developing particular topics. Such experiences outside the platform broaden the context for informal reflection, in an area where in order to present ideas, it is also necessary to select and organise material, and to summarise the main concepts at issue (Parmigiani & Pennazio, 2012).

The main innovative aspect of LIRA, however, lies in providing multiple feedback. The user can compare answers given by community members from different sociocultural groups, or by native and non-native speakers. As a repository, LIRA is mainly designed for self-learning, and so it is primarily through the correction of activities and the feedback received that users must understand the links between forms, functions, and contexts. Because of the nature of language use, it is often difficult to give learners a single right answer, nor is it possible to exemplify possible uses exhaustively. For this reason, the materials are designed to suggest a range of different reference models to users of the platform, related to what Italians of different ages, sexes, and perhaps of different geographical origins, have said or written in the situations presented in the activities. In this way, the user is stimulated to reflect on the ways in which different pragmatic meanings can be attributed to an expression like *Complimenti!*. LIRA allows users to compare their answers not only with the solutions proposed by the authors of the activities, but also with the answers of other native or non-native members of the community, where the latter are selected as having similar socio-biographical features to those listed by the user when registering on the platform.

The informal strategies provided on the platform are particularly appropriate with respect to 'marked' language uses, such as the use of a compliment as a rebuke, or as an ironic insult, and in cases where users can report personal learning experiences (e.g. use of slang or dialect, linguistic and cultural stereotypes, and misunderstandings of the formality or informality of the context, etc.). Collective discussions like the one cited above offer opportunities to increase users' awareness of phenomena which we can consider central to learning the pragmatics of a second language (Bettoni, 2006).

4. Conclusions

LIRA is a learning tool, which illustrates how today's technologies can provide users with the means to respect each other's individualities, emphasising personal characteristics and peculiarities, and allowing learning both in independent space-time and within a community which offers ongoing ideas and materials for reflection.

Promoting the social dimension of e-learning allows us to re-consider the potential of online platforms like LIRA, which can not only distribute content but also support interaction at a distance. Such informal e-learning, which has its roots in web 2.0, can provide a motivational and relational environment which may be able to self-sustain for considerable periods of time, supporting users during the consolidation of their foreign language competences and the deepening of their sociocultural knowledge.

References

Bettoni, C. (2006). *Usare un'altra lingua. Guida alla pragmatica interculturale.* Roma/ Bari: Laterza.

Bonaiuti, G. (2006). *E-learning 2.0. Il futuro dell'apprendimento in rete tra formale ed informale*. Trento: Erickson.

Brown, A., & Campione, J. (1990). Communities of learning and thinking or a context by any other name. *Contributions to Human Development, 21*, 108-126. Retrieved from http://dx.doi.org/10.1159/000418984

Deng, L., & Yuen, A. H. K. (2009). Blogs in higher education: implementation and issues. *TeachTrends, 53*(3), 95-98.

Downes, S. (2005). E-learning 2.0. *E-learn Magazine, 2005*(10). Retrieved from http://dx.doi.org/10.1145/1104966.1104968

Lave, J., & Wenger, E. (1991). *Situated learning. Legitimate peripheral participation*. Cambridge: Cambridge University Press. Retrieved from http://dx.doi.org/10.1017/CBO9780511815355

Manca, S., & Sarti, L. (2002). Comunità virtuali per l'apprendimento e nuove tecnologie. *TD-Tecnologie Didattiche, 1*, 11-19.

Mazzoni, E. (2005). La Social Network Analysis a supporto delle interazioni nelle comunità virtuali per la costruzione di conoscenza. *TD-Tecnologie Didattiche, 2*, 54-63.

Muukkonen, H., Hakkarainen, K., & Lakkala, M. (1999). Collaborative technology for facilitating progressive inquiry: the future learning environment tools. In C. Hoadley & J. Roschelle (Eds.), *Proceedings of the CSCL '99 conference* (pp. 406-415). Mahwah NJ: Lawrence Erlbaum. Retrieved from http://dx.doi.org/10.3115/1150240.1150291

O'Reilly, T. (2005). *What is Web 2.0: design patterns and business models for the next generation of software*. Retrieved from http://oreilly.com/web2/archive/what-is-web-20.html

Parmigiani, D., & Pennazio, V. (2012). Web e tecnologie 2.0 a scuola: strategie di apprendimento formali ed informali. *TD-Tecnologie Didattiche, 20*(2), 99-104.

Preece, J. (2001). *Comunità online. Progettare l'usabilità, promuovere la socialità*. Milano: Tecniche Nuove.

Rheingold, H. (2001). Memoria in rete e interazioni sociali. In F. Casalingo (a cura di), *Memoria quotidiana* (pp. 209-217). Pescara/Milano: Le Vespe.

Scardamalia, M., & Bereiter, C. (1993). Technologies for knowledge-building discourse. *Communications of the ACM, 36*(5), 37-41. Retrieved from http://dx.doi.org/10.1145/155049.155056

Scardamalia, M., & Bereiter, C. (1994). Computer support for knowledge-building communities. *Journal of the Learning Sciences, 3*(3), 265-283. Retrieved from http://dx.doi.org/10.1207/s15327809jls0303_3

Treccani (2014). *Complimenti – Vocabulario online*. Retrieved from http://www.treccani.it/vocabolario/tag/complimenti/

Vygotsky, L. S. (1978). *Mind in society. The development of higher psychological processes.* Cambridge MA: Harvard University Press.

Wilson, T., & Whitelock, D. (1997). Come lo hanno usato? Il coinvolgimento degli studenti di informatica in un ambiente CMC creato per l'apprendimento a distanza. *TD-Tecnologie Didattiche, 12,* 15-20.

Zanoni, G. (2014). Il repository multimediale LIRA: analisi della partecipazione della comunità di utenti. In C. Cervini & A. Valdivieso (a cura di), *Dispositivi formativi e modalità ibride per l'apprendimento linguistico*. Bologna: Edizioni CLUEB (Collana Contesti Linguistici, dir. Felix San Vicente).

13 Grammar processing through English L2 e-books: distance vs. face-to-face learning

Mª Ángeles Escobar-Álvarez[1]

Abstract

For university teachers in Distance Education, e-books should be an optimum solution since they do not have the opportunity to flip through the pages of print texts together with their students in the same classroom. College students usually use criteria such as cost, efficiency and personal comfort. Working with e-textbooks can be a tough decision for them. However, we present the advantages of an e-grammar book approach to foreign language teaching, and put forward a learning-efficient way to work with e-textbooks with the purpose of improving student motivation in a distance learning context.

Keywords: distance learning, e-textbooks, English grammar, L2 acquisition, student motivation.

1. Introduction

Many researchers assume that most adults never master a foreign grammar. Moreover, for foreign language instruction in distance contexts where learners can hardly be exposed to the second language in the natural environment and where acquisition of communicative skills is not face-to-face through the foreign language, the situation may be even more difficult.

---

1. Universidad Nacional de Educación a Distancia, Madrid, Spain; maescobar@flog.uned.es

How to cite this chapter: Escobar-Álvarez, M. Á. (2016). Grammar processing through English L2 e-books: distance vs. face-to-face learning. In A. Pareja-Lora, C. Calle-Martínez, & P. Rodríguez-Arancón (Eds), *New perspectives on teaching and working with languages in the digital era* (pp. 153-160). Dublin: Research-publishing.net. http://dx.doi.org/10.14705/rpnet.2016.tislid2014.430

Chapter 13

The aims of this paper are first of all to expose college students' textbook preferences in the context of distance learning in Spain, and, on the other hand, to take the challenge issued and show the type of e-textbooks that may be determinant in such a distance learning environment. The procedure consists firstly in summarising the pros and cons about print textbooks and e-books, and how they are influencing the acquisition of the subject under study: English grammar through learning tasks in Tourism studies. Then we will try to contrast how the affective factor and motivation exert an important influence on students when they are using the type of textbook that meets most of their preferences in the subject under study.

A mixed method is used in aiming at researching the easiest learning way which an e-textbook may offer in order to enhance the acquisition of our subject. Using a cross-sectional survey conducted with our students, we will demonstrate that the type of textbook is not the most important factor to guarantee the successful acquisition of a particular subject in distance education, but motivation and affective learning. This can serve to encourage teachers to publish their textbooks while paying attention to their students' preferences in either form. It can also have important pedagogical implications on distance education, such as increasing the offer of e-books to their students.

2. Pros and cons of print books and e-books

Traditionally written texts represent an ancient way to preserve knowledge. In fact, ancient books have lasted many years. So the question is whether e-books overlook this. Therefore, important information can be lost in a matter of seconds just because of a simple mistake of pressing the wrong button.

On the other hand, mistakes can be corrected and information can be updated quickly. The permanence of a written book is far beyond a standard e-book, so are their mistakes. From an affective perspective, an e-book may not give the reader the intellectual feeling that a written book can.

Textbooks are usually heavy and carrying multiple books may result in a strain on your back. With e-books, one only needs to carry one device that will house all of them. Moreover, today one can have access to cloud-based digital libraries from any electronic device (mobile phone or tablet). These digital libraries do not only offer knowledge to their academic clients but a digital platform which is an open and collaborative learning space where students can personalise their selections for study.

The textbook used in our research is *English Grammar and Learning Tasks for Tourism Studies* (Escobar-Álvarez, 2011). Students have used this textbook since early 2012, where the subject of *English II for Tourism* was launched within the Degree of Tourism at UNED. We had to wait until January 2014 for the corresponding e-book to be available for our students.

In order to conduct our research we asked our students to write an essay on the advantages and disadvantages of using the textbook or the e-book to prepare this subject. Most students turned out to prefer the textbook to the e-book, mainly because they feel they can write notes on its pages more easily that in an e-book. In what follows, we will be discussing the factors that should be considered in order to offer students a user-friendly e-book approach which enables them to process the L2 grammar in a natural way.

3. Student motivation

There is abundant literature on the scope of motivation in the learning of foreign languages. Krashen's (1982) Affective Filter theory during the 1970-80s showed that "learners with high motivation, self-confidence, a good self-image, and a low level of anxiety are better equipped for success in second language acquisition [. In contrast,] low motivation, low self-esteem, and debilitating anxiety [… may] form a mental block that prevents comprehensible input from being used for acquisition" (Rannut, n.d., n.p.). According to Dörnyei (2001), the teacher behaviour is a prevailing motivational tool: "[t]he teacher stimulus is diverse in that it ranges from the empathy with student-teacher attitudes that conquer students to engross in undertakings" (p. 120). Ellis (1994), in an attempt to explore motivation, merely emphasises that the motivation allows learners to be aware of their own learning process.

In our study we assume that if our students freely write a voluntary essay showing their textbook preferences, they will also indicate their grade of motivation. In this way, we were not only measuring their personal taste with respect to their personal choices to use a textbook or an e-book, but also their motivation to be explicitly active in their own learning process. Moreover, our students were also told that their participation would have a positive impact in their final grade. As pointed out by Lin and Warschauer (2011),

> "[t]he most influential theory in the field of language learning motivation is the socio-educational model proposed by Gardner (1985). This model highlights the impact of attitudes towards (L2) communities on motivation and student achievement. […] This model also identifies two types of motivational orientation: integrative and instrumental. Integrative orientation is defined as 'a sincere and personal interest in the people and culture represented by the other language group' […], while instrumental orientation pertains to the potential pragmatic gains of L2 proficiency, such as to get a better job or to pass a required examination […] Masgoret and Gardner (2003) found that there was a positive correlation between both types of orientation and achievement. Both integrative and instrumental orientation had an indirect effect on achievement through motivation" (p. 59).

4. Grammar and its benefits for autonomous learning

Grammar may be defined as the linguistic system of a language. Traditionally, grammar was associated to rules which dictated what one should say or write to speak a language well. However this perspective is no longer followed by more current grammar approaches to L2 teaching. Many recent grammar accounts pay attention to how the linguistic system of a particular language is acquired and used. Clearly, one can learn a foreign language in a more natural way by looking at how sounds or words are combined and how sentences are formed by native speakers from birth.

As for L2 use, any adult learner can realise that practice is key to performance. Since adult learners do not start from scratch because they have already acquired their first language, they may try – to no avail – to target the foreign language with their own L1 grammar. For some teachers, negative feedback is always required to acquire the target-like linguistic system. Others adopt a more eclectic method and claim that a natural grammar approach along with a task oriented performance results in a more natural way to use the L2 successfully. To do so, an active, autonomous attitude to language learning is clearly required. Following Escobar-Álvarez (2011),

> "it is clear that the explicit study of some constructions that form the grammar of the target language can support the learning of such a language in a quicker and more efficient way. In this sense, it's important to think of grammar as something that can help, like any tool, rather than something that has to be memorised. When one understands the grammar (or the particular constructions) of a language, one can immediately apply this explicit knowledge to other related linguistic facts without having to ask a teacher or look in a book, which is also essential, for example, in a case of self-study" (p. 14).

User-friendly e-books allow learners to work in a natural environment and in an autonomous way. For example, an e-grammar book can tell when a mistake is made and which grammar point needs revising, whenever and wherever learners are. Practice is therefore guaranteed.

5. Dealing with example generation tasks

An e-book should provide a comprehensive treatment of the examples used in teaching and learning grammar in the foreign language. It should focus on learner generated examples, a teaching strategy of asking L2 learners to construct their own examples in the L2 language under given constraints. Clearly, learner generated examples in the L2 serve as a powerful pedagogical tool for enhancing the learning of grammar at a variety of levels. Likewise, the resources provided would result in a motivating introduction to the study of the L2 grammar. As argued above, grammar points should not just be part of a comprehensive grammatical syllabus, but intended to revise and consolidate what the student already knows and will need to know for succeeding in a particular learning task.

Obviously, descriptive rules are often forgotten and what more importantly, they do not really help to raise the students' level of accuracy to perform well in the writing and speaking part of the exam. One of the goals of the learning tasks contained in a good grammar e-book is to develop, improve and practice the knowledge of English grammar required for the practice of all language skills.

It is well-known that Task-Based Language Teaching (TBLT) or Task-Based Instruction (TBI) attempts to make students do meaningful tasks using the target language, cf. Long (1991), Ellis (2003), Gass and Selinker (2008), among many others. Nowadays, interdisciplinarity and 'task-based approach' are the terms appearing in the new curricula of L2 teaching across the board since there is a general need to teach languages with a topic-content. According to the grammatical approach outlined so far, Escobar-Álvarez's (2011) e-textbook puts forward learning tasks that are related to a topic-content in the Tourism industry. The way to develop such tasks implies:

- understanding each task, i.e. reading through the input material and seeing what is required by it;

- selecting ideas, i.e. deciding what specific information is needed from the input material but taking care to avoid 'lifting' phrases from the texts;

- making notes, i.e. highlighting who the target reader or audience for the writing task is and what register is most appropriate;

- planning a final answer, i.e. deciding on the outline for the task, how to structure it, thinking about paragraphs and using some linking devices.

6. Conclusion

In considering learning from tasks in the context of foreign language grammar, the self-study approach of an e-book, like the one we discuss here, seems to be on the right track. First, students are active in their own learning process by having a key to all tasks. In addition, the grammar constructions include 'worked examples', that is, explicit solutions to activities provided in real professional texts, which may be highlighted thanks to the specific techniques provided by e-readers or electronic libraries. In either way, students generate examples which mirror their conceptions of grammar involved in all example generation tasks. In this way, students will process all grammatical rules by themselves in a very effective way, since it provides a 'window' into a learner's mind.

References

Dörnyei, Z. (2001). *Teaching and researching motivation*. Harlow, England: Pearson Education.

Ellis, R. (1994). *The study of second language acquisition*. Oxford: Oxford University Press.

Ellis, R. (2003). *Task-based language learning and teaching*. Oxford, New York: Oxford Applied Linguistics.

Escobar-Álvarez, M. Á. (2011). *English grammar and learning tasks for tourism studies. Unidad Didáctica*. Madrid: Universidad Nacional de Educación a Distancia (e-book: bluebottlebiz.com).

Gardner, R. C. (1985). *Social psychology and second language learning: the role of attitudes and motivation*. London: Edward Arnold.

Gass, S., & Selinker, L. (2008). *Second language acquisition: an introductory course*. New York, NY: Routledge.

Krashen, S. D. (1982). *Principles and practice in second language acquisition*. Oxford: Pergamon.

Lin, C.-H., & Warschauer, M. (2011). Integrative versus instrumental orientation among online language learners. *Linguagens e Diálogos, 2*(1), 58-86. Retrieved from http://linguagensedialogos.com.br/2011.1/textos/16-art-lin-warschauer.pdf?

Long, M. (1991). Focus on form: a design feature in language teaching methodology. In K. De Bot, R. Ginsberg, & C. Kramsch (Eds.), *Foreign language research in cross-cultural perspective*. Amsterdam: John Benjamins. Retrieved from http://dx.doi.org/10.1075/sibil.2.07lon

Masgoret, A. M., & Gardner, R. C. (2003). Attitudes, motivation, and second language learning: a meta-analysis of studies conducted by Gardner and associates. *Language Learning, 53*(1), 123-163. Retrieved from http://dx.doi.org/10.1111/1467-9922.00227

Rannut, U. (n.d.). Psychological factors influencing the integration of new immigrants in Estonia. *ImmiSoft - Integration Research Institute*. Retrieved from http://www.integrationresearch.net/research-projects.html?

Section 1.3.
Interaction design, usability and accessibility

14 A study of multimodal discourse in the design of interactive digital material for language learning

Silvia Burset[1], Emma Bosch[2], and Joan-Tomàs Pujolà[3]

Abstract

This study analyses some published interactive materials for the learning of Spanish as a first language and English as a Foreign Language (EFL) commonly used in primary and secondary education in Spain. The present investigation looks into the relationships between text and image on the interface of Interactive Digital Material (IDM) to develop learners' language skills. Screen design is evaluated with regards to the following formal units of analysis: graphic elements (shape, colour, size, resolution, significance), typography (style, colour, size, readability), composition (location, ratio) and action (recognition and effects) to assess their functionality in various learning activities. A discussion is also presented on the way these features of multimodal discourse can influence the language learning processes.

Keywords: interactivity, design, multimodality, language learning.

1. Universitat de Barcelona, Barcelona, Spain; sburset@ub.edu

2. Universitat de Barcelona, Barcelona, Spain; emmabosch@ub.edu

3. Universitat de Barcelona, Barcelona, Spain; jtpujola@ub.edu

How to cite this chapter: Burset, S., Bosch, E., & Pujolà, J.-T. (2016). A study of multimodal discourse in the design of interactive digital material for language learning. In A. Pareja-Lora, C. Calle-Martínez, & P. Rodríguez-Arancón (Eds), *New perspectives on teaching and working with languages in the digital era* (pp. 163-172). Dublin: Research-publishing.net. http://dx.doi.org/10.14705/rpnet.2016.tislid2014.431

Chapter 14

1. Introduction

The growing publication of digital educational materials for language learning in primary and secondary school is mainly due to two factors. On the one hand, it is logical that the teaching-learning situations benefit from all the advantages that digital environments provide in their multiple facets. On the other hand, it is evident that twenty-first century children and youngsters are active participants in the so called digital era, which entails that the forms of communication which they are now engaged in have changed considerably to previous generations, and therefore, an adjustment is needed to formalise the contents of digital materials to the new needs of the users.

Taking this into consideration, a key dimension that differentiates digital materials is the concept of interactivity. In this context, interactivity is identified as the relationship established by the users with the interface to process information actively, and thus increase learners' motivation, which results in more effective learning.

From this perspective and in the framework of a wider research tackling interactive material for the learning of Spanish as a first language and EFL, the present study looks in particular into the relationships between text and image on the interface of IDMs for language learning.

The analysis of screen design deals with the following formal units and features (in parenthesis): graphic elements (shape, colour, size, resolution, significance), typography (style, colour, size, readability), composition (location, ratio), and action (recognition and effects). Besides, their functionality in language learning activities is also discussed.

The study of the design of interactive digital materials for language learning is a research issue that should be addressed from different perspectives. To ensure meaningful interactivity between the learner and the digital material, courseware design should be analysed taking into account the usability of the learning material from the study of multimodal discourse (Han, Yun, Kwahk,

& Hong, 2001; Marzal, Colmenero, & Morato, 2003; Nielsen & Morkes, 1998; Nokelainen, 2006).

2. The concept of interactivity

The concept of interactivity is investigated from several different fields, such as Human Computer Interaction (HCI), instructional design, artificial intelligence, e-learning, or multimedia. From the instructional design research, some studies indicate interactivity has a positive influence on learning (Najjar, 1998; Ohl, 2001; Robertson, 1998; Sims, 1997; Yacci, 2000) and motivation (Stocks & Freddolino, 2000; Teo, Oh, Liu, & Wei, 2003). Increased user control, as reported by Brady (2004), "should increase learning and […] satisfaction. Similarly, increasing active processing should result in increased learning outcomes" (para. 2). Thus, it is crucial to study the interactivity of IDMs to understand how it applies, how it can enhance the process of learning and when better performance can be achieved to improve this process.

Will students learn more and better with IDMs? With the same content, IDMs have more potential to promote learning and language acquisition than traditional materials may provide. The answer lies in interactivity, which can capture the attention of learners and motivate them to learn. Students are asked to act at various times, keeping their attention throughout the whole process.

Sims (1997) classifies interactivity in various non-exclusive concepts (object, linear support, construct, reflexive, simulation, hypertext, contextual without immersion and virtual immersion), which refer to various instructional tasks and help understand the relationship between the digital material and the learner. Later, Sims (2000) analyses the elements of online interactivity through the four key components of any instructional design: the learner, the content, the pedagogy and the context. Furthermore, Kennewell, Tanner, Jones, and Beauchamp (2008) distinguish between two types of interactivity: technical and pedagogical. The first one refers to the relationship between a device (such as an Interactive Whiteboard (IWB), a tablet, or a computer) and the student, and the second one refers to the relationship of teacher-students through a strategy of content teaching in which the latter are active participants.

In the teaching and learning of languages, the four relations established by Moore (1993) are key to the development of communicative competence of students. The interactivity of the student and the material, the student and the interface, and the interaction between students and teacher and among students themselves generate enough practice to develop learners' communicative skills.

In a digital environment, teachers need to develop a particular pedagogy about the use of the material either for the IWBs, computers, tablets or *iPads*; that is, when they can be used and what for. This decision is determined by the characteristics of the digital materials available for teachers. IDMs are, therefore, a powerful tool for teaching and learning that acts as medium, which, in turn, allows for integration of other tools, such as the ones provided by the so-called web 2.0 (Sessoms, 2008).

The new spaces of communication and interaction in web 2.0 imply substantial changes in the use of language (Yus, 2010). The language of the Internet is characterised by its multimodality, i.e. by the use of different modes for effective communication. In this sense, that must also be the subject of teaching and practice, according to the new interpretation and production processes involved in digital literacy (Cassany, 2011).

3. Multimodal discourse of the interface

Language is defined as a code, a system structured in ways that mean something in an independent medium, either from written text, music or art (Barthes, 1970). However, a new approach considers now that the codes are structured resources in the same message. The message is the meeting point of different codes. Thus, a mode is a means of expression used to convey meaning. Each message uses a number of modes thus becoming multimodal.

Following the social semiotics theory (Burn & Parker, 2001), multimodal discourse text analysis (where text here must be understood as any written or graphic document) is expressed according to a series of parameters and must consider three social functions: (a) the representation of an aspect of reality, (b) the orientation in which relationships are established between interlocutors (either real people, fictional or between fictional agents and readers), and (c) the way in which communication is organised with consistency and structure from a conceptual unit and a structural one.

Kress and van Leeuwen (2001) pioneered a proposal of a *grammar of the visual* based on Halliday's (1994) model. According to Halliday (1994), every text is a multifunctional semantic unit that produces meanings at three levels: one related to the ideas expressed by the ideational function, the other that refers to the attitudes of the addresser about the message and the addressee using the interpersonal function, and the last one refers to the linguistic structure of text expressed in the textual function. Thus, Kress and van Leeuwen (2001) translated this three-level model: ideational, interpersonal and textual to a three-dimensional visual grammar. The visual mode extends in three comparable mode dimensions: (a) the ideational function, as the ability of visual resources to represent objects and situations of the world; (b) the interpersonal function, understood as the ability of visual language to express the relationship between the producer and the recipient of a sign; and (c) the textual function, in which visual resources combine to form a grammar.

From the above it follows that the degree of interactivity of digital materials is determined largely by the quality of the interface design. Design is understood here as the adequacy of the formal presentation of the content (text and image) to develop optimal performance in the processes, phases and sequences of various activities. Therefore, the interface is a space in which the effectiveness of multimodal discourse will be successful if the formal components that structure the display follow some quality criteria that are determined by their functionality.

As far as digital materials for language learning are concerned, interactivity enhanced learning is determined by the ease and functionality of the management processes in the development of activities, which in turn are determined by the quality of the design elements that structure the screens.

4. Analysis of screen design: measuring interactivity from a multimodal discourse perspective

The quality of graphic design is a key element to facilitate interactive processes in the development of digital activity. The formalisation of typography and image, and the relationship between the two (i.e. multimodality) may influence the reception of messages and facilitate or hinder interactivity.

To assess the interactivity that screens can generate in a didactic sequence of digital material, four aspects of design are considered.

The first one is a graphic aspect, that is to say, the iconographic elements that compose the screen image. The categories analysed are

- *Shape*: all the features that define the appearance of iconographic elements (technical realisation, style, perspective, proportion, etc.);

- *Colour*: chromatic properties of the iconographic element (hue, saturation, lightness);

- *Size*: proportions of the iconographic elements in relation to the space they occupy;

- *Resolution*: quality in the definition of the screen image;

- *Significance*: relevance and adequacy of iconographic elements in relation to the content.

The second aspect is typographic, and is analysed by means of the following components: (a) *style* (properties that define the look of the typographic element, that is, family, font, etc.); (b) *colour*; (c) *size*; and, last but not least, (d) *readability* (clarity in text reading).

The third aspect is composition, i.e. the relationship between the different elements, whether iconographic, typographical, or both simultaneously, which make up the screen image. Two categories are studied here:

- *Location*: place where the different elements are located;

- *Proportion*: harmony between elements regarding their dimensions.

The fourth aspect is devoted to the elements of action, i.e. graphic or typographic elements that must be activated to interact with the screen and allow the user to select, start, fast-forward, rewind, close, etc. The categories considered in this aspect are

- *Recognition*: identifying that the graphic or typographical elements will cause an action;

- *Visual effects* (if any): when activating the element, variations in colour, size, and lighting are displayed;

- *Sound effects* (if any): when activating the element, sounds are emitted.

The main criteria by which the different categories are analysed are functionality and consistency. Therefore, those components that hinder the interactive processes are identified. Interactivity impedes the teaching-learning processes in the graphic dimension when, for instance, the images have only a 'decorative' function, the colour combination is strident, or poor resolution prevents the proper display of the represented objects. Similarly, in the typographic aspect, the font chosen or an excessively small size may hinder readability, as may a colour that does not stand out enough from the background. Likewise, at a compositional level, images and texts can be pressed to each other or not distributed harmoniously. And finally, regarding the elements of action, they might be difficult to identify, and visual or sound effects (if any) might be gratuitous or too distractive.

Each screen is considered a 'unit of analysis', and the categories defined above are described for each one. However, independent analysis of each screen is not sufficient to assess the interactive processes, as activities are formed into a chained sum of screens. Thus, another criterion is introduced to analyse the *coherence* between screens of the same material. On the one hand, the existence of coherence between screens of the same unit (the subsequent unit of the analysed material) and, on the other hand, between the screen that is evaluated and considered to serve a similar role in the second unit analysed.

Examples of interactivity that impede teaching-learning processes are baffling the user with unexpected typographic, chromatic and compositional changes, or random changes occurring in the shape and location of an element of action in the same unit screens or with similar function.

5. Conclusion

In the interactive processes come into play several factors, such as learner, content, pedagogy and context (Sims, 2000). In the present study of language learning in digital environments, the learner should receive content from a clear and precise multimodal discourse so that interactivity can prompt learning. Clarity of content is key both in the educational design of the activity and its formal aspect of the design. In this sense, graphic design affects not only aesthetic considerations, but focuses primarily on issues related to functionality.

The main function of IDMs for language learning is, obviously, to learn and practise language using an active methodology in which interactivity promotes learning from effective multimodal discourse. The multimodal discourse is generated on the screen from the established interrelation between the written text and image. In this sense, graphic design directly affects the interactive processes, not only regarding the instructions of the activities but also the learning of the content.

In summary, analysing the criteria related to (a) the formal presentation of screens (graphic elements, typography, composition, and action); and (b) the coherence in IDMs, determines the quality of their interactivity and, consequently, their effectiveness for language learning.

References

Barthes, R. (1970). *S/Z*. Paris: Editions du Seuil.
Brady, L. (2004). The role of interactivity in web-based educational material. *Software Usability Research Laboratory*. Whichita State University. Retrieved from http://usabilitynews.org/the-role-of-interactivity-in-web-based-educational-material/
Burn, A., & Parker, D. (2001). Making your mark: digital inscription, animation, and a new visual semiotic. *Education, Communication and Information*, *1*(2), 155-179. Retrieved from http://dx.doi.org/10.1080/14636310120091913
Cassany, D. (2011). *En_línia. Llegir i escriure a la xarxa*. Barcelona: Graó.
Halliday, M. A. K. (1994). *An introduction to functional grammar*. London: Arnold.
Han, S. H., Yun, M. H., Kwahk, J., & Hong, S. W. (2001). Usability of consumer electronics products. *International Journal of Industrial Ergonomics*, *28*(3-4), 143-151. Retrieved from http://dx.doi.org/10.1016/S0169-8141(01)00025-7
Kennewell, S., Tanner, H., Jones, S., & Beauchamp, G. (2008). Analysing the use of interactive technology to implement interactive teaching. *Journal of Computer Assisted Learning*, *24*(1), 61-73. Retrieved from http://dx.doi.org/10.1111/j.1365-2729.2007.00244.x
Kress, G., & van Leeuwen, T. (2001) *Multimodal discourse*. London: Arnold.
Marzal, M. A., Colmenero, M. J., & Morato, J. (2003). Selección de recursos didácticos en red: accesibilidad y usabilidad como elementos de un sistema de evaluación para la educación. In *Segunda Conferencia Iberoamericana en Sistemas, Cibernética e Informática. Orlando: CISCI*.
Moore, M. (1993). Theory of transactional distance. In D. Keegan (Ed.), *Theoretical principles of distance education*. London & New York: Routledge.
Najjar, L. (1998). Principles of educational multimedia user interface design. *Human Factors*, *40*(2), 311-323. Retrieved from http://dx.doi.org/10.1518/001872098779480505

Chapter 14

Nielsen, J., & Morkes, J. (1998). *Applying writing guidelines to web pages. Universitat de Barcelona*. Retrieved from http://www.useit.com/papers/webwriting/rewriting.html

Nokelainen, P. (2006). An empirical assessment of pedagogical usability criteria for digital learning material with elementary school students. *Educational Technology & Society*, 9(2), 178-197.

Ohl, T. (2001). An interaction-centric learning model. *Journal of Educational Multimedia and Hypermedia*, 10(4), 311-332.

Robertson, J. (1998). Paradise lost: children, multimedia and the myth of interactivity. *Journal of Computer Assisted Learning*, 14(1), 31-39. Retrieved from http://dx.doi.org/10.1046/j.1365-2729.1998.1410031.x

Sessoms, D. (2008). Interactive instruction: creating interactive learning environments trough tomorrow's teachers. *International Journal of Technology in Teaching and Learning*, 4(2), 86-96.

Sims, R. (1997). Interactivity: a forgotten art? *Computers in Human Behavior*, 13(2), 157-180. Retrieved from http://dx.doi.org/10.1016/S0747-5632(97)00004-6

Sims, R. (2000). An interactive conundrum: constructs of interactivity and learning theory. *Australian Journal of Educational Technology*, 16(1), 45-57.

Stocks, J., & Freddolino, R. (2000). Enhancing computer-mediated teaching through interactivity: the second iteration of a World Wide Web-based graduated social work course. *Research on Social Work Practice*, 10(4), 505-518.

Teo, H., Oh, L., Liu, C., & Wei, K. (2003). An empirical study of effects of interactivity on web user attitude. *International Journal of Human Computer Studies*, 58(3), 281-305. Retrieved from http://dx.doi.org/10.1016/S1071-5819(03)00008-9

Yacci, M. (2000). Interactivity demystified: a structural definition for distance education and intelligent computer-based instruction. *Educational Technology*, 40(4), 5-16.

Yus, F. (2010). *Ciberpragmática 2.0. Nuevos usos del lenguaje en Internet*. Barcelona: Ariel.

15. Audiovisual translation and assistive technology: towards a universal design approach for online education

Emmanouela Patiniotaki[1]

Abstract

Audiovisual Translation (AVT) and Assistive Technology (AST) are two fields that share common grounds within accessibility-related research, yet they are rarely studied in combination. The reason most often lies in the fact that they have emerged from different disciplines, i.e. Translation Studies and Computer Science, making a possible combined approach quite a demanding task due to their interdisciplinarity and the need for exploration of various parameters. Moreover, by focusing on certain needs and modes, several angles are added to the investigation. At the same time, due to their specific characteristics, the possibility of practical and applicable proposals towards the achievement of accessible education can be high. This paper aims to present some basic connections between the different disciplines involved in the 'Accessible Online Education Research', whose goal is to provide a theoretical framework for the joint investigation of AVT and AST-based approaches to accessible online education, and suggest possible implementations of the two disciplines for the creation of universal educational environments.

Keywords: audiovisual translation, assistive technology, universal design, online education.

---

1. Imperial College London, University College London, London, UK; e.patiniotaki@ucl.ac.uk

How to cite this chapter: Patiniotaki, E. (2016). Audiovisual translation and assistive technology: towards a universal design approach for online education. In A. Pareja-Lora, C. Calle-Martínez, & P. Rodríguez-Arancón (Eds), *New perspectives on teaching and working with languages in the digital era* (pp. 173-183). Dublin: Research-publishing.net. http://dx.doi.org/10.14705/rpnet.2016.tislid2014.432

Chapter 15

1. Defining the research cluster

Since the understanding of this paper lies in the establishment of connections among more than one field, it is important to explain the meanings they carry within the particular research.

As a branch that has gained its place within the field of Translation Studies since the 1990s, AVT "is often defined as translation of text that (1) is transmitted through two simultaneous and complementary channels (acoustic and visual) and (2) combines several signifying codes" (Martínez-Sierra, 2008, p. 29). AVT consists of several translation practices, among which are Subtitling for the Deaf and Hard-of-hearing (SDH) and Audio Description (AD) for the blind and visually impaired, which are used mainly to serve their intended audiences. SDH is interlingual or intralingual subtitling that adheres to different norms from those of conventional subtitling with regard to reading speed and syntax. It includes additional information that is necessary in order for the audience to receive all the auditory elements initially provided by the source material. AD, on the other hand, "provides a narration of the visual elements" – "the visual made verbal" (Snyder, 2011, p. 1). Although other AVT practices have also proved their function as access services (e.g. voice-over), the current analysis focuses on these two as they are considered the basic forms of AVT used for such purposes and their morphology could allow for further application of research outcomes to other practices.

AST has been assigned various definitions, among which is "any item, piece of equipment, or system, whether acquired commercially, modified, or customised, that is commonly used to increase, maintain, or improve functional capabilities of individuals with disabilities" (ADA, 2004, Section 508). Although in the past AST was synonym to hardware, it has gradually started to encompass a variety of software used by disabled users with the aim to either substitute or facilitate hardware, while in many cases AST appliances move further to provide new innovative ways of access or satisfy emerging needs. Further categorisation of AST also varies, with the example of Cook and Hussey's (1995, pp. 6-12) differentiation between assistive and rehabilitative or educational technologies, low to high technology, hard and soft technologies, appliances and tools, minimal to maximal technology, general or specific, and commercial versus custom technologies.

'Computer-assisted education' and 'computer-based instruction' are two terms that have been used to describe the initial phases of educational computing (Alessi & Trollip, 1991; Gibbons & Fairweather, 1998). Through several stages dating as far back as the 1960s, when the first virtual classroom was formed in the University of Illinois, we have now come to what is called Online Education, e-Learning or Online Learning. Aggarwal (2000) differentiates between three models of Web-based learning: Web-support for information storage, dissemination and retrieval; Web-support for two-way interaction; and Web-based teaching. Instances of these models can be found in the practices followed by the various dominant players in education, from traditional (non-)profit universities to distance or e-learning organisations around the world, and Online Education is now studied separately from the general field of education in many aspects due to its distinctive characteristics.

2. Accessibility on web material through AVT and AST

Within this context, accessibility refers to the availability of online products, services or material to people with disabilities – physical, cognitive, mental, sensory, emotional, developmental or a combination of the above. This paper discusses accessibility from the point of view of sensory impairments, although the notion of accessibility is quite often seen as 'unintentionally' flexible and inclusive, since what has once been designed to cater for the needs of the deaf may also be used for other disabilities through its development.

Having been established as one of the main means of communication, information and entertainment, the Web has become part of people's lives. According to Dutton, Blank, and Groselj (2013), OxIS, one of the most recent surveys on disabilities and the Internet, found that over half (51%) of British people with a disability use the Internet, although in half of these cases their disability limits its use. The vast movement of the last decade towards an accessible Web has emerged from several sources following various directions, while focus on audiovisual material has already dominated different discussions of standards related to accessible online material. Nowadays, the most recent version of the AST Act of 2004[2], the Europe 2020 Initiative (European Commission, 2010) of the European Commission along with the e-Inclusion and e-Accessibility Policies engaged under the i2010 framework of the EU, combined with Web accessibility standards, the most prominent being the W3C Web Accessibility Initiative, bring the need for equal access to the Web to the surface.

Due to its nature as a branch within Computer Science, AST has been present in Web accessibility considerations during its own development. However, what began as a set of 'plugged-in' assisting tools is now acquiring a more integrated form, with the example of websites designed based on screen reading requirements. In their account of the fundamental approaches to sensory aids, Cook and Hussey (1995) identify two primary intrinsic human enablers in sensory communication, sensing and perception, the limitation or absence of which demands the use of AST. They distinguish between augmentation and substitution methods for limited or absent senses respectively. While such a definition seems to emerge from medicine and has been used to refer to aids, such as magnifiers and speech-to-text converters, it is interesting how this also applies to AVT. SDH and AD are also destined for users with partial loss. With the gradual development of software that can be used for navigation and speech-to-text or text-to-speech conversion, often combined with physical aids, the Web has somewhat automatically developed the feature of accessibility, with such demands putting pressure on governments and developers.

In parallel to that, although SDH and AD are commonly known as traditional features of television or cinema, with the more accessible Web, audiovisual material inevitably follow in the queue of 'online wealth' that needs to become

---

2. One Hundred Eighth Congress of the United States of America; Assistive Technology Act of 2004. H. R. 4278. U.S. Government Publishing Office.

accessible. As a result, with the latest World Wide Web Consortium (W3C) guidelines developers are requested to provide alternatives for time-based media on their websites. These alternatives include equivalents for pre-recorded audio-only and video-only media, captions, conventional or extended/descriptive audio description for pre-recorded media, as well as live captions for live audio content in synchronised media, allowing SDH and AD to establish their role as access services in online contexts. With the HTML5 <video> and <audio> elements, this process becomes easier for developers. This demand proves the necessity of both AST and AVT practices for the accessibility of online environments. What is more, the BBC has published Accessibility Guidelines aiming at the provision of accessible editorial content and user experience, including the provision of caption/subtitles and the USA Government has incorporated a New Video & Multimedia Accessibility Guide under Section 508 including guidance on both captioning and AD with the use of 508-compliant players.

It is important to notice a transfer of duty towards providers in general with regard to Web content, with a possible aim to free the users of the need to buy different software and equipment since AST is often reactive in design and advances very fast, making a priori implementations more functional and necessary. Another parameter that needs to be considered is that non-accessible online environments might discourage users, which can also be argued based on the results of research conducted by Dobransky and Hargittai (2006) suggesting that "while over half of people without disabilities use a computer at home, less than a third of those with disabilities do so" and "while over half of people without impairments access the network in their homes, just over a quarter of those with disabilities do so, highlighting considerable disparities" (p. 14). Finally, although AST and AVT might seemingly have little in common, it could be argued that under the scope of accessibility, they supplement each other, while it is not rare that they exchange routes throughout their development. For example, re-speaking, speech recognition and text-to-speech conversions as well as speech processing, synthesisers and automatic translation have been developed through both fields, maybe with a different approach and at a different pace and mode, making the joint study of findings in both fields a unique research opportunity.

3. Online education: accessibility and universal design

Not much research has been conducted in Online Learning with regard to accessible online environments. The reason often lies in the fact that such a study alone requires consideration of several aspects and a variety of theoretical approaches, since education itself is a multidisciplinary field of research. Teaching methodologies, learning environments, strategies, curriculum development and management, evaluation and assessment are only a few of the parameters considered in the design of a teaching process. When such a process is transferred from the traditional classroom to the Web, a new series of parameters that need to be considered is automatically included in the design process. According to Kearsley (2000), the elements of Online Learning include email, threaded discussions, forums, real-time conferencing, transfer of material, application software, etc. The requirements for Online Learning, e.g. computer literacy, managements of behavioural or learning difficulties, etc., also affect the choice of methods applied. In any case, training and technical support by the hosting body are a prerequisite.

When aiming at Accessible Online Education, taking the design of complete online courses or supplement material as a model case, requirements grow, since more needs have to be satisfied. With regard to sensory impairments, we could briefly refer to the need for the hosting online environment to be fully accessible, while its content and design should be following accessibility standards (including navigation, alternative texts, cross-platform application, alternative texts, etc.). Tools to enhance students' performance should be provided through the online environment. In 2010, The 'DARE to Care: Disability Accommodations tRaining Environment' project website provided tips for best enhancing accessibility of online training courses. Other American universities, including the George Washington University and the University of Colorado, formed guidelines for accessible online courses based on Section 508. More recently, CANnect (2014), a non-profit consortium with the aim of raising awareness on the needs of disabled Internet users, published a detailed guide on Accessible Online Learning Content, including both AST and AVT practices.

In the last two decades, several attempts indicate the move towards accessible online environments, both on commercial and research bases. This paper discusses holistic attempts, i.e. complete educational environments rather than specific tools, such as the SSTAT. Among the commercial platforms available, Panopto, Tegrity, MediaSite and Echo306 belong to the most popular choices of universities as systems which form learning environments that capture video, audio and screen activity, support captions and other editing features. Interesting recent research projects include DELE, a fully-iconic e-learning environment through which tutors can "define, generate and test e-learning courses for deaf people, which are automatically managed, published and served by the system itself" (Bottoni et al., 2012, p. 780), and MVP that can be used by students in class to edit lecture visuals through their own devices or cooperate in groups. European projects, like ClipFlair and the Accessible e-Learning Platform for Europe indicate the realisation of the need for holistic educational environments. Finally, open-source platforms like Moodle and LANCELOT might provide some accessibility features, yet they were not initially designed to that end. With the integration of several AST tools, Moodle attempts to offer an accessible online environment. Assessing the accessibility level of a sample online course based on principles of Universal Instructional Design, Elias (2010) indicates the lack of AST and AVT tools available to students, stressing the need for integration of tools within the platform.

It is not rare that through technological advancements, barriers might be erected where solutions should be given. As happens with websites, platforms and other online educational environments need to integrate accessibility features in their structure. This idea could capture the essence of Universal Design (UD), that is, "the concept of designing all products and the built environment to be aesthetic and usable to the greatest extent possible by everyone, regardless of their age, ability, or status in life" (NCSU, 2012, n.p.), as introduced by architect Ronald L. Mace. UD in education "goes beyond accessible design for people with disabilities to make all aspects of the educational experience more inclusive for students, parents, staff, instructors, administrators, and visitors with a great variety of characteristics" (Burgstahler, 2012, p. 1). According to McGuire, Sally, and Shaw (2006), educational applications of UD include UD for Learning, UD for Instruction and Universal Instructional Design. Through their discussion on the framework of Considering Alternative Paradigms based on Shaw, McGuire, and Scott (2004), it seems that principles like universally designed instruction available to all students, inclusive curriculum and alternative methods for accessing teaching materials that have evolved from the reauthorisation of the IDEA Act have brought about significant changes in Education (McGuire et al., 2006).

UD has already been discussed within Online Education. In most cases, evaluation of accessibility in terms of UD is based on the principles discussed above, with alterations for application to the different mode of provision, the Web. Boyd (2006) combines UD principles and Web Accessibility guidelines, adding more elements for Web instruction in order to present an account of Guidelines for Accessible Design in Online Education. This proves that the issue of Online Education is rather complex due to the many parameters that need to be considered for the design and effective use of online educational environments. However, usability being the aim of UD seems to have the potential to provide the required educational framework for this research. AVT offers specific techniques to access services and AST tools can focus on the Web and educational aims, offering their own account in a potential combined theoretical background for Accessible Online Education. However, such an account can never be inclusive of all the aspects related to such tasks (e.g. physiological, medical, sociological, etc.).

The process of creating material for the purpose of Accessible Online Education is another step that involves adherence to various norms in order for the material itself to be accessible to all students. According to de Macedo and Ulbricht (2013), the most common deficiencies found in web access include visual and auditory deficiencies. Digital learning objects, i.e. "any digital or not entity, that can be used, reused and referenced during learning supported by technology" (IEEE-LTSC-LOM, 2005), include media content, instructional content, software, and software tools, which should be made accessible within a holistic educational context. Towards that end, de Macedo and Ulbricht (2013) have employed UD principles, as well as the W3C and IMS guidelines for accessible identical or equivalent content based on the idea that "learning objects built considering the factors of accessibility and universal design can be used by people with disabilities just as effectively as if used by any other user" (p. 185).

4. Considerations and conclusion

The complexity of research in Accessible Online Education due to various parameters of consideration makes such an attempt hard, but also unique. Several more aspects need to be considered, including the use of automated language processes, quality in the use of AST and AVT practices, training of the subjects interacting through the education process, or the value of AVT practices for the development of learning skills, just to name few. Yet, it cannot be denied that the future of Online Education is bright and the need for accessible contexts that will allow universal access by most potential users is a necessity. Accessibility of the whole educational context as well as the learning objects need to be the focus of the task, while a solid background for the implementation of AVT and AST practices seems to be able to form a flourishing ground for relevant studies through the successful combination of theories within the various fields involved.

References

ADA. (2004). Information and technological assistance of the Americans with disabilities Act. Section 508 Surveys and Reports.

Aggarwal, A. (2000). Web-based education. In A. Aggarwal (Ed), *Web-based learning and teaching technologies: opportunities and challenges.* Hersley & London: Idea Group Publishing. Retrieved from http://dx.doi.org/10.4018/978-1-878289-60-5.ch001

Alessi, S., & Trollip, S. (1991). *Computer based instruction: methods and development.* Englewood Cliffs, NJ: Prentice-Hall.

Bottoni, P., Capuano, D., De Marsico, M., Labella, A., & Velialdi, S. (2012). Experimenting DELE: a deaf-centered e-learning visual environment. Paper presented at the *AVI'12. May 21-25* (pp. 780-781). Capri Island. Retrieved from http://dx.doi.org/10.1145/2254556.2254711

Boyd, K. R. (2006). Universal design for online education: access for all. In D. Monolescu, C. Schifter, & L. Greenwood (Eds.), *The distance education evolution: issues and case studies* (pp. 67-115) Hershey: Information Science Publishing (Idea Group Inc.).

Burgstahler, S. (2012). *Universal design in education: principles and application.* University of Washington: DO-IT.

CANnect. (2014). *How-to guide for creating accessible online learning content.* Web site: http://projectone.cannect.org/index.php

Cook, A. M., & Hussey, S. M. (1995). *Assistive technologies: principles and practice.* USA: Mosby – Year Book, Inc.

De Macedo, S. M. C., & Ulbricht, R. V. (2013). Universal design and accessibility standards. In C. Stephanidis & M. Antona (Eds.), *Online learning objects.* UAHCI/HCII 2013, Part III, LNCS 8011 (pp. 179-186). Berlin Heidelberg: Springer-Verlag.

Dobransky, K., & Hargittai, E. (2006). The disability divide in internet access and use. *Information, Communication & Society, 9*(3), 313-334. Retrieved from http://dx.doi.org/10.1080/13691180600751298

Dutton, W. H., Blank, G., & Groselj, D. (2013). *Cultures of the internet: the internet in Britain. Oxford Internet Survey 2013.* University of Oxford. Retrieved from http://oxis.oii.ox.ac.uk/blog/almost-half-people-disabilities-dont-use-internet-why#sthash.WeYIJnbZ.dpuf

Elias, T. (2010). Universal instructional design principles for Moodle. *The International Review of Research in Open and Distance Learning, 11*(2). Retrieved from http://www.irrodl.org/index.php/irrodl/article/view/869/1575

European Commission. (2010). *Europe 2020: a strategy for smart, sustainable and inclusive growth.* Retrieved from http://eur-lex.europa.eu/LexUriServ/LexUriServ.do?uri=COM:2010:2020:FIN:EN:PDF

Gibbons, A., & Fairweather, P. (1998). *Designing computer based instruction.* Englewood Cliffs, NJ: Educational Technology Publications.

IEEE-LTSC-LOM. (2005). The learning object metadata standard. In *IEEE Learning Technology Standards Committee.* Retrieved from http://goo.gl/flxYaA

Kearsley, G. (2000). *Online education: learning and teaching in cyberspace.* Canada: Nelson Thomson Learning, Inc.

Martínez-Sierra, J. J. (2008). *Humor y traducción. Los Simpson cruzan la frontera.* Castellón de la Plana: Jaume I University.

McGuire, M. J., Sally, S. S., & Shaw, F. S. (2006). Universal design and its applications in educational environments. *Remedial and Special Education, 27*(3), 166-175. Retrieved from http://dx.doi.org/10.1177/07419325060270030501

NCSU. (2012). *Ronald L. Mace*. Retrieved from https://www.ncsu.edu/ncsu/design/cud/about_us/usronmace.htm

Shaw, F. S., McGuire, J. M., & Scott, S. S. (2004). *A framework for considering alternative paradigms*. Storrs: University of Connecticut, Center of Postsecondary Education and Disability.

Snyder, J. (2011). Fundamentals of audio description. Teaching audio description: an on-line approach. *4th International Conference Media for All 4*. July 01. London: Imperial College.

Section 2.

New trends in the application of ICTs to language learning

Section 2.1.
Mobile-assisted language learning

16 Mobile learning: a powerful tool for ubiquitous language learning

Nelson Gomes[1], Sérgio Lopes[2], and Sílvia Araújo[3]

Abstract

Mobile devices (smartphones, tablets, e-readers, etc.) have come to be used as tools for mobile learning. Several studies support the integration of such technological devices with learning, particularly with language learning. In this paper, we wish to present an Android app designed for the teaching and learning of Portuguese as a foreign language. We aim to promote new experiences in the field of mobile learning, based on the concept of Social Learning (Mondahl & Razmerita, 2014).

Keywords: mobile devices, languages, social learning, learning management system.

1. Mobile devices in the language classroom

Research on language learning using mobile devices such as mobile phones or Personal Digital Assistants (PDAs) has increased exponentially in the last decade. Most of this research showed that students have positive perceptions about the use of their own mobile phone as a learning tool. Connected seamlessly to the Internet via wireless access, these mobile technologies open up a range of possibilities for teaching and learning languages (both native and foreign). Mobile phones or smartphones are being used to enable the development not only of lexical skills (Lu, 2008; Moura & Carvalho, 2013) and grammar (Wang

---

1. Universidade do Minho, Guimarães, Portugal; nelsongomes@outlook.com

2. Universidade do Minho, Guimarães, Portugal; sergio.lopes@dei.uminho.pt

3. Universidade do Minho, Braga, Portugal; saraujo@ilch.uminho.pt

How to cite this chapter: Gomes, N., Lopes, S., & Araújo, S. (2016). Mobile learning: a powerful tool for ubiquitous language learning. In A. Pareja-Lora, C. Calle-Martínez, & P. Rodríguez-Arancón (Eds), *New perspectives on teaching and working with languages in the digital era* (pp. 189-199). Dublin: Research-publishing.net. http://dx.doi.org/10.14705/rpnet.2016.tislid2014.433

& Smith, 2013), but also of speaking and listening skills (Lys, 2013) in formal and informal contexts. Students have only tapped into the educational potential of mobile phones, and it appears that the technology is not a barrier for them. In fact, learners nowadays are carrying new literacies and digital technology (Web 2.0 environments, iPods, mobile communication, etc.) into schools. Mobile phones now have GPS, texting, voice, and multimedia capabilities which can be used to improve language learning performance (Bloch, 2008; DuBravac, 2012; Moura, 2010; Moura & Carvalho, 2011; Sykes & Reinhardt, 2013, among others).

The possibilities that Web 2.0 and mobile technologies offer the language teacher are countless, with new applications and services being launched every day. Applications such as *Duolingo*, *Babbel*, *Mosalingua*, *Memrise*, *Voxy* and *Busuu* are available for download from the App Store or Google Play. These apps provide a stress-free work environment for learners and help them to be more responsible for their learning process. As for informal language learning through social interactions, there are several websites that use social networks like *Babbel* (www.babbel.com), *LiveMocha* (www.livemocha.com) or *Palabea* (www.palabea.net). These e-learning platforms allow students to hone practical skills and conversational fluency via videoconference. *Verbling* for example offers immersive language learning through Google+ Hangouts. *Italki* or *Mixxer* connect people online to practice speaking skills together via Skype. As mentioned by Eaton (2013), *Duolingo* has come up with an innovative "way to combine social media-based language learning with crowd-sourced efforts [in order] to translate the Web" (n.p.). All these platforms offer increasingly powerful applications (like multimedia and social networking) which make language learning practice resemble real-life communication. It is generally believed that language learning can be most effective when language practice occurs in real and meaningful conversations (with other learners who share the same interests) instead of isolated linguistic settings. Some of the relevant concepts found in the literature on mobile learning ('social interactionism', 'social constructivism' or 'connectivism') call our attention to the role of social interaction in language learning (Lisbôa, Coutinho, & Bottentuit Júnior, 2013; Verga & Kotz, 2013).

Although there is a greater proliferation of applications for the English language, we can find several apps which combine online instructional content with a global community of language learners in a very wide range of languages. *Livemocha*, for example, offers languages learning programs in over 35 languages. Without leaving home, students can learn foreign languages like English, French or more exotic languages. Portuguese, however, is very poorly represented and whatever few courses exist are often taught in Brazilian Portuguese. Spoken by 244 million people worldwide, Portuguese is the sixth most spoken language in the world, the fifth most used on the Internet and third on the social networks Facebook and Twitter, according to Portuguese newspaper *Público*.

2. Presentation of the prototype
I want to learn Portuguese

Within the course of *Technologies Applied to Language* offered in 2012-2013, eight students of the Master's in *Non-Native Portuguese Language - Portuguese as a Foreign Language and Second Language* at the University of Minho have created contents for the national symbol of Portugal – *Galo de Barcelos*. From these contents, we have developed an Android app for Portuguese language learners, which is illustrated in Figure 1.

Figure 1. Interface of application with Galo de Barcelos

Chapter 16

We tried to develop different language skills (vocabulary, grammar, listening and reading skills, etc.) through a wide variety of activities (true/false, filling in the blanks, matching, multiple choice, etc.) and using authentic audio-visual materials (Figure 2).

Figure 2. Listening and vocabulary activities

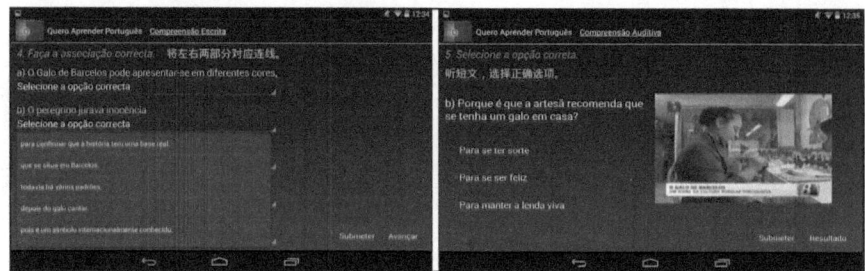

A bilingual dictionary was inserted to help Chinese students grasp the meaning of words considered difficult (Figure 3).

Figure 3. Chinese-Portuguese dictionary

Students receive specific feedback on their performance with respect to each activity or at the end of each lesson (Figure 4).

Figure 4. Visualisation of final results

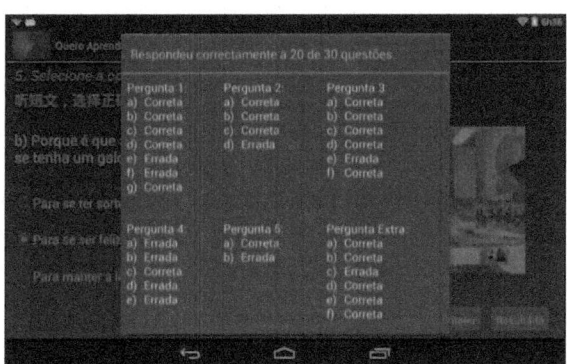

This feedback is useful for learners because it is a tool for active, self-directed involvement, which is essential for developing communicative competence.

3. Extension of this prototype

The application described in the previous section was merely a first prototype that we want to develop in partnership with the Department of Industrial Electronics Engineering of the University of Minho. Our intention is to create a flexible teaching and learning environment in which teachers and students can navigate as they wish, (passively) querying content or (actively) creating and sharing content.

3.1. Technological aspects

The system under development should be able to take full advantage of mobile platforms, namely by offering enhanced speed and battery usage. Consequently, it is built around a native Android application, but it also features a web interface which can be accessed from any platform (mobile or desktop).

Another goal of the system is to easily support delivery of new learning materials. Since mobile platforms are not appropriate for content production, it will feature a web application to help teachers to produce new activities. When contents are introduced in this web application, they will be immediately available to all mobile application users connected to the Internet. Drawing on HTML5 new features such as drag and drop, this web application will be plugin-free and usable virtually in any platform.

To summarise, the system is composed of (1) an Android application for learners, (2) an alternative web application for learners, offering the same features as the previous one, and (3) a web application for teachers and institutions supporting course management and creation of materials. The system architecture is illustrated in Figure 5.

Figure 5. System architecture

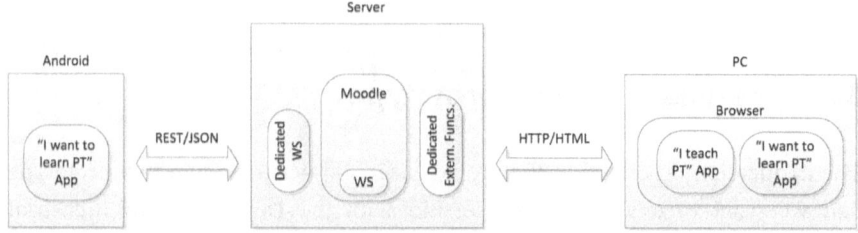

The server side of this system is therefore central because it stores the contents that are made available to learners in both the web and Android client applications. To implement the system we (naturally) considered existing Learning Management Systems (LMS). Moodle is a widely used and free LMS, along with all related development tools, and it features a modular design that can be extended by plugins. It was thus chosen as the basis for the server implementation.

Moodle is a complete LMS that features customisation of web site design, collaboration tools that make it easier to build communities, configurable grading and reports, and it supports different learning methods. The most important feature of Moodle for the purpose of this project is that it provides a web service access using different protocols and formats. Therefore, Moodle's web services are the interface for the Android application, namely REST web services and JSON data to reduce both processing load and network bandwidth (Mohamed & Wijesekera, 2012).

Moodle will be extended to support the Android app in a more efficient way, as well as the concepts of the pedagogical approach proposed in the following section. More specifically, it will be extended with a web service for the Android app and a back-office supporting additional kinds of activities (or quizzes) and functionalities, for example, games. These extensions are implemented as dedicated external functions. New kinds of quizzes consist of templates for both web and Android interfaces, and a database schema. The web interface will make use of some of the newest HTML features like animations.

Although the project includes a web application with similar goals to the Android App, in this paper we focus on the latter. Since internet connectivity is not always available, the app will store offline content using a local database that is later synchronised with the Moodle database. Users will be able to choose different levels of offline content download (and a cache size limit), for example, the current learning path or the entire course. Offline content has to be managed, which will be done automatically. When activities are finished, the results are saved in the local database and any other data can be deleted. Users will have the option to delete no longer needed data, or it will be automatically deleted when cache exceeds size limit. When the mobile device gets connected to the Internet again, the application automatically sends any results data to the server. This data is short and it is kept as part of the user profile and has to be deleted explicitly in the mobile application.

Pronunciation activities will be supported by the system but with manual assessment. Both teachers and material designers often forget that intonation is an important aspect of phonetics which carries meaning. The segmental (i.e. vowels and consonants) and suprasegmental (i.e. rhythm and intonation) features of speech clearly cannot be neglected in foreign language learning and teaching. The online language learning platform *Babbel* tries to give learners an 'instant evaluation' of how close their pronunciation is to that of a native speaker, but this speech recognition tool sometimes does not work. This can be frustrating, especially when it prevents progressing in the learning process. In fact, assessing the proficiency of non-native speakers poses a big challenge for researchers dealing with speech recognition technologies for pronunciation learning, particularly pronunciation evaluation and error detection (AbuSeileek, 2007). For these reasons, the introduction of 'real-time' speech recognition to aid users to improve their pronunciation skills was left for future developments. However, the platform saves the speech produced by learners for later assessment by teachers (Bottentuit & Coutinho, 2008).

3.2. Pedagogical aspects

The app will provide users with a guided path that allows for the contextualised development of different skills (lexical, grammatical, written and spoken comprehension) based on self-correction activities structured according to their level of difficulty.

The web platform will also feature a functional and intuitive application to create and view a wide range of contents with different templates. These templates will be customised according to input from teachers, who may additionally suggest new types of activities to encourage novel ways of perception and learning stimuli. The proposed tools are simple to use, intuitive and friendly, providing a pleasant experience to the user. From a technological and social perspective, these tools will enhance new ways of creating, publishing and managing educational content in virtual contexts. It should be noted that we will support the insertion of games namely for training of grammar or vocabulary (Cornillie, Thorne, & Desmet, 2012). These types of games are not only motivational, but they also support incidental and informal learning (Marsick & Watkins, 2001).

These content creation applications may be used by any teacher who wants to create learning objects for their class(es), and teachers/schools interested in developing (more complete) language learning paths for one or more levels of the Common European Framework of Reference for Languages (CEFR, 2001). Both teachers and learners will have access to all produced content via their phones, tablets and via their computers whenever and wherever, using the two learning applications.

The 'private' digital resource created by teachers as part of their professional practice can be made public at any time if they so wish. Likewise, educational institutions registered on the platform will have their learning objects/paths made freely available. Thus, the platform will also help teachers/institutions to promote and internationalise their courses with rankings (which will be accomplished through specific feedback on the students' learning results; teachers' feedback, external expert committee, among others).

4. Conclusion

To think about strategies for language learning through mobile devices is becoming more effective and easy given the popularity of these devices among students. Whereas there are teachers who accept challenges and are willing to incorporate this type of technology in the classroom, others are more reluctant and resist changes in their educational practices (Lancha, 2010). To improve mobile learning effectiveness, teachers need to be adequately prepared to implement technology in their teaching and learning practice.

When we propose a learning environment supported by emerging digital technologies, we intend to reinforce the adoption of these technologies in order to form a wide community of teachers who share experiences and digital material. In fact, while updating their knowledge, users of this platform will certainly rethink pedagogies and focus on teaching methods that extend the classroom beyond the traditional learning environments (Wang & Smith, 2013). Our aim is to foster the standardisation across the online teaching network, encouraging teachers to actively work together to enrich the quality of the pedagogical strategies and contents presently available for teaching. It is really important that the teacher may, without advanced technical knowledge, design and publish visually attractive materials that are appropriate to the profile and age of the students. More than offering intuitive and friendly tools for design and publication of digital contents, the major advantage of this project is that all materials and developers will be evaluated with several criteria in order to encourage teamwork and creativity among the teaching community. This step is crucial to provide an optimal learning process for students and to help them find the adequate course according to their needs.

References

AbuSeileek, A. F. (2007). Computer-assisted pronunciation instruction as an effective means for teaching stress. *The JALT CALL Journal, 3*(1-2), 3-14.

Bloch, J. (2008). *Technology in the L2 composition classroom*. Ann Arbor: University of Michigan Press.

Bottentuit, J. B., & Coutinho, C. P. (2008). Recomendações para Produção de Podcasts e Vantagens na Utilização em Ambientes Virtuais de Aprendizagem. *Revista Prisma.com, 6*, 158-179.

CEFR. (2001). *Common European framework of reference for languages: learning, teaching, assessment*. Cambridge: Cambridge University Press.

Cornillie, F., Thorne, S. L., & Desmet, P. (2012). Editorial: digital games for language learning: from hype to insight? *ReCALL special issue: digital games for language learning: challenges and opportunities, 24*(3), 243-256. Retrieved from http://dx.doi.org/10.1017/S0958344012000134

DuBravac, S. (2012). *Technology in the L2 curriculum*. Boston, MA: Prentice-Hall.

Eaton, K. (2013, March 26). Online language learning firm babbel lands $10 million investment. FastCompany. Retrieved from http://www.fastcompany.com/3007480/tech-forecast/online-language-learning-firm-babbel-lands-10-million-investment?

Lancha, F. S. (2010). *As Tecnologias Móveis no Contexto da Aprendizagem Formal*. Trabalho de Projecto de Mestrado em Gestão de Sistemas de e-Learning. Universidade Nova de Lisboa.

Lisbôa, E. S., Coutinho, C. P., & Bottentuit Júnior, J. B. (2013). Rede social de aprendizagem colaborativa em Línguas Estrangeiras. *Actas da VII Conferencia Internacional de TIC na Educação, Challenges 2013*, (pp. 995-1008). Braga: Universidade do Minho.

Lu, M. (2008). Effectiveness of vocabulary learning via mobile phone. *Journal of Computer Assisted Learning, 24*(6), 515-525. Retrieved from http://dx.doi.org/10.1111/j.1365-2729.2008.00289.x

Lys, F. (2013). The development of advanced learner oral proficiency using IPADS. *Language Learning and Technology, 17*(3), 94-116.

Marsick, V. J., & Watkins, K. E. (2001). Informal and incidental learning. *New Directions for Adult and Continuing Education Special Issue: The New Update on Adult Learning Theory, 89*, 25-34. Retrieved from http://dx.doi.org/10.1002/ace.5

Mohamed, K. E., & Wijesekera, D. (2012). A lightweight framework for web services implementations on mobile devices. *IEEE First International Conference on Mobile Services* (pp. 64-71). Retrieved from http://dx.doi.org/10.1109/mobserv.2012.19

Mondahl, M., & Razmerita, L. (2014). Social media, collaboration and social learning – a case-study of foreign language learning. *The Electronic Journal of e-Learning, 12*(4), 339-352.

Moura, A. (2010). *Apropriação do Telemóvel como Ferramenta de Mediação em Mobile Learning: estudos de caso em contexto educativo*. Tese de doutoramento em Ciências da Educação – Especialidade de Tecnologia Educativa. Braga: Universidade do Minho.

Moura, A., & Carvalho, A. A. (2011). Aprendizagem mediada por tecnologias móveis: novos desafios para as práticas educativas. In P. Dias e A. Osório (Eds.), *Actas da VII Conferência Internacional de TIC na Educação – Challenges 2011*, Braga: Universidade do Minho (pp. 233-246).

Moura, A., & Carvalho, A. A. (2013). Framework for mobile learning integration into educational contexts. In L. B. Zane & M. Lin (Eds.), *Handbook* of *mobile learning* (pp. 58-69). London: Routledge.

Sykes, J. M., & Reinhardt, J. (2013). *Language at play: digital games in second and foreign language teaching and learning*. Upper Saddle River, NJ: Pearson.

Verga, L., & Kotz, S. A. (2013). How relevant is social interaction in second language learning? *Frontiers in Human Neuroscience, 7*. Retrieved from http://dx.doi.org/10.3389/fnhum.2013.00550

Wang, S., & Smith, S. (2013). Reading and grammar learning through mobile phones. *Language Learning & Technology, 17*(3), 117-134.

17 Critical visual literacy: the new phase of applied linguistics in the era of mobile technology

Giselda Dos Santos Costa[1] and Antonio Carlos Xavier[2]

Abstract

In our society, which is full of images, visual representations and visual experiences of all kinds, there is a paradoxically significant degree of visual illiteracy. Despite the importance of developing specific visual skills, visual literacy is not a priority in school curriculum (Spalter & van Dam, 2008). This work aims at (1) emphasising the importance of integrating visual literacy as the fifth linguistic skill in English classes, and (2) showing a visual activity exploring a video called Price Tag. We will show some strategies that can be applied in foreign language classes in order to teach students a way to encode and decode the artifacts of their own culture and perceive the affordances of multimodal composition. In this research, the students' cell phones were used with which we developed activities using videos as multimodal texts.

Keywords: critical visual literacy, material designing, mobile learning, modal affordance.

---

1. Federal Institute of Piauí - IFPI, Teresina, Brazil; giseldacostas@hotmail.com

2. Federal University of Pernambuco - UFPE, Recife, Brazil; xavierufpe@gmail.com

How to cite this chapter: Santos Costa, G., & Xavier, A. C. (2016). Critical visual literacy: the new phase of applied linguistics in the era of mobile technology. In A. Pareja-Lora, C. Calle-Martínez, & P. Rodríguez-Arancón (Eds), *New perspectives on teaching and working with languages in the digital era* (pp. 201-212). Dublin: Research-publishing.net. http://dx.doi.org/10.14705/rpnet.2016.tislid2014.434

Chapter 17

1. Introduction

Integrating visual ability in the language classroom is beneficial for the teacher because it allows students to think in more complex ways, since new technologies lead to new forms of information, thus requiring new vocabulary and new methods for a more critical interpretation. However, our educational reality is different. Spalter and van Dam (2008) point out that the practice of visualisation is neglected in our classrooms, especially in the curriculum of foreign language teaching in an era in which the development of visually literate citizens is fundamental. Spalter and van Dam (2008) state that students are engaged in a constant cycle of consuming and producing visual media, but, as mentioned by Metros (2008), "they are not visually literate. They do not have the skills to understand how to decipher an image and make ethical decisions [about the] validity and [value of information]" (p. 98).

This work will help teachers to develop learning experiences in language classrooms using the concepts of critical visual literacy. It is organised into the following sections: Firstly, we will begin with a brief introduction to our theoretical framework presentation of the concept of modal affordance. Secondly, it will be explained what a multimodal text is. In the following section, we will present a linguistic/pedagogical activity using a video clip as a multimodal text. Finally, the article concludes pointing out the contributions of the integration of visual literacy in the curriculum of English teaching.

2. Modal affordance

The term affordance has its origins in Gibson's (1979) studies, it indicates that the context offers an opportunity to the agent to do an action, independently of whether the agent makes use of it or not, in other words, he defines affordance as all possible action in the context.

What do we see when we look, hear, smell or hold something? Gibson (1979) answered this question by saying that what we perceive are the values and meanings of things. What we perceive are not necessarily objects, but the possibilities of action that they provide for some kind of agent's behaviour. For us, affordance is an interactive process between the individual and the environment, and the latter is a set of resources for actions available to the agent who needs to perceive their potentialities and initiate action (Figure 1).

Figure 1. Affordance concept (adapted from Şahin et al., 2006)

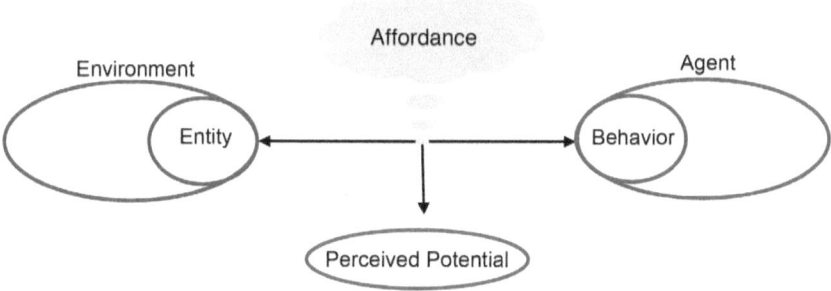

Kress (2010) developed the notion of modal affordances in which modes have particularities and limitations in terms of affordances that offer different potentials for communication and meaning of the text, such as Linguistic Affordance for example, which involves the oral and written language (vocabulary, punctuation, grammar); visual affordance, which includes stationary and moving images (colour, vector, line, plane); gestural affordance, which comprises facial expressions and body language (movement and speed, body position); auditory affordance, which involves music and sound effects (volume, tone, rhythm, silence, pause); and spatial affordance, which involves the layout and organisation of objects in space (proximity, direction, position in space).

According to Santos (2013), in the process of interaction, the modes of communication have different meanings for each person because affordances are not the same for all learners. We perceive different potential meanings depending on goals, interests, intentions, background knowledge and cultures. The concept of affordance was introduced recently in the research of second language and foreign language teaching and researchers have been challenged to perform it. In the current studies, modal affordance is accomplished as any discursive movement that provides sociolinguistic information or intends to enable the critical consciousness of the student about the language phenomena and social power, mainly through multimodal texts, which refers to the use of different semiotic resources to produce meanings.

3. Multimodal text

Kress (2010) also argues that the shift toward literacies or multiliteracies has led to the inclusion in our classrooms of multimodal denomination or text that moves beyond alphabetic print to utilise additional modes as well, such as video, audio, or still image. Any discipline can explore different aspects of multimodality. This is not a theory.

These approaches are concerned with the social and cultural construction of meaning, and can be applied to investigate the power, inequality and ideology in human interactions and artefacts. According to Knoblauch, Schenettler, Raab, and Soeffner (2006), the interest in multimodality is a consequence of the use of digital photography and video that is becoming a standard practice in qualitative research.

The definition of multimodality from the New London Group (1996) is the combination of semiotic modes in a single composition to take effect or meaning. However, in order to be considered a semiotic mode, there must be a cultural sense shared within a community and all these modes perform social functions that are organised to make sense. For example, a gesture, an intonation of voice and a look are part of the way for the construction of meaning. Halliday (1978) suggests that all modes simultaneously tell us something about our ideas of the world (ideational meaning), enactment of our social relations (interpersonal meaning) and produces a structured and coherent text (textual meaning).

Multimodality arises as a combination of semiotic modes and ways of culturally created organisation.

The modes have different affordances and people always use different modes simultaneously to make meanings or senses. There is a general view that multimodal texts attempt to persuade through the use of various visual modes, words, sounds and other ways of communicating. Kress and van Leeuwen (1996), for example, argue that in multimodal texts, the meaning refers to all modes, and a unified interpretation makes a cohesive argument, giving many voices to the reader. The authors of a multimodal text as a video clip use many ways to strengthen their arguments and realise that several semiotic modes contain unique possibilities and limitations that make them particularly able to communicate specific meanings.

4. Design of a critical activity

We will show some strategies that can be applied in foreign language classes in order to teach students a way to encode and decode the artefacts of their own culture. In this research, we used the students' cellphones with which we developed activities using videos as multimodal texts. We chose videos because they are one of the participants' favorite cellphone affordances. In fact, 52 % of them told us that they send or receive videos through their cellphones on a daily basis. The video Price Tag was downloaded from the YouTube site and processed in 3pg format for mobile technology and transferred by Bluetooth to the students' cellphones (Figure 2). This video features a song by the British singer Jessie J, released on January 30, 2011, criticising over-consumption. Jessie J sings with rapper B.o.B.

The critical part of this task is the analysis and discovery of the social and political interests in the production and reception of images in relation to social, cultural effects of power and domination in the context of students' lives. In the section below, we analyse five answers from a high school student. Carlos is a fictitious name chosen to preserve his identity.

Chapter 17

Figure 2. The video "Price Tag" in cell phone

Activity

1. What was the author's purpose in beginning this clip with these images? Use evidences from the text and your ideas to support your answer.

Figure 3. Image from video clip

Carlos says that the image shows the simplicity of childhood in relation to adulthood. Adults are blinded by money and very consumerist. Therefore, the bear beside the child is happy, and the one next to the adult is blind, sad and amputated. In his comments, Carlos reveals a critical view of real life experiences. He notes the shapes and figures of the bear as a symbolic element reflecting two meanings: one of innocence and the other of consumerism nowadays. According to the observations made by the student in his reply in relation to the video image, we can infer that the bear, in the first image, is in the foreground, a position of importance in relation to the child and, in the second image, the bear is secondary in relation to the adult (middle ground). With this observation, we emphasise the importance of teachers having knowledge about how the different modes of image, sound and movement can influence or not in the way that meaning is constructed. In addition, this meaning is constructed along with the sequence of overlapping images in the clip.

2. What kind of proverb or expression does that image refer to? And in what situations are they employed in real life?

Figure 4. Image from video clip

Carlos answered: "Money does not grow on trees. It is usually used when someone asks for money. Then, someone uses the phrase to emphasise that it

Chapter 17

is difficult to get money". This answer shows that visual literacy helps students to appreciate the multiple ways of representing life experiences, and that our interpretation of images is linked to culture: the images we see interact with our culture, attitude and belief systems so that our perceptions and interpretations depend on culture and context, as mentioned before. According to Beare (2008), ideas, experiences and cultural perspectives found in verbal and nonverbal texts help us to shape our worldviews. The vision we gain allows us to understand our cultural, linguistic and literary entail.

3. In our society, there are certain prejudices and/or behavioral differences in our daily lives. See the pictures and mention some prejudices and differences of life explored in the video clip (and discuss these images with a classmate).

Figure 5.   Image from video clip

The question about the symbolism of colours and toys that were exemplified by the clip also got a positive response. Carlos said that the video clip criticises the differences observed in our real life: the girl plays with dolls and the boy with cars and war. The feminine colour is pink, and the male is blue, the woman is more consumerist than the man because of the quality and quantity of clothes, shoes, jewellery and toys shown in the clip. Therefore, the colour of the objects can carry symbolic connotations. All these symbolisms associated with colours and objects in particular together with all observations are Carlos's culture examples. He critically evaluates the visual senses of his real life.

4. What kind of message did the author want to convey with these images? And to whom was it addressed?

Figure 6. Image from video clip

When we asked Carlos about these images, the student said that the author was inviting people to give less importance to consumerism, and getting rid of the expensive labels. Thus, it should be clear and we should reconsider when students have the opportunity to discover the meaning of images with critical thinking, it will allow them to see world in which they live with critical eyes. Carlos responds positively to this visual text, because text analysis is coherent with his daily experiences. We also note that the personal interpretation is not isolated from social and political forces as said Kress (2002).

5. Was this activity difficult to answer? Explain a little about it.

Many of the students said that this visual activity was more difficult than expected, not because of technology, but because critical literacy emphasises the need to use language as a vehicle of social change and writing requires students to think about their opinions and feelings before writing (Wood, Soares, & Watson, 2006, p. 57). Besides, one of Carlos's concerns in this answer is to emphasise that the teacher has a different analysis. We note that he was awaiting for confirmation of a correct answer from the teacher. It is important to highlight that, in this type of exercise, the analysis of the answers is not intended to be as either right or wrong, but to give feedback about the student's critical thinking, as teachers cannot give the correct interpretation of a specific visual element. Thus, the visual activity requires students to be aware of the intentionality of the text and allows them to see that interpretations are determined by their culture.

5. Conclusion

The conclusion reached, during the analysis, was that visually literate students could read, decode, create, question, and interpret the purpose and intended meaning of a variety of text forms associated with mobile multimedia technologies. The learners developed a more socially conscious way to evaluate images. This is crucial, because through these kinds of activities students become not only technologically literate but also visually literate. Critical visual literacy, as the fifth linguistic skill in English classes can be developed through a variety of activities. It might help a learner achieve positive results in any field, foreign language included. We should not forget that each person has a unique way of perceiving the world. The visual image is one more tool to facilitate understanding of the social world (Freire, 2007).

The videos also had an impact on the motivation and interest of students. They were tools to demonstrate the significance and meaning of daily scenes and culture of the students. According to their statements, the cellphone helped and made the interpretation of images easier, especially because mobile technology has helped to improve language learning. It placed students in a more realistic context and made this process more attractive, interesting and motivating.

With mobile technology, the students were able to maximise the acquisition of skills, linguistic competences and to optimise their time of study. They were also able to have access to their didactic activities anywhere and anytime. Thus, the use of cell phones in teaching and learning foreign languages has enabled a variety of ways of teaching and learning which were not possible in an atmosphere of traditional or formal teaching.

References

Beare, K. (2008). *YouTube in the classroom*! Retrieved from http://esl.about.com/od/listeninglessonplans/a/youtube.htm

Freire, P. (2007). *Pedagogy of autonomy: knowledge necessary for educational practice* (35th edition). São Paulo: Paz e Terra.

Gibson, J. J. (1979). *The ecological approach to visual perception.* Hillsdale, NJ: Lawrence Erlbaum.

Halliday, M. A. K. (1978). *Language as a social semiotic.* London: Edward Arnold.

Kress, G. (2002). English for an era of instability: aesthetics, ethics, creativity and design. *English in Australia, 134*, 15-23.

Kress, G. (2010). *Multimodality: a social semiotic approach to communication.* London: Routledge.

Kress, G., & van Leeuwen, T. (1996). Reading *images: the grammar of visual design.* London: Routledge.

Knoblauch, H., Schenettler, B., Raab, J., & Soeffner, H. G. (2006). *Video analysis: methodology and methods. Qualitative audiovisual data analysis in sociology.* Frankfurt: Peter Lang.

Metros, S. E. (2008). Digital literacies in the age of sight. *Theory Into Practice, 47*(2), 102-109. Retrieved from http://dx.doi.org/10.1080/00405840801992264

New London Group (1996). Pedagogy of multiliteracies: designing social futures. *Harvard Educational Review, 66*(1), 60-93. Retrieved from http://dx.doi.org/10.17763/haer.66.1.17370n67v22j160u

Şahin, E., Çakmak, M., Doğar, M. R., Uğur, E., & Üçoluk, G. (2006). To afford or not to afford: formalizing affordances for robot control. *Dagstuhl Seminar: Towards Affordance-based Robot Control, June 5-9, 2006.*

Santos, G. (2013). *Mobile learning: exploring the potential of using mobile phone in teaching - learning of English as a foreign language with public school students.* PhD dissertation in Linguistics. Federal University of Pernambuco: Brazil. [English translation]

Spalter, A., & van Dam, A. (2008). Digital visual literacy. *Theory into Practice, 48*(2), 93-101. Retrieved from http://dx.doi.org/10.1080/00405840801992256

Wood, K. D., Soares, L., & Watson, P. (2006). Empowering adolescents through critical literacy. Middle School Journal, 1, 55-59. Retrieved from http://middlesecondarytoolkit.pbworks.com/w/file/fetch/38699626/Empowering%20Adolescen?

18 Virtual learning environments on the go: CALL meets MALL

Jorge Arús Hita[1]

Abstract

This paper presents *Eating out*, a Moodle-based digital learning resource for English as a Foreign Language (EFL) teaching that can be run both on computers and mobile devices. It is argued that Mobile Assisted Language Learning (MALL) resources do not necessarily need to be specifically designed for such platforms. Rather, a carefully planned methodology and a well-grounded theoretical basis for the explanation of lexicogrammatical issues are posited as the keys to the creation of Foreign Language Teaching (FLT) digital resources for which computer as well as mobile device users feel they are getting their time's worth.

Keywords: CALL, MALL, Moodle, systemic functional linguistics, teaching methodology, VLE.

1. Introduction

This paper defends the use of a solid theoretical and methodological basis for the design and development of digital learning resources for FLT as a way to make them useful on both PC and mobile platforms. To that end, it presents and discusses *Eating out*, a digital learning resource with strong theoretical and methodological underpinnings. Several e-learning areas are concerned here, notably a) Virtual Learning Environments (VLEs), as *Eating out* uses Moodle, one of the most widely-used VLEs nowadays, b) Computer Assisted Language

---

1. Universidad Complutense de Madrid, Madrid, Spain; jarus@ucm.es

How to cite this chapter: Arús Hita, J. (2016). Virtual learning environments on the go: CALL meets MALL. In A. Pareja-Lora, C. Calle-Martínez, & P. Rodríguez-Arancón (Eds), *New perspectives on teaching and working with languages in the digital era* (pp. 213-222). Dublin: Research-publishing.net. http://dx.doi.org/10.14705/rpnet.2016.tislid2014.435

© 2016 Jorge Arús Hita (CC BY-NC-ND 4.0) 213

Learning (CALL), as the resource is used for language learning, and c) MALL, since *Eating out* can be run on a mobile device.

The use in FLT of VLEs, also known as Learning Management Systems (LMSs), has already gone a long way, as shows the literature on the subject. Publications from only a few years ago, such as Baten, Bouckaert, and Khan (2009), which would be fairly recent in other disciplines, feel much older in the fast-moving e-learning world. Bueno-Alastuey and López Pérez (2013), Ernest, Heiser, and Murphy (2013), Hubackova and Semradova (2013) or Xiaoqiong, Guoqing, and Zeng (2013) are but a few examples of the more recent literature on the use of VLEs for FLT. A good number of researchers specifically look at the use of Moodle for FLT, e.g. Ono, Ishihara, and Yamashiro (2014), Sun (2014), da Costa Pinho et al. (2013), even devoting a whole volume to it, as Stanford (2009) did a few years ago (for Moodle 1.9; unfortunately, there seems to be no follow-up for more recent Moodle versions). There is even literature on the use of Moodle for teaching Languages for Specific Purposes (LSPs), which is of interest to us here because *Eating out*, a general EFL unit in itself, is intended as part of a more comprehensive Business English course. Some of the most recent references on Moodle and LSP are Breeze (2014), Martín-Monje and Talaván (2014), Perea-Barberá and Bocanegra-Valle (2014) and Rodríguez-Arancón and Calle-Martínez (2014), all of them within the monograph edited by Bárcena, Read and Arús (2014).

If we turn our attention to the use of mobile devices for FLT, i.e. MALL, the proliferation of research papers and book chapters is staggering, as attested, for instance, by the 65-page-long annotated bibliography in Burston (2013). One of the big issues when speaking of MALL coincides with the main concern of this paper, i.e. the methodology underlying mobile applications. The literature is unsurprisingly quite abundant here, too, e.g. Baleghizadeh and Oladrostam (2010), Burston (2014, 2015) and Xin (2014). Among the methodological issues discussed in the MALL literature, there is one which triggers frequent disagreement, i.e. whether MALL activities must be specifically designed for mobile devices or they can be safely adapted from general CALL activities, even paper-based ones. Ballance (2012, 2013) makes a point for the use of activities specifically designed for MALL platforms. According to this author, failure to do this explains the results of experiments such as the one reported by Stockwell (2010), where students took longer to perform the same activity on a mobile device than on a PC. Stockwell's (2010) comparison of student performance in the same task on CALL and MALL closely relates to some of the research work based on *Eating out* (Arús & Rodríguez-Arancón, 2015), which will be mentioned later on.

The rest of this paper is structured as follows: section 2 presents *Eating out*, focusing on its strong theoretical and methodological background, whereas section 3 provides some discussion in the light of the description in the previous section, as well as offering some concluding remarks.

2. Eating out

This digital learning resource is the result of work carried out within the Spanish government-funded SO-CALL-ME (*Social Ontology-driven Cognitively Augmented Language Learning Environment*) project (ref. FFI2011-29829). Within this project, a number of mobile applications have been created for English language teaching in the broader context of LSP. The apps so far developed are ANT, for oral comprehension practice through the news; FANCLUB, for the same skill but through audio-books; BUSINESS APP, focusing on the listening comprehension of business-related situations; MARLUC, for the pronunciation of specific words; VIOLIN, for the audiovisual comprehension of videos; VISP, for oral production; and *Eating out*, which, as said, is not an app in itself but rather a teaching resource for listening comprehension and communicative practice (CEFR[2] level A2-B1) amenable to use both on computers and mobile devices.

Previous work by SO-CALL-ME members, in which a number of EFL-teaching apps and digital resources were evaluated, identified the need for the reinforcement

---

2. Common European Framework of Reference for Languages

of the pedagogical aspect of this kind of resources (Arús, Rodríguez-Arancón, & Calle-Martínez, 2013; Calle-Martínez, Rodríguez-Arancón, & Arús, 2014; Martín-Monje, Arús, Rodríguez-Arancón, & Calle-Martínez, 2013; Pareja-Lora et al., 2013; Rodríguez-Arancón, Arús, & Calle-Martínez, 2013). In this light, we undertook the creation of *Eating out*, which stems from a didactic unit previously designed and meant for traditional textbook-based teaching. However, due to the interactive nature of the unit, it was considered that it could lend itself to adaptation as a digital learning resource. The challenge at that point was to test whether the solid theoretical and methodological work underlying the original didactic unit would make up for the dramatic platform change, i.e. from textbook to computer to mobile devices.

Eating out[3] uses Systemic Functional Grammar (SFG) as a theoretical framework both for the methodological conceptualisation of the entire resource and for the explanation of the lexicogrammar necessary to achieve the unit's learning goals. This theory describes languages by means of system networks. These system networks try to capture the fact that speakers are constantly making choices from the different possibilities available in the lexicogrammar of their language. For instance, in the case of mental transitivity, which is important to this lesson (see below), speakers can choose to express a cognitive process (e.g. *I know…*), an emotive process (e.g. *I like…*), a perceptive process (e.g. *I feel…*) or an intentional process (e.g. *I'm thinking of…*), each one with an associated set of rules. By using this approach, *Eating out* seeks to familiarise students with the options available for each area of the grammar, as well as the associated rules, so they use the target language with the same mechanisms applied when they speak their mother tongue, i.e. making meaningful selections. Additionally, SFG considers that linguistic choices are dependent on choices made outside language, i.e. at the level of context. We will not delve into the complexity of this interdependency; it will suffice to say that contextual choices are based on criteria related to the nature of the interactants, the subject matter at stake and the role of language in negotiating a given situation. If the SFG-based lexicogrammatical approach accounts for the theoretical strength of *Eating out*,

---

3. Available at https://cv4.ucm.es/moodle/course/view.php?id=32765

the context-language interdependency is at all times present in this resource: all activities are contextualised within the general notion-functional goals, as described below, thus accounting for *Eating out*'s methodological robustness. Arús (2008) offers a detailed account of how to exploit SFG in EFL teaching.

Eating out consists of four sections preceded by an introduction to the unit's notio-functional goals – ordering and eating unknown food, something with which one often has to cope when travelling for business – as well as the learning goals, which are: a) identify unfamiliar words from the context on topics related to his/her interests; b) deal with situations likely to arise whilst travelling in an area where the language is spoken; and c) socialise simply but effectively using simple common expressions and following basic routines.

The four sections of the unit are: 1. 'Listening Comprehension'; 2. 'Vocabulary'; 3. 'Lexicogrammar'; and 4. 'Over to you'. The listening comprehension section consists of a recording where three characters go to get a cheesesteak in Philadelphia for the first time, followed by a number of comprehension questions on the listening activity. If students do not reach a minimum scoring they are then advised to listen to the situation once more and answer another battery of questions; if they still have trouble understanding and answering the comprehension questions, they are then asked to read the script.

In the vocabulary section, students are presented with a list of the most relevant vocabulary to the unit. This list is supported by a glossary accessible by clicking on each word, and is then followed by a matching activity where vocabulary items have to be matched with their definitions.

The lexicogrammar section is *Eating out*'s *piece de resistance*. As said above, it uses SFG to introduce students to the transitivity of mental processes, i.e. expressions of cognition, perception, intention and emotion, as described, for instance, in Halliday and Matthiessen (2004). These processes are extensively used in the situation to which students listen at the beginning of the lesson, as ordering food requires the use of expressions such as *I'd like (a drink)*, *I don't know (what to order)*, *I love (meat)*, etc. This is an example of how everything in *Eating out* is contextualised. Two sets of questions for lexicogrammatical practice, created by means of Moodle's short answer questions, follow the lexicogrammatical explanation. As previously with the listening comprehension practice, students are advised to go through the second round of questions if they perform poorly on the first round. Before undertaking this second attempt, they can consult a more detailed lexicogrammatical explanation of mental transitivity.

The last section, 'Over to you', tries to provide more creative practice for the unit's lexicogrammar. All activities in *Eating out* are designed to be automatically corrected by the program, so students can have immediate feedback. Therefore it is not really possible to provide really open-ended, creative activities, which would require human supervision for correction and feedback. As said above, however, the unit tries at all times to integrate the materials into the notio-functional goals specified and an attempt is made to gradually move students into more productive language use. Inter- and intra-activity contextualisation as well as the transition throughout the unit from more controlled to more creative use of the language, with the limitations just mentioned, are recognised as two key methodological requirements for successful FLT (see, e.g. Omaggio-Hadley, 2000).

3. Discussion and concluding remarks

That *Eating out* is indeed successful in achieving its goals is attested by Arús and Rodríguez-Arancón (2015), who report on an experiment in which 32 university students worked with *Eating out* – some of them on a computer, some on a mobile device – and then completed a questionnaire containing a number of methodological and technical questions. The experiment did not look at results in terms of students' scores but rather at the students' perception of their experience using the resource, which was meant to complement previous work which, as mentioned in the description of *Eating out*, evaluated apps from the point of view of researchers.

The experiment revealed that students gave *Eating out* an average rating of 4 out of 5, 3.6 being the lowest score. Interestingly, the average scores for the resource on PC and on mobile devices was the same, 4 out of 5 in both cases, and the technical ratings in the MALL experience were very similar to those in the CALL experience, which means that students were not troubled by the specificities of MALL platforms, with their smaller screens and keyboards or touch-screen interfaces, more than by CALL platforms. This seems to suggest that activities, even whole units as in this case, which have not been designed exclusively for mobile devices can still be as satisfactorily perceived by MALL users as by CALL users. Pending further experimentation that confirms the results in Arús and Rodríguez-Arancón (2015), we can now tentatively claim that a) the reason for the good overall results in user satisfaction, and notably the similar results obtained from CALL and MALL users, is that *Eating out* is a good teaching resource; and b) what makes it good is its well-planned methodological deployment and sound theoretical background, as described in this paper. This does not mean that the technical aspects do not count, but rather that if the contents are good, users are ready to obviate technical hindrances – as long, obviously, as they are not blatantly hard to surmount. And, in the case of FLT applications, as in FLT in general, good contents mean a good methodology and an appropriate theoretical deployment.

4. Acknowledgements

The research described in this paper has been partly funded by the *Spanish Ministry of Science and Innovation, Grant* **FFI2011-29829**: Social Ontology-based Cognitively Augmented Language Learning Mobile Environment (SO-CALL-ME).

References

Arús, J. (2008). Teaching modality in context: a sample lesson. *Odense Working Papers in Language and Communication, 29*, 365-380.

Arús, J., & Rodríguez-Arancón, P. (2015). Autonomous learning resources for the teaching of EFL: what learners think. *Encuentro 23*, 1-15.

Arús, J., Rodríguez-Arancón, P., & Calle-Martínez, C. (2013). A pedagogic assessment of mobile learning applications. In *Proceedings of ICDE 2013*.

Baleghizadeh, S., & Oladrostam, E. (2010). The effect of mobile assisted language learning (MALL) on grammatical accuracy of EFL students. *MEXTESOL Journal, 34*(2), 77-86.

Ballance, O. J. (2012). Mobile-language learning: more than just 'the platform'. A commentary on: using mobile phones for vocabulary activities: examining the effect of the platform, Stockwell, 2010. *Language Learning and Technology, 16*(3), 21-23.

Ballance, O. J. (2013). MALL– somewhere between the tower, the field, the classroom and the market: a reply to professor Stockwell's response. *Language Learning and Technology, 17*(1), 37-46.

Bárcena, E., Read, T., & Arús, J. (Eds.). (2014). *Languages for specific purposes in the digital era*. New York: Springer. Retrieved from http://dx.doi.org/10.1007/978-3-319-02222-2

Baten, L., Bouckaert, N., & Khan, Y. (2009). The use of communities in a virtual learning environment. In M. Thomas (Ed.), *Handbook of research on Web, 2.0 and second language learning* (pp. 137-155). London: IGI Global. Retrieved from http://dx.doi.org/10.4018/978-1-60566-190-2.ch008

Breeze, R. (2014). Moodle glossary tasks for teaching legal English. In E. Bárcena, T. Read, & J. Arús (Eds.), *Languages for specific purposes in the digital era* (pp. 111-128). New York: Springer International Publishing. Retrieved from http://dx.doi.org/10.1007/978-3-319-02222-2_6

Bueno-Alastuey, M. C., & López-Pérez, M. V. (2013). Evaluation of a blended learning language course: students' perceptions of appropriateness for the development of skills and language areas. *Computer Assisted Language Learning, 27*(6), 1-19. Retrieved from http://dx.doi.org/10.1080/09588221.2013.770037

Burston, J. (2013). Mobile-assisted language learning: a selected annotated bibliography of implementation studies. *Language Learning & Technology, 17*(3), 157-225.

Burston, J. (2014). The reality of MALL: still on the fringes. *CALICO Journal, 31*(1), 103-125. Retrieved from http://dx.doi.org/10.11139/cj.31.1.103-125

Burston, J. (2015). Twenty years of MALL project implementation: a meta-analysis of learning outcomes. *ReCALL, 27*(1), 4-20. Retrieved from http://dx.doi.org/10.1017/S0958344014000159

Calle-Martínez, C., Rodríguez-Arancón, P., & Arús, J. (2014). A scrutiny of the educational value of EFL mobile learning applications. *Cypriot Journal of Educational Sciences, 9*(3), 137-146.

Da Costa Pinho, I., Epstein, D., Reategui, E. B., Correa, Y., & Polonia, E. (2013). The use of text mining to build a pedagogical agent capable of mediating synchronous online discussions in the context of foreign language learning. In *Frontiers in Education Conference, 2013* (pp. 393-399). *IEEE*. Retrieved from http://dx.doi.org/10.1109/FIE.2013.6684853

Ernest, P., Heiser, S., & Murphy, L. (2013). Developing teacher skills to support collaborative online language learning. *The Language Learning Journal, 41*(1), 37-54. Retrieved from http://dx.doi.org/10.1080/09571736.2011.625095

Halliday, M. A. K., & Matthiessen, C. M. I. M. (2004). *An introduction to functional grammar* (3rd ed.). London: Arnold.

Hubackova, S., & Semradova, I. (2013). Comparison of on-line teaching and face-to-face teaching. *Procedia-Social and Behavioral Sciences, 89*, 445-449. Retrieved from http://dx.doi.org/10.1016/j.sbspro.2013.08.875

Martín-Monje, E., & Talaván, N. (2014). The I-AGENT project: blended learning proposal for professional English integrating an AI extended version of Moodle with classroom work for the practice of oral skills. In E. Bárcena, T. Read, & J. Arús (Eds.), *Languages for specific purposes in the digital era* (pp. 45-67). New York: Springer International Publishing. Retrieved from http://dx.doi.org/10.1007/978-3-319-02222-2_3

Martín-Monje, E., Arús, J., Rodríguez-Arancón, P., & Calle-Martínez, C. (2013). REALL: rubric for the evaluation of apps in language learning. In *Proceedings of ML13* (pp. 1-12).

Omaggio-Hadley, A. (2000). *Teaching language in context*. Boston: Heinle & Heinle.

Ono, Y., Ishihara, M., & Yamashiro, M. (2014). Instant text-based feedback systems–the development of a text-based feedback system and its potential use in foreign language teaching. *Journal of Information Technology and Application in Education, 3*(1), 1-8. Retrieved from http://dx.doi.org/10.14355/jitae.2014.0301.01

Pareja-Lora, A., Arús, J., Martín-Monje, E., Read, T., Pomposo-Yanes, L., Rodríguez-Arancón, P., Calle-Martínez, C., & Bárcena, E. (2013). Toward mobile assisted language learning apps for professionals that integrate learning into the daily routine. In L. Bradley & S. Thouësny (Eds.), *20 Years of EUROCALL: Learning from the Past, Looking to the Future* (pp. 206-210). Dublin Ireland: Research-publishing.net. Retrieved from http://dx.doi.org/10.14705/rpnet.2013.000162

Perea-Barberá, M. D., & Bocanegra-Valle, A. (2014). Promoting specialised vocabulary learning through computer-assisted instruction. In E. Bárcena, T. Read, & J. Arús (Eds.), *Languages for specific purposes in the digital era* (pp. 129-154). New York: Springer International Publishing. Retrieved from http://dx.doi.org/10.1007/978-3-319-02222-2_7

Chapter 18

Rodríguez-Arancón, P., Arús, J., & Calle-Martínez, C. (2013). The use of current mobile applications in EFL. In *Proceedings of IETC 2013* (pp. 1219-1225).

Rodríguez-Arancón, P., & Calle-Martínez, C. (2014). A practical application of wikis for learning business English as a second language. In E. Bárcena, T. Read, & J. Arús (Eds.), *Languages for specific purposes in the digital era* (pp. 155-173). New York: Springer International Publishing. Retrieved from http://dx.doi.org/10.1007/978-3-319-02222-2_8

Stanford, J. (2009). *Moodle 1.9 for second language teaching*. Birmingham: Packt Publishing.

Stockwell, G. (2010). Using mobile phones for vocabulary activities. Examining the effects of the platform. *Language Learning and Technology, 14*(2), 95-110.

Sun, L. (2014). Investigating the effectiveness of Moodle-based blended learning in college English course. *International Journal of Information Technology and Management, 13*(1), 83-94. Retrieved from http://dx.doi.org/10.1504/IJITM.2014.059152

Xiaoqiong, Y., Guoqing, Y., & Zeng, Z. (2013). Personalized teaching model based on Moodle platform. In Z. Zhong (Ed.), *Proceedings of the International Conference on Information Engineering and Applications (IEA) 2012* (pp. 27-35). New York: Springer International Publishing. Retrieved from http://dx.doi.org/10.1007/978-1-4471-4856-2_4

Xin, J. (2014). The effectiveness of m-learning in the form of smart phones in English grammar teaching. *Sino-US English Teaching, 11*(1), 13-17.

19. Exploring the application of a conceptual framework in a social MALL app

Timothy Read[1], Elena Bárcena[2], and Agnes Kukulska-Hulme[3]

Abstract

This article presents a prototype social Mobile Assisted Language Learning (henceforth, MALL) app based on Kukulska-Hulme's (2012) conceptual framework. This research allows the exploration of time, place and activity type as key factors in the design of MALL apps, and is the first step toward a systematic analysis of such a framework in this type of app in the future. Firstly, the selected conceptual framework is discussed, emphasising the adequacy of its development (or even adaptation) for the systematised design of mobile apps for second language learning. Secondly, the prototype of the Audio News Trainer (ANT) app, which aims at developing oral and written competences in a mixed individual-social modality, is presented in terms of its formal features and its functionality. Finally, some preliminary findings are presented together with suggestions for further development.

Keywords: mobile learning, MALL, conceptual framework, social media, oral reception, written interaction.

1. UNED, Madrid, Spain; tread@lsi.uned.es

2. UNED, Madrid, Spain; mbarcena@flog.uned.es

3. The Open University, UK; agnes.kukulska-hulme@open.ac.uk

How to cite this chapter: Read, T., Bárcena, E., & Kukulska-Hulme, A. (2016). Exploring the application of a conceptual framework in a social MALL app. In A. Pareja-Lora, C. Calle-Martínez, & P. Rodríguez-Arancón (Eds), *New perspectives on teaching and working with languages in the digital era* (pp. 223-232). Dublin: Research-publishing.net. http://dx.doi.org/10.14705/rpnet.2016.tislid2014.436

1. Introduction

In most modern cities it is hard to take any form of public transport, such as the underground/metro or bus, without seeing a significant percentage of the public on board with their heads craned forward while they interact with some kind of mobile device, be it a smartphone, tablet, netbook, or personal media player. It was just a question of time before users turned to using these devices for their educational needs. It has been estimated that at this moment in time there are over 80,000 educational mobile apps available[4], a proportion of which are intended for Second Language Learning (henceforth, SLL). To get a very general idea of how many, and how difficult it is to find suitable apps, just searching for 'learn English' on the iOS and Android app stores returns almost 800 results. From an academic perspective, it is hard to assess the real value of these apps and even harder to see if they have been designed and developed using any underlying conceptual or pedagogic framework. Talking to app developers and even reading background information about some of those that are available online suggests an essentially ad hoc methodology, which may reflect some teaching/learning experience on the part of the development team, but is far from what the scientific literature has to say on the subject.

If there were a single aspect of mobile devices that characterises them, it would arguably be their ability to enable us to communicate with other people. Historically, this was undertaken by phone calls but gradually, as the Web gave rise to Web 2.0 and the dominance of social media, the majority of the communication undertaken on these devices today is via these social tools (Evans, 2013). Kaplan (2012) highlights the importance of their use and introduces the notion of *mobile social media*, where he goes on to define four types: firstly, *Space-timers* (location and time sensitive), with apps like Facebook Places or Foursquare for interchanging messages that are relevant for a specific location at one specific point in time. Secondly, *Space-locators* (only location sensitive), with apps like Yelp or Qype for interchanging messages that are relevant for one specific location (tagged as such to be read later by others at the same location).

---

4. http://noticias.universia.es/ciencia-nn-tt/noticia/2014/04/07/1093782/ya-existen-mas-80-000-aplicaciones-educativas.html

Thirdly, *Quick-timers* (only time sensitive), with apps like Twitter or Facebook for increasing immediacy. Fourthly and finally, *Slow-timers* (neither location, nor time sensitive), with apps like YouTube or Wikipedia for transferring traditional social media applications to mobile devices.

In this article, Kukulska-Hulme's (2012) conceptual framework is considered and applied to a prototype social MALL app as the first step toward a systematic analysis of this type of app in the future.

2. The need for a conceptual framework

Kukulska-Hulme (2012) argues that the design of mobile apps for SLL requires the development (or even adaptation) of a conceptual framework to systematise their design. She goes on to define such a framework in terms of the temporal and spatial characteristics of mobile learning scenarios, highlighting a series of questions that should be answered for any given mobile SLL app, as can be seen in Figure 1.

Figure 1. Conceptual framework for next generation mobile SLL apps (based on Kukulska-Hulme, 2012)

Next generation designs	Time	• Specific time or anytime? • Routine or spontaneous? • Instant access or leisurely? • How much available time? • Dependent on sufficient time? • Interruptible?
	Place	• Specific location or anywhere? • Private or public place? • Relaxing, energising? • Stationary or moving? • Walking, running? • Driver or passenger?
	Activity	• Challenging or easy? • Suitable for multitasking? • Receptive or productive? • Involves speaking aloud? • Writing or gestures? • Individual or social?

Arguably, some of these questions can be asked before developing the app, but others would need to be answered by a student as and when they are using it. In this article, a modified version of a MALL app developed by the authors is applied to explore this framework, or at least a part of it.

As well as the temporal and spatial criteria, it is important to consider what pedagogic context the activity/ies would need for a given app to be developed. A thorough analysis of this question goes beyond the scope of this article, and it should be noted that there are a great many such analyses available (e.g Rodríguez-Arancón, Arús-Hita, & Calle-Martínez, 2013; Traxler & Kukulska-Hulme, 2005). However, in the SLL literature, as well as work on e-Learning in general, a differentiation has been made between instructivist and constructivist learning approaches. Mesh (2010) argues that the former is useful to provide beginners with basic language structures, lexicon and pronunciation. Laurillard (2007) argues that the latter can be related to discursive processes (dialogue, concept exchange), interactive processes (task-based experimentation, meaningful feedback), adaptive processes (linking or adapting ideas from theory to practice) and reflective processes (thinking about the interactive process and feedback to achieve task objectives). Given what was identified above about the importance of social media use from mobile devices, it is arguably important to include aspects of social-functionality in apps within a given learning scenario. For example, Yeager, Hurley-Dasgupta, and Bliss (2013) identify four types of activities that can be undertaken: aggregation/curation (bringing together links to existing resources), remixing (documentation, blogging, etc.), repurposing/constructivism (where users arguably build their own internal connections) and feeding forward (sharing new content, resources, summaries, etc. with others). The incorporation of one or more of these activities would facilitate the pro-active learning of the app's users.

3. The ANT app

ANT has been developed to enable a student to develop both his/her oral and written competences from a mobile device, running either iOS or Android. It has been developed using a cross-platform development technology. The news domain was selected by the authors as one of the most popular subjects for the general population and, as such, inherently motivating to be used on a daily basis, something that is crucial to ensure the continued use of an educational app. This is important because the authors have observed that the majority of MALL apps are left to one side after an initial period of exploration and use because the app had no connection to the everyday lives of the users and no interest beyond the academic goal of SLL. ANT aims to encourage sustained language practice that is integrated with daily life. It also aims to capture information about the user's experience.

ANT contains previously classified audio news podcasts available online to present a list in terms of three levels of difficulty (which is colour-coded following the standard traffic light system: green – easy, yellow – medium and red – difficult). The app has three functional phases: firstly, after logging in and reading the guidelines (Figure 2a and Figure 2b), the user listens to an audio news podcast (Figure 2c and Figure 2d) and answers questions about the experience (Figure 2d and Figure 2e). Secondly, s/he connects to Facebook to note what has been understood as the main argument of the news item. Thirdly, the user scours other social media to find supporting material for his/her understanding of the news as presented in step two, which s/he can then include on Facebook.

Regarding the questions mentioned as part of stage 1, three come from the conceptual framework presented by Kukulska-Hulme (2012) and three are directly related to the task in hand, that of listening to the audio recording:

- Is this routine or spontaneous use?

- Are you in a private or public place?

- How much available time do you have?

- What is the volume level used?

Chapter 19

- How much background noise is there around you?

- How much have you understood of what you have heard?

These data about the factors that affect audio comprehension are logged on the ATLAS server and the student is returned to the list to listen to other recordings. The questions that come from the framework are of a more general nature and have been included to provide empirical data on the usage habits of students as a way to support their presence in the model.

Figure 2. ANT screens

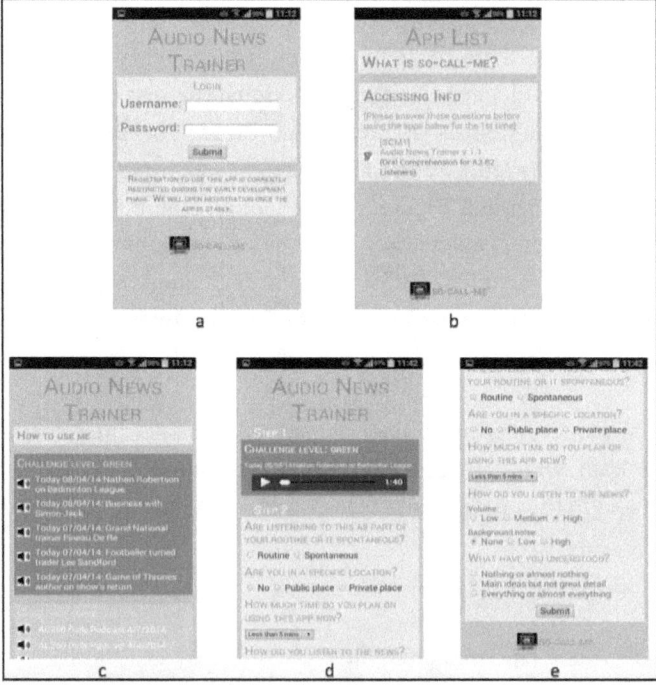

The others have been included to explore criteria identified to have an impact on audio (Cutler & Clifton, 1999) i.e. the lower the volume of the audio input and the greater the background noise, and the harder it is to understand as the hearer has to use their knowledge of the language and experience of the real world to substitute the unheard segments in their mind). Furthermore, all six questions are needed to assess the real world use of the app to help the designers improve the current version and work towards the next one as and when necessary. Apart from these questions, a number of brief answer-only-once questionnaires have been designed on different aspects of the underlying learning process (e.g. on the importance of audio skills in language use; on the use of mobiles for educational/training purposes) once again to give the designers data as part of a needs analysis.

Figure 3. Sample Facebook post to ANT group summarising what a student might have learnt from listening to a news item and liking an existing entry

Although functionally speaking ANT is currently quite simple, it offers three pedagogic advantages over just listening to the radio news on a mobile directly from the website: firstly, the sequencing of podcasts in order of difficulty according to accent and speed, since level adequacy of the SLL input has been identified by the experts to be fundamental for effective learning (Krashen, 1985). Secondly, the pedagogic structure of the interface enhances self-regulation and metacognition, which are particularly relevant processes within adult SLL. Thirdly, the way students can work collaboratively afterwards with other users on a given social network to refine what they think they have understood after listening to a recording, following a constructivist approach.

As was noted above, once the user has worked with the app s/he leaves a note of his/her understanding on the ANT Facebook page. There are two possibilities here: firstly, if no one has the same interpretation as him/her, then the student can create a new entry, as can be seen in Figure 3a. Secondly, if someone else has already concluded the same, then s/he can click on the Like button, to show their support for the entry, as can be seen in Figure 3b.

As was also noted above, once a student has participated on Facebook, depending on the other interpretations of the recording and notes that have been added there, the student should use other social media and websites to search for supporting evidence for his/her understanding, which should also be added back to Facebook with further comments as necessary (in the target language), as can be seen in Figure 3c. The complementary information and data obtained by the different users about a given news story are expected to lead to a fruitful debate on Facebook or in the classroom. Arguably, this form of written digital interaction is useful practice as it represents a major means of communication today (Maggiani, 2014).

4. Preliminary findings

Given the early stage of the work presented in this paper and the desire to further explore the importance of time, place and activity type in the design of MALL apps, only the first of the three steps described above was tried. The data entered by the students were logged on the ATLAS research group server (atlas.uned.es). An early pilot has been undertaken with ten students from a first year university course in Professional English. The results gathered can be divided into two groups: the data about the temporal and spatial conditions of the way in which the student worked with the app and the data about the actual listening activity. Regarding the former, given the prototypical nature of the trial undertaken, the students arguably had not had time to internalise the use of the app and all had reported using it spontaneously, following a request for participation that had reached them by email. There was an even split between the app's use in public or private places, as expected. Most users had only listened to one recording, so given the typical duration of 2–3 minutes, and the additional time needed to answer the questions, then 5 minutes was marked as the duration of use. For the latter, it was evident that most of the students did have some difficulty following the podcast. As was expected, background noise was also a naturally occurring factor for oral comprehension, which students have to get used to. Even though, as was noted above, the app was developed using a cross-platform technology, the majority of difficulties that the students had were due to usability problems. For example, on some devices the play button had to be pressed several times to get the recording running and on others it would just not work.

5. Conclusion and future work

The initial results obtained here have helped the authors plan a subsequent more comprehensive test to be undertaken that should provide finer grained evidence about the adequacy of applying Kukulska-Hulme's (2012) temporal – spatial – activity-based conceptual framework for the next generation of MALL SLL apps. Furthermore, language teachers could also use these data to plan appropriate blended or distance learning activities to make the most of the way in which the students actually use these apps.

6. Acknowledgements

The research presented in this article has been supported by the SO-CALL-ME Project (with funding from the Spanish Ministry of Science and Innovation; FFI2011-29829).

References

Cutler, A., & Clifton, Jr., C. (1999). Comprehending spoken language: a blueprint of the listener. In C. M. Brown & P. Hagoort (Eds.), *The neurocognition of language* (pp. 123-166). Oxford: Oxford University Press.

Evans, B. (2013). Mobile is eating the world. *Benedict Evans Blog*. Retrieved from http://ben-evans.com/benedictevans/2013/11/5/mobile-is-eating-the-world-autumn-2013-edition

Kaplan, A. M. (2012). If you love something, let it go mobile: mobile marketing and mobile social media 4x4. *Business Horizons*, *55*(2), 129-139. Retrieved from http://dx.doi.org/10.1016/j.bushor.2011.10.009

Krashen, S. D. (1985). *The input hypothesis: issues and implications*. London: Longman.

Kukulska-Hulme, A. (2012). Language learning defined by time and place: a framework for next generation designs. In J. E. Díaz-Vera (Ed.), *Left to my own devices: learner autonomy and mobile assisted language learning. Innovation and leadership in English language teaching, 6.* (pp. 1-13). Bingley, UK: Emerald Group Publishing Limited. Retrieved from http://dx.doi.org/10.1163/9781780526478_002

Laurillard, D. (2007). Designing for connectedness: principles for e-learning. *Rethinking the Teaching of Science H*, *806*.

Maggiani, R. (2014). *Social media and its effect on communication: multidimensional interactions have altered the basic rules of communication*. Solari. Retrieved from www.solari.net/documents/position-papers/Solari-Social-Media-and-Communication.pdf

Mesh, L. J. (2010). Collaborative language learning for professional adults. *Electronic Journal of E-learning*, *8*(2).

Rodríguez-Arancón, P., Arús-Hita, J., & Calle-Martínez, C. (2013). The use of current mobile learning applications in EFL. In D. Korkut (Ed.), *Investigation of problematic internet usage of university students with different spychosocial levels*. Proceedings of IETC 2013 (pp. 1219-1225). Kuala Lumpur, Malaysia.

Traxler, J., & Kukulska-Hulme, A. (2005). Evaluating mobile learning: reflections on current practice. In *mLearn 2005: Mobile technology: The future of learning in your hands, Cape Town, South Africa*.

Yeager, C., Hurley-Dasgupta, B., & Bliss, C. A. (2013). CMOOCs snd global learning: an authentic alternative. *Journal of Asynchronous Learning Networks*, *17*(2).

20 Design and implementation of BusinessApp, a MALL application to make successful business presentations

Cristina Calle-Martínez[1], Lourdes Pomposo Yanes[2], and Antonio Pareja-Lora[3]

Abstract

Little by little, Mobile Assisted Language Learning (or, simply, MALL) is taking force in the field of education, as it supports language blended learning and language learning ubiquity. The study presented here belongs in the Social Ontology-based Cognitively Augmented Language Learning Mobile Environment (SO-CALL-ME) research project, whose final aim is to design and create English as a Foreign Language (EFL) mobile applications (henceforth, apps) that apply a solid pedagogy to teaching technical and language skills. Thus, these apps provide a very flexible form of learning that is also practical, interactive, adaptive, dynamic and deeply rooted in daily socio-cultural situations and contexts. In particular, our study has aimed at designing and implementing an app to help its users create and perform successful business presentations. Thus, the potential users of our app are both professionals and students in general, since business presentations are a compulsory and essential activity in most professional environments nowadays. Using our app will allow them to learn these skills ubiquitously and autonomously, since it contains self-evaluating (automatically corrected) exercises.

Keywords: EFL, mobile, application, language learning, MALL, app, business, BusinessApp.

---

1. Universidad Complutense de Madrid / ATLAS (UNED), Madrid, Spain; cristinacalle@filol.ucm.es

2. ATLAS (UNED), Madrid, Spain; lpomposo@ucjc.edu

3. Universidad Complutense de Madrid / ATLAS (UNED), Madrid, Spain; aplora@ucm.es

How to cite this chapter: Calle-Martínez, C., Pomposo Yanes, L., & Pareja-Lora, A. (2016). Design and implementation of BusinessApp, a MALL application to make successful business presentations. In A. Pareja-Lora, C. Calle-Martínez, & P. Rodríguez-Arancón (Eds), *New perspectives on teaching and working with languages in the digital era* (pp. 233-243). Dublin: Research-publishing.net. http://dx.doi.org/10.14705/rpnet.2016.tislid2014.437

Chapter 20

1. Introduction

More and more students (and learners, in general) combine their learning tasks with other multiple activities every day. These other activities (work, fellowships, child care and other domestic responsibilities, etc.) are not less important for them and require their attention several hours a day. This reduces to a great extent the amount of time that they can devote to learning and/or practicing what they have learnt.

In such cases, they mostly find odd moments and time left between their other multiple activities throughout the day. In other words, they learn when and wherever they can (for instance, at home, at university, or on public transport). This is what the term *ubiquitous learning* means (Kukulska-Hulme, 2012; Peng, Su, Chou, & Tsai, 2009).

This scenario has made the application of new technologies and educational modalities and trends to learning become a hot topic (Vázquez Cano & Martín Monje, 2014). This has given rise to two new types of important Open Educational Resources (OERs), namely Massive Open Online Courses (MOOCs) and apps. Both MOOCs and apps clearly enable not only ubiquitous learning, but also *blended learning*, that is, a mixture of face-to-face and online learning (Bueno-Alastuey & López Pérez, 2014; Rodríguez-Arancón, Bárcena, & Arús, 2012). The main catalysts for this change are, obviously, smartphones and PC tablets, which combine portability and full computational power and frequently allow for an almost ubiquitous web access.

Recent statistics show that the ratio of mobile phones per person is even higher than that of PCs or laptops. Besides, according to the Spanish Statistics Institute (INE, Press release, October 2013 http://www.ine.es/prensa/np803.pdf), the number of mobile data plan contracts has increased enormously lately. Mobile phones are already an unavoidable component of the life of European citizens regardless of their age. Citizens use them both for leisure (playing games, communicating with their family and friends, personal scheduling, etc.) and for academic and/or professional purposes (web searching, learning, etc.).

Therefore, the need to add either new MOOCS or new apps to the current repertoire of OERs becomes more urgent every day. Both types of OERs have a place in the development of any learning module (cf. Vázquez Cano & Martín Monje, 2014). However, MOOCs are more adequate when presenting theoretical content, since (a) they are not supposed to be interactive and (b) MOOC learners do not necessarily have to play an active role when they learn. On the other hand, apps are more suitable not only when providing theoretical background and knowledge, but also when practicing what has been or is being learnt, since they are usually more interactive and are less restricted than MOOCs, e.g. by virtue of their presentation format. Accordingly, apps are more versatile and adaptable and also allow for a more *autonomous learning* than MOOCs.

For this reason, the work presented here aimed at developing an app (*BusinessApp*) from its inception. This app helps learn English for a specific purpose in a particular domain, that is, the domain of business and the purpose of creating and performing successful business and/or professional presentations (presentations of e.g. goods, services and companies). The topic of business presentations has never been dealt with in any other freely available app up to now (Calle-Martínez, Rodríguez-Arancón, & Arús-Hita, 2013), since freely available apps are usually more basic and not so specific).

In the next section we summarise the most relevant details of *BusinessApp* development.

2. The development of *BusinessApp*

BusinessApp is part of a whole set of MALL apps, built within the SO-CALL-ME research project (ref.: FFI2011-29829 – see the Acknowledgements). The main objective of SO-CALL-ME is to develop apps with a solid pedagogic base that can help to learn content and develop skills in English. More broadly speaking, it aims at providing a set of OERs for English learning that are flexible, practical, interactive and dynamic, while also deeply rooted in daily socio-cultural situations and contexts (Pareja-Lora et al., 2013).

In particular, the purpose of *BusinessApp* is twofold: it can be broken down into a general purpose and a specific purpose. The general purpose of *BusinessApp* is to help improve its users' oral skills in English (basically, their oral expression and their oral comprehension skills). Its specific purpose is to help its users put these oral skills into practice in order to create and perform successful presentations of products, goods, services, businesses and/or companies in their professional environment.

Even though the target users of this app are thought to be only the authors' English University students at the beginning, it soon became obvious that the range of target users was much wider. On the one hand, business presentations are an almost compulsory and essential activity in most professional environments nowadays. In a more and more globalised world, the language most frequently used for these presentations is English, the *lingua franca* in business, international companies, science and technology. On the other hand, some authors, such as Cotton and Robbins (1993), Ellis and Johnson (1994) or Matthews (1987), point out the importance of carrying out practical activities when learning a language, since they help acquire oral skills to be put into practice in future professional situations.

Thus, *BusinessApp* has been developed to be useful either for (a) people that need to learn how to make good business presentations in English for their work, and (b) students at all levels, who have to learn and/or to create and perform good presentations in any area of their current studies (not necessarily in English). All these target users, to a lesser or to a greater extent, do or will need the skills and knowledge that can be developed and learnt with *BusinessApp* at some point in their professional career.

From a more technical point of view, *BusinessApp* has been developed following the Rapid Application Development (RAD) methodology (Maurer & Martel, 2002). In this methodology, the development of applications is driven by the implementation phase, and the other usual phases of software development are subject and secondary to implementation. The main aim of this methodology is to finish a first prototype of the application as soon as possible. Then, the first prototype evolves and is transformed, within an iterative process, into several different, increasingly improved versions of the prototype. This improvement process is fed with the results of the evaluation tests, which are run by some selected typical users of the final application. This process ends when the evaluation tests are fully successful and, then, the last prototype implemented is considered the first actual version of the application. Accordingly, the design phase in RAD is reduced to a minimum, and its results are, basically, the specifications of (a) the different screens that constitute the human-machine interface, and (b) the actions that have to be taken when any of the components of these screens is selected, clicked on and/or played.

2.1. The design of *BusinessApp*

In this light, the design of *BusinessApp* had to specify only the main blocks of the application, the screens that would have to be shown, and the different actions that had to be taken in each case. Accordingly, *BusinessApp*'s design was structured around four main modules or screens, namely (1) the STRUCTURE module, (2) the BODY LANGUAGE module, (3) the GRAPH & TREND DESCRIPTION module, and (4) the GOOD & BAD PRESENTATIONS module.

Firstly, the design of the STRUCTURE module includes all the necessary screens to explain (a) how a good business presentation is structured, that is, the macrostructure of a successful business presentation (which are the main blocks that such a presentation should include, and in which order), as well as (b) what should the contents of each of these blocks refer to.

Secondly, the design of the BODY LANGUAGE module contains a number of screens giving some clues and hints about what are considered good and bad manners and postures when performing a business presentation, that is, the right body language that should be used during a presentation.

Thirdly, the design of the GRAPH & TREND DESCRIPTION module includes some additional screens that provide the common vocabulary (a) to describe graphs and tables, which are quite usual in business presentations, and (b) to provide further information about trends using these two elements.

Finally, the design of the GOOD & BAD PRESENTATIONS module includes a supplementary set of screens that present some accompanying but important issues that can enhance a business presentation (good intonation and rhythm, making jokes, etc.). In addition, the design of the *BusinessApp* included the specification of yet another secondary module of the application, the GLOSSARY module, which should help learners manage the vocabulary they are taught when using the app.

All the screens and the actions specified in the design of *BusinessApp* were extracted from a didactic unit previously created by the authors, according to the usual linguistic and pedagogic standards of quality to get an effective oral and written communicative competence. The method followed is the Communicative Language Teaching (CLT) approach, which stems from the socio-cognitive perspective of socio-linguistic theory, with an emphasis on meaning and communication, and a goal to develop learners' communicative competence (Canale & Swain, 1980). Consequently, the design of each module block (that is, of each sub-screen) portrays a set of suitable examples and the most useful and usual lexical and discursive units associated to that block. Reading and listening to these examples, as well as learning the units mentioned, greatly helps to create and perform successful business presentations. All in all, this provides the app with a solid linguistic and pedagogical basis. Besides, each module also includes a set of self-evaluating (and automatically corrected) exercises, which facilitate the autonomous learning of the content and the development of the skills addressed by the app.

2.2. The implementation of *BusinessApp*

Some recommendations and standards for mobile learning[4] put the emphasis in the need to implement apps so that they can be run on any selected platform (e.g. a mobile phone, a PC tablet or a laptop) and/or regardless of the device's operating system (*Android*, *iOS*, *Windows*, etc.). Usually, this means that (a) the contents of the *app* must be represented in HTML5 and (b) these HTML5

---

4. For instance: http://e-standards.flexiblelearning.net.au/documents/2014-recommended-vet-estandards_v1.1.docx

contents must be managed and presented on the screen of the device by means of some form of Java (e.g. JavaScript).

We however have not followed these recommendations, because we wanted to evaluate the suitability of *MIT App Inventor Classic* (http://appinventor.mit.edu/explore/classic.html) for the implementation of MALL *apps*. The reason to carry out such an evaluation is that *MIT App Inventor* is a semiautomatic development environment with quite a user-friendly interface for people not used to programming (which might be the case of linguists programming MALL *apps*). Besides, it is most appropriate for the implementation of applications following the methodology selected (RAD). Therefore, *BusinessApp* has been implemented by means of *MIT App Inventor Classic*.

MIT App Inventor Classic consists of three main modules: (a) the module to implement the different screens of the app, conveniently specified in the design phase (not shown here for the sake of space); (b) the module to program the actions that must be performed when any of the components of the screen (such as a button or a textbox) is selected, clicked on or played (see Figure 1); and (c) the module that simulates the behaviour of the app in a standard (or basic) smartphone, which is useful for testing what was already implemented (Figure 2). The main advantage of this tool is that it has been conceived for almost fully drag-and-drop programming. In particular, the module to perform the actions associated to screen components makes programming almost as easy as doing a jigsaw puzzle. In fact, the different elements that can be combined to program the application are represented on the screen as pieces of jigsaw puzzles (Figure 2).

The main disadvantage of *MIT App Inventor Classic* (inherited by *BusinessApp*) is that it generates apps that can only run on Android. However, this disadvantage is a bit secondary, since Android (a) is one of the most used mobile operating systems, and (b) provides a lot of built-in pre-defined services, like the text-to-speech and the speech recogniser services, which are quite useful to develop MALL apps. In particular, the Android text-to-speech built-in service is pervasively used in *BusinessApp*, in order to read aloud the texts that learners have to listen to, with a more than satisfactory intonation at a minimum cost.

Chapter 20

Figure 1. Implementation of the *BusinessApp* screen actions with *MIT App Inventor*

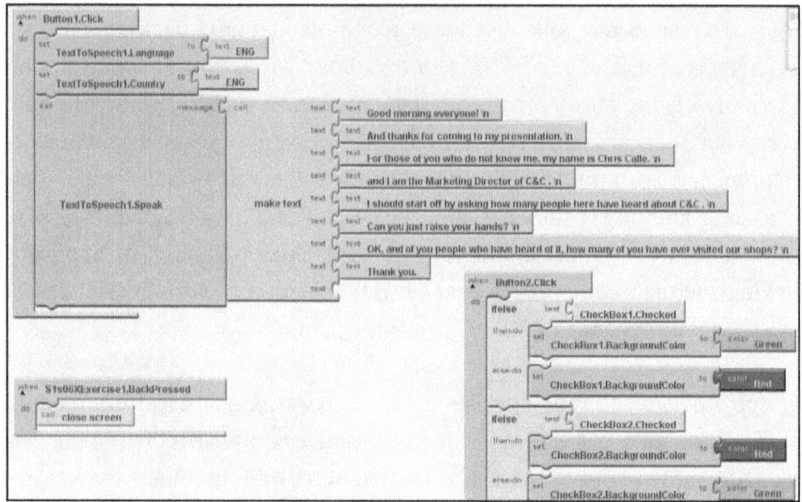

Figure 2. Simulating the execution of the *BusinessApp* screen with *MIT App Inventor*

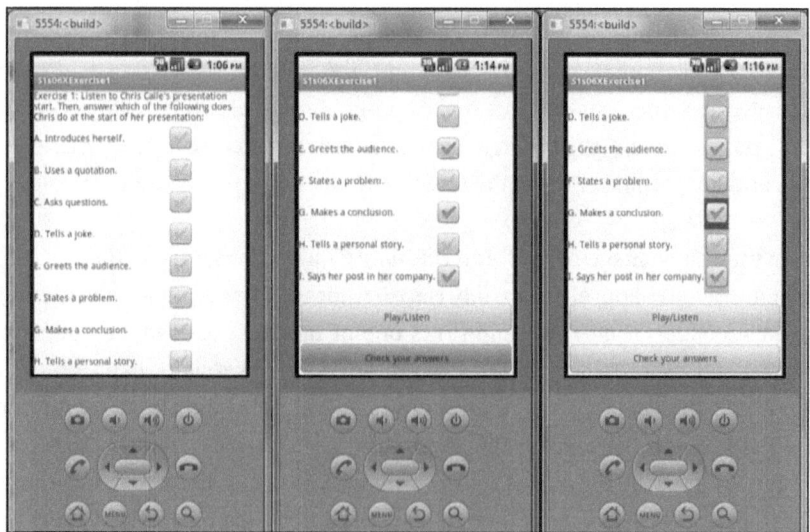

3. Future work

Some evaluation and testing of *BusinessApp* has already been accomplished by the authors themselves in order to develop a fully functional version of the app. However, a real evaluation phase with actual users is still to be performed. The users in this real evaluation phase will be our students.

Towards this end, *BusinessApp* will be uploaded to the virtual space of their courses. Students will then download and test it themselves. After testing it, they will have to create and perform a business presentation, which will be scored according to the criteria for good presentations presented in the app. This will help evaluate the suitability of *BusinessApp* to learn its associated content and develop the corresponding English skills. In addition, students will have to fill a questionnaire about more technical issues of the app (such as its usability). This questionnaire will be elaborated with the rubric presented in Martín-Monje, Arús, Rodríguez-Arancón, and Calle-Martínez (2013) as a basis. The data so obtained will help improve the implementation of *BusinessApp* in the future (if necessary).

4. Conclusions

In this paper, we have presented *BusinessApp*, a mobile application that we have developed (a) to help its users create and perform successful business presentations in English, and (b) also, from a more general perspective, to improve their oral and communication skills in this language.

This mobile application has been designed according to solid pedagogical and linguistic criteria, and can be used for the ubiquitous and blended learning of the aforementioned content and skills.

Autonomous learning is also enabled in the application by means of the self-evaluation exercises that accompany each of the modules of *BusinessApp* and which can be automatically corrected by the application.

5. Acknowledgements

The research described in this paper has been partly funded by the *Spanish Ministry of Science and Innovation, Grant **FFI2011-29829***: Social Ontology-based Cognitively Augmented Language Learning Mobile Environment (SO-CALL-ME).

We would like to thank the ATLAS (UNED) research group as well, for their constant inspiration, encouragement and support.

References

Bueno-Alastuey, M. C., & López Pérez, M. V. (2014). Evaluation of a blended learning language course: students' perceptions of appropriateness for the development of skills and language areas. *Computer Assisted Language Learning, 27*(6), 509-527. Retrieved from http://dx.doi.org/10.1080/09588221.2013.770037

Calle-Martínez, C., Rodríguez-Arancón, P., & Arús-Hita, J. (2013). A Scrutiny of the educational value of EFL mobile learning applications. In *Proceedings of the 4th World Conference on Learning, Teaching and Educational Leadership, Barcelona* (pp. 25-27).

Canale, M., & Swain, M. (1980). Theoretical bases of communicative approaches to second language teaching and testing. *Applied Linguistics, 1*(1), 1-47. Retrieved from http://dx.doi.org/10.1093/applin/I.1.1

Cotton, D., & Robbins S. (1993). *Business class*. London: Nelson.

Ellis, M., & Johnson, C. (1994). *Teaching business English*. Oxford: Oxford University Press.

Kukulska-Hulme, A. (2012). Language learning defined by time and place: a framework for next generation designs. In J. E. Díaz-Vera (Ed.), *Left to my own devices: learner autonomy and mobile assisted language learning. Innovation and leadership in English language teaching, 6* (pp. 1-13). Bingley, UK: Emerald Group Publishing Limited. Retrieved from http://dx.doi.org/10.1163/9781780526478_002

Martín-Monje, E., Arús-Hita, J., Rodríguez-Arancón, P., & Calle-Martínez, C. (2013). REALL: rubric for the evaluation of apps in language learning. In *Proceedings of ML13* (pp. 1-12).

Matthews, C. (1987). *Business interactions*. Hemel Hempstead: Prentice Hall.

Maurer, F., & Martel, S. (2002). Extreme programming: rapid development for web-based applications. *IEEE Internet Computing, 6*(1), 86-91. Retrieved from http://dx.doi.org/10.1109/4236.989006

Pareja-Lora, A., Arús, J., Martín-Monje, E., Read, T., Pomposo-Yanes, L., Rodríguez-Arancón, P., Calle-Martínez, C., & Bárcena, E. (2013). Toward Mobile Assisted Language Learning apps for professionals that integrate learning into the daily routine. In L. Bradley & S. Thouësny (Eds.), *20 Years of EUROCALL: learning from the past, looking to the future* (pp. 206-210). Dublin: Research Publishing. Retrieved from http://dx.doi.org/10.14705/rpnet.2013.000162

Peng, H., Su, Y.J., Chou, C., & Tsai, C. (2009). Ubiquitous knowledge construction: mobile learning re-defined and a conceptual framework. *Innovations in Education Technology, 46*(2), 171-183. Retrieved from http://dx.doi.org/10.1080/14703290902843828

Rodríguez-Arancón, P., Bárcena, E., & Arús, J. (2012). A novel approach for the development of communicative competence in English in a blended learning context. *Journal of Language Teaching and Research, 3*(2), 256-272.

Vázquez Cano, E., & Martín Monje, E. (2014). *Nuevas tendencias en la elaboración y utilización de materiales digitales para la enseñanza de lenguas*. Aravaca (Madrid): McGraw-Hill/Interamericana de España, S.L.

21 Using audio description to improve FLL students' oral competence in MALL: methodological preliminaries

Ana Ibáñez Moreno[1], Anna Vermeulen[2], and Maria Jordano[3]

Abstract

During the last decades of the 20th century, audiovisual products began to be audio described in order to make them accessible to blind and visually impaired people (Benecke, 2004). This means that visual information is orally described in the gaps between dialogues. In order to meet the wishes of the so-called On Demand (OD) generation that wants 'anything, anytime, anyplace', we implemented Audio Description (AD) as a tool to promote oral production skills by means of mobile devices (android smart phones) and designed an app named VIdeos for SPeaking (VISP). In this paper we describe the methodological steps followed until the achievement of this first version of VISP, and we present the first prototype, which will be applied to distance education students and in other ubiquitous learning environments.

Keywords: audio description, oral competence, foreign language learning, FLL, mobile assisted language learning, MALL, mobile apps.

---

1. UNED, Madrid, Spain; aibanez@flog.uned.es

2. Ghent University, Ghent, Belgium; anna.vermeulen@ugent.be

3. UNED, Madrid, Spain; mjordano@flog.uned.es

How to cite this chapter: Ibáñez Moreno, A., Vermeulen, A., & Jordano, M. (2016). Using audio description to improve FLL students' oral competence in MALL: methodological preliminaries. In A. Pareja-Lora, C. Calle-Martínez, & P. Rodríguez-Arancón (Eds), *New perspectives on teaching and working with languages in the digital era* (pp. 245-256). Dublin: Research-publishing.net. http://dx.doi.org/10.14705/rpnet.2016.tislid2014.438

1. Introduction: AD and Foreign Language Learning (FLL)

As mentioned by Krejtz et al. (2012) and the *Dual Coding Theory* (Paivio, 1986; Sadoski & Paivio, 2004), we have the capacity to store and retrieve information in verbal as well as non-verbal ways; when this is done simultaneously, learning is facilitated since the same data is available through several channels.

In the same vein, the Cognitive Theory of Multimedia Learning (Mayer, 2001) states that the processing of information improves when it is provided by two channels, namely the auditory and the visual. That makes audiovisual texts, which combine the verbal sign with images and sound, an attractive and stimulating tool for language learners, since their multimodal nature provides information through multiple channels, which strengthens memory retrieval (Moreno & Mayer, 2007).

AD, as a modality of multimodal audiovisual translation, was created for a specific audience, the blind and visually impaired people, and for a specific purpose: to make the visual content of an event accessible by conveying it into spoken words (Benecke, 2004). Back in 1992, studies on multimodal learning which compared learning with and without AD indicated that students with no narration performed significantly worse on problem-solving tests than those who heard the AD (Mayer & Anderson, 1992).

Recently, AD has been applied as a tool to promote the writing skills of English translation students (Clouet, 2005) and to enhance self-learning vocabulary (Martínez, 2012). The Ghent University-based project *Audiodescripción como Recurso Didáctico en ELE* (ARDELE) – that is, AD as a Didactic Resource for Spanish as a Foreign Language (hereafter FL) – also explores different aspects of the use of AD in the FLL classroom. To date, its results show that AD enhances the lexical and the phraseological competence (Ibáñez & Vermeulen, 2013). Since AD can be rendered, recorded (based on a written script, the socalled *AD script*, hereafter ADS), as well as live, it serves to train both written and oral competences (Ibáñez & Vermeulen, 2014).

2. The use of Mobile Assisted Language Learning (MALL) to improve oral competences

Some authors set the emergence of MALL in 2009 with the appearance of the first mobile application ('app') to learn languages, developed by the British Council (Hockly, 2013). More recently, MALL has been defined by Kukulska-Hulme (2013) as "mobile technologies in language learning, especially in situations where device portability offers specific advantages" (cited in Stockwell & Hubbard, 2013, p. 2). This concept is intimately linked to the deep development that mobile technology has experienced in the last decade, as well as to the wide variety of mobile devices, users and uses included, in this growing world.

Kukulska-Hulme and Shield (2007) stated that the implementation of collaborative oral activities in a mobile context would only be possible through synchronous communication based on chatting. They claim that although nowadays it is possible to maintain voice dialogues using mobile devices, this would violate the 'anytime, anyplace' principle of mobile learning (m-learning) in some specific context, for instance a bus full of people talking to each other. Siskin (2009) proposed a comprehensive classification of different ways to teach languages through m-learning. Kim, Rueckert, Kim, and Seo (2013) successfully set up a project based on the use of the mobile phone outside the classroom. One of the activities consisted of recording and sharing videos on *YouTube* to practice students' speaking competence.

There are different ways to practice and improve student's competences in FL by using mobile technology. Some of them are listed below:

    1.1 Mobile-based Synchronous Computer Mediated Communication (M-SCMC).

    1.2 Mobile versions of websites designed to practice foreign languages.

    1.3 Podcasting and other ways of subscription.

1.4 Authoring tools to create new material.

1.5 English as a Foreign Language (EFL) applications ('apps').

Out of these resources, those dealing with oral competences are (1.3) and (1.5). As regards podcasting (1.3), it is one of the pioneering MALL activities to improve oral competences. Rosell-Aguilar (2013) shows its benefits for FLL students in a study about different aspects of their language development derived from their exposition to podcasts. Another option is subscribing to an RSS channel by speaking. This has been applied in a MALL app called *ANT*, created to listen to the news (see Pareja-Lora et al., 2013).

As for (1.5), nowadays, there are dozens of apps created to learn English. However, very few promote spoken language. A selection of the most comprehensive apps is provided below:

- *Sounds*, The Pronunciation App.

- *English conversations*.

- *Speak English* (Listen, repeat and compare).

- *Talk English*.

- *Vaughan System*.

As for apps that have been specifically developed within the academic world, there is almost nothing available, and apart from a few proposals that are being tested, there is not much material (Godwin-Jones, 2011). Moreover, there are no empirical studies based on testing these apps, especially with regards to oral competences. Given that this field is still under development, our aim is to propose a MALL app with strong academic grounds and pedagogically solid, as well as motivating and stimulating for FLL students.

3. Proposal and description of a mobile app: VISP

In line with the current trend of applying audiovisual translation to FLL and teaching and following the principles of the communicative approach to language teaching, we have designed a MALL application based on AD that can be used to improve oral production skills in English: VISP v1. This first prototype has been initially conceived for B1 students of English. The theoretical background of this mobile app, as well as recent research on the field of FLL, establishes the solid base for its conception, departing from the following series of premises.

First, from the FLL perspective, exposing learners to audiovisual material containing specific lexicon will help them to learn and use it more efficiently (Tight, 2010). As stated elsewhere, "[e]ven if ubiquitous learning environments have increased and new technologies have been developed to adapt to the new learning styles (Jones & Ho, 2004), we believe that there are fewer chances for the average user, in [a ubiquitous] context, to practice oral production. In this [respect], AD has showed to be a useful tool to promote oral skills in the [FLL] classroom" (Ibáñez Moreno & Vermeulen, 2015, p. 250). However, it has not yet been tested in the field of MALL. Therefore, VISP v1 would be the first MALL application based on AD.

Second, from the perspective of MALL, we depart from the premise that ubiquitous learning environments can improve motivation and promote learning (Keramidas, 2010; Lee & Hammer, 2011). In this sense, this application is conceived to meet the needs of the OD generation: learning anytime, anywhere. Figure 1 shows its home screen.

VISP v1 is framed within the communicative approach, especially within the task-based approach, in the sense that VISP v1 consists of communicative activities whose goal is to achieve a specific learning objective (Ellis, 2003). Tasks are the backbone of VISP v1.

Chapter 21

Figure 1. Home screen of VISP v1

For this first version, we chose a 30" clip of the film *Moulin Rouge* (Luhrmann, 2001). Following the conventions of AD, an audio describer is allowed to use 180 words per minute. In VISP v1, however, users should employ around 60 words only. The clip was selected on the basis of its absence of dialogue and little action. This gives users time to describe what they see. The ADs of the whole clip are provided below (as originally recorded):

> "A handsome young man, Christian, in his twenties, with dark hair and beard, takes a new line on his typewriter. He puts his hand to his forehead. Through his open window lies Paris at night. Tearfully, he stares out of the window at the Moulin Rouge. He turns back to the typewriter; the Paris cityscape".

Second, the instructions for the usability of VISP v1 were designed. They consisted of several steps, beginning with a very brief introduction to AD. A great effort was done in order to select the most essential information about AD, so as to comply with smartphones' and tablets' usability and readability (Fling, 2009).

From the introduction screen the user can access a real AD sample: a clip of 4", extracted from *Memoirs of a Geisha*, so users can first listen to a real AD. Finally, a button at the bottom of the screen directs users to a pre-questionnaire where they fill in their personal data: name, surname and email. They also complete a short language test.

The pre-questionnaire has several purposes: 1) to obtain data from the users (with the corresponding disclaimer informing about the confidential use of such data) and keep track of their progress; 2) to obtain data about the users' previous knowledge of English so that their progress can be assessed and the validity of VISP v1 can be confirmed; and 3) to provide users with some background knowledge of the vocabulary that will be necessary to accomplish an accurate exercise.

Once users have been introduced to AD, watched and listened to an example, and filled in their data, they can continue to the next step by clicking on the *Instructions* button.

The instructions are very simple, brief and direct, so as to keep the user's attention and interest. Also, tips are given, as well as three basic rules of audio describing. Finally, users are reminded that there are no time limits to perform the task. They can repeat the task as many times as they want before sending their recording. The next step is the practice itself. The screen included in Figure 2 shows the core of the whole activity, and of the application.

In this screen, users can watch the clip as many times as they want, by clicking on *Play* and *Rewind*, until they feel ready to record their own AD. When this moment comes, they will have to click on *Record*. After the recording, they have the option of listening to their performance. Once users are satisfied with their AD, they go back to the *Home* screen and click on the button *Finish* (see Figure 1).

Figure 2. Practice screen of VISP v1

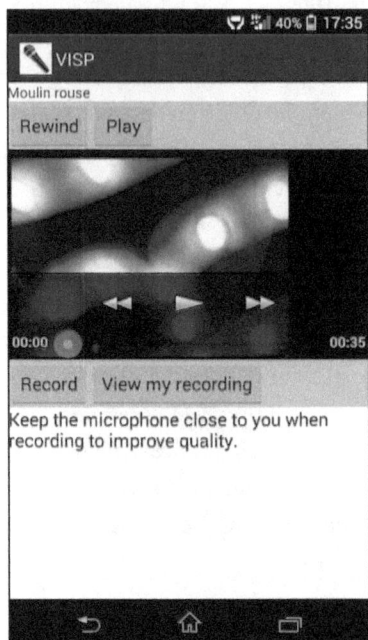

In the *Finish* screen, users fill in their name, and send their recording. If the users have filled in their personal data in the initial questionnaire, we can also send some feedback on their performance by taking into account their improvement. Besides, this screen also includes a self-evaluation section, accessible by clicking on the button below *Send*. This button directs the users to another post-questionnaire, where they can listen to the original clip with AD (among other activities), which are aimed at an autonomous assessment of their performance.

4. Concluding remarks and future research

In this work we have presented the methodological steps taken by three members of the research group Applying Technology to LAnguageS (ATLAS). ATLAS is a UNED-based research group working on MALL, Computer-Assisted Language Learning (CALL) and Massive Open Online Courses (MOOCs), among other areas, to develop a MALL app (VISP v1) that aims to help B1 English language learners to work their oral skills, especially speaking. VISP v1 has been developed from the idea that the use of AD, which offers the same information that is accessible visually in an oral way, can create an effective multimodal learning environment. VISP v1 is already one of the pioneering MALL apps that has used AD as a technique to practice oral production skills in FLL; however, it is still a prototype that has to be tested on distance learning students of English. Therefore, very soon the results will show its benefits and limitations. These limitations will lead us to its further development, for instance by implementing level A1, A2 and B2 tasks, and by removing all the elements that are not useful.

5. Acknowledgements

The research presented in this chapter has been written in the wide context of the SO-CALL-ME project, funded by the Spanish Ministry of Science and Innovation (ref. no. FFI2011-29829).

References

Benecke, B. (2004). Audio-description. *Meta, 49*(1), 78-80. Retrieved from http://dx.doi.org/10.7202/009022ar

Clouet, R. (2005). Estrategia y propuestas para promover y practicar la escritura creativa en una clase de inglés para traductores. In *Actas del IX Simposio Internacional de la Sociedad Española de Didáctica de la Lengua y la Literatura* (pp. 319-326).

Ellis, R. (2003). *Task-based language learning and teaching*. Oxford: Oxford University Press.

Fling, B. (2009). *Mobile technology and development: practical techniques for creating mobile sites and web apps*. Sebastopol, CA: O'Reilly Books.

Godwin-Jones, R. (2011). Mobile apps for language learning. *Language Learning & Technology, 15*(2), 2-11. Retrieved from http://llt.msu.edu/issues/june2011/emerging.pdf

Hockly, N. (2013). Mobile learning. *English Language Teaching Journal*, *67*(1), 80-84. Retrieved from http://dx.doi.org/10.1093/elt/ccs064

Ibáñez, A., & Vermeulen, A. (2013). Audio description as a tool to improve lexical and phraseological competence in foreign language learning. In D. Tsagari, & G. Floros (Eds.), *Translation in language teaching and assessment* (pp. 45-61). Newcastle upon Tyne: Cambridge Scholars Publishing.

Ibáñez, A., & Vermeulen, A. (2014). La audiodescripción como recurso didáctico en el aula de ELE para promover el desarrollo integrado de competencias. In R. Orozco (Ed.), *New directions in Hispanic linguistics* (pp. 263-292). Newcastle upon Tyne: Cambridge Scholars Publishing.

Ibáñez Moreno, A., & Vermeulen, A. (2015). VISP 2.0: methodological considerations for the design and implementation of an audio-description based app to improve oral skills. In F. Helm, L. Bradley, M. Guarda, & S. Thouësny (Eds), *Critical CALL – Proceedings of the 2015 EUROCALL Conference, Padova, Italy* (pp. 249-253). Dublin: Research-publishing.net. Retrieved from http://dx.doi.org/10.14705/rpnet.2015.000341

Jones, V., & Jo, J. H. (2004). Ubiquitous learning environment: an adaptive teaching system using ubiquitous technology. *Proceedings of the Annual Conference of the Australian Association for Computers in Learning in Tertiary Education*.

Keramidas, K. (2010). What games have to teach us about teaching and learning: game design as a model for course and curricular development. *Currents in Electronic Literacy*. Retrieved from http://currents.dwrl.utexas.edu/2010/keramidas_what-games-have-to-teach-us-about-teaching-and-learning

Kim, D., Rueckert, D., Kim, D., & Seo, D. (2013). Students' perceptions and experiences of mobile learning. *Language Learning & Technology*, *17*(3), 52-73. Retrieved from http://llt.msu.edu/issues/october2013/kimetal.pdf

Krejtz, K., Krejtz, I., Duchowski, A., Szarkowska, A., & Walczak, A. (2012). Multimodal learning with audio description: an eye tracking study of children's gaze during a visual recognition task. *SAP'12 Proceedings of the ACM Symposium on Applied Perception* (pp. 83-90). Retrieved from http://dx.doi.org/10.1145/2338676.2338694

Kukulska-Hulme, A. (2013). Mobile assisted language learning. In C. Chapelle (Ed.), *The encyclopedia of applied linguistics* (pp. 3701-3709). New York: Wiley.

Kukulska-Hulme, A., & Shield, L. (2007). Can mobile devices support collaborative practice in speaking and listening? *Paper presented at the EuroCALL 2007, Limerick, Ireland* (pp. 1-20). Retrieved from http://vsportal2007.googlepages.com/collaborativepractice

Lee, J. J., & Hammer, J. (2011). Gamification in education: what, how, why bother? *Academic Exchange Quarterly, 12*(5), 1-5.

Luhrmann, B. (2001). Moulin Rouge. Twentieth Century Fox.

Martínez, S. (2012). La audiodescripción (AD) como herramienta didáctica: Adquisición de la competencia léxica. In M. Cruces Del Pozo, A. Luna, A. Álvarez (Eds), *Traducir en la Frontera*. Granada, Atrio.

Mayer, R. E. (2001). *Multimedia learning*. New York: Cambridge University Press. Retrieved from http://dx.doi.org/10.1017/CBO9781139164603

Mayer, R., & Anderson, R. (1992). The instructive animation: helping students build connections between words and pictures in multimedia learning. *Journal of Educational Psychology, 84*(4), 444- 452. Retrieved from http://dx.doi.org/10.1037/0022-0663.84.4.444

Moreno, R., & Mayer, R. (2007). Interactive multimodal learning environments. *Educational Psychology Review, 19*(3), 309-326.

Paivio, A. (1986). Mental representations: a dual coding approach. Oxford: Oxford University Press.

Pareja-Lora, A., Arús-Hita, J., Martín-Monje, E., Read, T., Pomposo-Yanes, L., Rodríguez-Arancón, P., Calle-Martínez, C., Bárcena-Madera, E. (2013). Toward mobile assisted language learning apps for professionals that integrate learning into the daily routine. In L. Bradley & S. Thouësny (Eds.), *20 Years of EUROCALL: Learning from the Past, Looking to the Future* (pp. 206-210). Dublin Ireland: Research-publishing.net. Retrieved from http://dx.doi.org/10.14705/rpnet.2013.000162

Rosell-Aguilar, F. (2013). Podcasting for language learning through iTunes U: the learner's view. *Language Learning and Technology, 7*(3), 74-93. Retrieved from http://llt.msu.edu/issues/october2013/rosellaguilar.pdf

Sadoski, M., & Paivio, A. (2004). A dual coding theoretical model of reading. In R. B. Ruddell, & N. J. Unrau (Eds.), *Theoretical models and processes of reading* (5th ed.) (pp.1329-1362). Newark, DE: International Reading Association. Retrieved from http://dx.doi.org/10.1598/0872075028.47

Siskin, C. B. (2009). Language learning applications for smartphones, or small can be beautiful. *Edvista*. Retrieved from http://www.edvista.com/claire/pres/smartphones/

Stockwell, G., & Hubbard, P. (2013). *Some emerging principles for mobile-assisted language learning* (pp. 1-15). Monterey, CA: The International Research Foundation for English Language Education. Retrieved from http://www.tirfonline.org/wp-content/uploads/2013/11/TIRF_MALL_Papers_StockwellHubbard.pdf

Chapter 21

Tight, D. (2010). Perceptual learning style matching and L2 vocabulary acquisition. *Language Learning Research Club, 60*(4), 792-833. Retrieved from http://dx.doi.org/10.1111/j.1467-9922.2010.00572.x

Section 2.2.

ICTs for content and language integrated learning

22. ICT in EMI programmes at tertiary level in Spain: a holistic model

Nuria Hernandez-Nanclares[1] and Antonio Jimenez-Munoz[2]

Abstract

The European Higher Education Area (EHEA) in Spain has increased the number of degrees taught through English, although secondary schools do not ensure an appropriate set of linguistic skills for bilingual degrees. A holistic, accountable model for Information and Communications Technology (ICT)-supported learning can give students the adequate scaffolding to perform better in their module-related tasks. Using Content and Language Integrated Learning (CLIL) blended with pre- and post-lecture online tasks, social networks and micro-blogging as tools for further practice as well as integrating these into in-class practices, student performance improves. Contrasting the impact of these interventions reveals the need to cater for mixed learning styles and abilities.

Keywords: EMI, blended learning, ICT-enhanced learning, bilingualism, economics.

1. The expansion of English as the medium of instruction

An increasing number of universities around the globe now offer modules or full degrees taught through a foreign language, usually English. Particularly in Europe, this is a direct consequence of EHEA, though in some countries, such as

---

1. Universidad de Oviedo, Oviedo, Spain; nhernan@uniovi.es

2. Universidad de Oviedo, Oviedo, Spain; jimenezantonio@uniovi.es

How to cite this chapter: Hernandez-Nanclares, N., & Jimenez-Munoz, A. (2016). ICT in EMI programmes at tertiary level in Spain: a holistic model. In A. Pareja-Lora, C. Calle-Martínez, & P. Rodríguez-Arancón (Eds), *New perspectives on teaching and working with languages in the digital era* (pp. 259-268). Dublin: Research-publishing.net. http://dx.doi.org/10.14705/rpnet.2016.tislid2014.439

Germany or Sweden, there is a tradition of tertiary programme instruction through English and some other nations such as France or Spain have shown a recent interest in CLIL programmes (Wächter & Maiworm, 2008). This widespread adoption of English as the Medium of Instruction (EMI) has confirmed English as the language of a more global education, rooted in widened competition among institutions and graduates at tertiary level (Doiz, Lasagabaster, & Sierra, 2011; Smit & Dafouz, 2012). Most Spanish universities, however, have streamlined their EMI degrees in various ways, but not through total immersion. Some have offered a double route (one cohort to be taught primarily in English, the other in Spanish), often in a mixed programme (some EMI modules, but core modules in Spanish) or just mixed modules in such a way that there is no cross-curricular or no full undergraduate programme offered through English (Cots, 2012).

While the introduction of bilingual programmes opens a window for the revision of instructional design, a considerable number of participants have observed the problems of this rapid and widespread adoption of EMI. Instructors have often complained about the challenge of teaching content through a foreign language, particularly for solving "language-related issues" (Airey, 2013, p. 64). Code-switching between native and foreign language is not automatic for either lecturer or learner, and students show a "lack of sophistication" in their "school English", against the academic English required at university (Erling & Hilgendorf, 2006, p. 284). Furthermore, many academic instructors have complained about the need to water down and simplify content in order to make it comprehensible to students (Costa & Coleman, 2010). English has also been said to have a "limiting effect" on students' final performance (Clegg, 2001, p. 210), unless the whole degree is simplified, and thus inadequate to stiffer, more globalised competition.

All these strong reservations make EMI pale in comparison to those modules where language is not a barrier. These readymade misconceptions fail to notice that the preponderance of English as a lingua franca is indisputable in an increasingly connected world where work, communication, research and transactions take place through English. Separating concepts and facts from the language they are presented in becomes a duplicity that cannot be afforded in times of teeth-to-nail competition for jobs; just as ICT skills, these must be learnt simultaneously (Rienties, Brouwer, & Lygo-Baker, 2013). The inherent advantages of teaching "two for the price of one" and the "added value" of EMI (Bonnet, 2012, p. 66) need to be supported by evidence. The quality of learning under EMI will depend greatly on a number of socio-economic and curricular factors, but there is also the need to identify those best (and time-efficient) practices. In most EMI provisions, teaching time is limited to a reduced number of contact hours which are not devoted to language, but content. Consequently, students must work on their language skills independently (often without expert support), and there is no provision for independent language study time, which is often a transparent need.

How much English a first-year student knows and needs will vary greatly from country to country (Jenkins, Cogo, & Dewey, 2011); in Spain the minimum level after secondary school is A2.2 in the Common European Framework of Reference for Languages (CEFR), which states A1.1 starter level to C2.2 native-like level. Students can "understand very basic personal and family information" as well as "communicate in simple and routine tasks" and "describe in simple terms aspects of his/her background, immediate environment and matters in areas of immediate need" (Council of Europe, 2001, p. 24). Our own research (Hernandez-Nanclares & Jimenez-Munoz, 2015) shows that government expectations are exceeded by high-school achievers, but also that implicit requirements in first-year modules are much higher than the ablest students can manage. Testing a cohort of 90 first-year students at the beginning of the year, their overall performance exceeded educational design, from B2.1 in reading to B1.1 in all other skills, while stark differences among low-performing and top-performing students were found (8.2% of students were rounded-up A2, while 3.2% were B2 and 1.2% C1). However, analysing the lectures, seminars and tasks to be performed by students in two EMI first-year modules (World Economic History, or WEH, and World Economy, or WE) and mapping their implicit skills to CEFR descriptors, the gap between these skills and the ones required by instructors was tremendous: most skills implied a B2.2, C1.1 or C1.2 level, which would require between 250 and 750 additional hours of English language instruction.

2. ICT-mediated interventions

For the Degrees in Business Administration, Economics, and Accountancy and Finance, there are two parallel cohorts, one Spanish-taught (SMI) and another one English-taught (EMI), which sit the same exams in their respective languages and are graded using the same criteria. Global academic results for 2010-2011 and 2011-2012 (Table 3 below) showed SMI students outperforming EMI undergraduates in all bands, with better pass rates (77.2% to 66.4%) and average grades (68.5% to 59.5%). SMI students followed the same high-school system but they are native speakers (CEFR C2), which would indicate that EMI students are doomed to underachieve on purely linguistic grounds, unless their language level approaches that of natives. Remedying that disparity is paramount; we offer here the analysis of the impact of ICT-enhanced and other pedagogical interventions during the academic year 2012-2013 on the learning of an EMI cohort (90 students, 50 female, 8 overseas). Their results are contrasted with an EMI cohort of 220 (114 male, no overseas).

To improve student results and ascertain best practices among EMI staff, lecturers in WE and WEH liaised through 2012-2013 with a linguist and technology expert in order to analyse and tackle the problems at hand. There was room for improvement upon the WEH teacher-led instructional design which had a negative impact on EMI grades. More student-centred learning and more in-class participation was needed, so that the target skills for the EMI module could be fostered. Also, a flexible method to compensate English-language mixed abilities was needed, so that students maximised their independent study time and could remedy their individual shortcomings, rather than being put through a whole separate programme. In this sense, only ICT could offer that level of granularity and adaptability in a way that we would need the students to create their Personal Learning Environment (PLE) within the existent Virtual Learning Environment (VLE). The idea was to offer traceable materials for content, skills and language, to be chosen by each student, which allowed tracking of the particular effect of these on academic performance; similarly, students would be exposed to differentiated instructional techniques and approaches, so their efficacy were quantifiable.

Both WEH and WE students shared common problems: a general lack of knowledge about supranational bodies and global economic flows, a very Spanish-centred world view, an inadequate level of productive English in most cases, lecturer dependence, and a marked lack of research skills. However, each module demanded different abilities from students, and as a consequence, particular problems in previous years had also been different. WEH, more teacher-led and with written-only exams, suffered from low in-class participation, while attainment was only average because content treatment on the part of students was usually superficial. Problems in WE, which aimed at being more participative, revolved around the linguistic quality of student responses, their lack of oral ability and a corresponding low attainment in both oral and written answers requiring a degree of linguistic complexity. These differences led to the use of an array of techniques (see Table 1).

Table 1. Outline of methodology for each module

Methodology	WEH	WE
Method of instruction	Teacher-centred lectures, content-based	Student-centred seminars, skills-based
Instructor	1 Senior lecturer	Team teaching (1 senior lecturer, 1 English-native lecturer)
Expected student interaction	Low, occasional, extended commentary, reflection-oriented	High, frequent, brief comment, task-oriented
Blended Learning	Pre-session, preparatory materials	Post-session, exploratory resources
Skills practice and student participation	Out-of-class, online asynchronous and individual	In-class, online synchronous group follow-up
Social networks	Twitter-based topic-centred discussions, m-learning	In-class face-to-face workshops and group debates
English support	Online tutorials on demand	In-class tutorials and online PLEs

Although a frequent shortcoming (Rienties et al., 2012), we have aimed at making ICT choice and pedagogical approach cohere. Deliberately, non-ICT and an ICT-enhanced method or their usages are contrasted, so that results are differentiated.

Also, synchronous and asynchronous learning is combined to support learners more widely. Thus, lectures are confronted to seminars and single-teaching to team-teaching, but also the educational sequence and the role of ICT-powered learning is differentiated. Also, synchronous and asynchronous learning is combined to support learners more widely, offering a model answer to the "open question" of "how to best design online learning with a blend of synchronous and asynchronous communication opportunities over time" (Giesbers, Rienties, Tempelaar, & Gijselaers, 2014, p. 30).

In WEH, interventions are pre-session, except Twitter-based discussions and online tutorials. In WE, the focus is in-session and post-session, aiming at improving the quality of students' responses. These students were closely monitored to observe their evolution in both content (grades) and language (CEFR). Students self-graded their progress using a standardised survey (Jimenez-Muñoz, 2014), and also evaluated other aspects (Table 2).

Table 2. Student evaluation for each aspect of the module (1-5 LIKERT)

Methodology	Evaluation (WEH)	Impact on learning (WEH)	Evaluation (WE)	Impact on learning (WE)
Method of instruction	3.7	3.6	4.2	4.1
Instructor	3.3	3.4	4.6	4.8
Expected student interaction	2.7	2.2	4.1	3.9
Blended Learning	4.6	4.3	3.7	3.4
Skills practice and student participation	4.5	4.5	4.8	4.7
Social networks	4.8	4.4	4.4	4.3
English support	4.2	4.1	4.6	4.4

The divide between hands-on and non-participatory methods of instruction, as well among ICT-enhanced and non-ICT instruction seems evident from student responses. Those implementations promoting student participation and interaction, as well as those involving the use of technology, fare better in student evaluation. However, a better valuation of face-to-face over online learning is also noticeable, which contrasts with academic results (Lopez-

Zapico & Tascon-Fernandez, 2013). The key question was, however, whether that motivational gauge showed a tangible link to academic results and whether students' assessment could predict the influence of those interventions on their final academic achievement for these modules.

3. Results and conclusions

Comparing outcomes with those of previous years, a marked improvement in student grades was evident for EMI students (Table 3). In a reversal of roles, EMI students outperformed SMI students. The EMI cohort yields progress, while the SMI cohort shows a slight regression, unearthing common prejudice against EMI modules as groundless.

Table 3. Module results – pass rate (average grade)

Year	WEH (SMI)	WEH (EMI)	WE (SMI)	WE (EMI)
2010-2011	88.2 (69%)	83.4 (61%)	66.1 (68%)	60.6 (63%)
2011-2012	89.7 (72%)	76.7 (58%)	64.9 (65%)	44.9 (56%)
2012-2013	85.3 (65%)	94.9 (78%)	54.9 (64%)	78.9 (69%)
Variance after interventions	-3.7 (-6.1%)	+14.9 (+18.5%)	-1.1 (-2.5%)	+26.2 (+9.5%)

With regard to those ICT-mediated interventions specifically, students who used these frequently achieve higher grades (except online English-language tutorials for students who did not need them frequently); in some cases, heavy users of English tutorials were those who also ranked lowest (Table 4).

Table 4. Average grades for WEH students per usage

Usage	Online preparatory reading	Online preparatory activities	Twitter-based debates	English online tutorials
Very low	52%	59%	51%	73%
Occasional	64%	61%	55%	80%
Frequent	88%	82%	78%	65%
Daily	91%	89%	92%	-

In WE, however, heavy users achieve better grades, with no significant variation among content and language usage. It points to high levels of motivation rather than focusing on remedial language support (Table 5).

Table 5. Average grades for WE students per usage

Online usage	Expansion activities	Language-centred tools
Very low	48%	47%
Occasional	55%	57%
Frequent	63%	67%
Daily	78%	80%

Attributing student success to the method of delivery and instruction should always be tentative. From these academic results, the impact of these interventions on student performance seems evident, but it seems also clear that all pedagogical modifications to instructional design played a role in success.

Despite the various uses these systems can offer, a single form of ICT-enhanced learning, synchronous or not, would only cater for a number of learning styles. Also, linking the student groups per technology (Table 4 and Table 5) to the results of the subjective evaluation of those technologies (Table 2) shows that students give prominence to ICT-enhanced tasks, which is coherent with recent findings on motivation (Tempelaar et al., 2012). However, the direct impact on their learning is not different from other non-technological interventions, nor is there a clear divide between these in terms of excellence and achievement.

Consequently, this research shows that a holistic method, one which combines varied pedagogically-geared ICT with face-to-face educational practices, can not only remedy, but maximise students' chances of achievement. Conversely, it shows that without these remedial interventions being performed (for which ICT is key), the long-term prosperity of bilingual programmes and their benefits are severely compromised against those degrees taught entirely through a native language.

References

Airey, J. (2013). "I don't teach language." The linguistic attitudes of physics lecturers in Sweden. *AILA Review, 25*(1), 64-79. Retrieved from http://dx.doi.org/10.1075/aila.25.05air

Bonnet, A. (2012). Towards an evidence base for CLIL. *International CLIL Research Journal, 1*(4), 65-78.

Clegg, J. (2001). Towards successful English-medium education in Southern Africa. In D. Marsh, A. Ontero, & Tautiko Shikongo (Eds.), *Enhancing English-medium education in Namibia* (pp. 11-13). University of Jyväskylä and Ongwediva, College of Education, Jyväskylä.

Costa, F., & Coleman, J. A. (2010). Integrating content and language in higher education in Italy: ongoing research. *International CLIL Research Journal, 1*(3), 19-29.

Cots, J. M. (2012). Introducing English-medium instruction at the university of Lleida, Spain: intervention beliefs and practices. In A. Doiz, D. Lasagabaster, & J. M. Sierra (Eds.), *English-medium instruction at universities. Global challenges*. Multilingual Matters.

Council of Europe. (2001). *The common European framework of reference for languages: learning, teaching, assessment*. Cambridge: Cambridge University Press.

Doiz, A., Lasagabaster, D., & Sierra, J. M. (2011). Internationalisation, multilingualism and EMI. *World Englishes, 30*(3), 345-359. Retrieved from http://dx.doi.org/10.1111/j.1467-971X.2011.01718.x

Erling, E., & Hilgendorf, S. (2006). Language policies in the context of German higher education. *Language Policy, 5*(3), 267-293. Retrieved from http://dx.doi.org/10.1007/s10993-006-9026-3

Giesbers, B., Rienties, B., Tempelaar, D., & Gijselaers, W. (2014). A dynamic analysis of the interplay between asynchronous and synchronous communication in online learning: the impact of motivation. *Journal of Computer Assisted Learning, 30*(1), 30-50. Retrieved from http://dx.doi.org/10.1111/jcal.12020

Hernandez-Nanclares, N., & Jimenez-Munoz, A. (2015). English as a medium of instruction: evidence for language and content targets in bilingual education in Economics. *International Journal of Bilingual Education and Bilingualism*. Retieved from http://dx.doi.org/10.1080/13670050.2015.1125847

Jenkins, J., Cogo, A., & Dewey, M. (2011). Review of developments in research into English as a Lingua Franca. *Language Teaching, 44*(3), 281-315. Retrieved from http://dx.doi.org/10.1017/S0261444811000115

Jimenez-Munoz, A. (2014). Measuring the impact of CLIL on language skills: a CEFR-based approach for HE. *Language Value, 6*(1), 28-50.

Lopez-Zapico, M. A., & Tascon-Fernandez, J. (2013). El uso de twitter como herramienta para la enseñanza universitaria. *Teoría de la Educación: Educación y Cultura en la Sociedad de la Información, 14*(2), 316-345.

Rienties, B., Brouwer, N., & Lygo-Baker, S. (2013). The effects of online professional development on higher education teachers' beliefs and intentions towards learning facilitation and technology. *Teaching and Teacher Education, 29*, 122-131. Retrieved from http://dx.doi.org/10.1016/j.tate.2012.09.002

Rienties, B., Kaper, W., Struyven, K., Tempelaar, D. T., Van Gastel, L., Vrancken, S., et al. (2012). A review of the role of ICT and course design in transitional education practices. *Interactive Learning Environments, 20*(6), 563-581. Retrieved from http://dx.doi.org/10.1080/10494820.2010.542757

Smit, U., & Dafouz, E. (2012). Integrating content and language in higher education. An introduction to English-medium policies, conceptual issues and research practices across Europe. *AILA Review, 25*(1), 1-12. Retrieved from http://dx.doi.org/10.1075/aila.25.01smi

Tempelaar, D. T., Niculescu, A., Rienties, B., Giesbers, B., & Gijselaers, W. H. (2012). How achievement emotions impact students' decisions for online learning, and what precedes those emotions. *Internet and Higher Education, 15*(3), 161-169. Retrieved from http://dx.doi.org/10.1016/j.iheduc.2011.10.003

Wächter, B., & Maiworm, F. (2008). *English-taught programmes in European higher education. The picture in 2007.* Bonn: Lemmens, ACA Papers on International Cooperation in Education.

23 Vocabulary Notebook: a digital solution to general and specific vocabulary learning problems in a CLIL context

Plácido Bazo[1], Romén Rodríguez[2], and Dácil Fumero[3]

Abstract

In this paper, we will introduce an innovative software platform that can be especially useful in a Content and Language Integrated Learning (CLIL) context. This tool is called Vocabulary Notebook, and has been developed to solve all the problems that traditional (paper) vocabulary notebooks have. This tool keeps focus on the personalisation of the learning process as a key element, but it also provides the advantages of technology, solving paper-related problems and providing additional multimedia features. Moreover, we will describe the current state-of-the-art in the implementation of CLIL (using Spain as an example) and afterwards we will discuss the benefits that this digital tool provides in a CLIL context. Nowadays, teachers are worried because they devote too much time to the teaching of CLIL vocabulary and not to the application of those words in social tasks, which are a way of consolidating knowledge and key competences at the same time. With Vocabulary Notebook, we will show how this problem can be tackled in a very successful way. Vocabulary Notebook is currently being used for educational purposes in more than 127 countries by more than 17,000 individuals, as well as several educational institutions around the globe.

Keywords: vocabulary, CLIL, MALL, educational software, key competences, personalisation, formative assessment.

---

1. University of La Laguna, La Laguna, Spain; pbazom@ull.edu.es

2. Langproving, S. C. Tenerife, Spain; romen@langproving.com

3. Consejería de Educación, S. C. Tenerife, Spain; fumero.dacil@gmail.com

How to cite this chapter: Bazo, P., & Rodríguez, R., & Fumero, D. (2016). Vocabulary Notebook: a digital solution to general and specific vocabulary learning problems in a CLIL context. In A. Pareja-Lora, C. Calle-Martínez, & P. Rodríguez-Arancón (Eds), *New perspectives on teaching and working with languages in the digital era* (pp. 269-279). Dublin: Research-publishing.net. http://dx.doi.org/10.14705/rpnet.2016.tislid2014.440

Chapter 23

1. Introduction

Traditionally, paper notebooks have been used by students to create personalised vocabulary lists. Teachers have usually encouraged students to add their own definition and sample sentences to the terms. As reported by Walters (2009), "[v]ocabulary notebooks are frequently suggested as effective tools for students to use, to take charge of, organise and manage their vocabulary learning" (p. 112, see also Fowle, 2002; Schmitt & Schmitt, 1995). We reckon that this is so with CLIL vocabulary too. In the digital era, we propose that the old paper vocabulary notebooks evolve into a technological tool.

This paper deals with the use of a commercial platform called Vocabulary Notebook that is currently being used for educational purposes by individuals as well as educational institutions around the globe.

With Vocabulary Notebook, students can review and edit their personal vocabulary everywhere and using any device (smartphones, tablets or PCs); all devices are synchronised at all times, with their vocabulary safe in the cloud. Moreover, special teacher features are provided for educational institutions. These features for teachers provide useful metrics that allow them to successfully guide students during the learning process, facilitating their vocabulary acquisition and even facilitating formative assessment, thanks to the feedback about students' habits and interests provided by the tool.

When applied to a CLIL context, Vocabulary Notebook can help teachers reduce the excessive time that is usually dedicated to teaching specific vocabulary in class. This is often caused by the lack of students' organisation during the vocabulary acquisition process. By means of this platform, students are able to keep an organised and personal glossary of the new terms they learn, facilitating autonomous study. This approach leads to an improved retention of the vocabulary, saving time in class. Thereby, teachers are able to devote this extra time to the application of the vocabulary in practical activities that can lead to a better understanding and a productive learning of the concepts, such as in the case of social tasks.

2. Vocabulary Notebook

This software platform represents a digital vocabulary notebook. It is designed to help students to improve their vocabulary by replacing the traditional paper notebooks. This tech tool includes not only native mobile apps for both Android and iOS, but also provides a web application with cloud storage that offers extended functionality, including more types of tests and special features for teachers.

2.1. Students

Vocabulary Notebook keeps the focus on the personalisation of the learning process as a key element of vocabulary acquisition. However, apart from keeping this principle – that was also present in the traditional approach represented by paper notebooks – the proposed platform also enhances functionality by providing the benefits of technology, such as multimedia features, automatic backups, ubiquity, easy editions, advanced filtering options for studying and several self-assessment tests to make study more pleasant.

At first, Vocabulary Notebook looks like a blank notebook that allows students to write down the new words they learn – as easily as they would do it in traditional notebooks – allowing them to include several optional fields, such as sample sentences, translations or definitions. Later on, students will be able to comfortably review their vocabulary, using many features that make studying easier, such as sorting words alphabetically, reviewing vocabulary by importance or categories, searching within the list of words, etc. as well as doing self-assessment tests or listening to the right pronunciation of the words.

Additional optional fields and marks for the vocabulary are provided by the platform, such as the dichotomy fields 'known/not-known' and 'important/not-important', that are used as pre-built categories to tag words. The former field ('known/not-known') is automatically updated when students do a test. The terms in which the student has failed are automatically marked as not-known and the terms that have correctly been used in the tests are marked as 'known'.

That being said, it is important to mention that students can change these fields at any moment and that they can even create custom categories such as 'very important' or 'partially known' to group their vocabulary in a more specific way.

The main advantage of Vocabulary Notebook is that it solves paper-related problems such as space and edition issues, limited number of pages, difficulties when sorting words alphabetically or reviewing vocabulary by categories, etc. Thus, Vocabulary Notebook becomes a close and comfortable/convenient tool to keep our personal vocabulary in. Moreover, the additional technological features represent a clear advantage in comparison to paper alternatives. In addition, students do not have to carry heavy and uncomfortable notebooks anymore (Roda, Rodríguez, & López, 2014).

One of the most interesting features is the ability to group words by topics/categories that are customised by the student (Figure 1). This feature allows them to filter the list while studying; being able to review only the words they want, such as the unknown words, the words within the category 'Science' or the important words in the category 'Maths'.

Figure 1. Main section of Vocabulary Notebook for iOS: the list of terms

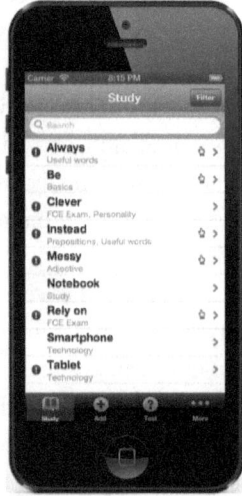

Through the web application (Figure 2), students can access additional features, such as five different types of tests (e.g. matching words with their corresponding definitions or selecting the right word from 3 options), that extend the functionality provided in the mobile apps. All these tests use the student's knowledge base, that is, their own vocabulary notebook. Furthermore, in the web application, additional sorting features are provided (most recent first, from A to Z, Z to A, etc.). Moreover, student-teacher interaction takes place through the web application, saving time during lessons at school. Thus, the suggestions for new words that teachers can send to students can be received by them through the web application at home.

Figure 2.   Web application interface for students

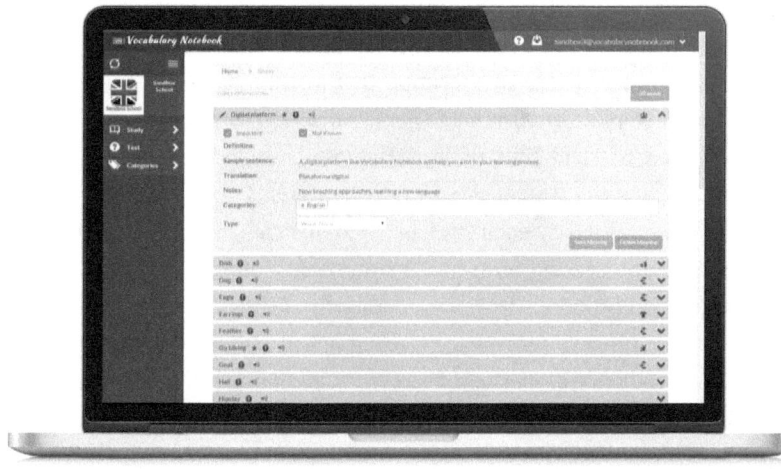

It is important to mention that the interaction that self-assessment tests provide offers a more enjoyable way for students to review vocabulary, since it has a gaming component. In the near future, additional gamification features will be added to the tool, including badges and symbolic awards that will be obtained by students when achieving different milestones in their learning process. Moreover, an image field for each term will be included too, which is specially interesting for younger students.

2.2. Teacher's dashboard

As mentioned above, the web application also includes special tools for teachers. These features allow them to organise their classes better and more efficiently, and to help their students learn vocabulary faster, as well as to increase students' motivation.

Teachers can organise students in groups through the platform. The most common organisation is by level. This organisation allows teachers to obtain valuable feedback about each specific group, as well as send specific suggestions according to the level of each group.

As mentioned above, among other features, the teacher's account includes the option of sending lists of vocabulary to the different groups of students he/she has. This feature is particularly interesting when a teacher wants to make sure that students are aware of the important vocabulary of a specific lesson. However, since the platform promotes personalisation as a key element, teachers are only allowed to send lists of important/recommended terms to students, but definitions, sample sentences and all other fields of each term should be personal, and thus added by each student. Students can also decide whether they want to include a suggested term in their personal notebooks or not, as part of the personalisation process. However, among the feedback information offered to teachers, the number of terms each student has accepted from the suggestions that have been sent to him/her can be seen. We consider this information very useful to bring teachers closer to students and promote communication between the parties.

Additionally, the tool for teachers displays a great amount of additional information about the usage their students make of their digital Vocabulary Notebook, which makes formative assessment much easier to implement, since the real needs and interests of the students are shown on the dashboard. Teachers can see the words their students mark as 'not known' to review them in class later; they can also see the words that students consider important, or the topics/categories most used by them. This latter information shows the interest of students and allows teachers to gear their classes to those topics. A few additional individual stats are shown, such as the number of words each student has, the number of logins he/she does and the number of self-assessment tests each student has performed.

By analysing the data that are collected and displayed in the teacher dashboard, not only about the groups but also about the individual students, teachers can save a considerable amount of time in detecting their real needs and difficulties. Moreover and most importantly, effective actions and activities to solve those problems can be prepared carefully and be carried out in class at an early stage, thus preventing a loss of students' attention and interest. Since these actions can be performed either in group or individually – allowing curricular adaptation – these actions can be very effective to engage students in the learning process.

This feedback tool for teachers contributes greatly to the role of the teacher as a facilitator, and if teachers perform the right corrective actions based on the data provided, a substantially better outcome can be achieved when it comes to vocabulary acquisition (Figure 3).

Figure 3.   Teacher dashboard through the web application

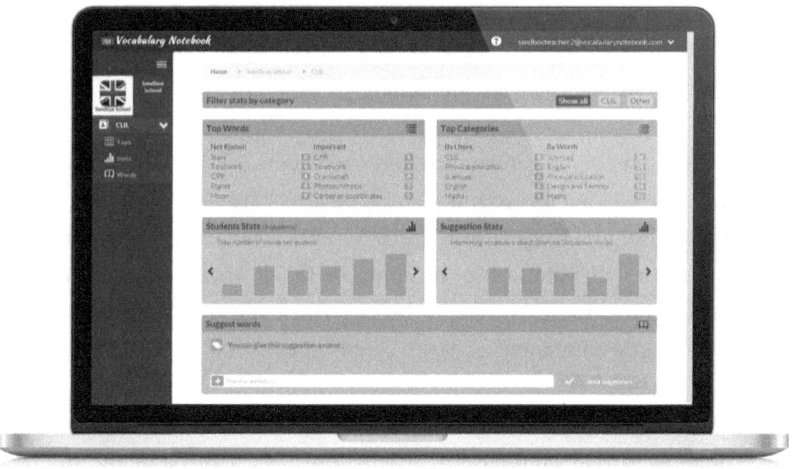

3. CLIL

Vocabulary learning is a very important process in the acquisition of a foreign language. As Wilkins (1972) stated: "[w]ithout grammar very little can be conveyed, without vocabulary nothing can be conveyed" (pp. 111-112).

Most learners of English acknowledge the importance of vocabulary learning; however, vocabulary teaching has not always been responsive to that problem. It is only in recent years that vocabulary teaching and research on vocabulary teaching and learning has emerged as an important field of study.

In the last decade, many Spanish schools have incorporated CLIL to the curriculum. CLIL is a dual-focused educational approach where a foreign language is used for both the teaching of that foreign language and of another subject of the school curriculum. CLIL has proved to be useful because of its transferability not only across countries but also across different types of schools. The term CLIL was adopted in 1994 (mentioned in Marsh, Maljers, & Hartalia, 2001), and it tries to define good practice in schools where another language is used to teach content. Marsch, Enner and Sigmund (1999) stated that

> "[t]eachers have found that content and language integrated learning is about far more than simply teaching non [subject language matters] in an additional language in the same way as the mother tongue [... is] not a matter of simply changing the language of instruction" (p. 17).

Nevertheless, in many Spanish schools, problems with specific vocabulary have arisen as it has been recognised by Dobson, Pérez Murilo, and Johnstone (2010) in the Bilingual Project evaluation report. Teachers are worried because they devote too much time to the teaching of CLIL vocabulary and not to the application of those words in social tasks, which are a way of consolidating knowledge and key competences at the same time.

Deep learning nowadays involves retention of concepts that can be used to solve problems in real contexts. Learners must learn through the interaction of perception and action. They must see learning as a continuous construction process in a social context. They must be aware of the interaction of the body, mind, emotions and reasoning, and that knowledge is constructed in a social and emotional way. In the 21st Century, we need citizens who can analyse and diagnose complex situations, who can act in flexible, sensible and creative ways and can reflect thoughtfully and formulate proposals accordingly. They need to live in a democracy in heterogeneous human groups and act autonomously and constructively to fulfil their life goals.

This implies a methodology where students fulfil very time-consuming tasks leaving very little time to specific CLIL vocabulary. These tasks are related to the key competences which understand teaching and learning in a different way from the traditional point of view. Teaching is seen as research, and it must integrate learning and experience (sense and significance). Learners must personalise their learning (metacognition and self-regulated learning with cooperation and empathy) and they must acknowledge the purpose and value of digital products.

4. Vocabulary Notebook and CLIL

With Vocabulary Notebook, the problem of teaching CLIL vocabulary can be tackled in a very successful way.

As we have shown in the previous section of this paper, with Vocabulary Notebook, learners can move their CLIL specific vocabulary to the cloud, being able to use this web application through any device, from iOS and Android smart phones/tablets to any computer. This tool allows students to write down all the new vocabulary they learn, with personalised definitions, translations, sample sentences, categories of their choice, and many other fields and marks (such as known, important, etc.), as they do with paper notebooks. However, with this tool, students can also sort their vocabulary from A-Z and review vocabulary by knowledge or categories. They can do self-assessment tests or even listen to the right pronunciation of the words. It saves time for teachers and learners, and they can always have the tool at hand to solve the questions that arise while performing social tasks. It also provides them with long-term retention of those CLIL concepts so that they can later use them for problem solving in unfamiliar contexts outside the school. Consequently, CLIL vocabulary becomes meaningful; students use it in tasks instead of keeping endless lists of vocabulary they never practise.

Vocabulary Notebook can also be associated to the key competencies (linguistic, digital, social and civic, autonomy and entrepreneurship, and learning to learn). This tool is a very important help for the shift that the digital era is producing in teaching and learning; that is, to move from a curriculum based on areas of study to a curriculum based on problems or situations (Pérez, 2013).

5. Conclusion

Our research has proved that by using the application Vocabulary Notebook, the students were able to tackle the problem of incorporating specialised vocabulary derived from the use of CLIL in their classes. The tool proved to be an important element in the incorporation of vocabulary and development of 'learning to learn' and digital competences. Both students and teachers were very satisfied with the results.

References

Dobson, A., Pérez Murilo, M. D., & Johnstone, R. (2010). *Bilingual education project Spain: evaluation report.* British Council/Ministerio de Educación (IFIIE).

Fowle, C. (2002). Vocabulary notebooks: implementation and outcomes. *ELT Journal,56*(4), 380-388. Retrieved from http://dx.doi.org/10.1093/elt/56.4.380

Marsch, D., Ennser, C., & Sygmund, D. (1999). *Pursuing plurilingualism.* Jyväskylä: University of Jyväskilä.

Marsh, D., Maljers, A., & Hartalia, A-K. (2001). *Profiling European CLIL classrooms.* Jyväskylä: University of Jyväskylä.

Pérez, A. (2013). *Educarse en la Era Digital.* Madrid: Ediciones Morata S.L.

Roda, J. L., Rodríguez, R., & López, A. F. (2014). A Process and a tool to assess vocabulary learning for computer science engineers. *IEEE Global Engineering Education Conference, Istanbul* (pp. 659-666).

Schmitt, N., & Schmitt, D. (1995). Vocabulary notebooks: theoretical underpinnings and practical implications. *ELT Journal, 49*(2), 133-143. Retrieved from http://dx.doi.org/10.1093/elt/49.2.133

Walters, J. (2009). The effect of keeping vocabulary notebooks on vocabulary acquisition. *Language Teaching Research, 13*(4), 403-423. Retrieved from http://dx.doi.org/10.1177/1362168809341509

Wilkins, D. (1972). *Linguistics in language teaching*. London: Arnold.

Section 2.3.

Computerised language testing and assessment

24 Using tablet PC's for the final test of Baccalaureate

Jesús García Laborda[1] and Teresa Magal Royo[2]

Abstract

Online testing is becoming a popular way to deliver language tests, partly because of its reduced cost, partly because of the high quality of test data collection. In language tests, interface validation has received a limited attention in professional literature (García, Magal, da Rocha, & Fernández, 2010). This paper will show the validation process of the OPENPAU application, which aims at language testing exam delivery through an attitudinal study. The real importance of this project is that it offers reliable solutions at a low cost for the needs of a nationally delivered online test that can serve to assess all the traditional language skills (namely speaking, listening, reading and writing) in an efficient, simple and cost-effective manner. Our paper presents the design, development, and evaluation of a tablet PC software application for assessing both productive and receptive skills in foreign languages for its prospective use in the Final Test of Baccalaureate. The software development has been carried out within the OPENPAU project (FFI2011-22442), funded by the Ministry of Economy and Competitiveness.

Keywords: computer system design, computer software, usability, computer assisted testing, internet, computer software evaluation, educational technology.

---

1. Universidad de Alcalá, Alcalá de Henares, Madrid, Spain; jesus.garcialaborda@uah.es

2. Universitat Politècnica de València, Valencia, Spain; tmagal@degi.upv.es

How to cite this chapter: García Laborda, J., & Magal Royo, T. (2016). Using tablet PC's for the final test of Baccalaureate. In A. Pareja-Lora, C. Calle-Martínez, & P. Rodríguez-Arancón (Eds), *New perspectives on teaching and working with languages in the digital era* (pp. 283-292). Dublin: Research-publishing.net. http://dx.doi.org/10.14705/rpnet.2016.tislid2014.441

Chapter 24

1. Introduction

The English section of the University Entrance Examination (PAU) is a challenge in Spain even today. A number of projects and studies have intended to show some of its main assets and pitfalls. Fernández and Sanz (2005) probably did one of the best diachronic studies on the topic. Their paper reflected many of the different sound research articles that it included. Whittaker (2006) mentioned that there are some historical reasons why the foreign language paper was included in the PAU. It is also clear that the revision of the Foreign Language section of the University Entrance Examination seems totally necessary.

In 2009, the Ministry of Education suggested the introduction of a number of tasks by 2011. In that year, the Ministry of Education, Culture and Sports decided to postpone those changes to 2013 and later the LOMCE was passed and finally the exam will disappear in 2017 (Ministry of Education, Culture & Sports, 2013). However, despite the experts' opinions, as years go by, it is also self-evident that the different national and regional governments have no interest to improve an old fashioned test that can hardly provide any information on the student's competence (Amengual, 2005, 2006; García, 2010, 2012). It does not matter whether newer ideas have been provided to increase the validity of the test. In this sense, a few years ago Catalunya began to deliver the listening comprehension tasks, later Galicia did the same. Very few studies, however, have addressed whether this change has actually had any impact in the classroom (Wall, 2000). What certainly seems true is that the level required to Catalan students is higher than that demanded of the rest of the Spanish students. Thus, maybe the inclusion of certain tasks has the power to change the educational approach in language testing (Alderson & Wall, 1996; Wall, 2005).

2. Literature review

The effect of tests has been long documented in professional literature (Knudson, 1975; Kohonen & Nummenmaa, 1976; Messick, 1996; Pimsleur,

1975; Shohamy, 1992 – among many others). The concern in these papers was on the negative effects on teaching by jeopardising language learning to give ground for test scores and accountability. In 1989, Hughes defined backwash as "[t]he effect of testing on teaching and learning" (p. 1). Spolsky (1994) considers that backwash relates to the side-effects of testing in the classroom. One of the first documented changes introduced by positive washback is described by Wall (2005), who performed a total change in education in Sri Lanka in accordance to a totally new high school leaving exam. This experience helped to create a positive construct by Alderson and Wall (1993). According to Weir (2005), this construct does not just include the task rubrics, but a much larger set of variables and conditions in which the way of delivery has a significant role (Figure 1).

According to Weir (2005), all the factors included in the context validity group may have a potential effect in changing the results of a test. The theory also states that the use of different means of delivery, however, should have a minimal effect in the final score. Indeed, the documented number of learning experiences on the use of tablet PC limits the capacity to discern whether they have a potential positive or negative affect (Chapelle, 2001). According to van Oostveen, Muirhead, and Goodman (2011), there is little evidence to support that comfort and familiarity with a tablet PC or iPad. For them, "[i]t is important to note that the introduction of a new technology, even if it makes a wide variety of affordances available for use, cannot by itself instigate redefinition of learning tasks to allow for meaningful learning to occur" (van Oostveen et al., 2011, p. 78). However, Crichton, Pegler, and White (2012) consider that the use of a tablet PC requires the familiarisation with the purpose of use as well as with the new educational technology. This also means that although students might be familiarised with the use of mobile technology for leisure and social networking, its use for educational purposes (especially for testing) may seem unusual or even odd for them. Similar results are found by Waters (2010), who considers that iPads may be way behind in usability versus netbooks or even laptops, especially in writing (Sullivan, 2013). Although some of these studies remark the idea of students' limitations to use traditional tablets, up to now, no studies have addressed the use of tablets with an external keyboard.

Figure 1. Theoretical framework of the OPENPAU project (based on García, Magal, Litzler, & Giménez, 2014 and Weir, 2005)

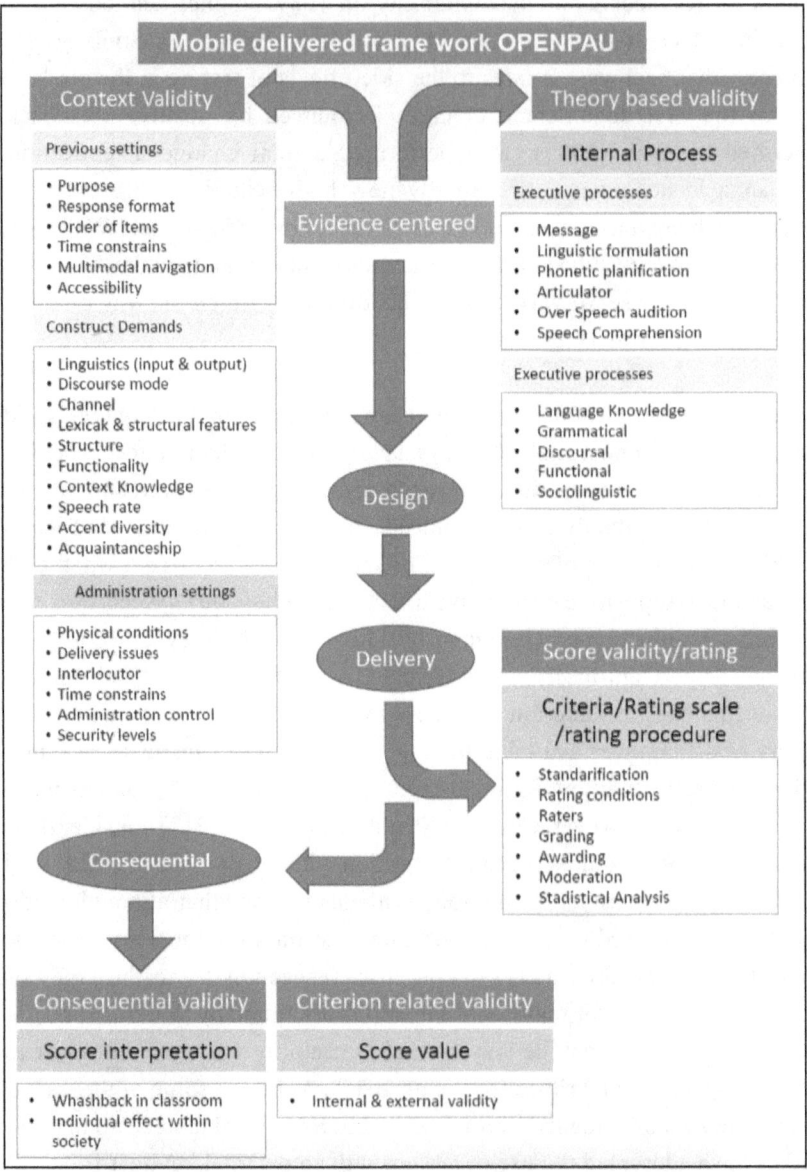

As for their use in testing, there are very few. For instance, Siozos, Palaigeorgiou, Triantafyllakos, & Despotakis (2009) said that the use of tablets in their experiment in secondary education proved their validity. On the contrary, in one of the most interesting papers on the topic, Schaffhauser (2012) states that it is necessary to consider "the challenges of security, usability, and content that might arise when students are taking tests on tablet devices and discussing how these might be resolved" before sound high stakes exams can be delivered by tablet or iPad (p. 16).

3. Methodology

In order to observe the degree of satisfaction of using a tablet PC as a delivery system for the University Entrance Examination, an online questionnaire was delivered to 31 first year university students at Universidad Politécnica de Valencia in January 2014, with a primary version of the OPENPAU prototype of tablet-delivered online test. The test is intended to be taken with 10 inch tablets with a Windows 8 environment (see Figure 2).

Figure 2. Student taking the tablet-based language test through the OPENPAU application

4. Results

The questionnaire revolved around three main items.

1) Considero que los exámenes on-line de la aplicación OPENPAU son útiles (I consider that the online tests delivered through the OPENPAU application are useful). The results indicated that students were mostly sceptical towards the use of this type of test (Figure 3). This response can be due to the lack of previous experience. Low-stakes tests are not usually delivered online, and the only high-stakes that most students may have had to take in their school life in Spain is the PAU, which obviously is not computer-based. As a consequence, many may feel strange when taking an online foreign language test. Another issue could be their own attitude towards how foreign languages should be assessed. A third reason for this response would be the lack of specific preparation and skills to take such tests despite its user-friendly design and usability.

Figure 3. Response to 'I consider that the online tests delivered through the OPENPAU application are useful'

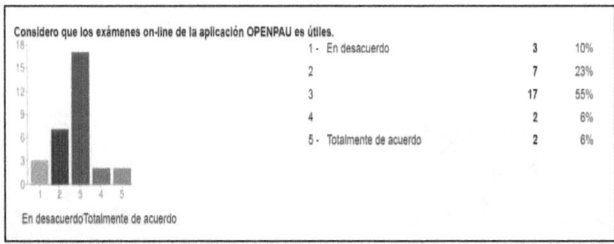

2) Tengo la sensación de control de los exámenes online de la aplicación OPENPAU (I have the sensation of control of the online tests of the OPENPAU application). The responses to this item indicate the same tendency as in the previous item (Figure 4). The most evident indication is that there is a great number of undetermined responses and a slight tendency towards a negative feeling of control. Test taker training may be the key issue in this case. It is important to note that participants in this research had never had any contact with the application before. Thus, their negative responses could have been expected.

Figure 4. Response to 'I have the sensation of control of the online tests of the OPENPAU application'

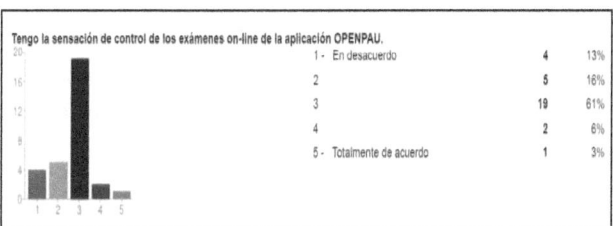

3) Considero que los exámenes online son útiles para mejorar mis conocimientos y competencias de un idioma (I consider that online tests are useful to improve my knowledge and competence in the language). Item 3 may contrast with Item 1, since students were more positive towards using tests than to the platform. However, although the results are slightly better, no significant conclusions could be drawn. As in the two items before, the largest response was the subjects' inability to take a position and the central tendency was the largest response (Figure 5).

Figure 5. Response to 'I consider that online tests are useful to improve my knowledge and competence in the language'

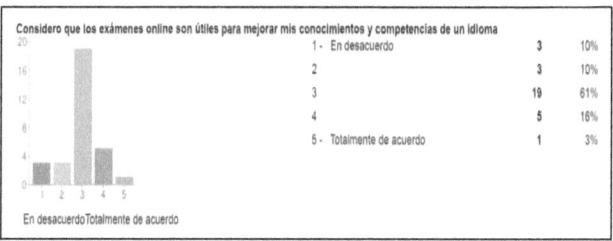

5. Conclusions

Although the results of this short study did not evidence the interest of the students in this application, given the current tendency of research in the use of tablets for education, we consider it of high interest at a national level to continue with the current research. This work is just a first approach towards this issue but, as indicated by Item 3, if the adequate conditions are present, students could be receptive to tablet-based language tests and recognise the value of online-delivered language tests. In this sense, given the current state of affairs in contemporary education, it would be interesting to study responses to similar studies in a few years. Besides, further studies should focus on the other stakeholders' (teachers, administrators, educational boards and so) attitudes towards the implementation of this delivery system. Additional studies should study the impact of training on the new tasks, the presence of underdeveloped skills (especially speaking) in instruction and organisation, and administration issues.

This paper provided the theoretical framework and a very brief description of the OPENPAU tool. Further publications will provide more detailed information on the importance for ubiquitous language learning through training, advantages of mobile based-testing, and types of semi-assisted speaking interaction with tablet-based delivery. The use of tablets in the Final Test of Baccalaureate will depend to a large extent on budgets and the whole framework of this exam in the future. At this point, our hopes are high, but only time will tell.

6. Acknowledgements

The researchers would like to express their gratitude to the Ministry of Economy and Competitiveness (MINECO), with co-founding with ERDF funds under the 2008-2011 plan, for supporting the development and implementation of the OPENPAU project (MINECO FFI2011-22442).

References

Alderson, C., & Wall, D. (1993). Does washback exist? *Applied Linguistics, 14*(2), 115-129. Retrieved from http://dx.doi.org/10.1093/applin/14.2.115

Alderson, J. C., & Wall, D. (1996). Examining washback: the Sri Lankan impact study. In A. Cumming & R. Berwick (Eds.), *Validation in language testing*. Clevedon, England: Multilingual Matters.

Amengual, M. (2005). Posibles sesgos en el examen de Selectividad. In H. Herrera Soler & J. García Laborda (Eds.), *Estudios y Criterios para una evaluación de calidad* (pp. 121-148). Valencia: Universidad Politécnica de Valencia.

Amengual, M. (2006). Análisis de la prueba de inglés de Selectividad de la Universitat de les Illes Balears. *Ibérica, 11*, 29-59.

Chapelle, C. A. (2001). *Computer applications in second language acquisition*. Cambridge: Cambridge University Press. Retrieved from http://dx.doi.org/10.1017/CBO9781139524681

Crichton, S., Pegler, K., & White, D. (2012). Personal devices in public settings: lessons learned from an iPod Touch/iPad project. *Electronic Journal of e-Learning, 10*(1), 23-31.

Fernández, M., & Sanz, I. (2005). Breve historia del examen de Selectividad. In H. Herrera Soler & J. García Laborda (Eds.), *Estudios y criterios para una Selectividad de calidad en el examen de Inglés* (pp. 19-26). Valencia: Editorial Universidad Politécnica de Valencia.

García, J. (2010). ¿Necesitan las universidades españolas una prueba de acceso informatizada? El caso de la definición del constructo y la previsión del efecto en la enseñanza para idiomas extranjeros. *Revista de orientación y Psicopadagogía, 21*(1),71-80.

García, J. (2012). De la Selectividad a la Prueba de Acceso a la Universidad: Pasado, presente y un futuro no muy lejano. *Revista de Educación, 357*, 17-28.

García, J., Magal, T., da Rocha, J. M., & Fernández, M. (2010). Ergonomics factors in English as a foreign language testing: The case of PLEVALEX. *Computers & Education, 54*(2), 384-391. Retrieved from http://dx.doi.org/10.1016/j.compedu.2009.08.021

García, J., Magal, T., Litzler, M. F., & Giménez, J. L. (2014). Mobile phones for a University Entrance Examination language test in Spain. *Educational Technology & Society, 17*(2), 17-30.

Hughes, A. (1989). *Testing for language teachers*. Cambridge and New York: Cambridge University Press.

Knudson, R. L. (1975). Emphasis: use and misuse of standardized testing. *The English Record, 26(2)*, 114.

Kohonen, V., & Nummenmaa, L. (Eds.). (1976). Special issue on teaching and testing communicative competence. *Language centre news, 4*.

Messick, S. (1996). Validity and washback in language testing. *Language Testing, 13*(3), 241-256. Retrieved from http://dx.doi.org/10.1177/026553229601300302

Ministry of Education, Culture & Sports. (2013). *Ley Orgánica 8/2013, de 9 de diciembre, para la mejora de la calidad educative* (p. 97858-97921). Madrid, Spain: Boletín Oficial del Estado. Retrieved from https://www.boe.es/boe/dias/2013/12/10/pdfs/BOE-A-2013-12886.pdf

Pimsleur, P. (1975). Criterion vs. norm-referenced testing. *Language Association Bulletin, 27*(1), 21-24.

Schaffhauser, D. (2012). You may now open your test tablets. *T.H.E.Journal, 39*(7), 16-23.

Shohamy, E. (1992). Beyond performance testing: a diagnostic feedback testing model for assessing foreign language learning. *The Modern Language Journal, 76*(4), 513-521. Retrieved from http://dx.doi.org/10.1111/j.1540-4781.1992.tb05402.x

Siozos, P., Palaigeorgiou, G., Triantafyllakos, G., & Despotakis, T. (2009). Computer based testing using "digital ink": Participatory design of a tablet PC based assessment application for secondary education. *Computers & Education, 52*(4), 811-819. Retrieved from http://dx.doi.org/10.1016/j.compedu.2008.12.006

Spolsky, B. (1994). Conditions for second language learning in Israel. *English Teacher's Journal, 47*(May), 45-54.

Sullivan, R. M. (2013). The tablet inscribed: inclusive writing instruction with the iPad. *College Teaching, 61*(1), 1-2. Retrieved from http://dx.doi.org/10.1080/87567555.2012.700339

Van Oostveen, R., Muirhead, W., & Goodman, W. M. (2011). Tablet PCs and reconceptualizing learning with technology: a case study in higher education. *Interactive Technology and Smart Education, 8*(2), 78-93. Retrieved from http://dx.doi.org/10.1108/17415651111141803

Wall, D. (2000). The impact of high-stakes testing on teaching and learning: can this be predicted or controlled? *System, 28*(4), 499-509. Retrieved from http://dx.doi.org/10.1016/S0346-251X(00)00035-X

Wall, D. (2005). *The impact of high-stakes examinations on classroom teaching: a case study using insights from testing and innovation theory*. Cambridge: Cambridge University Press.

Waters, J. K. (2010). Enter the iPad (or not?). *T.H.E. Journal, 37*(6), 38-40.

Weir. C. J. (2005). *Language testing and validation: an evidence-based approach*. New York, NY: MacMillan.

Whittaker, R. (2006). Review of Estudios y Criterios para una Selectividad de calidad en el examen de inglés. *Estudios Ingleses de la Universidad Complutense, 14*, 198-206.

25 The implications of business English mock exams on language progress at higher education

Rocío González Romero[1]

Abstract

Language learning has been increasingly influenced by technology over the last decades thanks to its positive effects on language acquisition. It is thanks to the technology's supportive role towards language learning that an increasing number of online foreign language courses have appeared. Besides, foreign language courses are more and more specialised covering a wide range of topics, from nursing to agricultural studies. However, this study is exclusively concerned with a well-known Language for Specific Purposes (LSP) subject: Business English. The objective of this research is twofold: on the one hand, to describe the implications of mock exams on foreign language learning; on the other hand, it aims at contributing to the field of computerised language testing by properly analysing the effects of these kinds of exams on learners' foreign language progress. Previous studies have focused on the development of specific language skills (Dunkel, 1991; Larson, 2000), or have reported the improvement of computer adaptive testing on official language exams (Alderson, 2000), or have simply described the advantages and disadvantages of computer-based tests (Alderson, 2000; Brown, 1997; Dunkel, 1999). However, few studies have considered the role of mock exams as scaffolding activities for language learning. The present study involves adult participants at the higher education context undertaking online Business English as a compulsory subject of their degree on Economics. The paper discusses the importance of scaffolding activities such as mock exams and self-

---

1. Centro de Educación Infantil y Primaria La Moraña, Arévalo, Ávila, Spain; rgoromero@gmail.com

How to cite this chapter: González Romero, R. (2016). The implications of business English mock exams on language progress at higher education. In A. Pareja-Lora, C. Calle-Martínez, & P. Rodríguez-Arancón (Eds), *New perspectives on teaching and working with languages in the digital era* (pp. 293-302). Dublin: Research-publishing.net. http://dx.doi.org/10.14705/rpnet.2016.tislid2014.442

assessment activities in order to ensure learners' language progress and makes reference to supporting articles in the field at the same time that it presents some materials illustrating these developments.

Keywords: information and communication technologies, ICT, language for specific purposes, LSP, online learning, assessment, higher education.

1. Introduction

Integrating the use of technology into education requires the adaptation of good teaching materials into digital format in the simplest and most cost-effective way. This is the case with assessment since it is an essential part of any course because it checks students' understanding of the course's content. Tests and examinations are widely used as assessment tools for being objective indicators of a student's performance.

In the current teaching context, the increasing use of e-learning platforms has triggered the need of automatic tests to check students' progress. Given the growing variety of Information and Communication Technology (ICT) tools involved in education, it is becoming a challenge to monitor students' progress. That is why this article attempts to justify the positive effects of mock exams on language learning and gives evidence of this practice as scaffolding activities.

2. The relationship between online learning and LSP

Online learning has become an established way of teaching and learning over the last decade. The particularity of this type of education is the use of technology by both the tutor and the learners with the objective of designing digital learning content, offering interaction among participants, and fostering the process of learning. Until recently, online learning was just an excellent way of enlarging the target audience of a course; however, it now requires getting closer to each student by offering different interactive possibilities, such as counselling or individual feedback.

Turning to the issue of LSP, the same circumstances have arisen regarding the new virtual challenges that tutors face. Not only do the tutors need to master the course's content, but they also have to be computer literate. According to Arnó-Macià (2011), "in the context of [...] LSP, technology also becomes a gateway to specialised discipline knowledge and to students' relevant discourse communities" (p. 24). Hence, the tutor must collect the latest language resources within a specialised field.

2.1. The potential benefits of online learning

Online learning contributes to LSP teaching and learning by providing a great variety of resources to improve grammar and the four main language skills: reading, listening, writing and speaking. In addition to these skills, there are several ways in which online learning is beneficial: it caters for students' specific needs; it provides access to the digital resources at any time; it fosters students' autonomy; it develops awareness and learning strategies; and it is based on students' own responsibility.

All in all, online education requires the use of technology to personalise a course's content so that students get the most out of it, given their particular characteristics.

2.2. Online learning and assessment

When designing an online course, one needs to consider whether the course would mainly be exam-based or assignment-based. This means asking yourself which are the most important elements within the course. If it is the exam, the course will likely prioritise the acquisition of knowledge. However, if the course is assignment-based, students will be probably expected to put knowledge into practice over the length of the course. This is the view of James and Fleming (2005), who think that students tend to perform in a better way at coursework assignments rather than at examinations. What lies beneath is the importance of providing enough tools and opportunities for students to check their knowledge through the course. In fact, most of the courses currently created tend to include both types of assessment.

2.3. The importance of feedback

On numerous occasions, students within an online learning course require feedback in order to properly obtain the course's objectives. This feedback could come from different areas, like answering doubts about grammar, providing the accurate answers for exercises, correcting a written composition, or specifying the course's assessment criteria for beginners, among others. Some authors, like Hattie (1987), argue that feedback is the main interactive component in many forms of online learning. For example, Gibbs and Simpson (2004) claim that "[students] can cope without much, or even any, face-to-face teaching, but they cannot cope without regular feedback on assignments. […] Regular assignments and comprehensive feedback is understood to be central to distance education" (p. 9). In this case, online tutors should provide comprehensive feedback on regular assignments as frequently as possible.

2.4. Automatic assessment tools

Marking may become a tedious task if tutors find they have a large amount of work to correct. Within online education, automatic assessment tools are increasing in order to save the tutors' precious time and give students immediate feedback. Among these automatic assessment tools, this article will briefly describe the mock exams and the self-assessment tests.

Regarding mock exams, one can consider them as a kind of examination under similar conditions as the final exam, but usually shorter. The objective of mock exams is to provide feedback to the student without having to wait until very late in the course, or even after the final exam. That is the reason why they can be used as scaffolding activities supporting students' learning. Mock exams have indeed many advantages, they:

- support learning by checking what students have learnt;

- give learners the opportunity to practice and consolidate what they think they know;

- provide instant knowledge of results and feedback;

- help students to monitor their own progress;

- develop learners' self-evaluation skills;

- guide the choice of further learning resources to increase mastery;

- give learners a sense of accomplishment;

- provide tutors with the necessary materials to monitor and evaluate students' progress.

Concerning the self-assessment tests, it is highly recommended to use them when the tutor wants to know students' perceptions and beliefs. The need for self-assessment fosters the reflection on one's own learning, which not only helps to know the areas one needs to study more, but also facilitates the development of critical thinking.

It is a common belief among tutors that a percentage of the final mark has to be devoted to assessment activities, such as mock exams and self-assessment tests, in order to encourage students to do them. Evidence on the field, like the research performed by Forbes and Spence (1991), show that without the input of motivation given by marks students did not solve practically any activity, and as a consequence, their final grade was noticeably low compared to students who were used to assessing their peers' work. Gibbs and Simpson (2004) state that "coursework does not have to be marked to generate the necessary learning. [...] The trick when designing assessment regimes is to generate engagement with learning tasks without generating piles of marking" (p. 8). Thus, the use of automatic mock exams and self-assessment tests helps students improve their learning while the teacher saves marking time.

3. Methodology and results

3.1. Setting and participants

The present research was carried out to study the relationship between mock exams and the students' final exam achievement. To do so, the work reported here has been carried out at the Universidad Católica Santa Teresa de Jesús de Ávila, Spain, where participants were adult learners enrolled in an online official degree on Economics. As part of their compulsory curriculum, students took Business English. This subject's level is pre-intermediate to intermediate and it is worth six credits, which is equivalent to a hundred and fifty hours. Participants who were involved in the research were twenty in total and were all Spanish. They had a basic knowledge of English but had never studied any LSP class before. This is why all of them were considered novel learners in this respect.

3.2. Procedure

Before beginning the study, the mock exams were designed according to the course's content. Each mock exam included five multiple-choice questions learnt in the lesson: two of the items requested specific business vocabulary, another one checked a linguistic expression, and the last two items were about grammatical features. There were a total of twenty-four mock exams, which corresponded to the total number of lessons. After having created the mock exams, they were uploaded into the course's virtual platform. Students did not have a fixed deadline to take the mock exams, nor did they have a time limit to complete them. On the very first day of the course, students were highly recommended to take each mock exam after studying the lesson, but they were not obliged to do so. Hence, two groups were accordingly created: the experimental and the control ones. Once data was collected, it was analysed by calculating the average marks of the students who took the mock exams and the ones who did not, and later on, they were compared to the final exam's grade of all students. The last step consisted in creating a graph to show the results.

3.3. Results and discussion

Comparing participants' answers of both students who took the mock exams and the ones who did not, it was realised that the fact of taking the mock exams had significant correlation with students' academic achievement. Those who took the mock exams had higher final grades than those who decided not to take them, as can be seen in Figure 1.

Figure 1. Influence of mock exams on final exam's grade

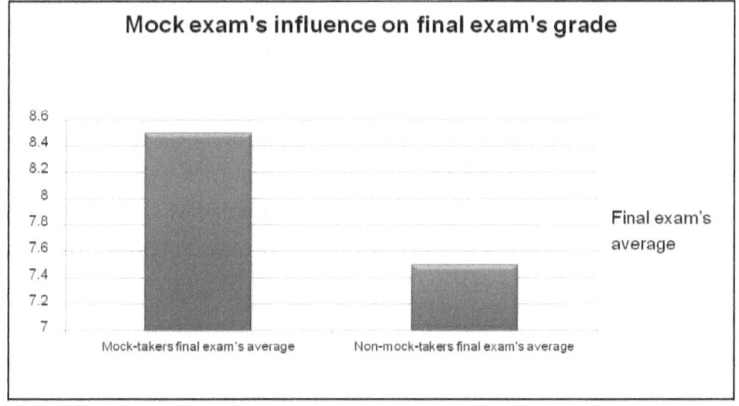

The preceding graph shows an interesting finding too. Considering the final exam to be worth from one to ten points, where five is the passing grade, the difference between students who did not take the mock exams and the ones who did so is almost one point. Since this difference is notably large, it seems that taking mock exams as scaffolding activities improves learning.

An appealing insight into the findings of this research is the fact that many participants took all the mock exams, even though they were not marked (as mentioned above). The number of these participants is quite high, especially with respect to the low number of participants that either did not take any mock exam or did not complete all the mock exams. There are several possible reasons that could explain this situation. One could be that students may have been highly motivated to acquire as much knowledge as they could in this subject, given that they were all novel LSP learners; hence, they took all the mock exams because they might want to check their understanding before the final exam. Another feasible explanation could be that those students who completed all the mock exams considered it important (1) to check their progress, so that they knew in advance those aspects that they needed to study harder for the final exam, or (2) to build up the content they thought they knew. Yet, there might be students who did not entirely understand (or were not fully confident) that they would not receive any mark for taking the mock exams; and, for this reason, they completed all the mock exams.

Unfortunately, it is not possible to know the reason(s) that moved students to complete all the mock exams since no survey was conducted to check students' inner motivations. This issue could become an interesting starting point for a future research. All in all, whether it is for one reason or another, what matters is that those participants who completed all the mock exams greatly surpassed the ones who did not take them, proving that this assessment tool can support students' learning and progress.

Another consideration that can be done in light of the previously stated results is that mock exams were the only learning resource tested in this research. This means that the present study is limited by the number of different learning strategies applied. However, mock exams can be combined with many other resources, such as self-assessment tests, individual or collaborative projects, or even educational activities or games like quizzes, mazes, crosswords, guessing the object, and so on.

To sum up, the information presented before provides some support for the view that not only do students who take mock exams achieve a brilliant final grade in a given subject, but they also outperform those students who decided not to take the mock exams. Moreover, these results might endorse Gibbs and Simpson's (2004) opinion about not assessing coursework, but rather engaging students in doing the course tasks since it reports large benefits for their learning process even though the reasons for their motivation could be imprecise.

Indeed, a promising line of study regarding the field of online LSP learning and language progress could be taking into consideration sociolinguistic variables like age, gender, language level, and so on, affecting the performance of mock exams. Another attainable research could focus on the importance of motivation for language learning, but this seems to be a well-established area of research (Dörnyei, 1998; Fernández Orío, 2013; Pourhosein Gilakjani, Leong, & Banou Sabouri, 2012; Ushida, 2005). In addition, further investigations could feasibly tackle the issue on other LSP disciplines.

4. Conclusions

Online learning is now an extended everyday practice in which many disciplines are taught, including the one this article is about: Business English. In online higher education, feedback is what makes a difference on students' achievement; however, it is difficult to provide detailed feedback when the tutor has countless students. It is thanks to technology that automatic assessment tools, such as mock exams, can be used to give immediate and helpful feedback to students. This article has outlined and verified the benefits of mock exams as scaffolding activities to foster language learning. Results indicate that these types of activities promote outstanding final grades as well as prove to be an effective way of engaging students in learning tasks.

References

Alderson, J. C. (2000). Technology in testing: the present and the future. *System, 28*(4), 593-603. Retrieved from http://dx.doi.org/10.1016/S0346-251X(00)00040-3

Arnó-Macià, E. (2011). Approaches to information technology from an LSP perspective: challenges and opportunities in the new European context. In N. Talaván Zanón, E. Martín Monje & F. Palazón Romero (Eds.), *Technological innovation in the teaching and processing of LSPs: Proceedings of TISLID'10* (pp. 23-40). Madrid: Universidad Nacional de Educación a Distancia.

Brown, J. D. (1997). Computers in language testing: present research and some future directions. *Language Learning and Technology, 1*(1), 44-59. Retrieved from http://llt.msu.edu/vol1num1/brown/default.html

Dörnyei, Z. (1998). Motivation in second and foreign language learning. *Language Teaching, 31*(3), 117-135. Retrieved from http://dx.doi.org/10.1017/S026144480001315X

Dunkel, P. (1991). Computerized testing of nonparticipatory L2 Listening comprehension proficiency: an ESL prototype development effort. *Modern Language Journal, 75*(1), 64-73. Retrieved from http://dx.doi.org/10.1111/j.1540-4781.1991.tb01084.x

Dunkel, P. (1999). Considerations in developing or using second/foreign language proficiency computer-adaptive tests. *Language Learning and Technology, 2*(2), 77-93.

Fernández Orío, S. (2013). *Motivation and second language acquisition*. Retrieved from Universidad de La Rioja, Servicio de Publicaciones. Retrieved from http://biblioteca.unirioja.es/tfe_e/TFE000342.pdf

Forbes, D., & Spence, J. (1991). An experiment in assessment for a large class. In R. Smith (Ed.), *Innovations in Engineering Education*. London: Ellis Horwood.

Gibbs, G., & Simpson, C. (2004). Conditions under which assessment supports students' learning. *Learning and Teaching in Higher Education, 1*, 3-31.

Hattie, J. A. (1987). Identifying the salient facets of a model of student learning: a synthesis of meta-analyses. *International Journal of Educational Research, 11*, 187-212.

James, D., & Fleming, S. (2005). Agreement in student performance in assessment. *Learning and Teaching in Higher Education, 1*, 32-50.

Larson, J. W. (2000). Testing oral language skills via the Computer. *CALICO Journal, 18*(1), 53-66.

Pourhosein Gilakjani, A., Leong, L. M., & Banou Sabouri, N. (2012). A Study on the role of motivation in foreign language learning and teaching. *International Journal of Modern Education and Computer Science, 4*(7), 9-16. Retrieved from http://dx.doi.org/10.5815/ijmecs.2012.07.02

Ushida, E. (2005). The role of students' attitudes and motivation in second language learning in online language courses. *CALICO Journal, 23*(1), 49-78.

26 Assessing pragmatics: DCTs and retrospective verbal reports

Vicente Beltrán-Palanques[1]

Abstract

Assessing pragmatic knowledge in the instructed setting is seen as a complex but necessary task, which requires the design of appropriate research methodologies to examine pragmatic performance. This study discusses the use of two different research methodologies, namely those of Discourse Completion Tests/Tasks (DCTs) and verbal reports. Research has shown that the use of DCTs in combination with verbal reports can increase the trustworthiness of the results (Félix-Brasdefer, 2010). Hence, taking into account the potential of verbal reports, the present study aims to investigate the cognitive processes undertaken by a group of English language learners as regards their pragmatic performance. Findings regarding the value of retrospective verbal reports are discussed together with practical recommendations for the use of DCTs and verbal reports to assess speech act performance in the instructed setting.

Keywords: pragmatics, speech acts, assessment, DCTs, retrospective verbal reports.

1. Introduction

Assessment of Second Language/Foreign Language (SL/FL) pragmatics is a growing area in the field of Interlanguage Pragmatics (ILP). Several researchers have drawn their attention to this particular aspect, especially in recent years (see Beltrán-Palanques, 2013, 2014; Félix-Brasdefer, 2010; Roever, 2010, 2011; Ross

---

1. Universitat Jaume I, Castellón de la Plana, Spain; vbeltran@uji.es

How to cite this chapter: Beltrán-Palanques, V. (2016). Assessing pragmatics: DCTs and retrospective verbal reports. In A. Pareja-Lora, C. Calle-Martínez, & P. Rodríguez-Arancón (Eds), *New perspectives on teaching and working with languages in the digital era* (pp. 303-312). Dublin: Research-publishing.net. http://dx.doi.org/10.14705/rpnet.2016.tislid2014.443

& Kasper, 2013; Usó-Juan & Martínez-Flor, 2014). Pragmatics, which is one of the main components of the communicative competence model (Bachman, 1990; Usó-Juan & Martínez-Flor, 2006), should be appropriately introduced in the instructed setting in order to teach and assess this competence successfully. In this paper, I will focus on the issue of assessing pragmatics in the online instructed setting combining two different research methodologies: Discourse Completion Tests/Tasks (DCTs) and retrospective verbal reports. In the first part of the paper, I will provide a theoretical framework which focuses on the use of the two aforementioned research methodologies in the field of ILP. In the second part I will explain how the study was developed and the results derived from it. Finally, I will briefly discuss practical recommendations for the use of DCTs and verbal reports to assess speech act performance in the instructed setting.

2. Theoretical framework

Verbal reports have been used in the field of ILP in combination with other research instruments, particularly those of role-plays (Beltrán-Palanques, 2013; Cohen & Olshtain, 1993; Félix-Brasdefer, 2008a, 2008b; Widjaja, 1997; Woodfield, 2012) and DCTs (Beltrán-Palanques, 2013; Robinson, 1992; Woodfield, 2008, 2010). However, for reasons of space, this paper is restricted to focus on the studies in which verbal reports were employed in combination with DCTs (see Beltrán-Palanques, 2013, 2014; Félix-Brasdefer, 2010).

One of the pioneering studies which used verbal reports in combination with written DCTs was conducted by Robinson (1992). The author combined concurrent (single-subject think-aloud) and retrospective verbal reports (i.e. interviews). The data obtained by means of verbal reports provided specific information about the planning process of refusal semantic formulae, evaluation of different utterances, pragmatic and linguistic difficulties, and knowledge sources. Woodfield (2008) employed paired concurrent verbal reports and retrospective verbal reports with three pairs of native speakers of English to provide insights concerning issues of validity noticed during the reconstruction of requests in 18 written DCTs. Woodfield (2010) explored the role of paired concurrent and retrospective verbal reports to examine the cognitive processes of advanced learners of English as a SL on written DCTs which elicited status-unequal requests. The data obtained from concurrent verbal reports revealed that the social context of the discourse situation affected the pragmalinguistic and sociopragmatic choices and language-related episodes showed participants' negotiation of lexical and grammatical elements when planning the request strategies. Regarding retrospective reports, the author reported that they offered information about participants' language of thought and the difficulties that participants experienced with the research methodology employed. More recently, Beltrán-Palanques (2013) conducted a study employing retrospective verbal reports in combination with both open role-plays and interactive written DCTs. In this study, the speech act under investigation was that of apologies. Results revealed that retrospective verbal reports appeared to be instrumental in gathering information regarding participants' pragmatic production.

In short, studies using verbal reports, either concurrently or retrospectively, in combination with DCTs, have shown the positive effects of this particular research methodology. Verbal reports seem to be instrumental in providing information as regards the participants' cognitive process, perceptions of speech act performance, validation of research instruments, sociocultural and sociolinguistic knowledge, as well as politeness issues. Hence, taking into account the literature review sketched above, the present study aims to contribute to this specific field of research by examining the potential of using interactive written DCTs in combination with retrospective verbal reports in an online instructed setting.

3. The study

3.1. Participants

This small explanatory study included 30 adult learners (12 male and 18 female) of an online English as a Foreign Language (EFL) course (mean age: 28.3). Participants were first asked to complete the UCLES Quick Placement Test

(Oxford University Press) to test their proficiency level. Results revealed that their proficiency level was B1, according to the Common European Framework of Reference for Languages (CEFR – http://www.coe.int/t/dg4/linguistic/source/framework_en.pdf). This particular result was expected, as participants were taking an online B1 course. Nevertheless, it was necessary to administer this placement test to appropriately identify participants' proficiency level. In addition to this, a background questionnaire was also administered in order to gather information regarding participants' personal information (e.g. age, gender, mother tongue) and FL learning experience (adapted from Beltrán-Palanques, 2013). Data gathered from the questionnaire revealed that participants were bilingual (i.e. Catalan and Spanish) and had studied English at school, secondary school and university.

3.2. The speech act under investigation

The pragmatic aspect under investigation in this study is the speech act of apologies. According to Searle (1979), apologies fall into the category of expressives, since they "express the psychological state specified in the sincerity condition about a state of affairs specified in the propositional content" (p. 15). Apologies are here defined as a "compensatory action to an offense in the doing of which S (the speaker) was causally involved and which is costly to H (the hearer)" (Bergman & Kasper, 1993, p. 82). Then, apologies can be used as remedial exchanges to restore harmony between speakers after a given offense (Goffman, 1971).

People often take part in remedial actions in which they attempt to save face (Brown & Levinson, 1987) and restore the social harmony of the speech community (Goffman, 1971). Following Brown and Levinson (1987), an apology is typically viewed as negative politeness whose main goal is that of providing a redressive action. From the domain of politeness, an apology is seen as a communicative event in which the speaker (i.e. the apologiser) should take into account the other interlocutor's face (i.e. the apologisee) in order to restore the situation (Brown & Levinson, 1987). Hence, apologising, as mentioned by Bataineh and Bataineh (2006), is a face-saving act for the hearer and a face-threatening act for the speaker.

3.3. Instruments and procedure

The research methodology employed in this study consisted of interactive written DCTs (Beltrán-Palanques, 2013). This consists of eight different situations containing the following variables: social status (i.e. equal and hearer-dominant), social distance (i.e. stranger and acquaintance), and level of offense (high and low). However, in the present study, only four of the eight situations used in the aforementioned study were selected, specifically those involving the following variables: social status (i.e. equal), social distance (i.e. stranger and acquaintance), and level of offense (high and low). Table 1 shows the different situations.

Table 1. Situations

Context of the situation		Variables		
		Social status	Social distance	Level of offense
Sit. 1	Bookshop	Equal	Stranger	Low
Sit. 2	University	Equal	Acquaintance	High
Sit. 3	Student's flat	Equal	Acquaintance	Low
Sit. 4	University	Equal	Stranger	High

Participants were grouped in pairs and they were asked to complete the interactive written DCTs in pairs. Immediately after the completion of each written cognitive task, participants took part in the retrospective verbal report. Tasks were performed using *Skype*. However, due to the interactive nature of the written DCTs, only one participant of each pair elicited the speech act under investigation (i.e. apologies). Participants could read back their written production before engaging them in the verbal probes. In so doing, participants were exposed to their own production, in order to make them aware of what they produced. Participants were allowed to use Catalan, Spanish and/or English during the verbal probes, since in this case, the major goal was to examine participants' thoughts while performing the tasks, rather than exploring their spoken competence in English. Furthermore, it was believed that allowing them to use their L1 would facilitate the verbal reporting. Verbal reports were recorded in order to further examine participants' contributions. The retrospective verbal reports were transcribed following Jefferson's (2004) transcript notation.

4. Results and discussion

This section provides an overview of the results of this study. Table 2 displays the results derived from the retrospective verbal reports.

Table 2. Situations

Verbal reports	Situations			
	Situation 1	Situation 2	Situation 3	Situation 4
Grammar and lexicon	7	6	7	9
Social status	7	4	5	8
Social distance	8	5	5	9
Level of offense	9	12	10	15

Each participant was asked to take part in the verbal report, which focused on aspects related to grammar and lexicon, and pragmatic knowledge. As mentioned above, only one of the participants in each pair took part in the apology production. Therefore, only the data derived from the participants who produced apology sequences are shown here.

Regarding grammar and lexicon, retrospective verbal reports revealed that, in general, participants focused on aspects related to grammar and lexicon when planning their pragmatic production, especially in the fourth situation (i.e. nine participants out of 15). This could be related to the fact that this situation in particular could be more demanding for participants since it involved the following context: two equal participants who were strangers and whose level of offense was high. As a matter of fact, most participants indicated that this situation was very offensive for the other interlocutor since it involved damaging students' class notes. It is worth mentioning that participants were students, so perhaps they perceived this as very offensive.

Concerning social status, participants indicated that in situations 1 and 4 this particular variable seemed to have affected the way they addressed their interlocutors. In this case, all the participants shared the same social status, and they revealed that the fact that they had the same status affected their production.

According to them, having a different social status could involve apologising in a different manner, thus, using more strategies to restore the situation. As regards this specific variable, participants did not provide much information, probably due to the fact that they all shared the same social status.

Social distance, according to the results obtained in the verbal reporting, appeared not to have a great impact on participants' pragmatic production. As a matter of fact, eight and nine participants mentioned this specific variable in the situations 1 and 4, in which social distance was that of stranger. According to the verbal reporting, in the other remaining two situations (i.e. 2 and 3), containing acquaintance social distance, a lower number of participants seemed to have paid attention to this issues, particularly five participants in each one.

Finally, retrospective verbal reports revealed that the severity of offence played a paramount role. As a matter of fact, those situations whose level of offense was classified as high seemed to have received the attention of the majority of the participants. Particularly, situations 2 and 4, in which the severity of offense was classified as high, called participants' attention as they involved situations which violated social norms.

The results of this study are in line with previous works in the field, in which verbal reports were also instrumental in revealing participants' information regarding their speech act performance in DCTs (Beltrán-Palanques, 2013; Robinson, 1992; Woodfield, 2008, 2010). Robinson (1992) indicated that verbal reports were useful to obtain information about attended aspects, and indications of linguistic and pragmatic difficulties, among others. Woodfield (2008) found that verbal reports were instrumental in identifying participants' attention while working on the tasks. Similarly, Woodfield's (2010) study revealed that retrospective verbal reports provided information regarding participants' cognitive processes while on task. Beltrán-Palanques (2013) found that verbal reports were instrumental in providing information regarding participants' pragmatic knowledge. In this explanatory study, retrospective verbal reports were also useful to obtain information related to participants' attention to grammar and lexicon features as well as pragmatic knowledge.

5. Conclusions

The aim of this explanatory study was to contribute to the growing body of literature that employs verbal reports in combination with other research instruments, particularly DCTs. Results from this study are consistent with previous research in the field, since retrospective verbal reports were instrumental in providing further information concerning participants' speech act production. Several studies have concluded that verbal reports, in their various forms (i.e. concurrent and retrospective) can be of paramount interest, given that researchers can obtain further information related to learners' pragmatic performance. This, in turn, can benefit language teachers in their tasks of developing instructional approaches aim to (i) integrate speech acts; and (ii) better understand how learners at different levels process and perform pragmatic utterances in contextualised situations. Empirical studies whose goal is to obtain participants' thoughts while performing cognitive tasks, such as DCTs, should employ verbal reports, since this tool allows researchers to better understand participants' pragmatic behaviour. Moreover, the use of DCTs and verbal reports can also be of paramount interest for instruction, as a tool to obtain information about learners' pragmatic performance, and to improve instructional approaches as well as design them drawing on empirical findings.

6. Acknowledgements

The research conducted in this paper is part of the Education and Innovation Research Project "Proyecto de Innovación Educativa Universitat Jaume I 2779/13, Parámetros de aproximación a la evaluación de las destrezas orales en lengua inglesa: tipología, diseño de tests y criterios de validación".

References

Bachman, L. F. (1990). *Fundamental considerations in language testing.* Oxford: Oxford University Press.

Bataineh, R. F., & Bataineh, R. F. (2006). Apology strategies of Jordanian EFL university students. *Journal of Pragmatics, 38*(11), 1901-1927.

Beltrán-Palanques, V. (2013). *Exploring research methods in interlanguage pragmatics. A study based on apologies.* Saarbrücken: Lambert Academic Publishing.

Beltrán-Palanques, V. (2014). Methodological issues in interlanguage pragmatics: some food for thought. In G. Alcaraz-Mármol & M. M. Jiménez-Cervantes Arnao (Eds.), *Studies in philology. Linguistics, literature and cultural studies in modern languages.* Cambridge: Cambridge Scholars Publishing.

Bergman, M. L., & Kasper, G. (1993). Perception and performance in native and nonnative apology. In G. Kasper & S. Blum-Kulka (Eds.), *Interlanguage pragmatics* (pp. 82-107). Oxford: Oxford University Press.

Brown, P., & Levinson, S. C. (1987). *Politeness. Some universals in language usage.* Cambridge: Cambridge University Press.

Cohen, A. D., & Olshtain, E. (1993). The production of speech acts by EFL learners. *TESOL Quarterly, 27*(1), 33-56. Retrieved from http://dx.doi.org/10.2307/3586950

Félix-Brasdefer, J. C. (2008a). Perception of refusals to invitations: exploring the minds of foreign language learners. *Language Awareness, 17*(3), 195-211.

Félix-Brasdefer, J. C. (2008b). *Politeness in Mexico and the United States: a contrastive study of the realization and perception of refusals.* Amsterdam: John Benjamins Publishing Company. Retrieved from http://dx.doi.org/10.1075/pbns.171

Félix-Brasdefer, J. C. (2010). Data collection methods in speech act performance: DCTs, role-plays, and verbal reports. In A. Martínez-Flor & E. Usó-Juan (Eds.), *Speech act performance. Theoretical, empirical and methodological issues* (pp. 41-56). Amsterdam: John Benjamins Publishing Company. Retrieved from http://dx.doi.org/10.1075/lllt.26.03fel

Goffman, E. (1971). *Relations in public. Microstudies of the public order.* Harmondsworth: Penguin.

Jefferson, G. (2004). Glossary of transcript symbols with an introduction. In G. Lerner (Ed.), *Conversation analysis: studies from the first generation* (pp. 13-31). Amsterdam: John Benjamins Publishing Company. Retrieved from http://dx.doi.org/10.1075/pbns.125.02jef

Robinson, M. A. (1992). Introspective methodology in interlanguage pragmatics research. In G. Kasper (Ed.), *Pragmatics of Japanese as a native and target language* [Second Language Teaching and Curriculum Center Technical Report No. 3] (pp. 27-82). Honolulu HI: University of Hawai'i Press.

Roever, C. (2010). Researching pragmatics. In B. Paltridge & A. Phakiti (Eds.), *Continuum companion to research methods in applied linguistics* (pp. 240-255). London: Continuum International Publishing Group.

Roever, C. (2011). Testing of second language pragmatics: past and future. *Language Testing*, *28*(4), 463-481. Retrieved from http://dx.doi.org/10.1177/0265532210394633

Ross, S., & Kasper, G. (Eds.). (2013). Assessing second language pragmatics. Basingstoke: Palgrave Macmillan.

Searle, J. (1979). *Expression and meaning: studies in the theory of speech acts*. Cambridge: Cambridge University Press. Retrieved from http://dx.doi.org/10.1017/CBO9780511609213

Usó-Juan, E., & Martínez-Flor, A. (2006). Approaches to language learning and teaching: towards acquiring communicative competence through the four skills. In E. Usó-Juan & A. Martínez-Flor (Eds.), *Current trends in the development and teaching of the four language skills* (pp. 3-25). Berlin: Mouton de Gruyter. Retrieved from http://dx.doi.org/10.1515/9783110197778.1.3

Usó-Juan, E., & Martínez-Flor, A. (2014). Reorienting the assessment of the conventional expressions of complaining and apologising: from single-response to interactive DCTs. *Iranian Journal of Language Testing*, *4*(1), 113-136.

Widjaja, C. (1997). A study of date refusal: Taiwanese females vs. American females. *University of Hawai'i Working Papers in ESL*, *15*(2), 1-43.

Woodfield, H. (2008). Problematising discourse completion task: voices from verbal report. *Evaluation and Research Education*, *21*(1), 43-69. Retrieved from http://dx.doi.org/10.2167/eri413.0

Woodfield, H. (2010). What lies beneath?: Verbal report in interlanguage requests in English. *Multilingua*, *29*(1), 1-27. Retrieved from http://dx.doi.org/10.1515/mult.2010.001

Woodfield, H. (2012). Pragmatic variation in learner perception: the role of retrospective verbal report in L2 speech act research. In J. C. Félix-Brasdefer & D. A. Koike (Eds.), *Pragmatic variation in first and second language contexts. Methodological issues* (pp. 209-238). Amsterdam: John Benjamins Publishing Company.

Section 3.
Applying computational linguistics and language resources to language teaching and learning

27 An updated account of the WISELAV project: a visual construction of the English verb system

Andrés Palacios Pablos[1]

Abstract

This article presents the state of the art in WISELAV, an on-going research project based on the metaphor Languages Are (like) Visuals (LAV) and its mapping Words-In-Shapes Exchange (WISE). First, the cognitive premises that motivate the proposal are recalled: the power of images, students' increasingly visual cognitive learning style, and the importance of grammar in L2 learning. Then an updated report follows on WISE's analysis of the English verb system, an interpretation in terms of a transfer of morphological-functional information, represented through a series of fitting shapes. These are purposely assigned, as certain basic iconicity principles are applied to associate verb grammar meanings and graphic forms. The shapes so described appear with the steps taken to develop a pilot computer programme and to both highlight the visual aspects of the system and eventually enable its use online.

Keywords: English verb, applied linguistics, construction grammar, cognitive learning, verbo-graphic metaphor.

---

1. Universidad de Burgos, Burgos, Spain; apalacio@ubu.es

How to cite this chapter: Palacios Pablos, A. (2016). An updated account of the WISELAV project: a visual construction of the English verb system. In A. Pareja-Lora, C. Calle-Martínez, & P. Rodríguez-Arancón (Eds), *New perspectives on teaching and working with languages in the digital era* (pp. 315-326). Dublin: Research-publishing.net. http://dx.doi.org/10.14705/rpnet.2016.tislid2014.444

Chapter 27

1. Introductory foundations of WISELAV

WISELAV is a research project whose purpose is to study the implications of the proposed metaphor (LAV/WISE), and to develop a set of suitable supports for assessing its potential pedagogic value. As an on-going project, it aims to explore how its proposed visual framework can account for analysing and teaching English verb phrases, rather than becoming a grammar of the English verb on its own or a comparative study of other existing analyses. Because of this and space restrictions, this paper includes hardly any references to the huge number of existing works dealing with verbs and tense in English.

For a better understanding of the project and its scope, it seems convenient to first acknowledge the cognitive premises that set it off. The first one is the power of images. Through multiple arrangements, they have always proved to be useful to illustrate and explain the often-complex processes of science; and now, with the new technologies, hypertext and the digital era, images have also taken over outside the academic world in our everyday lives. Thus, this expansion of image usage is bringing about some changes for our cognitive learning styles. This phenomenon, of particularly decisive pedagogic consequences for the younger generation, has not been unnoticed by researchers: Myers (2003), for example, suggested the incorporation and explanation of non-verbal elements within visual texts; Littlemore (2004) verified students' increasingly visual cognitive learning style; and Jiang and Grabe (2007) explored the linguistic usage of some graphic organisers to represent text structure.

Another premise of WISE was to acknowledge that nowadays grammar teaching – although considered an essential component in L2 learning – is frequently neglected, a situation often aggravated in brief English for Specific Purposes (ESP) courses that focus on specific content and hardly cover students' grammatical needs. However, as Dudley-Evans and St. John (1998, pp. 74-80) make quite clear, teaching Languages for Specific Purposes (LSP) should not give *carte blanche* to overlook knowledge gaps in grammar. In an attempt to improve this state of affairs, WISE merges these two referred premises, searching for a way to take advantage of the illustrative power of images as a support for language grammar teaching.

While metaphor theory can provide some theoretical rationale to explain the cognitive extent to which visuals are mappable onto languages, it suffices here to outline the following notion: if graphic supports help to understand complex concepts (in our case, grammatical), it is because some common conceptual metaphors like 'understanding is seeing' can ease the mapping of our commonplace knowledge about visuals onto students' own knowledge of grammar (cf. Lakoff, 1987, p. 222). Then, recognising the power visuals have, we can map them onto our understanding of language and deploy proposals that, like WISE, can draw on students' visual knowledge and help them improve their frequently blurred idea of grammar.

If these were the premises that somehow made the conceptualisation of WISE possible, the stimulus that initiated its conception and ultimately defined its goal however, was the frequent verb-related mistakes made by low-level English as a Second Language (ESL) and ESP students alike. Many of them are false beginners with a rudimentary grammar base. As failing to use verbs properly can undermine communication seriously, it seemed worthwhile to pay verbs due attention and take into account any new insights of their performance to relieve or upgrade students' learning. That was exactly the project's final target.

2. From WISE analysis to the WISELAV web application

WISE (Palacios, 2009) is a verbo-graphic analogy developed to describe the English verb by means of a system of fitting shapes. It exemplifies verbs as they combine to produce different verb phrases or groups (henceforth VGs). This construal of verb structure through fitting shapes, in turn, involved a thorough analysis of verb rules at work so that their functional and morphological performance could be conveyed onto the parallel, purposely-created visual system. As a result, it works rather well illustrating many operational aspects of verbs such as the different degree of inflection and periphrasis VGs have in order to produce grammatical forms and meanings, the subject-verb agreement, modals' different operation and the distinct telescoping arrangement of English verb structure. All these features often lead to the verb mistakes referred to before and so, in principle, WISE could meet a good deal of students' verb grammar needs and increase their linguistic awareness.

Table 1. Principles and contrast between the English verb system and WISE

Principles and contrast	English verb system	Graphic WISE scheme
Typical paradigm of information flow	Each unit (word/shape) has 2 codes (transmitter and receptor). Some code is passed forwards to the next unit.	
Reversion of transfer system	Morphological codes: (Transmitting stems + receptive endings).	Graphic codes: (Receptive backs + transmitting fronts).
	Inverted or non-continuous: Stem+(...)→ (...)+Receptive ending Stem1+ending0 → Stem2+ending1 ...	Direct-contact or flat transfer: Back0+Front1 → Back1+Front2 ...
Functional value of units	There are several functional verb categories.	WISE units represent forms of functional status.
	Some auxiliary verbs can vary their functions and thus their categories.	Those verbs have different WISE shapes depending on their function.
	Compound structures have the functional value given by the combination of units. Even if shortened or omitted, they are disambiguated by context.	Whether they are explicit or not, WISE always represents their functional value.
Irregular morphologies	Some forms are metamorphosed into irregular morphologies or have receptive code Ø.	Yet their representation with WISE is always regular.
Values of the first verb (operator, in compound structures)	Subject-verb agreement (rarely displayed in English) and mode/ tense disjunction.	Both variables displayed in the active core of first shape.

The process to develop a computer program has brought about some improvements to WISE's first interpretation of the English verb. These improvements, together with the on-going software development and some preliminary trials, account for WISELAV's current state of the art. Before referring this, it is highly convenient to recover some basic principles of its graphic analysis, here briefly related to their analysed target. WISE's graphic approach allows a higher level of representational meaning than linguistic instances: rather than precise VG examples alone, WISE also produces the patterns of verb structure to which any discrete example belongs. This can easily be explained: the last link of the VG chain (unless there is an ellipsis or omission) must always be a lexical verb, and that lexical verb, even if it is a single concrete one, is seen as a category with no further distinction.

An important improvement has been the reduction of WISE verb assignments provided by Palacios (2009, p. 106). The initial system of six possible backs and six possible fronts has been simplified to just five fronts and five backs (Figure 1). Whereas the backs are related to the morphological receptors of verb endings (except for the subject-verb agreement, which appears in the shape cores), the fronts are associated with the six functional verb categories (modals and auxiliary 'do' share the same front and hence merge in just one front, F_1). These ten graphic contour codes can be considered the WISE basic constituent parts that make up single-shaped verb units together with their structural extended patterns. To increase distinction, different colours have been given to the six verb categories.

Apart from the contour assignments resulting in five backs and five fronts, WISE makes use of a few other useful distinctions in order to produce its graphic shapes. First, to distinguish between unchanging and variable assignments and thus resemble verbs' mentioned functional variability at times, some contours can be represented with **continuous or broken lines**, depending on whether they represent fixed or variable verb functional categories. Following these criteria, for example, the front of lexical verbs has a continuous line, which shows this category is always depicted this way (Figure 1, F_5). At sentence level, we could take into account transitivity and so make some graphic distinction for such a feature. However, to focus on the verb phrase, WISELAV neglects that variable.

Figure 1. WISE's upgraded assignments of backs and fronts

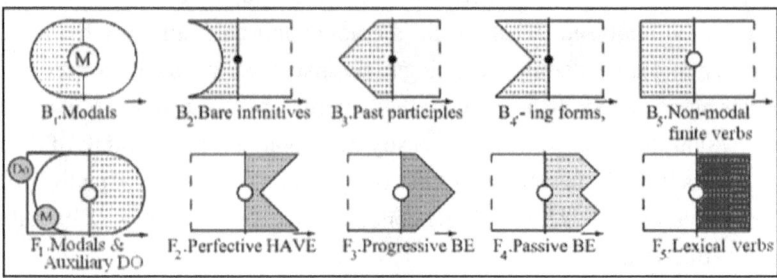

Another WISE distinction is the one made for **cores**. Finite verbs, apart from their intrinsic grammatical meanings (in Figure 1), carry the specific values of finiteness: subject-verb agreement (although not so much in English) and conveying either tense or modality. These features can only be expressed by the verbs appearing in VG first position within sentences. In order to depict these meanings, WISE distinguishes finite verbs with an active core (Figure 2a) that can symbolically differentiate among all the mutually exclusive values each of these two variables can take. On the other hand, verbs become non-finite when occurring in whatever other circumstances, therefore carrying neither subject agreement nor any tensed or modal load. This condition is shown through a black non-active core (Figure 2b). Actually, in a strict sense, it is the non-finite backs (Figure 1, B_{2-4}) that can be considered the only three possible receptive shapes in an extended VG, the other two backs being finite receptors (Figure 1, $B_{1\,\&\,5}$) and therefore carriers of subject agreement. This fact can prove of interest when teaching the system.

Figure 2. Patterns of finiteness and telescopic arrangement

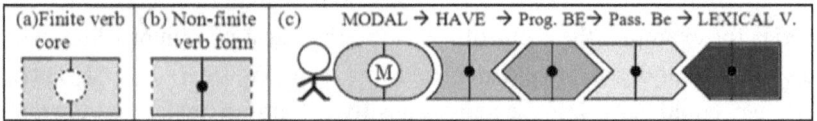

These distinctive criteria (front/back shape, colour, line type and core) work together to provide an accurate description of verbs. In the case of modals, for instance, as they can only perform as finite modal auxiliaries, that quality always makes them finite-core shapes with both back and front of continuous round contour. Similarly, we can check the shapes of the three non-finite verb simple forms (Figure 1, B_{2-4}) and easily visualise it in other possible extended structures (see the schematic WISE telescopic verb arrangement in Figure 2c). In this way, when a verb is conjugated, it will necessarily follow the sequence of first finite then non-finite cores.

It must also be reminded that the ten graphic assignments were not given capriciously but, up to what was feasible, by considering the time semantic value each adds to the VG and trying to convey some mnemonic strategy. In order to ease the visual proposal and make the most of its cognitive possibilities, everything was carefully looked into, deliberately pursuing some principles of iconicity (such as conciseness, generalisation, autonomy, and structure). Their correct assembly allows us to project at a glance **the five basic verb** combinations (cf. Downing & Locke, 2006; Quirk, Greenbaum, Leech, & Svartvik, 1985) while mirroring their restrictions (Figure 3).

Figure 3.   The five basic verb combinations

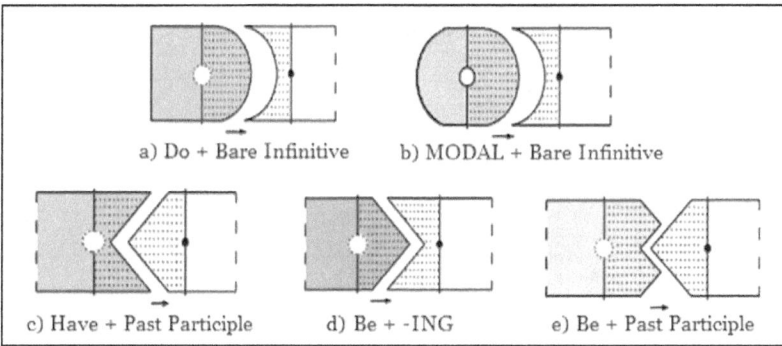

Thus, by following grammar rules and applying the explained distinctions of continuous-broken line and core type, we have what can be regarded as the nine

Chapter 27

WISE basic verb shapes (Figure 4). As they need proper understanding and learning to deal easily with the different verb patterns, it is worth recollecting their **mnemonic** support:

1) Infinitive: back of forward semicircle, neutral semantic value.

2) Past participle: back of backward arrow, value of completed action.

3) –ing form: back of forward arrow, value of action in progress.

4) Auxiliary 'do': Shape that recalls its capital D.

5) Auxiliary 'have': backward-arrow front linkable to the perfective aspect.

6) Progressive 'be': forward-arrow front linkable to the progressive aspect.

7) Modal: Invariable shape that may remind us of a circle.

8) Passive 'be': zigzag front that may recall the passive role drift to the subject as verb action addressee.

9) Lexical verbs: vertical front that usually closes the verb chain.

Figure 4. The nine WISE basic verb forms

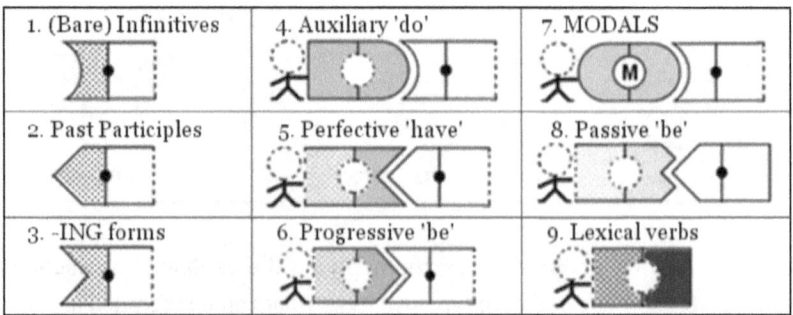

The continuous-broken line distinction is useful for synthesis and research purposes when studying the different patterns of structure. However, it is not so when describing concrete VGs whose components have concrete functions. Therefore, broken lines are not generated with the WISELAV application, intended to create plain shapes of particular examples with fixed contours.

The first version (http://www3.ubu.es/wiselav) already highlights the visual aspects of the system but has just partly developed some of the necessary subsystems: an introduction; the example builder, meant to upload an assortment of examples designed to practise and validate WISE pedagogical interest; a user's application, to allow interaction with the system and perform the designed learning tasks; and a teacher's management application, to allow teachers to control the different possibilities the platform offers. Underlying the example builder and the user's application is the WISELAV Figures Generator (henceforth WFG, Figure 5), a subsystem that holds all the concepts defined in WISE as interactive icons to be used and form the different shapes.

Figure 5. WFG

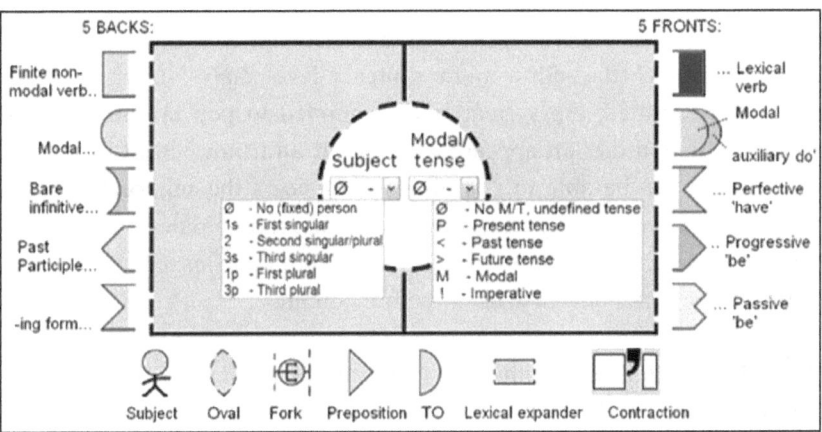

At the sides, the **backs** and **fronts** appear to generate verb shapes. Clicking on the **subject** displays the subject-dummy and activates the core, conceived to mark subject agreement and tense-modal value of the first verb by choosing among the different options of the **core's left and right tabs**. The **contraction** icon allows to show both the negative contractions (clicking on contraction + oval + NOT), and the operator contractions (clicking on subject + contraction + front). Finally, between subject and contraction appear the **non-verbal elements** that can intervene and interact with verbs.

The **oval** displays those elements which do not alter the verb's morphological transfer (inverted subject, negation, intervening adjuncts and, occasionally, the object), as in the role of double dominoes. Rather than ovals, they actually become strips replicating the preceding front. The **fork** reproduces the effect that certain coordinators (AND, OR, BUT, the comma, etc.) have in inter-verbal position. Its two variable sides allow for graphic adjustments in order to integrate the morphological changes these coordinators bring about in the VG.

Prepositions have the shape of a forward arrow triangle, which fits in the back of –ing forms, thus imitating their linguistic behaviour. The **TO particle** is represented by a forward semicircle that fits the back of infinitives. The **lexical expander** is a rectangular band, which is narrower than verb shapes and which can represent both intervening non-verbal elements and other components external to the VG (thus allowing for sentence level analysis). When a lexical verb front is formed, the system is programmed to pop up the interactive **addition** icon. On the left appears the **explicit addition**, meant to represent examples like 'to be able to'; on the right appears the **inherent addition**, which can be employed for cases whose internal morphological transfer is not explicit, cases such as 'to stop + –ing'. If both addition icons remain unclicked, the next shape is not attached, as in 'before coming'.

All in all, being provided with these interactive icons, the WFG can represent both the mainstream English verb conjugation and other off-mainstream verb arrangements, like lexical auxiliaries, catenative verbs and phrasal verbs. What is most revealing is that the WFG can do this without betraying WISE principles, and hence, show English verb grammar at work.

However, in order to offer a complementary teaching resource, WISELAV also includes a smaller analysis of tense functions through a series of diagrams correlated to each particular tense and deliberately simple (based on the communicative power of arrows, brief labels and examples). These slides can emerge along with examples and thus offer a quick functional hint for students. Figure 6 charts the diagrams corresponding to the present progressive.

Figure 6.   Uses of present progressive

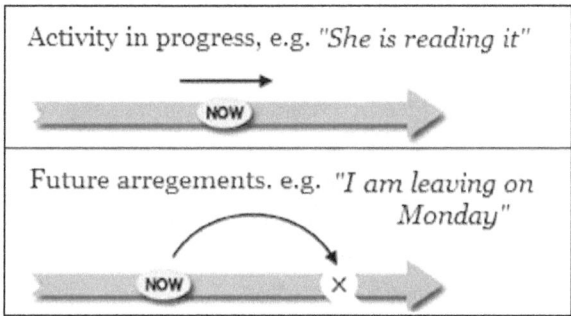

3. WISELAV's progress and future implementation

The software system has been designed to detect and show mistakes and, by doing so, it is expected to increase users' linguistic awareness and cut down on their mistakes. In any case, WISELAV objectives must not be misunderstood. The project is not meant to produce an alternative, complete grammar, or to replace conventional teaching methodology. Rather, it is meant to provide some auxiliary support and increase the learning of some grammatical issues.

In a second phase (http://www3.ubu.es/wiselav2), the program has been redesigned and upgraded to allow for a better management of exercises and results. For instance, an exercise builder can now upload specific tasks associated to selected examples (avoiding random example occurrence), manual sound recording of examples is added, the colour distinction of verb categories has been implemented, and a score-keeping application registers exercise results as accessible data for subsequent analysis. However, important advances remain to be implemented: the future software should allow us to record sound and manage sentence segments better and, overall, it should be more user-friendly. Once these features are integrated into a smoothly-run application, the different shapes will be close to having 'their own life'. This will enable an appropriate use online, providing a valuable learning tool. The results obtained in some preliminary trials seem to support this prospect.

References

Downing, A., & Locke, P. (2006). *English grammar. A university course.* New York: Routledge.

Dudley-Evans, T., & St. John, M. J. (1998). *Developments in English for specific purposes.* Cambridge: Cambridge University Press.

Jiang, X., & Grabe, W. (2007). Graphic organizers in reading instruction: research findings and issues. *Reading in a Foreign Language, 19*, 34-55.

Lakoff, G. (1987). Image metaphors. *Metaphor and Symbolic Activity, 2*(3), 219-222. Retrieved from http://dx.doi.org/10.1207/s15327868ms0203_4

Littlemore, J. (2004). Item-based and cognitive-style-based variation in students' abilities to use metaphoric extension strategies. *Ibérica, 7*, 5-31.

Myers, G. (2003). Words, pictures and facts in academic discourse. *Ibérica, 6*, 3-13.

Palacios, A. (2009). Languages are (like) visuals: linguistic considerations and potential usage. *Ibérica, 17*, 99-118.

Quirk, R., Greenbaum, S., Leech, G., & Svartvik, J. (1985). *A comprehensive grammar of the English language.* London: Longman.

28 Generating a Spanish affective dictionary with supervised learning techniques

Daniel Bermudez-Gonzalez[1], Sabino Miranda-Jiménez[2], Raúl-Ulises García-Moreno[3], and Dora Calderón-Nepamuceno[4]

Abstract

Nowadays, machine learning techniques are being used in several Natural Language Processing (NLP) tasks such as Opinion Mining (OM). OM is used to analyse and determine the affective orientation of texts. Usually, OM approaches use affective dictionaries in order to conduct sentiment analysis. These lexicons are labeled manually with affective orientation (polarity) of words such as positive or negative. There are few dictionaries of affective orientation for Spanish; also, the size of these dictionaries is small. Thus, we propose a method for building a large affective Spanish dictionary for subjectivity and sentiment analysis. Supervised learning techniques are used to classify the entries from a lexical dictionary according to their affective orientations based on their definitions. We combine three classifiers (decision trees, naive Bayes, and a support vector machine) to determine the final polarity of each entry, that is, positive or negative.

Keywords: opinion mining, subjectivity and sentiment analysis, affective orientation, polarity detection.

---

1. Prospectiva en Tecnología e Integradora de Sistemas SA de CV, Ciudad de México, Mexico; danielbermudez30@gmail.com

2. INFOTEC- Centro de Investigación e Innovación en Tecnologías de la Información y Comunicación, Aguascalientes, México; sabino.miranda@infotec.mx

3. Services & Processes Solutions, Ciudad de México, México; raulgm00@gmail.com

4. UAEM UAP Nezahualcóyotl, Estado de México, México; dmcalderonn@uaemex.mx

How to cite this chapter: Bermudez-Gonzalez, D., Miranda-Jiménez, S., García-Moreno, R.-U., & Calderón-Nepamuceno, D. (2016). Generating a Spanish affective dictionary with supervised learning techniques. In A. Pareja-Lora, C. Calle-Martínez, & P. Rodríguez-Arancón (Eds), *New perspectives on teaching and working with languages in the digital era* (pp. 327-338). Dublin: Research-publishing.net. http://dx.doi.org/10.14705/rpnet.2016.tislid2014.445

1. Introduction

In recent years, the automatic processing of opinions has increased because of its potential applications. One of them is sentiment analysis (Pang & Lee, 2008) in social networks. Most people write their opinions in forums, review sites, and microblogging (Twitter, Facebook, among others). This information is useful for companies, governments, and individuals who want to obtain global feedback for their activities or products.

Machine learning techniques have been used to face sentiment analysis problems, namely, to determine the affectivity of texts: their positive or negative orientation. As stated by Banea, Mihalcea, and Wiebe (2011), "[m]uch of the research work [...] on sentiment and subjectivity analysis has been applied to English, but work on other languages is [a] growing [need]" (p. 1).

In this paper, we propose a new method to build a subjectivity and sentiment dictionary for Spanish based on the definitions from an explanatory dictionary and three classifiers, which will be employed to perform sentence level sentiment classification.

2. Related work

Lexicons have been used for subjectivity and sentiment analysis because they can be applied to identify opinions or emotions by means of rule-based opinion classifiers. For example, there are several popular lexicons for subjectivity and sentiment analysis for English, such as the OpinionFinder lexicon (Wiebe & Riloff, 2005), which contains 6,856 unique entries associated with a polarity label (positive, negative, neutral). SentiWordNet (Esuli & Sebastiani, 2006) is another popular lexicon, which is based on WordNet (Miller, 1995) and encompasses more than 100,000 words. It was automatically generated, starting with a small set of manually labeled *synsets*. A *synset* represents a group of cognitive synonyms (nouns, verbs, adjectives, or adverbs) that express a distinct concept.

In the case of the Spanish language, there are few dictionaries of affective orientation. One of them, the Spanish Emotion Lexicon (SEL), has 2,038 words (Díaz-Rangel, Sidorov, & Suárez-Guerra, 2014; Sidorov et al., 2012). This dictionary was manually classified into 6 affective categories (joy, anger, fear, sadness, surprise, and disgust). The Polarity Lexicon (PL) presented in Saralegi and San Vicente (2013) has 4,738 words classified as positive or negative. Another lexicon, the Spanish Sentiment Lexicon (Pérez-Rosas, Banea, & Mihalcea, 2012) uses a cross-language expansion approach based on WordNet to determine the polarity. This lexicon has 3,843 words, classified as positive or negative.

Our approach is different: we used the entry definition of an explanatory dictionary to determine the polarity of the entry itself. We used two affective dictionaries manually labeled (SEL and PL) to train the classifiers in order to classify the entries from a large explanatory dictionary.

3. Building the affective dictionary

We were interested in discovering the positivity or negativity of dictionary entries in order to use them in opinion mining tasks. Thus, our objective was to automatically build an affective dictionary for Spanish with two categories: positive and negative. However, other works have used more categories to determine semantic orientation of messages or documents.

The number of classes used depends on the particular purposes and the domains of these works. For instance, Pang, Lee, and Vaithyanathan (2002) used two classes (positive and negative) for movie reviews, and Pérez-Rosas et al. (2012) used these two classes for generating sentiment lexicons in a target language using annotated English resources. Three classes (positive, negative, and neutral) were the base to predict contextual polarity of subjectivity phrases in a sentence in Agarwal, Biadsy, and Mckeown (2009); four classes (positive, negative, neutral, and informative) to determine the semantic orientation on Twitter data (Sidorov et al., 2012); and six classes helped determine a fine-grained affective orientation in sentences (joy, anger, fear, sadness, surprise, and disgust) in Díaz-Rangel et al. (2014).

In our approach, we used three dictionaries in order to obtain the resulting affective dictionary: an explanatory dictionary, which has the words (entries) to be classified, and two lexicons, labeled by hand with different affective categories.

3.1. The affective lexicons

Two labeled affective dictionaries were used to train the classifiers: the SEL lexicon (Díaz-Rangel et al., 2014; Sidorov et al., 2012) and the PL lexicon (Saralegi & San Vicente, 2013). In our approach, we used only two categories; thus, we mapped SEL's categories to a positive or negative category, that is, *joy* and *surprise* to positive, *anger*, *fear*, *sadness*, and *disgust* to negative.

3.2. Preprocessing of the explanatory dictionary

We used the words from Anaya explanatory dictionary of Spanish as input data to be classified (30,228 entries). Also, we used the entry definitions in two different ways: first, the definitions of words from the affective dictionaries were used to train the classifiers, and second, the definitions of the remaining entries were used to classify the entry itself.

In order to prepare the dictionary entries for classification, we removed from the entries all phrases and words with no alphabetic symbols, suffixes, and prefixes (such as *mountain bike, modus vivendi, 'ido, ida', -a,* or *neumo-*). Also, we removed stop words such as articles, prepositions, and conjunctions. We just used content words, that is, single words such as *abeja, abrumar, rata,* etc.

To process the definition of each dictionary entry, we applied some rules. For example, if the entry definition had a text such as '**véase** CONCEPT' (**see** CONCEPT), then the definition of the CONCEPT was searched in the explanatory dictionary and was used instead of '**véase** CONCEPT'. In the following example, the definition of *alcohómetro* is replaced by the definition of *alcoholímetro*. Applying this rule the substitution is as follows:

ENTRY	DEFINITION
alcohómetro	*véase alcoholímetro*
alcohómetro	*Dispositivo para medir la cantidad de alcohol presente en el aire expirado por una persona.*

We also removed from definitions numbers, suffixes, prefixes, phrases with abbreviations, and abbreviations such as '*del lat.*', '*del ár.*', *FAM., vulg.*, among others. For example, this sort of particle is removed in the following definitions:

ENTRY	DEFINITION
ruborizar	*sonrojar, adquirir o producir rubor en el rostro.* ~~FAM~~. *ruborizado.*
palmar	~~del lat.~~ *palmare, golpear; o del caló palmar, acabar.*

Finally, in this step, if the words had multiple definitions, we used the most frequent ones, that is, we selected a percentage of the definitions, because different definitions of a same word have different affective orientations for the same word. In the following example, the word *perro* (dog) has multiple definitions and each definition has a different affective orientation; the definitions 2 and 3 have clearly negative meanings, and the definitions 5, 7, and 8 have positive meanings.

ENTRY	DEFINITION
perro	*1) Nombre común de cierto mamífero carnívoro, doméstico, del que hay infinidad de razas muy distintas entre sí por la forma, el tamaño y el pelaje*
	*2) **muy malo** [lleva una vida de perro]*
	*3) Dícese de la **persona vil, traidora y astuta** [no te fíes de él, es muy perro]*
	4) Persona que siempre va pegada a otra.
	*5) **Persona que acompaña tenazmente a otra para protegerla** de supuestos peligros.*
	6) Perro faldero. Perro pequeño que siempre acompaña a su amo.
	*7) Perro guardián. **Perro que guarda una propiedad.***

*8) Atar los perros con longaniza. Frase con que se da a entender la **abundancia o riqueza**.*

Because the linguistic resource that we have created aims at supporting other practical applications for opining mining, we classified the most frequent meanings of the explanatory dictionary in order to avoid too many semantic orientations of a same word. That is, we selected the first definitions up to a predetermined percentage. The explanatory dictionary lists its entries from the most frequent meanings to the least frequent meanings.

The percentage was defined using the following rules. If a word had 1-3 senses (definitions), all senses were used; if a word had 4-6 senses, 80% of the senses were used; if a word had 7-10 senses, 60% are used; if a word had more than ten senses, 40% are used. For instance, five senses were selected for the word *perro* mentioned above.

We used these percentages because the distribution of number of senses per word is substantially reduced after three senses in the Anaya dictionary. For example, words that had from one to three senses were 26,064; four senses, 1,792; and five senses, 774 (Gelbukh, Sidorov, & Ledo-Mezquita, 2003).

3.3. Preprocessing of the training data

In order to train the classifiers, we used the word definitions of SEL and PL. We used only the content words of the definitions, as we mentioned. In order to reduce their dimensionality, the Porter (2006) stemming algorithm for Spanish was applied to the definitions.

For example, after applying the preprocessing to the original text (1), we obtained a transformed text (2) which is used as a unigram model to train the classifiers, that is, we use single words (stems).

alegre dicese de la persona, gesto, etc., que tiene o denota alegría	**original text (1)**
alegr dices person gest tien denot alegr	**transformed text (2)**

3.4. Selected classifiers

Our method uses three machine learning classifiers. The selected machine learning classifiers were Naïve Bayes (NB), Decision Trees (DTs) and Support Vector Machines (SVMs).

We used the Waikato Environment for Knowledge Analysis (WEKA) software (Hall et al., 2009) that implements the machine learning algorithms mentioned above, and we implemented our version of the NB algorithm. WEKA implements SVM as a Sequential Minimal Optimisation (SMO), and DT with J48 algorithms.

Our input data is a vector. Each entry (stem) in the vector corresponds to a feature. For SVM and DT, a Term Frequency-Inverse Document Frequency (TF-IDF) weighting approach was used (Salton & Buckley, 1988), that is, we used not only the presence of each feature, but also its global importance in the explanatory dictionary.

We used a training set that consists of 5,222 words, which came from the two affective lexicons (SEL and PL). The training set has 1,924 positive words and 3,298 negative words.

Additionally, the test set consists of 3,000 words that were randomly selected from the explanatory dictionary in order to be labeled manually to assess our method. The resulting test set has 2,316 positive words and 684 negative words.

4. Experiments and results

As mentioned above, our method uses three machine learning classifiers and consists of three steps.

First, we generated the model for each classifier considering the training data. Second, we classified the entries from the explanatory dictionary using each model; thus, three affective dictionaries were generated, that is, one for each classifier. Third, we combined the results of the three classifiers in one affective dictionary using a voting scheme. For example, the word *hurgar* (delve) was labeled as positive (p) by NB, negative (n) by SVM, and negative (n) by DT; thus, the global orientation was negative because there were two votes for negative orientation. This strategy was applied for all entries from the Anaya dictionary.

We applied standard measures used in many NLP tasks. The *precision* (P) of a system is computed as the percentage of correct answers given by the automatic system. *Recall* (R) is defined as the number of correct answers given by the automatic system over the total number of answers to be given. *F-measure* is the harmonic mean of *precision* and *recall*. The coverage is 100%, thus precision and recall are equal (Navigli, 2009).

$$P = \frac{\text{\# correct answers provided}}{\text{\# answer provided}} \qquad R = \frac{\text{\# correct answers provided}}{\text{\# total answers to provide}}$$

The results obtained for each classifier are shown in Table 1. As shown in this table, we generally obtained better results when we combined the results of the classifiers. The precision obtained was 67%. The precision for the positive category was 71%, and for the negative category was 53.3%.

Table 1. Evaluation of the classifiers

Classifier	Category	Precision	Recall	F-measure
SVM	-	49.4%	49.4%	49.4%
	Positive	42.0%	42.0%	42.0%
	Negative	74.2%	74.2%	74.2%
DT	-	30.3%	30.3%	30.3%
	Positive	12.7%	12.7%	12.7%
	Negative	89.7%	89.7%	89.7%
NB	-	59.6%	59.6%	59.6%
	Positive	60.5%	60.5%	60.5%
	Negative	56.7%	56.7%	56.7%
Voting Scheme	-	**67.0%**	**67.0%**	**67.0%**
	Positive	71.0%	71.0%	71.0%
	Negative	53.3%	53.3%	53.3%

The results show that the performance for the negative category is reduced. Each classifier alone is better than the voting scheme because of discrepancies among classifiers. For example, if two classifiers vote for a positive polarity, the word will be classified as positive, even if the SVM classifies it correctly as negative.

The resulting lexicon has 30,773 affective words, including different meanings for each word. For example, the number accompanying the word *rosa* (3) indicates that the third meaning was used to determine its polarity.

In the resulting dictionary, we included the polarity, the word, and the gloss that describes the sense of the word. For example, in Table 2, we show some results of the dictionary. The first column indicates the polarity as positive (p) or negative (n), the second column indicates the classified word (*hurgar* / delve), and the last column indicates the meaning of the word.

Table 2. Excerpt from the affective Spanish dictionary

Results		
Polarity	Word	Gloss
n	*hurgar*	remover una cosa, escarbar.
n	*chorrear*	caer un líquido a chorro.
n	*roer*	raspar con los dientes una cosa, generalmente un alimento, arrancando parte de ella.
n	*rosa3*	mancha rosácea que sale en el cuerpo.
n	*aberrar*	andar errante, equivocarse, aberración, aberrante.
p	*comer2*	tomar la comida principal del día [en mi casa comemos a las dos].
p	*contribuir*	pagar las contribuciones o impuestos.

With respect to analysis of errors, we identified some errors when analysing the classified words. For example, if the word sense is related to a common animal (error type 1), the classified word has no positive or negative polarity at all; human annotators also hesitate how to classify these sorts of words. In the second error type, the definition is very short at word level; it is difficult that classifiers assign the correct label due to lack of context.

Table 3. Errors in the classification process

Error	Example
1. common animal	p|perro|nombre común, mamífero carnívoro, doméstico (p|dog| common animal, carnivorous mammal, domestic)
2. short definition	n|rivera|arroyo (n|stream|creek) n|revuelto|de revolver (n|mess-up|to mess up)

5. Conclusions

In this paper, we have presented a method that generates a large affective lexicon using supervised learning techniques for Spanish. We evaluated the results obtained using a test set with 3,000 words that were selected randomly and labeled by hand. The training set used consisted of 5,222 words from two affective lexicons (SEL and PL). The resulting lexicon has 30,773 words, classified as positive or negative words, including different meanings for each word. The precision obtained was 67.0%. It shows that the quality of our lexicon outperforms that of lexicons whose entries are classified using just one classifier.

In the future, we will not use stems to train the classifiers. In order to improve their performance, we will use lemmatisers, part of speech taggers, or syntactic n-grams (Sidorov et al., 2014) for example, since they have already been used for this purpose with good results.

References

Agarwal, A., Biadsy, F., & Mckeown, K. (2009). Contextual phrase-level polarity analysis using lexical affect scoring and syntactic n-grams. In *Proceedings of EACL 2009* (pp. 24-32). Greece: ACL. Retrieved from http://dx.doi.org/10.3115/1609067.1609069

Banea, C., Mihalcea, R., & Wiebe, J. (2011). Multilingual sentiment and subjectivity analysis. In D. Bikel & I. Zitouni (Eds.), *Multilingual natural language processing applications: from theory to practice.* Boston: IBM Press. Retrieved from http://people.cs.pitt.edu/~wiebe/pubs/papers/multilingualSubjBookChap2011.pdf?

Díaz-Rangel, I., Sidorov, G., & Suárez-Guerra, S. (2014). Creación y evaluación de un diccionario marcado con emociones y ponderado para el español. *Onomazein, 29*, 1-23. Retrieved from http://dx.doi.org/10.7764/onomazein.29.5

Esuli, A., & Sebastiani, F. (2006). SentiWordNet: a publicly available lexical resource for opinion mining. In *Proceedings of LREC 2006*, (pp. 417-422). Italy.

Gelbukh, A., Sidorov, G., & Ledo-Mezquita, Y. (2003). On similarity of word senses in explanatory dictionaries. *International Journal of Translation, 15*(2), 51-60.

Hall, M., Frank, E., Holmes, G., Pfahringer, B., Reutemann, P., & Witten, I. H. (2009). The WEKA data mining software: an update. *ACM SIGKDD Explorations Newsletter, 11*(1), 10-18. Retrieved from http://dx.doi.org/10.1145/1656274.1656278

Miller, G. A. (1995). WordNet: a lexical database for English. *Communications of the ACM, 38*(11), 39-41. Retrieved from http://dx.doi.org/10.1145/219717.219748

Navigli, R. (2009). Word sense disambiguation: a survey. *ACM Computing Surveys (CSUR), 41*(2). Retrieved from http://dx.doi.org/10.1145/1459352.1459355

Pang, B., Lee, L., & Vaithyanathan, S. (2002). Thumbs up?: sentiment classification using machine learning techniques. In *Proceedings of the ACL-02 conference on Empirical Methods in Natural Language Processing* (pp. 79-86). USA: ACL. Retrieved from http://dx.doi.org/10.3115/1118693.1118704

Pang, B., & Lee, L. (2008). Opinion mining and sentiment analysis. *Foundations and Trends in Information Retrieval, 2*(1-2), 1-135. Retrieved from http://dx.doi.org/10.1561/1500000011

Pérez-Rosas, V., Banea, C., & Mihalcea, R. (2012). Learning sentiment lexicons in Spanish. In *Proceedings of LREC 2012*, (pp. 3077-3081). Turkey: ELRA.

Porter, M. F. (2006). Spanish stemming algorithm. Retrieved from http://snowball.tartarus.org/algorithms/spanish/stemmer.html

Salton, G., & Buckley, C. (1988). Term-weighting approaches in automatic text retrieval. *Information Processing and Management, 24*(5), 513-523. Retrieved from http://dx.doi.org/10.1016/0306-4573(88)90021-0

Saralegi, X., & San Vicente, I. (2013). Elhuyar at TASS 2013. In *Proceedings of XXIX Congreso de la Sociedad Española de Procesamiento de lenguaje natural. Workshop on Sentiment Analysis at SEPLN (TASS2013)* (pp. 143-150). Madrid: SEPLN.

Sidorov, G., Miranda-Jiménez, S., Viveros-Jiménez, F., Gelbukh, A., Castro-Sánchez, N., Velásquez, F., Díaz-Rangel, I., Suárez-Guerra, S., Treviño, A., & Gordon, J. (2012). Empirical study of machine learning based approach for opinion mining in tweets. In *Advances in Artificial Intelligence (MICAI 2012)* (pp. 1-14). Mexico: Springer.

Chapter 28

Sidorov, G., Velasquez, F., Stamatatos, E., Gelbukh, A., & Chanona-Hernández, L. (2014). Syntactic N-grams as machine learning features for natural language processing. *Expert Systems with Applications, 41*(3), 853-860. Retrieved from http://dx.doi.org/10.1016/j.eswa.2013.08.015

Wiebe, J., & Riloff, E. (2005). Creating subjective and objective sentence classifiers from unannotated texts. In *Proceeding of CICLing-05, International Conference on Intelligent Text Processing and Computational* (pp. 486-497). Mexico: Springer. Retrieved from http://dx.doi.org/10.1007/978-3-540-30586-6_53

29. Transcription and annotation of a Japanese accented spoken corpus of L2 Spanish for the development of CAPT applications

Mario Carranza[1]

Abstract

This paper addresses the process of transcribing and annotating spontaneous non-native speech with the aim of compiling a training corpus for the development of Computer Assisted Pronunciation Training (CAPT) applications, enhanced with Automatic Speech Recognition (ASR) technology. To better adapt ASR technology to CAPT tools, the recognition systems must be trained with non-native corpora transcribed and annotated at several linguistic levels. This allows the automatic generation of pronunciation variants, new L2 phoneme units, and statistical data about the most frequent mispronunciations by L2 learners. We present a longitudinal non-native spoken corpus of L2 Spanish by Japanese speakers, specifically designed for the development of CAPT tools, fully transcribed at both phonological and phonetic levels and annotated at the error level. We report the results of the influence of oral proficiency, speaking style and L2 exposition in pronunciation accuracy, obtained from the statistical analysis of the corpus.

Keywords: non-native spoken corpora, spontaneous speech transcription, L1 Japanese, L2 Spanish, standards for transcription and annotation.

---

1. Universitat Autònoma de Barcelona, Barcelona, Spain; mario.carranza@uab.cat

How to cite this chapter: Carranza, M. (2016). Transcription and annotation of a Japanese accented spoken corpus of L2 Spanish for the development of CAPT applications. In A. Pareja-Lora, C. Calle-Martínez, & P. Rodríguez-Arancón (Eds), *New perspectives on teaching and working with languages in the digital era* (pp. 339-349). Dublin: Research-publishing.net. http://dx.doi.org/10.14705/rpnet.2016.tislid2014.446

Chapter 29

1. Introduction

Several studies have pointed out the possibility of efficiently adapting ASR systems to pronunciation assessment of non-native speech (Neri, Cucchiarini, & Strik, 2003) if technology limitations are compensated with a good design of language learning activities and feedback, and the inclusion of repair strategies to safeguard against recognition errors.

An ASR system can be adapted as an automatic pronunciation error detection system by training it with non-native speech data that generates

> "new acoustic models for the non-native realizations of L2 [phones], and by the systematization of L1-based typical errors by means of rules […]. In order to do so, phonetically transcribed non-native spoken corpora are needed; however, manual transcription of non-native speech is a time-consuming costly task, and current automatic transcription systems are not accurate enough to carry out a narrow phonetic transcription" (Carranza, 2013, p. 168).

In this paper we will introduce a corpus of non-native Spanish by Japanese speakers that contains spontaneous, semi-spontaneous and read speech. The corpus is transcribed at the orthographic, phonological and phonetic levels, and annotated with an error-encoding system that specifies the error type and its phonological context of appearance.

This database was compiled and annotated considering its future adaptation as a training corpus for developing ASR-based CAPT tools and applications for the teaching of Spanish pronunciation to Japanese speakers.

In section 1, we will present the general features of the corpus. Section 2 deals with the levels of transcription, the annotation standards, and the phone inventory used in the transcriptions. Finally, the results of the statistical analysis of errors are presented in section 3, followed by a discussion concerning our findings.

2. Corpus data description

The corpus features 8.9h of non-native speech, divided into semi-spontaneous speech (91'), spontaneous speech (214'), read speech (9') and conversational speech (201'). Spontaneous speech represents more than 80% of the recordings. The data was obtained from 10 male and 10 female Japanese students of L2 Spanish at the Spanish Department of the Tokyo University of Foreign Studies. They were selected according to their dialectal area (Kanto dialect) and none of them had previous academic contact with Spanish. The corpus contains the oral tests of the 20 informants throughout their two first academic years of Spanish study (from 1/4/2010 to 31/3/2012), which corresponds to the A1 and A2 levels in the Common European Framework of Reference for Language Learning (Council of Europe, 2001). Oral tests took place every six months, and consisted of different types of tasks that involved spontaneous, semi-spontaneous, and read speech. Semi-spontaneous speech was obtained from oral presentations prepared before-hand (in the 1st and 2nd semesters) and spontaneous speech was gathered from conversations between the student and the examiner and role-plays with no previous preparation (in all semesters). Oral proficiency was also taken into account by computing the mean of all the oral-test scores of each informant. Three proficiency levels were established according to this score: low ($N=6$), intermediate ($N=8$) and high ($N=6$).

The recordings were made with portable recorders and were segmented into individual audio files. The audio files were converted into WAV format and labelled with information regarding the student, the task type and the period of learning (semester). This allows the automatic computation of error rates according to proficiency level, learning stage and speaking style after the transcription and annotation of the corpus.

3. Levels of transcription

Transcription of non-native spontaneous speech is a complex activity due to its high degree of variability and the interference of the L1 and constant presence of vocalizations and other extra-linguistic phenomena. For this reason, transcribers should follow a set of rules to interpret and represent speech, aimed at maintaining consistency across all levels of transcription (Cucchiarini, 1993). Moreover, transcription is always bounded to a certain degree of subjectivity because it is based on individual perception and implies other sources of variation, such as familiarity of the transcriber with the L1 of the student, training and experience received, auditory sensitivity, quality of the speech signal, and factors regarding the speech materials to be transcribed, such as word intelligibility and length of the utterance.

Training corpora for ASR need to be transcribed in a very detailed way, preferably at a narrow phonetic level; acoustic non-linguistic phenomena that could interfere in the generation of the acoustic models should be correctly labelled. Furthermore, the narrow phonetic transcription of non-native speech must be compared to a reference transcription (i.e. a 'canonical' transcription) that represents the expected pronunciation of the utterance by native speakers. This will allow the system to automatically detect discrepancies between both levels and generate rules for pronunciation variants and acoustic models for non-native phones.

The corpus was transcribed and annotated using *Praat* (Boersma & Weenink, 2014). Two levels of representation – canonical phonemic and narrow phonetic transcriptions – were considered, and the resulting tiers were aligned with the orthographic transcription. Vocalizations and non-linguistic phenomena were also marked in two independent tiers. Finally, mispronunciations were encoded in a different tier, and every error label was aligned with the linguistic transcriptions.

3.1. Orthographic transcription

In the orthographic tier, every word is transcribed in its standardized form, but no punctuation marks are used due to the difficulty of establishing syntactic boundaries in spontaneous speech. Non-native spontaneous speech is characterized by a high number of filled pauses or hesitations, repetitions and truncations that tend to be employed when the speaker is confronted with some syntactic or lexical difficulty. The cases of fragmented speech are problematic for the orthographical transcription, especially truncations, when the word is never completed and the transcriber must guess the actual word that the informant intended to say. TEI-conformant (XML-like) tags were used for labelling these phenomena (Gibbon, Moore, & Winski, 1998; TEI Consortium, 2014), as well as unclear cases, missing words, foreign words and erroneous words (like regularized irregular verbs). Hesitations and interjections were also transcribed at this level according to their standardized forms in dictionaries. Only the speech of the informant is transcribed. The commentaries of the examiner are not considered, except when they overlap with the student's speech; in these cases, the overlapping speech is tagged with an XML label in the incident tier (the list of XML tags employed is shown in Table 4).

3.2. Canonical phonemic transcription

The canonical phonemic tier shows the phonological transcription of each word as pronounced in isolation. Northern Castilian Spanish (Martínez Celdrán & Fernández Planas, 2007; Quilis, 1993) was adopted as the standard reference for the transcription, considering that Japanese students had been taught mainly in this variety. Consequently, at this level, the phonemic opposition /s/–/θ/ is preserved, but not the opposition /ʝ/–/ʎ/, which is neutralized in favor of /ʝ/ (Gil, 2007). An adaptation of SAMPA to Spanish (Llisterri & Mariño, 1993) was chosen for the inventory of phonological units (see Table 1), since the obtained transcription had to be machine-readable.

3.3. Narrow phonetic transcription

The narrow phonetic level represents the actual pronunciation of the speaker in the most accurate way. In order to avoid transcriber's subjectivity, the transcription was based primarily on acoustic measurements and visual examination of the spectrogram and the waveform. We avoided perceptual judgment, except in cases where the decision cannot be taken from the methods stated before and should be reached upon auditorial perception. Coarticulatory phenomena (nasalization and changes in place or articulation) are considered here, as well as the Spanish allophonic variants of the phonemes presented in Table 1. We added a new set of symbols and diacritics taken from X-SAMPA (Wells, 1994) to account for these phenomena (see Table 2). Further symbols were also added to account for the L2 Spanish pronunciation of Japanese speakers. In total, 11 new symbols and 7 diacritics were needed for the narrow phonetic transcription (see Table 3).

3.4. Vocalizations and non-linguistic phenomena

Vocalized or semi-lexical elements, such as laughters, hesitations, and interjections were labelled in a separate tier. The acoustic realizations of these elements resemble linguistic sounds – hesitations are usually realized as vowels or nasal sounds, and interjections as short vowels – and can interfere in the acoustic modeling when training the recognizer.

Table 1. Our SAMPA inventory for phonemic transcription, based on Llisterri and Mariño (1993)

IPA	SAMPA	Description	IPA	SAMPA	Description
/a/	a	central open vowel	/m/	m	voiced bilabial nasal
/e/	e	front mid vowel	/n/	n	voiced alveolar nasal
/i/	i	front close vowel	/ɲ/	J	voiced palatal nasal
/i̯/	j	front close vowel (used in glides)	/t͡ʃ/	tS	voiceless palatal affricate
/o/	o	back mid rounded vowel	/f/	f	voiceless labiodental fricative
/u/	u	back close rounded vowel	/θ/	T	voiceless interdental fricative
/u̯/	w	back close rounded vowel (used in glides)	/s/	s	voiceless alveolar fricative
/p/	p	voiceless bilabial stop	/x/	x	voiceless velar fricative
/b/	b	voiced bilabial stop	/l/	l	voiced alveolar lateral
/t/	t	voiceless dental stop	/ɟ/	jj	voiceless palatal stop
/d/	d	voiced dental stop	/ɾ/	r	voiced alveolar flap
/k/	k	voiceless velar stop	/r/	rr	voiced alveolar trill
/g/	g	voiced velar stop			

Table 2. SAMPA inventory of Spanish allophones used in the narrow phonetic transcription

IPA	SAMPA	Description	IPA	SAMPA	Description
[β̞]	B	voiced bilabial approximant	[z]	z	voiced alveolar fricative
[ð̞]	D	voiced dental approximant	[d͡ʒ]	dZ	voiced palatal affricate
[ɣ̞]	G	voiced velar approximant	**Diacritics (X-SAMPA)**		
[ɟ]	J\	voiced palatal stop	[ã]	_~	nasalized
[j]	j	voiced palatal approximant	[ă]	_X	extra short
[ŋ]	N	voiced velar nasal	[i̯]	_^	non-syllabic (used in combination with full vowels in glides)

Table 3. X-SAMPA inventory of symbols used to represent Japanese and other sounds in the narrow phonetic transcription

IPA	X-SAMPA	Description	IPA	X-SAMPA	Description
[ɯ]	M	unrounded central-back vowel	[d͡z]	dz	voiced alveolopalatal affricate
[ə]	@	central mid vowel	[v]	v	voiced labiodental fricative
[ʃ]	S	voiceless postalveolar fricative	**Diachritics (X-SAMPA)**		
[ɸ]	p\	voiceless bilabial approximant	[ḁ]	_0	devoiced
[ç]	C	voiceless palatal fricative	[a̰]	_k	creaky voiced
[ʔ]	?	glottal stop	[aʲ]	_j	palatalized
[h]	h	voiceless glottal fricative	[aʰ]	_h	aspirated
[ʝ]	j\	voiced palatal fricative	[a̤]	_t	breathy voiced

This is why vocalizations were separated from the rest of speech. They were marked using XML tags to explicitly indicate that these segments should not be employed in the ASR training phase. Non-linguistic (or non-lexical) phenomena were marked in the incident tier. We considered laughs, breathing, external noise and overlapping speech of the examiner in this group. All tags used in the orthographic, vocalization and incident tiers are shown in Table 4.

4. Results and discussion

All the data from the *Praat* transcription tiers was recovered using *Praat* scripts, and data tables were generated for the statistical analysis. The resulting tables contain every mispronounced sound and all the information annotated in the transcriptions. Since the audio files varied in their duration, longer speech can make the possibility of committing errors rise. Consequently, we adopted a metric (error ratio) that takes into account the length of the file by counting the total number of mispronunciations and dividing it by the total number of words, after subtracting the number of hesitations and interjections. The adopted formula for obtaining the error ratio is shown in Figure 1. This metric indicates the total number of mispronunciations per linguistic word, and serves to better evaluate the speaker's performance in spontaneous non-prepared speech, as the duration of the audio files varies drastically from speaker to speaker.

Table 4. XML tags used for the annotation of extra-linguistic and non-linguistic phenomena, adapted from TEI Consortium (2014)

Tag	Explanation	Transcription tier
<repetition>	The following word is completely repeated at least once.	orthographic
<truncation>	The word is not completely uttered. Also used when repetitions are not complete.	orthographic
<unclear>	The word is recognized but cannot be phonetically transcribed due to problems in the signal.	orthographic
<foreign>	Foreign words articulated differently than target-language conventions.	orthographic
<gap\>	The marked segment cannot be recognized (no need to close).	orthographic
<sic>	Made-up word or non-existing word in target language.	orthographic
<noise>	External noise that interferes with speech.	incident

<breath>	Breathing of the speaker. It can happen alone or interfering with speech.	incident
<overlap>	The interviewer's speech overlaps with the informant's speech.	incident
<hesitation>	Filled-pause.	vocalization
<interjection>	Exclamation due to surprise, annoyance or other feelings.	vocalization
<laugh>	Inserted laughing or speech uttered while laughing.	vocalization

Figure 1. Formula for calculating the error ratio

$$ratio_e = \frac{N_e}{N_w - (N_h + N_i)}$$

Error ratio scores were obtained from each audio file and statistically analyzed considering three variables: oral proficiency, speaking style and period of learning. The statistical tests (ANOVA) showed no significant influence of the speaking style or time on the error ratio, which means that the number of pronunciation errors does not depend on the preparation or spontaneity of the discourse and does not vary throughout the first two years of language teaching (in a non-immersive L2 environment). However, oral proficiency had a clear influence on the error ratio ($df=2$, $F=7.431$, $p=0.00079$), which is lower in the high proficiency group and higher in the low proficiency group.

The mean error ratio actually varies in all the four learning stages when each proficiency group is analyzed separately (see Figure 2). Error ratio decreases specially in the period from 6 to 12 months of learning in all proficiency groups. From the 12th month, this tendency continues in intermediate and high proficiency groups, but not in the low proficiency group, which shows an error increase up to the first period level. These findings suggest that language exposure has a positive influence in intermediate and high proficiency learners, but not in low proficiency learners. Regarding the influence of speaking style on error ratio, it should be highlighted that spontaneous and conversational speech shows much more variability in the results than semi-spontaneous and read speech, as expected. Differences on mean error ratio by the speaking style are minimal.

Chapter 29

Figure 2. Mean error ratio by period of learning separated by oral proficiency groups

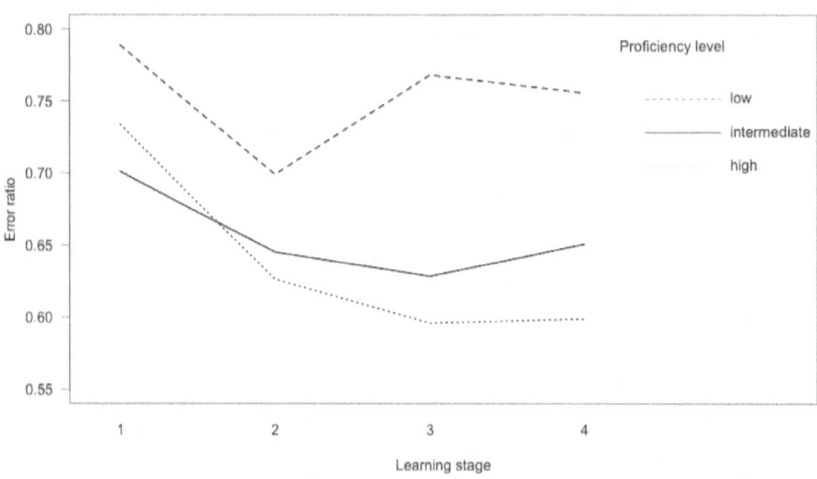

5. Conclusions

Our results show that the starting oral proficiency level of the student, due mainly to individual abilities, is the only variable that reported a positive impact on Spanish pronunciation acquisition. Although L2 exposure seems to reduce error ratios in intermediate and high proficiency groups – especially from the sixth month of instruction onwards –, the obtained differences did not prove to be statistically significant. Consequently, it seems that exposure to the target language is not enough to expect pronunciation accuracy improvement in foreign language students.

In further reports, we will focus on the specific errors found in the corpus and offer results by frequency of occurrence and error type. Future research will aim at the evaluation of erroneous utterances by means of native-speaker perceptual assessment and automatic evaluation by an ASR system.

References

Boersma, P., & Weenink, D. (2014). *Praat: doing phonetics by computer*. Retrieved from http://www.fon.hum.uva.nl/praat/

Carranza, M. (2013). Intermediate phonetic realizations in a Japanese accented L2 Spanish corpus. In P. Badin, T. Hueber, G. Bailly, D. Demolin, & F. Raby (Eds.), *Proceedings of SLaTE 2013, Interspeech 2013 Satellite Workshop on Speech and Language Technology in Education* (pp. 168-171). Grenoble, France. Retrieved from http://www.slate2013.org/images/slate2013_proc_light_v4.pdf

Council of Europe. (2001). *Common European framework of reference for languages: learning, teaching, assessment*. Cambridge, U.K: Press Syndicate of the University of Cambridge. Retrieved from https://www.coe.int/t/dg4/linguistic/Source/Framework_EN.pdf

Cucchiarini, C. (1993). *Phonetic transcription: a methodological and empirical study*. PhD dissertation, Radboud Universiteit Nijmegen.

Gibbon, D., Moore, R., & Winski, R. (1998). *Spoken language system and corpus design*. Berlin: Mouton De Gruyter. Retrieved from http://dx.doi.org/10.1515/9783110809817

Gil, J. (2007). *Fonética para profesores de español: de la teoría a la práctica*. Madrid: Arco/Libros.

Llisterri, J., & Mariño, J. B. (1993). *Spanish adaptation of SAMPA and automatic phonetic transcription*. ESPRIT PROJECT 6819 (SAM-A Speech Technology Assessment in Multilingual Applications).

Martínez Celdrán, E., & Fernández Planas, A. M. (2007). *Manual de fonética española: articulaciones y sonidos del español*. Barcelona: Ariel.

Neri, A., Cucchiarini, C., & Strik, H. (2003). Automatic speech recognition for second language learning: how and why it actually works. *Proceedings of the 15th International Congress of Phonetic Sciences* (pp. 1157-1160). Barcelona, Spain.

Quilis, A. (1993). *Tratado de fonología y fonética españolas* (2nd ed.). Madrid: Gredos.

TEI Consortium. (2014, January 20). *TEI P5: Guidelines for electronic text encoding and interchange – 8 Transcriptions of speech*. Retrieved from http://www.tei-c.org/release/doc/tei-p5-doc/en/html/TS.html

Wells, J. C. (1994). Computer-coding the IPA: a proposed extension of SAMPA. *Speech, Hearing and Language, Work in Progress*, 8, 271-289.

30 Using ontologies to interlink linguistic annotations and improve their accuracy

Antonio Pareja-Lora[1]

Abstract

For the new approaches to language e-learning (e.g. language blended learning, language autonomous learning or mobile-assisted language learning) to succeed, some automatic functions for error correction (for instance, in exercises) will have to be included in the long run in the corresponding environments and/or applications. A possible way to achieve this is to use some Natural Language Processing (NLP) functions within language e-learning applications. These functions should be based on some truly reliable and wide-coverage linguistic annotation tools (e.g. a Part-Of-Speech (POS) tagger, a syntactic parser and/or a semantic tagger). However, linguistic annotation tools usually introduce a not insignificant rate of errors and ambiguities when tagging, which prevents them from being used 'as is' for this purpose. In this paper, we present an annotation architecture and methodology that has helped reduce the rate of errors in POS tagging, by making several POS taggers interoperate and supplement each other. We also introduce briefly the set of ontologies that have helped all these tools intercommunicate and collaborate in order to produce a more accurate joint POS tagging, and how these ontologies were used towards this end. The resulting POS tagging error rate is around 6%, which should allow this function to be included in language e-learning applications for the purpose aforementioned.

Keywords: ontology, interoperability, POS tagging, accuracy, linguistic annotation, tools.

---

1. Universidad Complutense de Madrid / ATLAS (UNED), Madrid, Spain; apareja@sip.ucm.es

How to cite this chapter: Pareja-Lora, A. (2016). Using ontologies to interlink linguistic annotations and improve their accuracy. In A. Pareja-Lora, C. Calle-Martínez, & P. Rodríguez-Arancón (Eds), *New perspectives on teaching and working with languages in the digital era* (pp. 351-362). Dublin: Research-publishing.net. http://dx.doi.org/10.14705/rpnet.2016.tislid2014.447

Chapter 30

1. Introduction

Some of the most recent and interesting approaches to language e-learning incorporate an NLP module to provide the learner with, for example, "exercises, self-assessment tools and an interactive dictionary of key vocabulary and concepts" (Urbano-Mendaña, Corpas-Pastor, & Mitkov, 2013, p. 29). For these approaches to succeed, the corresponding NLP module must be based on some truly reliable and wide-coverage linguistic annotation tools (e.g. a POS tagger, a syntactic parser and/or a semantic tagger). However, "linguistic annotation tools have still some limitations, which can be summarised as follows:

> (1) Normally, they perform annotations only at a certain linguistic level (that is, morphology, syntax, semantics, etc.).

> (2) They usually introduce a certain rate of errors and ambiguities when tagging. This error rate ranges from 10% up to 50% of the units annotated for unrestricted, general texts" (Pareja-Lora, 2012b, p. 19).

The interoperation and the integration of several linguistic tools into an appropriate software architecture that provides a multilevel but integrated annotation should most likely solve the limitations stated in (1). Besides, integrating several linguistic annotation tools and making them interoperate can also minimise the limitation stated in (2), as shown in Pareja-Lora and Aguado de Cea (2010).

In this paper, we present an annotation architecture and methodology that (1) unifies "the annotation schemas of different linguistic annotation tools or, more generally speaking, that makes [a set of linguistic] tools (as well as their annotations) interoperate; and (2) [helps] correct or, at least, reduce the errors and the inaccuracies of [these] tools" (Pareja-Lora, 2012b, p. 20). We present also the ontologies (Borst, 1997; Gruber, 1993) developed to solve this interoperability problem. As with many other interoperability problems, they have really helped integrate the different tools and improve the overall performance of the resulting NLP module. In particular, we will show how we used these ontologies to interlink several POS taggers together, in order to produce a combined POS tagging that outperformed all the tools interlinked. The error rate of the combined POS tagging was around 6%, whereas the error rate of the tools interlinked was around 10%–15%.

2. The annotation architecture

The annotation architecture presented here belongs in the OntoTag's annotation model. This model aimed at specifying:

> "a hybrid (that is, linguistically-motivated and ontology-based) type of annotation suitable for the Semantic Web. [Hence, OntoTag's tags had to] (1) represent linguistic concepts (or linguistic categories, as they are termed within [ISO TC 37]), in order for this model to be linguistically-motivated[2]; (2) be ontological terms (i.e. use an ontological vocabulary), in order for the model to be ontology-based; and (3) be structured (linked) as a collection of ontology-based <Subject, Predicate, Object> triples, as in the usual Semantic Web languages (namely RDF(S) and OWL), in order for the model to be considered suitable for the Semantic Web" (Pareja-Lora, 2012b, p. 20).

Besides, as discussed above, it should be able to merge the annotation of several tools, in order to POS tag texts more accurately (in terms of precision and recall) than some tools available (e.g. Connexor's FDG, Bitext's DataLexica).

Thus, OntoTag's annotation architecture is, in fact, the methodology we propose to merge several linguistic annotations towards the ends mentioned above. This annotation architecture consists of several phases of processing, which are used to annotate each input document incrementally. Its final aim is to offer automatic, standardised, high quality annotations.

---

2. see http://www.iso.org/iso/standards_development/technical_committees/other_bodies/iso_technical_committee.htm?commid=48104, and also http://www.isocat.org

Chapter 30

Briefly, the five different phases of the annotation architecture are (1) distillation, (2) tagging, (3) standardisation, (4) decanting, and (5) merging. Yet, this last phase is sub-divided into two intertwined sub-phases: combination, or intra-level merging, and integration, or inter-level merging. They are described below, each one in a dedicated subsection.

2.1. Distillation

Most linguistic annotation tools do not recognise formatted (marked-up) text as input for annotation; hence, most frequently, the textual information conveyed by the input files (e.g. HTML, Word or PDF files) has to be distilled (extracted) before using it as input for an already existing linguistic annotation tool. The input of this phase is, thus, an unformatted document, consisting of only the textual information (the distilled, plain or clean text) of the input file to be annotated.

2.2. Tagging

In this phase, the clean text document produced in the distillation phase is inputted to the different annotation tools assembled into the architecture. It does not matter at this point the levels or the formats of the output annotations; it is left to the remaining phases of the architecture to cope with these issues. After this phase, the clean text document will be tagged or annotated (1) at a certain (set of) level(s), and (2) according to a tool-dependent annotation scheme and tagset.

2.3. Standardisation

In order for the annotations coming from the different linguistic annotation tools to be conveniently compared and combined, they must be first mapped onto a standard or guideline-compliant – that is, standardised – type of annotation, so that (1) the annotations pertaining to the same tool but to different levels of description are clearly structured and differentiated (or decanted, in OntoTag's terminology), (2) all the annotations pertaining to the same level of description but to different tools use a common vocabulary to refer to each particular phenomenon described by that level, and (3) the annotations pertaining to different tools and different levels of description can be easily merged later on in a one and unique overall standardised annotation for the document being processed.

It is at this point where OntoTag's ontologies play a crucial role. They have been developed following the existing standards, guidelines and recommendations for annotation (see some details about them below). Accordingly, annotating with reference to OntoTag's ontologies produces a result that uses a standardised type of tagset. For this reason, the tagsets and the annotations from each and every tool are mapped onto the terms of OntoTag's ontologies. Then, after this phase has been applied, all the tags are expressed according to a shared and standardised vocabulary. In addition, this vocabulary can also be considered formal and fully semantic from a computational point of view, since it is referred to ontologies. The level-driven, taxonomical and relational structure of OntoTag's ontologies is also right and proper for (1) structuring and distinguishing the information into different levels; and (2) summing up and interconnecting all of them later on again, by means of the relations already described in the ontologies themselves.

Yet, as commented above, the main contribution of this phase to the whole architecture is that it enables the model to handle the annotations from any tool, irrespective of the levels to which they pertain and the schemes (or the tagsets) employed for their generation. After the document being annotated is processed in this phase, the annotations for the same phenomenon coming from all the tools will follow the same scheme and will be, thus, comparable. A major drawback of including this phase, though, is that it requires a prior study of the output scheme and the tagsets of each of the tools assembled into the architecture. Indeed, their interpretation and mapping onto the standardised tagset obtained from OntoTag's ontologies cannot be automatically determined a priori. Consequently, an ad-hoc, tool dependent standardising wrapper must be implemented for each linguistic annotation tool assembled into an implementation of the architecture.

So, to summarise, the output of this phase is another set of documents, differing from the input ones in that they are tagged according to a standardised, tool-independent tagset and scheme (still, one document for each tool assembled into the architecture).

2.4. Decanting

A number of the linguistic annotation tools assembled into the architecture might tag at more than just one level of linguistic description. The annotations pertaining to the same tool but to a different level have to be decanted (that is, separated according to their levels and layers or types) in a way that:

- the process of the remaining phases is not complicated; but rather

- the comparison, evaluation and mutual supplement of the results offered at the same level by different tools is simplified; and

- the different decanted results can be easily re-combined, after they have been subsequently processed.

The solution to this problem (that is, how the annotations have to be partitioned and separated) was determined empirically, after carrying out several experiments (Pareja-Lora, 2012a). Eventually, it was found that, for each annotated document coming from the tagging phase (one for each tool), two different documents have to be generated to further process morphosyntactic annotations, that is:

- one document containing both the lemmas and the grammatical category tags (L+POS);

- one consisting of the grammatical category tags and the morphological annotations (POS+M).

2.5. Merging

At this point, all the standardised and decanted annotations have to be merged in order to yield a unique, combined and multi-level (or multi-layered) annotation for the original input document. This is the most complex part of the architecture, since it is responsible for two different tasks:

- uniting (*combining*) all the annotations that belong to the same level, but come from different tools;

- summing up and interconnecting (that is, *integrating*) the annotations that belong to different levels so as to bear a combined, integrated and unique set of annotations for the original input document.

As commented above, these two tasks are conceptually different and, thus, are considered two distinct (but intertwined) sub-phases in the architecture. Unfortunately, these two sub-phases, namely combination and integration, cannot be further described here for the sake of space.

3. The linguistic ontologies

As previously stated in Pareja-Lora (2012b, p. 326), the elements involved in linguistic annotation were formalised in a set (or network) of ontologies (OntoTag's linguistic ontologies). On the one hand, OntoTag's network of ontologies consists of:

- the Linguistic Unit Ontology (LUO), which includes a mostly hierarchical formalisation of the different types of linguistic elements (i.e., units) identifiable in a written text (across levels and layers);

- the Linguistic Attribute Ontology (LAO), which includes also a mostly hierarchical formalisation of the different types of features that characterise the linguistic units included in the LUO;

- the Linguistic Value Ontology (LVO), which includes the corresponding formalisation of the different values that the attributes in the LAO can take;

Chapter 30

- the OIO (OntoTag's Integration Ontology), which (1) includes the knowledge required to link, combine and unite the knowledge represented in the LUO, the LAO and the LVO; and (2) can be viewed as a knowledge representation ontology that describes the most elementary vocabulary used in the area of annotation.

On the other hand, OntoTag's ontologies incorporate the knowledge included in the different standards and recommendations regarding directly or indirectly morphosyntactic, syntactic and semantic annotation so far – not discussed here for the sake of space; for further information, see Pareja-Lora (2012a, 2012b).

4. Experimentation and results

We built a small corpus of HTML web pages (10 pages, around 500 words each) from the domain of the cinema reviews. This corpus was POS tagged automatically, and its POS tags were manually checked afterwards. Thus, we had a gold standard with which we could compare the test results. Then, we used two of these ten pages to determine the rules that had to be implemented in the combination module of the prototype, following the methodology described in Pareja-Lora and Aguado de Cea (2010). Eventually, we implemented in a prototype (called *OntoTagger*) the architecture described above (see Figure 1) in order to merge the annotations of three different tools, namely Connexor's FDG Parser (henceforth FDG, http://www.connexor.com/nlplib/?q=demo/syntax), a POS tagger from the LACELL research group (henceforth LACELL, https://www.um.es/grupos/grupo-lacell/index.php), and Bitext's DataLexica (henceforth DataLexica, http://www.bitext.com/whatwedo/components/com_datalexica.html). The prototype was then tested on the remaining eight HTML pages of the corpus.

In this test, in terms of precision, the prototype (93.81%) highly outperformed DataLexica (83.82%), which actually does not provide POS tagging disambiguation; improved significantly the results of LACELL (85.68% – OntoTagger is more precise in around 8% of cases); and slightly surpassed the results of FDG (FDG yielded a value of precision of 92.23%, which indicates that OntoTagger outperformed FDG in around 1.50% of cases).

In terms of recall, two different kinds of particular statistical indicators were devised. First, a group of indicators was calculated to show simply the difference in the average number of tokens which were assigned a more specific morphosyntactic tag by each tool being compared. For this purpose, for instance, the tags 'NC' (Noun, Common) and 'NP' (Noun, Proper) should be regarded as more specific than 'N' (Noun).

Figure 1. OntoTag's experimentation – OntoTagger's architecture

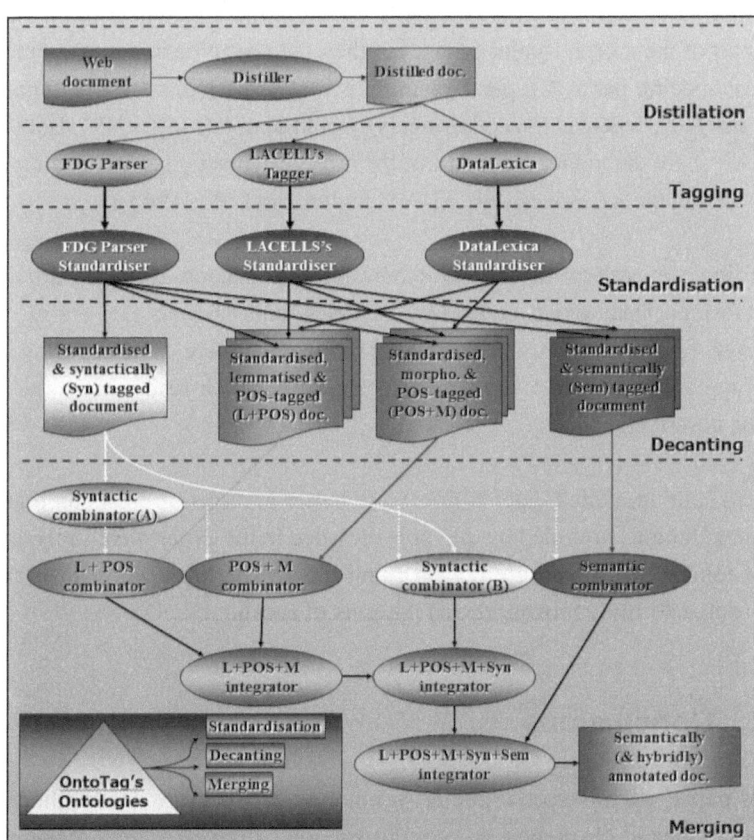

Regarding the values of the indicators in this first group, OntoTagger clearly outperformed DataLexica in 11.55% of cases, and FDG in 8.97% of cases. However, the third value of this comparative indicator shows that OntoTagger and LACELL are similarly accurate. This is due to the fact that, in fact, LACELL's morphosyntactic tags, when correct, are the most accurate of the three outputted by the three input tools. Hence, its recall can be considered the upper bound (or baseline) for this value, which is inherited somehow by OntoTagger.

On the other hand, a second group of indicators was calculated, in order to characterise the first one. Indeed, it measured the average number of tokens which are attached a more specific tag by a given tool than the others, but just in some particular cases. In these cases, the tools agreed in the assignment of the higher-level part of the morphosyntactic tag, but they did not agree in the assignment of its most specific parts. A typical example is that some tool(s) would annotate a token as 'NC', whereas (an) other one(s) would annotate it as 'NP'. Both 'NC' and 'NP' share the higher-level part of the morphosyntactic tag 'N', but not their most specific parts (respectively, 'C' = Common, and 'P' = Proper).

Regarding the values of the indicators in this second group, OntoTagger outperformed DataLexica in 27.32% of cases, and FDG in 12.34% of cases. However, once again, the third value of this comparative indicator shows that OntoTagger and LACELL are similarly accurate, which results from the same reasons described above.

Thus, to sum up, OntoTagger results were better in terms of precision than any of the annotations provided by the tools included in the experiment (only around 6% of tokens being wrongly tagged); and did not perform worse than any of them (outperforming most of them) in terms of recall.

5. Conclusions

In this paper, we have presented an annotation architecture and methodology that has helped us (1) make a set of linguistic tools (as well as their annotations) interoperate, and (2) reduce the POS tagging error rate and/or inaccuracy of these tools. We have also presented briefly the ontologies developed to solve this interoperability problem, and shown how they were used to interlink several POS taggers together, in order to attain the goals previously mentioned. As a result, the error rate of the combined POS tagging was around 6%, whereas the error rate of the tools interlinked was in the range of 10%–15%. The resulting error rate allows including this type of technologies within language e-learning applications and environments (e.g. mobile-assisted language learning) to automatically correct the exercises and/or the errors of the learner. This should help enhance and/or improve these language e-learning scenarios, and make them more powerful and effective.

6. Acknowledgements

We would like to thank the ATLAS (UNED) research group for their constant inspiration, encouragement and support, as well as Guadalupe Aguado de Cea and Javier Arrizabalaga, without whom this research would have never been completed.

References

Borst, W. N. (1997). *Construction of engineering ontologies.* PhD thesis. Enschede. Netherlands: University of Twente.

Gruber, T. R. (1993). A translation approach to portable ontologies. *Journal on Knowledge Acquisition,* 5(2), 199-220. Retrieved from http://dx.doi.org/10.1006/knac.1993.1008

Pareja-Lora, A. (2012a). *Providing linked linguistic and semantic web annotations – The OntoTag hybrid annotation model.* Saarbrücken: LAP – LAMBERT Academic Publishing.

Pareja-Lora, A. (2012b). *OntoTag: a linguistic and ontological annotation model suitable for the semantic web.* PhD thesis. Madrid: Universidad Politécnica De Madrid. Retrieved from http://oa.upm.es/13827/

Chapter 30

Pareja-Lora, A., & Aguado de Cea, G. (2010). Ontology-based interoperation of linguistic tools for an improved lemma annotation in Spanish. In *Proceedings of the 7th Conference on Language Resources and Evaluation (LREC 2010)* (pp. 1476-1482). Valletta, Malta: ELDA.

Urbano-Mendaña, M., Corpas-Pastor, G., & Mitkov, R. (2013). NLP-enhanced self-study learning materials for quality healthcare in Europe. In *Proceedings of the "Workshop on optimizing understanding in multilingual hospital encounters". 10th International Conference on Terminology and Artificial Intelligence (TIA'2013)* (pp. 29-32). Paris, France: Laboratoire d'Informatique de Paris Nord (LIPN).

31 The importance of corpora in translation studies: a practical case

Montserrat Bermúdez Bausela[1]

Abstract

This paper deals with the use of corpora in Translation Studies, particularly with the so-called '*ad hoc* corpus' or 'translator's corpus' as a working tool both in the classroom and for the professional translator. We believe that corpora are an inestimable source not only for terminology and phraseology extraction (cf. Maia, 2003), but also for studying the textual conventions that characterise and define specific genres in the translation languages. In this sense, we would like to highlight the contribution of corpora to the study of a specialised language from the translator's point of view. The challenge of our particular study resides in combining in a coherent way different linguistic issues with one aim in mind: looking for the best way to help the student acquire and develop their own competence on translation, and that this is reflected in the professional field.

Keywords: translation studies, *ad hoc* corpus, specialised languages.

1. Introduction

This paper shows how the compilation of an *ad hoc* corpus and the use of corpus analysis tools applied to it will help us with the translation of a specialised text in English. This text could be sent by the client or used by the teacher in the classroom.

---

1. Universidad Alfonso X el Sabio, Villanueva de la Cañada, Madrid, Spain; mbermbau@uax.es

How to cite this chapter: Bermúdez Bausela, M. (2016). The importance of corpora in translation studies: a practical case. In A. Pareja-Lora, C. Calle-Martínez, & P. Rodríguez-Arancón (Eds), *New perspectives on teaching and working with languages in the digital era* (pp. 363-374). Dublin: Research-publishing.net. http://dx.doi.org/10.14705/rpnet.2016.tislid2014.448

The corpus used for the present study is a comparable bilingual (English and Spanish) specialised corpus consisting of texts from the field of microbiology. Once our corpus is operative to be exploited using corpus processing tools, our aim is to study terminological, phraseological and textual patterns in both the English and the Spanish corpus to help us make the best informed decision as to the most appropriate natural equivalents in the Target Language (TL) in the translation process (cf. Bowker & Pearson, 2002; Philip, 2009). We intend to do so thanks to word lists, concordance, collocates and cluster searching. All these utilities are provided by the lexicographical tool *WordSmith Tools*.

2. Background

As Bowker and Pearson (2002) highlight, a corpus is a large collection of *authentic* texts, as opposed to 'ready-made' texts; they are in *electronic* form, which allows us to enrich them as we go along, and they respond to a *specific set of criteria* depending on the goals of the research in mind.

There are many fields of study in which linguistic corpora are useful, such as lexicography, language teaching and learning, sociolinguistics, and translation, to name a few. Using García-Izquierdo and Conde's (2012) words, "[i]n any event, regardless of their area of activity, most subjects feel the need for a specialised corpus combining formal, terminological-lexical, macrostructural and conceptual aspects, as well as contextual information" (p. 131). The use of linguistic corpora is closely linked to the need to learn Languages for Specific Purposes (LSPs). In this sense, translators are among the groups who need to learn and use an LSP, since they are non-experts of the specific field they are translating and they need to acquire both a linguistic and a conceptual knowledge in order to do so.

From the observation of specialised corpora, it is possible to identify specific patterns, phraseology, terminological variants, the frequency of conceptually relevant words, cohesive features and so forth. The access to this information will allow the translator to produce quality texts. Vila-Barbosa (2013) argues that Corpus Linguistics can be applied to the study of translation, among other disciplines. The line of research focusing on Corpus Translation Studies (CTS) stems from the descriptive approximations of Translation Studies, which consider the text as the unit of study depending on the context in which it is produced.

3. Methodology, corpus design and compilation

Cabré (2007) mentions the type of specialised texts that we need to include in our corpus so that it is balanced. Among the most relevant criteria highlighted by this author, we identify the topic, level of specialisation, textual genre, type of text, languages, sources, and, in the case of multilingual corpora, the relation established between the texts in the different languages. We could also add the communicative function, which is really implicit in the rest of the criteria mentioned by the author.

The whole process begins by choosing a specialised text in the Source Language (SL). It may be the text that the teacher and the students are working with in the classroom, or the actual text sent by the client to be translated. It could belong to any field: scientific, technical, legal, business, etc. In our particular case, we have taken as our Source Text (ST) the article entitled "Antibacterial activity of Lactobacillus sake isolated from meat" by Schillinger and Lücke (1989). We have chosen this one in particular because we think that it is a good example of a highly specialised text, scientific in this case, which is confirmed not only by its specialised terminology, but also by its macrostructure. It is an academic and professional type of discourse in which both the sender and the recipient are experts (high degree of shared knowledge) and it is an expositive and explicative type of text.

3.1. Corpus compilation in English

What we first need to know is the field of study and the level of specialisation of the ST. With this aim in mind, we have generated a wordlist (using the software *WordList*, provided by *WordSmith Tools*) of the most frequent words in the text, which will provide us with the specific terminology (*bacteriocin, strain, culture, agar, bacteria, plasmid, supernatant,* etc.). In order to start building our corpus, we search on the Internet for texts that include a number of the above mentioned terms. Each text has been saved individually in TXT format (the format supported by *WordSmith Tools*). All files have been stored in a folder named MEAT_INDUSTRY CORPUS with two subfolders, for the English and the Spanish texts. On most occasions, the texts were in PDF format and had to be converted into TXT, which implied a thorough and laborious cleaning process.

All the results obtained in our search are specific papers published in Journals. This is important since the results are going to be equally comparable with the ST regarding topic, level of specialisation, textual genre and type. The degree of reusability of our corpus is very high, since it has been created with the aim to be further enlarged and enriched with each new translation project.

The following are some interesting facts of the English compilation corpus:

- *Accuracy and reliability*: All the chosen texts (and this applies to both the English and the Spanish corpus) have passed a strict quality control, since they are published in well-known journals that have a peer-review process. Awareness has always been raised regarding the quality of the information found on the Internet. Harris (2007) points out the CARS Checklist (Credibility, Accuracy, Reasonableness and Support) as the criteria designed to guarantee high quality information on the Internet. We believe that even though we can never lower our guard, if the previous terminological job is done accurately and precisely, the results will very likely be knowledgeable, authentic and trustworthy, also due in great part to the development of the current search engines.

- *Limited accessibility*: It has not been an easy task to have free access to the academic texts. Therefore, apart from the free-downloadable ones, we have also included texts made up by *Abstracts*, which were, on all occasions, free.

- *Text originality*: Olohan (2004) defines bilingual or multilingual comparable corpora as "comparable original texts in two or more languages" (p. 35). But, can we be sure that all the texts that make up our corpus were originally written in English? However, even if these texts are *covert translations* (House, 2006), they are presented to the scientific community as originals, and they are totally acceptable and functional translations working in the target system as if they were originals. In fact, Baker (1995) does not refer to comparable corpora of texts as 'original' texts in two or more languages, since it is very hard to determine if they have really been written in the SL or they are translations in themselves. Apart from this, English is the *lingua franca* in scientific communication and it is the most frequent language of scientific scholarly articles published on the Internet.

3.2. Corpus compilation in Spanish

We now start building the Spanish corpus by searching for texts in Spanish that include the equivalents in Spanish of some of the most frequent and representative terms in the ST in English (we have searched for texts that included *bacteriocina, cepa, cultivo, agar, bacteria, plásmido, sobrenadante,* etc.). Some of the issues raised in the compilation of the Spanish corpus have been:

- *Wider variety of textual genres in the output*: We have not only gathered scientific articles, but also PhD theses and final year dissertations, which considerably enlarges the size of the Spanish corpus compared to the English one.

- *Cleaning*: The Spanish texts have required more 'cleaning' than the English texts. This is due to the fact that they included parts in English, such as the abstracts, the acknowledgments, or part of the bibliography.

We include in Table 1 statistical information regarding our corpus, where we can observe, among other data, the running words in the corpus (tokens) versus the different words (types), thus obtaining the resulting type/token ratio.

3.3. Asking the corpus the 'right' questions

The translator becomes a bit of an expert with each new translation brief. It is important to understand the meaning behind the term and learn something about the subject. In this context, corpora are of great importance, since we can search the corpus to find this kind of information (Table 1).

Table 1. Corpus statistical information

	English corpus. Statistical details	Spanish corpus. Statistical details
Number of files	29	27
Tokens	67.844	363.424
Types	6.466	18.994
Ratio Type/Token	10.73	5.87
Number of sentences	4.991	16.149

Sometimes it is also difficult for translators to locate equivalents, or to choose among several possible ones. Even if we are not using a parallel corpus, we can still identify a terminological equivalent, sometimes even guided by our intuition: we might suspect what the correct equivalent is, but we need to check it in our corpus. What we can do is generate a concordance and verify if our intuition was right. Towards this end, we recommend using an asterisk. This particular wildcard substitutes an unlimited number of characters. Like this, we will be able to rule out an incorrect equivalent and check the different varieties of the term.

The most frequent word in the ST has been *bacteriocin*, with a frequency of 0.98%. A corpus can help us identify terms shown in context, and the most frequent patterns of use. From the different concordance lines, collocates and clusters (retrieved thanks to the software *Concord*, a functionality provided by *WordSmith Tools*), we obtain relevant grammatical and lexicographical information. We show a very brief example of the terminological equivalents and the patterns found for *bacterio**.

The terminological English variants are:

- bacteriocin (401 entries), bacteriocins (238 entries);

- bacteriocinogenic (42 entries);

- bacteriocidal (1 entry).

The terminological Spanish variants are:

- bacteriocinas (1070 entries), bacteriocina (554 entries);

- bacteriostático/bacteriostática (31 entries);

- bacteriocinogénicas/bacteriocinogénicos (23 entries);

- bacteriolítica/bacteriolítico (13 entries);

- bacteriocidal (2 entries).

Please refer to Table 2 to see the most common patterns of *bacterio**.

Table 2. Contrastive study of the use of *bacterio** in English and Spanish

English	Spanish
bacteriocinogenic + noun (bacteriocinogenic activity, bacteriocinogenic strain)	noun + bacteriocinogénica/o (actividad bacteriocinogénica, cepa bacteriocinogénica)
bacteriocin + noun (bacteriocin activity, bacteriocin inhibition)	noun + bacteriocinas (actividad de las bacteriocinas, inhibición a las bacteriocinas)
Bacteriocin(s) + participial form (bacteriocins produced by, bacteriocin isolated from)	Bacteriocina(s) + participial form (bacteriocinas producidas por, bacteriocinas sintetizadas por)
bacteriocins + verb in passive voice (bacteriocins were first discovered, bacteriocins were defined by)	bacteriocinas + verb in active voice (las bacteriocinas presentan, las bacteriocinas inhiben)
bacteriocin + ing form (bacteriocin-producing strains, bacteriocin-producing lactococcus)	bacteriocinas + 'de' + type (bacteriocinas de Lactococcus, bacteriocinas de bacterias ácido lácticas)

We also learn about the most common verbs that are collocates of 'bacteriocina(s)' in the Spanish corpus: 'producir', 'codificar', 'aislar', 'presentar', etc.

All this information is of utmost importance for the translation of the text. A corpus can help us reflect the most natural style in our Target Text (TT). As Philip (2009) claims, TL norms should be borne in mind "when reproducing any idiosyncratic usage or innovative expressions that the SL text might include" (p. 59).

4. Using corpora in translation: an example

We would like to show an example of the direct contribution of corpora to translation practice. Let us look at this sentence taken from the abstract of the article we are using as our ST and suppose we need to translate it into Spanish:

> "In mixed culture, the bacteriocin-sensitive organisms were killed after the bacteriocin-producing strain reached maximal cell density, whereas there was no decrease in cell number in the presence of the bacteriocin-negative variant".

There are certain issues that catch our attention, such as how we could translate the following compound nouns:

- bacteriocin-sensitive organisms (see pattern 1);

- bacteriocin-negative variant (see pattern 2);

- bacteriocin-producing strain (see pattern 3).

Pattern 1: the first thing we do is conduct a concordance search in the Spanish corpus using 'sensible*' as our search word and including a context word, 'bacteriocina*'. A context word is used to check if it typically occurs in the vicinity of our search word in a specified horizon to the right and left of the search word. Also, we use a wildcard, the asterisk, in order to look for all the possible variants. We obtain a result of 10 concordance lines, from which we can deduce that the most frequent expression in Spanish is 'organismos sensibles a las bacteriocinas'.

Pattern 2: we conduct a concordance search using 'bacteriocina' as our search word and include the context word 'negativa'. In the outcome, we observe the concordance line: 'variante negativa para bacteriocina'.

Pattern 3: we look for the search word: 'bacteriocina*' and include the context word: 'productora*'. The results are astounding: 56 lines of concordances and in all of them we can observe that in Spanish the noun phrase 'cepa productora de bacteriocina' is very frequent (Figure 1).

Figure 1. Concordance lines of *bacteriocina**, context word *productora**

N	Concordance	Set	Word #	San San
1	productoras de sustancias antimicrobianas (bacteriocinas) que pudieran competir con		4,128	180 729
2	y del deterioro o bien, las cepas productoras de bacteriocinas pueden utilizarse como cultivos		620	46 861
3	a ensayar el potencial de cepas productoras de bacteriocinas en sistemas cárnicos, que han		8,155	512 429
4	las bacteriocinas o cepas productoras de bacteriocinas pueden emplearse para mejorar su		702	49 649
5	cepa de Lactobacillus plantarum productora de bacteriocinas inhibe el desarrollo de		9,651	582 419
6	que hayan sido descritas cepas productoras de bacteriocinas de todos los géneros de BL		10,614	435 579
7	de las bacterias lácticas productoras de bacteriocinas, frente a microorganismos		3,920	276 439
8	lácticas de origen cárnico productoras de bacteriocina así como de las bacteriocinas que		3,709	267 439
9	(halos de inhibición). Preparación del extracto de bacteriocina La cepa productora de bacteriocina		6,763	223 259
10	cepas de Pediococcus acidilactici productoras de bacteriocinas (González y Kunka 1987; Bhunia et		172	8 639
11	de Ped. acidilactici (Roger) no productora de bacteriocina. Después de 3 h de incubación el		2,513	91 100
12	meses. Dicha cepa potencialmente productora de bacteriocina así como su sobrenadante		2,374	88 309
13	de las cepas potencialmente productoras de bacteriocinas, por separado en un baño de agua a		1,270	47 369
14	extracto de bacteriocina La cepa productora de bacteriocina se deja crecer en caldo MRS (Oxoid)		5,788	223 469
15	cruzado entre todas las productoras de bacteriocinas que actuarán tambien como		121	1 899
16	para encontrar aquellas que sean productoras de bacteriocina. Bacterias productoras para el		5,595	217 100
17	químicos, las bacterias productoras de bacteriocinas o las bacteriocinas producidas por		3,432	256 519
18	microbiológico utilizado 3.1.1 Cepa productora de bacteriocina. 3. MATERIAL Y METODOS Se		6,714	280 100
19	diferentes especies de BAL productoras de bacteriocinas, entre ellas, C. piscicola, que s		13,553	606 569
20	que según el género de la bacteria productora de bacteriocina el peso molecular se encuentra		14,709	637 599
21	caracteristicas de estas bacterias productoras de bacteriocinas; 2. REVISION BIBLIOGRAFICA •		4,704	206 949
22	(1991), describen algunas BAL productoras de bacteriocinas comúnmente asociadas a los		4,665	201 729

As mentioned previously, specialised translation is not only about terminology, but also about style. Our translation should resemble other texts produced within that particular LSP. It must be stylistically appropriate as well as terminologically accurate. In this sense, we came across a difficulty in the translation of 'the bacteriocin-sensitive organisms were killed'. We did not find in our corpus any example of concordance of 'organismos eliminados' or 'fueron eliminados'. As it seems, we had come across the appropriate collocate but not the appropriate style. The verb 'eliminar' in the Spanish corpus follows the grammar pattern: verb + object (eliminar microorganismos) and in a large number of the cases, the noun 'eliminación' is used. Suggested translation:

> "En un cultivo mezclado, la eliminación de los organismos sensibles a la bacteriocina se produjo después de que la cepa productora de bacteriocina alcanzara la máxima densidad celular, mientras que no hubo disminución en el número de células en presencia de la variante negativa para bacteriocina".

5. Conclusions

There is a number of ways in which specialised corpora can help the translator. We can generate word lists to identify the field and level of specialisation of the ST. We can use them to learn about the subject we are translating, and about the most common lexical and grammatical patterns through the retrieval of concordances, collocates and clusters. Furthermore, it is an invaluable source regarding style: choosing the appropriate textual conventions and norms that the recipient of the TT expects to find reflected on the text is a guarantee that the text will have a high degree of acceptability. As Corpas-Pastor (2004, p. 161-62) points out, it involves a great development in the documentary sources for the translator, since the proper selection, assessment and use of those sources let the translator focus on developing strategies to consult the corpus and extract valuable information, optimizing time and effort. We believe that corpora help the student acquire and develop their own competence on translation, and that their use perfectly responds to the specialised translator's needs.

References

Baker, M. (1995). Corpus linguistics and translation studies: implications and applications. In M. Baker, G. Francis, & E. Tognini-Bonelli (Eds.), *Text and technology: in honour of John Sinclair* (pp. 17-45). Amsterdam/Philadelphia: John Benjamins.

Bowker, L., & Pearson, J. (2002). *Working with specialized language. A practical guide to using corpora*. London: Routledge. Retrieved from http://dx.doi.org/10.4324/9780203469255

Cabré, M. T. (2007). Constituir un corpus de textos de especialidad: condiciones y posibilidades. In M. Ballard & C. Pineira-Tresmontant (Eds.), *Les corpus en linguistique et en traductologie* (pp. 89-106). Arras: Artois Presses Université.

Corpas-Pastor, G. (2004). *La traducción de textos médicos especializados a través de recursos electrónicos y corpus virtuales*. Actas del II Congreso. Las palabras del traductor. Toledo, 2004. El español, lengua de traducción. Congreso internacional de ESLETRA. Retrieved from http://cvc.cervantes.es/lengua/esletra/pdf/02/017_corpas.pdf

García-Izquierdo, I., & Conde, T. (2012). Investigating specialized translators: corpus and documentary sources. *Ibérica, 23*, 131-156.

Harris, R. (2007). *Evaluating internet research sources*. Radnor Township School District. Retrieved from http://radnortsd.schoolwires.com/cms/lib/PA01000218/Centricity/ModuleInstance/2137/Evaluating_Internet_Research_Sources.pdf

House, J. (2006). Covert translation, language contact, variation and change. *SYNAPS, 19*, 25-47.

Maia, B. (2003). What are comparable corpora? In *Proceedings of pre-conference workshop multilingual corpora: linguistic requirements and technical perspectives* (pp. 27-34). Lancaster: Lancaster University.

Olohan, M. (2004). *Introducing corpora in translation studies*. London: Routledge.

Philip, G. (2009). Arriving at equivalence. Making a case for comparable general reference corpora in translation studies. In A. Beeby, I. Patricia-Rodríguez, & P. Sánchez-Gijón (Eds.), *Corpus use for learning to translate and learning corpus use to translate* (pp. 59-73). Amsterdam/Philadelphia: John Benjamins. Retrieved from http://dx.doi.org/10.1075/btl.82.06phi

Schillinger, U., & Lücke, F. K. (1989). Antibacterial activity of Lactobacillus sake isolated from meat. *Applied and Environmental Microbiology, 55*(8), 1901-1906.

Chapter 31

Vila-Barbosa, M. M. (2013). Corpus especializados como recurso para la traducción: análisis de los marcadores de la cadena temática en artículos científicos sobre enfermedades neuromusculares en pediatría. *Onomázein, 1*(27), 78-100.

32. Using corpus management tools in public service translator training: an example of its application in the translation of judgments

María Del Mar Sánchez Ramos[1] and Francisco J. Vigier Moreno[2]

Abstract

As stated by Valero-Garcés (2006, p. 38), the new scenario including public service providers and users who are not fluent in the language used by the former has opened up new ways of linguistic and cultural mediation in current multicultural and multilingual societies. As a consequence, there is an ever increasing need for translators and interpreters in different public service environments (hospitals, police stations, administration offices, etc.) and successful communication is a must in these contexts. In this context, Translation Studies has seen the emergence of a new academic branch called Public Service Interpreting and Translation (henceforth PSIT), which is present in a wide range of environments where communication (and mediation) is, as stated above, essential, such as healthcare, education and justice to name a few. In PSIT, legal translation principally involves the documents most commonly used in criminal proceedings, as in Spain legal aid is usually provided in criminal cases. Hence, PSIT legal translation training is intended to help trainees to develop their legal translation competence and focuses mainly on legal asymmetry, terminological incongruence, legal discourse, comparative textology and, fundamentally, on the rendering of a text which is both valid

---

1. FITISPos Research Group - Universidad de Alcalá, Alcalá de Henares, Madrid, Spain; mar.sanchezr@uah.es

2. FITISPos Research Group - Universidad de Alcalá, Alcalá de Henares, Madrid, Spain; francisco.vigier@uah.es

How to cite this chapter: Sánchez Ramos, M. d. M., & Vigier Moreno, F. J. (2016). Using corpus management tools in public service translator training: an example of its application in the translation of judgments. In A. Pareja-Lora, C. Calle-Martínez, & P. Rodríguez-Arancón (Eds), *New perspectives on teaching and working with languages in the digital era* (pp. 375-384). Dublin: Research-publishing.net. http://dx.doi.org/10.14705/rpnet.2016.tislid2014.449

in legal terms and comprehensible to the final reader (Prieto, 2011, pp. 12-13). Our paper highlights how corpus management tools can be utilised in the translation of judgments within criminal proceedings in order to develop trainees' technological competence and to help them to acquire expertise in this specific language domain. We describe how monolingual virtual corpora and concordance software can be used as tools for translator training within a PSIT syllabus to engender a better understanding of specialised text types as well as phraseological and terminological information.

Keywords: legal translation, specialised corpora, concordance programs.

1. Legal translation training in PSIT training

The ever-increasing mobility of people across boundaries, be it for economic, political or educational reasons, has led to the creation of multilingual and multicultural societies where the need for language and cultural mediation is also ever growing. Even if this is a worldwide phenomenon, it is most conspicuous in countries which have been traditionally considered as countries of emigration and have become countries of immigration in the last 20 years, thus evolving into complex multilingual and multicultural societies. This is also the case of Spain, a country where the high influx of immigrants and tourists poses challenges which require adequate responses to ensure a balanced coexistence (Valero-Garcés, 2006, p. 36). This need for translators and interpreters is even greater in public services like schools, hospitals, police stations, courts... where users who do not command the official language of the institution must be catered for up to the point where it has fostered the creation of a new professional activity and, subsequently, a new academic branch within Translation Studies, commonly referred to as PSIT. Hence, PSIT has a very wide scope, including healthcare, educational, administrative and legal settings. PSIT legal translation is mostly concerned with the documents which are most commonly used in criminal proceedings, such as summonses, indictments and judgments; probably because it is in criminal cases that legal-aid translation and interpreting services are provided (Aldea, Arróniz, Ortega, & Plaza, 2004, p. 89).

In an attempt to provide the education required in competent professionals, the University of Alcalá offers a program specifically designed for PSIT training, namely a Master's Degree in Intercultural Communication, Public Service Interpreting and Translation, which is part of the European Commission's European Master's in Translation network. This programme, which is offered in a wide variety of language pairs including English-Spanish, comprises a specific module on legal and administrative translation into both working languages. In line with the so-called competence-based training (Hurtado, 2007), this module is mainly intended to equip the students with the skills, abilities, knowledge and values required in a competent translator of legal texts. Based on previous multicomponent models and his own professional practice as a legal translator, Prieto (2011, pp. 11-13) offers a very interesting model for legal translation competence which encompasses the following sub-competences: (1) strategic or methodological competence (which controls the application of all other sub-competences and includes, among others, the identification of translation problems and implementation of translation strategies and procedures); (2) communicative and textual competence (linguistic knowledge, including variants, registers and genre conventions); (3) thematic and cultural competence (including but not limited to knowledge of law and awareness of legal asymmetry between source and target legal systems); (4) instrumental competence (documentation and technology); and (5) interpersonal and professional competence (for instance, teamwork and ethics). According to our experience in PSIT legal translation training, it is precisely in communicative and textual competence (especially as regards terminological and phraseological use of legal discourse in the target language) that many of our trainees show weaknesses, chiefly when translating into their non-mother tongue (in our case, English). As we firmly agree with the view that "being able to translate highly specialised documents is becoming less a question of knowledge and more one of having the right tools" (Martin, 2011, p. 5) and that we must ensure that our students "move beyond their passive knowledge of basic legal phraseology and terminology and take a more proactive stance in the development of their legal language proficiency" (Monzó, 2008,

p. 224), we designed the activity explained below to make our students aware of the usefulness of computer tools when applied to legal translation to overcome many of the shortcomings they face when translating legal texts.

2. Corpora in PSIT training

The pedagogical implications of using corpora in specialised translator training have been shown by various researchers (Bowker & Pearson, 2002, p. 10; Corpas & Seghiri, 2009, p. 102; Lee & Swales, 2006, p. 74), and also specifically in legal translator training (Biel, 2010; Monzó, 2008). Some of the main advantages identified are related to the development of instrumental sub-competence (PACTE Group, 2003, p. 53), or so-called information mining competence (EMT Expert Group, 2009). The need to know and use different electronic corpora and concordancing tools is also illustrated by Rodríguez (2010), who identifies a further sub-competence within the instrumental sub-competence of the PACTE model, namely "the ability to meet a number of learning outcomes: identifying the principles that lie at the basis of the use of corpora; creating corpora; using corpus-related software; and solving translation problems by using corpora" (p. 253).

Development of instrumental competence, including the use of documentation sources and electronic tools, is particularly relevant in PSIT, where translators need to manage different information sources in order to acquire sufficient understanding of the subject of a text and thus enable the accurate transfer of information. Given the importance of documentation in PSIT training to ensure production of a functionally adequate and acceptable target language text, we designed an activity focused on compiling and analysing monolingual virtual corpora to translate judgments issued in criminal proceedings. A virtual corpus is a collection of texts developed from electronic resources by the translator and compiled "for the sole purpose of providing information – either factual, linguistic or field-specific – for use in completing a translation task (Sánchez, 2009, p. 115). The compilation process would also help to develop our translation trainees' technical skills.

Of the different major corpus types (Bernardini, Stewart, & Zanettin, 2003, p. 6), we found monolingual corpora especially useful for our task as the students needed to compile a corpus containing texts produced in the target language. The final monolingual corpus would thus provide them with information about idiomatic use of specific terms, collocations, and other syntactic and genre conventions of the legal language.

Our students attended two training sessions of six hours in total. In the first session, they were introduced to the main theoretical concepts in Corpus-based Translation Studies, the main documentation resources for PSIT (lexicographical databases, specialised lexicographical resources and specialised portals) and different word search strategies needed to take advantage of search engines and Boolean operators. In the second session, they learned the differences between the so-called *Web for Corpus* (WfC) and *Web as Corpus* (WaC) approaches and were shown how to use retrieval information software, such as *SketchEngine* and *AntConc*. They also learned the basic functions of both software programs (generating and sorting concordancing, identifying language patterns, retrieving collocations and collocation clusters, etc.). After this training session, the students were each asked to compile a monolingual corpus (British English) as part of the module on Legal Translation, to translate a judgment issued in Spanish criminal proceedings into English. They were also asked to investigate genre and lexical conventions and to use their ad hoc corpus to solve terminological and phraseological problems when translating.

3. Compiling an ad hoc corpus in PSIT

The need for an initial determination of criteria for selection and inclusion is the starting point when designing and compiling a corpus. Our methodology was divided into three stages: source-text documentation, the compilation process and corpus analysis. In the first stage, we encouraged our students to read texts similar to the source text (in this case, a judgment passed by Spain's Supreme Court), which we provided to help them learn about the nature of this type of text and to familiarise them with the main linguistic and genre conventions. In the second stage, the students needed to be able to locate different Internet-based texts to be included in their own corpus. To do so, they needed to put into practice what they had learned about Boolean operators in previous sessions, that is, to search for information using keywords (e.g. 'appeal', 'constitutional rights', 'presumption of innocence'). It is of paramount importance at this stage to use very precise keywords – *seed words* – as filters, in order to exclude irrelevant information or 'noise'. Institutional web pages, such as that of the British and Irish Legal Information Institute (BAILII), can be used to download and save complete texts, namely UK Supreme Court's judgments. Students were also encouraged to use free software (i.e. *HTTrack*, *GNU Wget* or *Jdownloader*) so that they could automate the downloading process. As previously stated, "[o]nce the documents had been found and downloaded, the texts had to be converted to .txt files in order to be processed by corpus analysis software [like *AntConc*]. This task is especially necessary in the case of texts retrieved in .pdf format" (Lázaro Gutiérrez & Sánchez Ramos, 2015, p. 285). Finally, all documents were stored and the students were able to initiate an analysis of their materials.

The ad hoc corpora compiled by our students were highly useful in terms of all the terminological and idiomatic information they offered to aid the completion of the translation task. The students appreciated the immediate solutions their ad hoc corpora provided to different translation problems. For instance, they used the collocations and collocation cluster functions to identify the frequency of appearance of 'direct evidence' or 'direct proof' for the translation of 'prueba indiciaria'. The cluster/N-gram function was particularly useful for checking the collocational patterns of the most problematic words, such as those followed by a preposition (e.g. *judgment on/in*), where students positively evaluated the contextual information their ad hoc corpora offered (see Figure 1).

The concordance function was also a very attractive resource for our students. A simple query generated concordance lines listed in KeyWord In Context (KWIC) format. For instance, students looked up the appropriate English term for 'infracción de precepto constitucional'. The ad hoc corpus they had compiled offered a number of alternatives, such as 'breach', 'infringement', and 'violation', with 'violation' being the most frequent (see Figure 2).

Figure 1. Collocation cluster/N-gram function

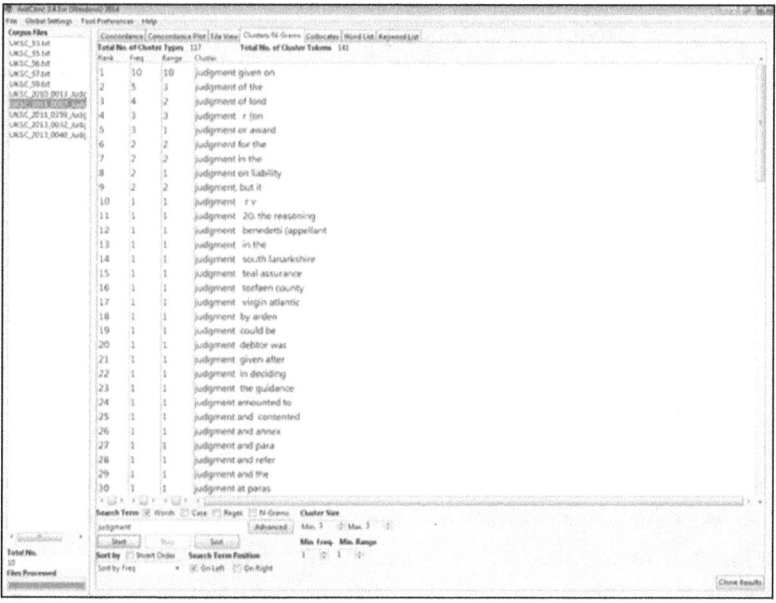

Figure 2. Concordance function

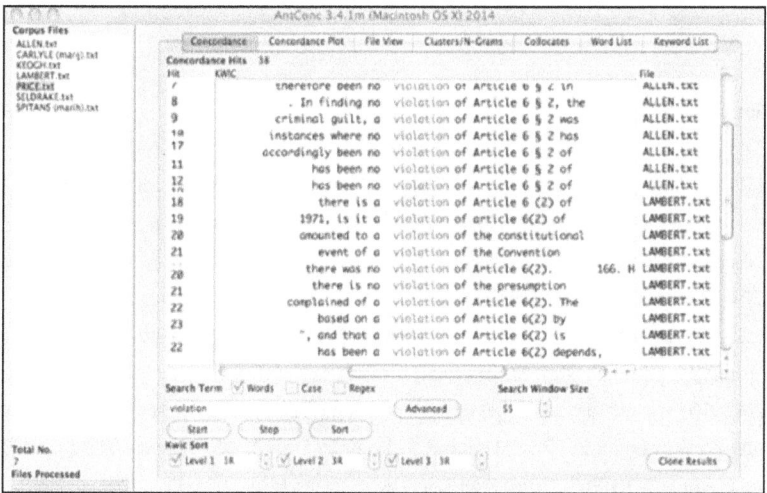

In general terms, the students' feedback was largely positive. They appreciated the usefulness of the different functions that a software tool such as *AntConc* can provide (e.g. frequency lists, collocates, clusters/N-grams, or concordancers). Compiling and using corpora made the students feel more confident in their technical skills and translation solutions. Altogether, corpus use was evaluated by our students as a valuable tool for developing their instrumental competence.

4. Conclusions

We have shown how we developed and exploited monolingual virtual corpora as a resource in the PSIT training environment. A corpus can be a valuable aid for specialised translation students, who can consult the corpus to acquire both subject field knowledge and linguistic knowledge, including information about appropriate (and inappropriate) terminology, collocations, phraseology, style and register. However, training is essential when compiling and using corpora, as this requires a variety of competences, both linguistic and technological. As we have commented, well-planned training on corpora and compiling methodology can contribute to the development of these competences, essential in the world of professional translation.

References

Aldea, P., Arróniz, P., Ortega, J. M., & Plaza, S. (2002). Situación actual de la práctica de la traducción y de la interpretación en la Administración de Justicia. In S. Cruces & A. Luna (Eds.), *La traducción en el ámbito institucional: autonómico, estatal y europeo* (pp. 85-126). Vigo: Universidade de Vigo.

Bernardini, S., Stewart, D., & Zanettin, F. (2003). (Eds.). *Corpora in translator education: an introduction*. Manchester: St. Jerome.

Biel, Ł. (2010). Corpus-based studies of legal language for translation purposes: methodological and practical potential. In C. Heine & J. Engberg (Eds.), *Reconceptualizing LSP. Online proceedings of the XVII European LSP Symposium 2009* (pp. 1-15).

Bowker, J., & Pearson, J. (2002). *Working with specialized language: a practical guide to using corpora*. London: Routledge. Retrieved from http://dx.doi.org/10.4324/9780203469255

Corpas, G., & Seghiri, M. (2009). Virtual corpora as documentation resources: translating travel insurance documents (English–Spanish). In A. Beeby, P. Rodríguez Inés, & P. Sánchez-Gijón (Eds.), *Corpus use and translating. Corpus use for learning to translate and learning corpus use to translate* (pp. 75-107). Amsterdam: John Benjamins. Retrieved from http://dx.doi.org/10.1075/btl.82.07cor

EMT Expert Group. (2009). *Competences for professional translators, experts in multilingual and multimedia communication*. European Master's in Translation Website of the DG Translation of the European Commission. Retrieved from http://ec.europa.eu/dgs/translation/programmes/emt/key_documents/emt_competences_translators_en.pdf

Hurtado, A. (2007). Competence-based curriculum design for training translators. *The Interpreter and Translator Trainer, 1*(2), 163-195. Retrieved from http://dx.doi.org/10.10 80/1750399X.2007.10798757

Lázaro Gutiérrez, R., & Sánchez Ramos, M. d. M. (2015). Corpus-based interpreting studies and public service interpreting and translation training programs: the case of interpreters working in gender violence contexts. In J. Romero-Trillo (Ed.), *Yearbook of Corpus Linguistics and Pragmatics 3* (pp. 275-292). Springer International Publishing Switzerland. Retrieved from http://dx.doi.org/10.1007/978-3-319-17948-3_12

Lee, D., & Swales, J. (2006). A corpus-based EAP course for NNS doctoral students: moving from available specialized corpora to self-compiled corpora. *English for Specific Purposes, 25*(1), 56-75. Retrieved from http://dx.doi.org/10.1016/j.esp.2005.02.010

Martin, C. (2011). Specialization in translation – Myths and realities. *Translation Journal*. Retrieved from http://www.bokorlang.com/journal/56specialist.htm

Monzó, E. (2008). Corpus-based activities in legal translator training. *The Interpreter and Translator Trainer, 2*(2), 221-252. Retrieved from http://dx.doi.org/10.1080/175039 9X.2008.10798775

PACTE Group. (2003). Building a translation competence model. In F. Alves (Ed.), *Triangulating translation: perspectives in process oriented research* (pp. 43-66). Amsterdam: John Benjamins. Retrieved from http://dx.doi.org/10.1075/btl.45

Prieto, F. (2011). Developing legal translation competence: an integrative process-oriented approach. *Comparative Legilinguistics – International Journal for Legal Communication, 5*, 7-21.

Rodríguez, P. (2010). Electronic corpora and other information and communication technology tools. An integrated approach to translation teaching. *The Interpreter and Translator Trainer*, 4(2), 251-282. Retrieved from http://dx.doi.org/10.1080/13556509.2010.10798806

Sánchez, P. (2009). Developing documentation skills to build do-it-yourself corpora in the specialized translation course. In A. Beeby, P. Rodríguez-Inés, & P. Sánchez-Gijón (Eds.), *Corpus use and translating. Corpus use for learning to translate and learning corpus use to translate* (pp. 109-127). Amsterdam: John Benjamins. Retrieved from http://dx.doi.org/10.1075/btl.82.08san

Valero-Garcés, C. (2006). *Formas de mediación intercultural: traducción e Interpretación en los Servicios Públicos.* Granada: Comares.

33. Integrating computer-assisted translation tools into language learning

María Fernández-Parra[1]

Abstract

Although Computer-Assisted Translation (CAT) tools play an important role in the curriculum in many university translator training programmes, they are seldom used in the context of learning a language, as a good command of a language is needed before starting to translate. Since many institutions often have translator-training programmes as well as language-learning programmes within one department or school, this paper explores the possibilities of expanding the usefulness of CAT tools from the Translation curriculum into the Foreign Language Learning curriculum. While it is not expected that CAT tools will replace any other methods of language learning, this paper hopes to show that CAT tools can nevertheless contribute to enhance the language learning experience.

Keywords: computer-assisted translation tools, foreign language learning.

1. Introduction

In professional translation, CAT tools have gradually become a staple tool and this is increasingly reflected in translator training programmes across universities and schools (e.g. Olohan, 2011, p. 342), often at both undergraduate and postgraduate level. In recent years, we have seen the proliferation of these tools, which can be described as a single integrated system allowing for a more efficient and consistent translation process (cf. Quah, 2006, p. 93).

---

1. Swansea University, Swansea, UK; m.a.fernandezparra@swansea.ac.uk

How to cite this chapter: Fernández-Parra, M. (2016). Integrating computer-assisted translation tools into language learning. In A. Pareja-Lora, C. Calle-Martínez, & P. Rodríguez-Arancón (Eds), *New perspectives on teaching and working with languages in the digital era* (pp. 385-396). Dublin: Research-publishing.net. http://dx.doi.org/10.14705/rpnet.2016.tislid2014.450

Despite their usefulness for translation, CAT tools are seldom used in the context of learning a language, since a good command of a language is usually needed before starting to translate. CAT tools are designed to facilitate the translation process rather than to facilitate language learning. However, since translator training programmes are often delivered in universities or schools where language learning programmes exist alongside translator training programmes, this paper explores the possibilities of expanding the usefulness of CAT tools from the Translation curriculum into the Foreign Language Learning curriculum. After providing an overview of the main features of CAT tools, this paper maps how some of the main components can be used to support and improve a number of skills in language learning.

2. Features of CAT tools

CAT tools can vary in the functionality provided, but at a basic level CAT tools offer at least *Translation Memory* (including *alignment*) tools or *Terminology Management* tools, or both. At a more advanced level, both the architecture and functionality of the tools are increased (cf. Fernández-Parra, 2014).

2.1. Translation memory (TM) and alignment tools

A TM consists of a database of texts and their corresponding translation(s), divided into segments, often at sentence level, for future reference or reuse. The main advantage of a TM is that "it allows translators to reuse previous translations" (Bowker, 2002, p. 111) quickly and efficiently. TMs are particularly suited to technical documentation because they allow a fast and easy retrieval of any previously used content (Bowker, 2002, p. 113) and work by comparing the current source text to translate to previously translated documents.

One method of creating a TM is by aligning a source text with its translation. *Alignment* is the process of comparing both texts and matching the corresponding sentences which will become segments, known as *translation units*, in the TM. In many CAT tools, the alignment is carried out automatically by the software.

In this case, it is almost inevitable that some of the segments will be misaligned (e.g. Bowker, 2002, p. 109), but some alignment tools cater for this possibility by allowing manual post-editing of the results of the alignment process.

2.2. Terminology management

Along with the TM, the terminology database, or *termbase*, is an essential component of CAT tools, as terminology is a crucial task in technical translation (cf. Bowker, 2002, pp. 104-106). A termbase is a database, but it differs from a TM in that it is used to store and retrieve segments at term level, e.g. phrases and single words, whereas the TM is typically used for sentences.

Depending on the level of sophistication of the CAT tool, the termbase can also be used to store and retrieve various kinds of information about the term, such as gender, definition, part of speech, usage, subject field, etc. In addition, the termbases in some CAT tools allow the storage and retrieval of multimedia files, e.g. graphics, sound or video files, etc., much more quickly and efficiently than spreadsheet software such as MS Excel. Further, they can allow for a hierarchical organisation of the information.

3. Using CAT tools in language learning

There is much literature on the skills needed in language learning, but a number of foundational skills are generally well established in language pedagogy, such as speaking, listening, reading, writing, grammar and vocabulary (e.g. Hinkel, 2011, p. xiii; Widdowson, 2013, p. 632). Similarly, the idea of using computers for language learning is not new. Although Kenny (1999) had already pointed out that the integration of CAT tools into university curricula could open up new areas of research and pedagogy, there has been little research on how CAT tools in particular might be applied to foreign language learning. However, as Rogers (1996) points out, foreign language learners and translators "have a good deal in common when it comes to dealing with words: each must identify new words, record them, learn them, recall them, work out their relationships with other words and with the real world" (p. 69). It is on the basis of this common ground between the tasks performed by translators and the tasks performed by language learners that this paper aims to 'recycle' the main components of CAT tools, such as the TM and the termbase, in order to support the various stages of the language learning process.

In the following sections, an overview is provided on how the TM and the termbase might support the various foundational language learning skills. However, given that CAT tools mainly deal with written text, focusing on skills such as listening and speaking rather falls outside the scope of this paper. They will nevertheless be hinted at when discussing multimedia files in the termbase. Translation skills have been added to the list of foundational skills, as translation is clearly another skill that CAT tools can contribute to.

It should also be pointed out that the list of suggested activities, which can be incorporated both to classroom learning and private study, remains open-ended in that new skills may be added and, as technology evolves, new CAT tool components may also be added. Further, new ways may be devised whereby a CAT tool feature might be able to support a skill currently not listed. Finally, this paper is not intended to suggest that the language skills should be approached in isolation. Therefore, each activity suggested in the following sections will typically integrate a number of the above skills.

The CAT tools explored in this paper are mainly the SDL Trados Studio 2011 suite, which includes SDL WinAlign and SDL MultiTerm, and Déjà Vu X2, not only because these are two important CAT tools in the translation industry and therefore widely taught in (at least UK) universities, but also because the useful components for language learning in these tools can be accessed as standalone features, without the need to launch the rest of the software.

3.1. TM, alignment and language learning

Since the TM deals mainly with segments at sentence level, it is particularly suited to supporting language learning skills such as reading, writing and translation, which are often employed at textual or sentential level. For the same reason, the more advanced language learners would particularly benefit from using TMs as an additional tool in their language learning. An example of TM that can be used for language learning is that of Déjà Vu X2. Figure 1 shows its typical use in translation.

Figure 1. Example of TM in translation

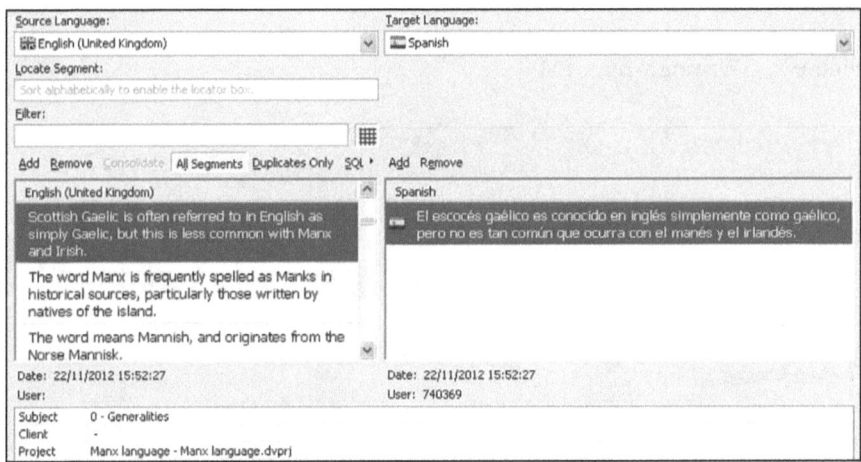

The column on the left corresponds to what translators would use as a source text to translate. This column shows the source text divided into segments.

The column on the right is where translators would type the translation. Language learners could obviously use this as an advanced translation exercise, where the lecturer can provide the text for students to translate either into or out of their first language.

The less advanced language learners can also carry out a variety of exercises, ranging from substitution and gap-filling exercises to all kinds of text manipulation exercises, such as partial or complete text reconstruction, re-ordering words in a sentence, unscrambling, etc., either in the source language or the target language, or both. In short, the students can carry out the type of computer activities typically associated to CALL or Computer-Assisted Language Learning as accounted for by Blake (2013), for example.

Another kind of activity where TMs can help the more advanced students is writing in the foreign language, for example by helping students to structure their writing and use fluent, natural ways of expressing themselves. One example is shown in Figure 2, where English is the source language and Spanish the target one.

Figure 2. Writing with a TM

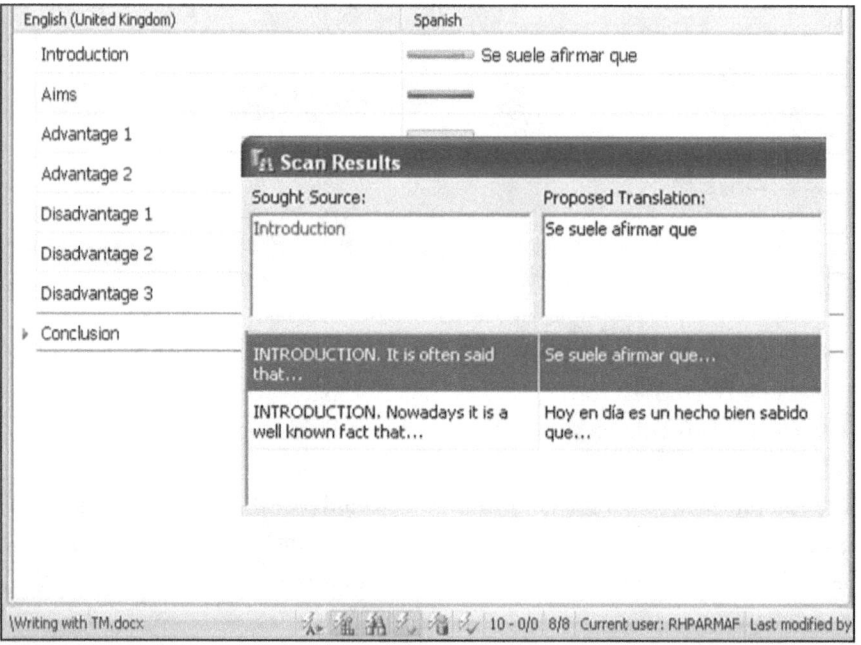

On the left of the screen, instead of a source text, the lecturer can create a file which will be used as a template with headings structuring the essay in a particular way, e.g. *Introduction, Disadvantage 1*, etc. There can be different templates for different tasks and students need not adhere to the templates very strictly. The example in Figure 2 shows a possible template for students to write an essay about the advantages or disadvantages of a chosen topic. Once the template is uploaded into the CAT tool, in this case Déjà Vu X2, the students can search the translation memory for phrases to start and end paragraphs, for example.

In order to do this, students would select the word *Introduction* in the English column and right-click it to search for that word in the TM. This will bring up the bilingual *Scan Results* dialog box also shown in Figure 2. In this case, the dialog box contains a couple of examples of good ways to start a paragraph in Spanish. Students would select one and copy it into the Spanish column and then finish the sentence with their own input.

Of course, this scenario requires a certain amount of preparation of the TM contents for the exercise. Figure 2 shows that every English segment in the TM has been amended to include the label *INTRODUCTION* at the start. This would indicate to students that the phrase can be used as an introductory phrase to start a paragraph. The use of uppercase is deliberate to distinguish the label from the actual phrase. Similarly, other labels could be PRESENTING AIMS, CONCLUSION, INTRODUCING AN OPPOSED VIEW, etc.

The TM in SDL Trados can also be used in this way. An example of the results obtained from searching an SDL Trados TM is shown in Figure 3.

Figure 3. Writing with SDL Trados

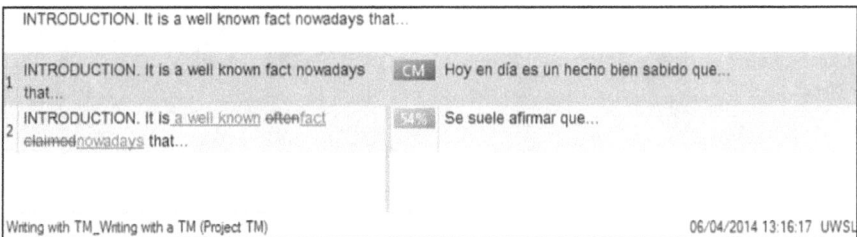

The automatic changes made by the software to the source text, as shown on the left in Figure 3, should not affect the writing task, as the label INTRODUCTION, placed at the start of the segment, remains unchanged and so do the contents of the target segment, which the students will decide whether they use in their writing task.

The lecturer need not be overwhelmed with the preparation of the TM contents in advance because this can be done by the students themselves using alignment. For example, the lecturer can simply direct the students to a bilingual resource such as the Collins Dictionary (2009), where the central pages contain a wealth of formulaic phrases in both languages. The students would simply need to create a separate file for each language with the required phrases and run both files through an alignment program. One such program to use in this scenario is SDL WinAlign. An example is shown in Figure 4.

Figure 4. Example of alignment

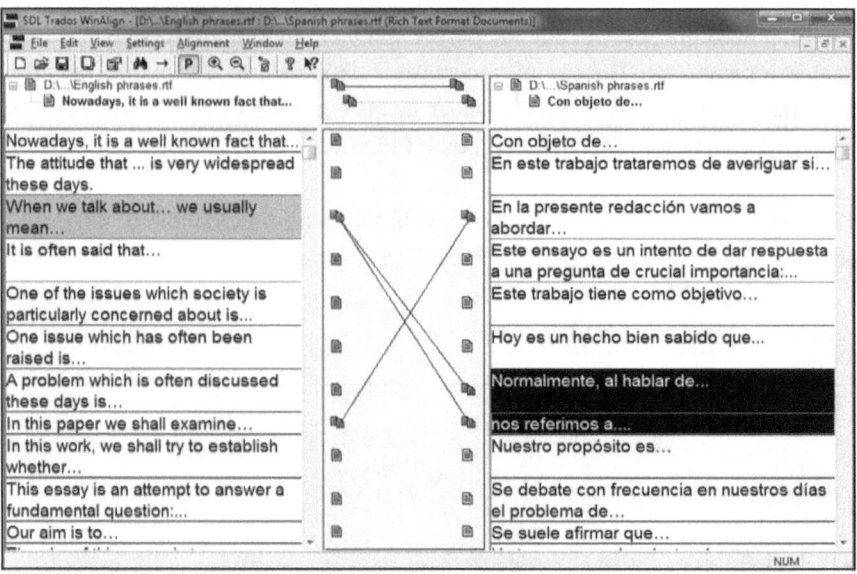

In Figure 4, the English phrases appear on the left, the Spanish on the right. Initially, the program will attempt to match the relevant phrases and it will display them joined with a dotted line. Dotted lines joining segments can easily be deleted by selecting the relevant option after right-clicking the icon of a particular segment. The suggestions can also be accepted by right-clicking and selecting the relevant option. In Figure 4, all dotted lines have been disconnected and several new re-connections are shown with a continuous line. An alignment exercise such as this could be used at all levels of language learning, as the level will depend on the contents to align, from single words to complete sentences or paragraphs.

Thus far we have assumed a one-to-one correspondence of segments but it may be that one segment matches two, as shown with the segments *Normalmente al hablar de...* and *nos referimos a...* in Figure 4. Both these segments correspond to one segment in English and can easily be joined by right-clicking the relevant option. Following the same procedure, a segment could be split if required.

Once all the segments are matched, the students can export the results as a TM, which they can then reuse in a variety of tasks as explained above. Déjà Vu X2 also has an alignment component, but it does not have the visual, drag-and-drop approach in SDL WinAlign to join the relevant segments which could be particularly helpful in language learning.

3.2. The termbase and language learning

In translation, the termbase is used to manage terminological tasks, a crucial aspect of the translation process. In language learning, the termbase can also support a crucial aspect: that of vocabulary acquisition, which in turn will support reading and writing tasks. The termbase facilities can vary widely from one CAT tool to another, but one good example of a useful terminological facility for language learning is that of SDL MultiTerm. An example of a terminological entry is shown in Figure 5.

An advantage of the SDL MultiTerm termbase over others, such as Déjà Vu X2, is that it allows the inclusion of multimedia information such as graphics, videos and sound files. The latter two, in particular, can be exploited in tasks such as pronunciation and role plays.

Figure 5. Example of terminological entry

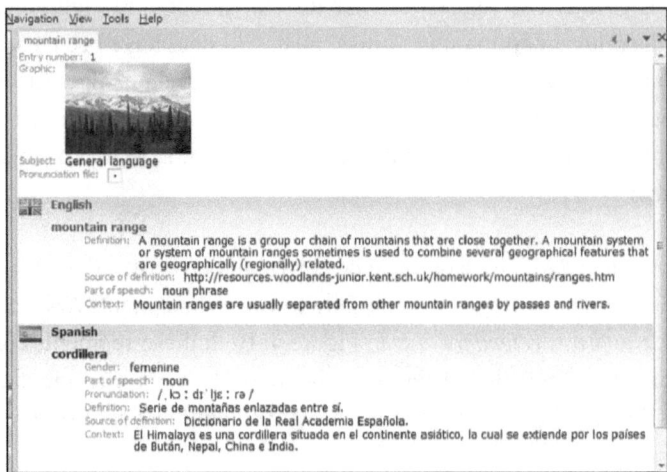

As with the TMs, termbases come empty to start with, and it is up to the user to decide whether a termbase should be bilingual or multilingual and which fields to include in each entry. Many of the fields often used in the termbases for translation, such as part-of-speech and definition can also be used in termbases for language learning. Learners may also benefit from fields such as grammatical information, e.g. regular/irregular verb, collocational restrictions, etc.

Termbases can be created by students themselves. In this case, much of the learning can take place by collecting the information needed and doing the necessary research to include the required information in the termbase. The learning, at any level, is further reinforced by consulting the termbase in subsequent tasks. Alternatively, lecturers can provide students with termbases to use in advanced reading or translation tasks.

4. Conclusion

This paper explored the possibilities of considering CAT tools as additional language learning tools, especially in universities or schools where CAT tools are already part of the curriculum, as both students and staff may already be familiar with the software. Some knowledge of the software is therefore assumed, although an effort has been made to present examples from components of CAT tools which can be accessed relatively quickly as standalone components.

The original idea of the suitability of CAT tools for technical translation based on lexical repetition can be recycled as repetition in language learning for the reinforcement of the learning. While it is not expected that CAT tools will ever replace other methods of language learning, this paper hopes to have shown that CAT tools can nevertheless co-exist with such methods and contribute to enhance the language learning experience.

References

Blake, R. J. (2013). *Brave new digital classroom. Technology and foreign language learning.* Georgetown: Georgetown University Press.
Bowker, L. (2002). *Computer-aided translation technology. A practical introduction.* Ottawa: University of Ottawa Press.
Collins Dictionary. (2009). *Spanish-English English-Spanish dictionary* (9th ed.). Glasgow: HarperCollins Publishers.
Fernández-Parra, M. (2014). *Formulaic expressions in computer-assisted translation.* Saarbrücken: Scholars' Press.
Hinkel, E. (Ed.). (2011). *Handbook of research in second language teaching and learning. Volume II*. Abingdon: Routledge.
Kenny, D. (1999). CAT tools in an academic environment: what are they good for? *Target, 11*(1), 65-82. Retrieved from http://dx.doi.org/10.1075/target.11.1.04ken
Olohan, M. (2011). Translators and translation technology: the dance of agency. *Translation studies, 4*(3), 342-357. Retrieved from http://dx.doi.org/10.1080/14781700.2011.589656
Quah, C. K. (2006). *Translation and technology.* Basingstoke: Palgrave Macmillan. Retrieved from http://dx.doi.org/10.1057/9780230287105
Rogers, M. (1996). Beyond the dictionary: the translator, the L2 learner and the computer. In G. Anderman & M. Rogers (Eds.), *Words, words, words. The translator and the language learner* (pp. 69-95). Clevedon: Multilingual Matters.

Widdowson, H. (2013). Skills and knowledge in language learning. In M. Byram & A. Hu (Eds.), *Routledge encyclopedia of language teaching and learning* (p. 631). Abingdon: Routledge.

Resources

Déjà Vu X2. Retrieved from www.atril.com
SDL Trados. Retrieved from http://www.sdl.com/products/sdl-multiterm/desktop.html

Author index

A
Araújo, Sílvia 12, 189
Arús Hita, Jorge 13, 213

B
Bárcena, Elena 13, 223
Bazo, Plácido 15, 269
Beltrán-Palanques, Vicente 17, 303
Bermúdez Bausela, Montserrat 20, 363
Bermudez-Gonzalez, Daniel 18, 327
Bosch, Emma 10, 163
Bueno Alastuey, Mª Camino 5, 27
Burset, Silvia 10, 163

C
Calderón-Nepamuceno, Dora 18, 327
Calle-Martínez, Cristina ii, viii, 1, 13, 233
Carranza, Mario 19, 339
Cassany, Daniel 6, 73

E
Escobar-Álvarez, Mª Ángeles 9, 153

F
Fernández-Parra, María 20, 385
Fumero, Dácil 15, 269

G
García Esteban, Soraya 7, 105
García Laborda, Jesús 5, 7, 16, 27, 105, 283
García-Moreno, Raúl-Ulises 18, 327
Gomes, Nelson 12, 189

Gómez, Susana 5, 39
González Otero, Rebeca 6, 83
González Romero, Rocío 16, 293
Gonzalez-Vera, Pilar 5, 51
Gutiérrez Pérez, Regina 7, 95

H
Hernandez-Nanclares, Nuria 15, 259

I
Ibáñez Moreno, Ana 14, 245

J
Jimenez-Munoz, Antonio 15, 259
Jordano, Maria 14, 245

K
Kukulska-Hulme, Agnes 13, 223

L
Lopes, Sérgio 12, 189

M
Magal Royo, Teresa 16, 283
Martín-Monje, Elena 9, 117
Miranda-Jiménez, Sabino 18, 327

P
Palacios Pablos, Andrés 18, 315
Pareja-Lora, Antonio ii, viii, 1, 13, 19, 233, 351
Patiniotaki, Emmanouela 11, 173
Pomposo Yanes, Lourdes 13, 233
Pujolà, Joan-Tomàs 10, 163

R

Rábano Llamas, Manuel 7, 105
Read, Timothy 13, 223
Rodríguez-Arancón, Pilar ii, viii, 1
Rodríguez, Romén 15, 269

S

Sánchez Ramos, María Del Mar 20, 375
Santos Costa, Giselda 12, 201

V

Vázquez Calvo, Boris 6, 73
Ventura, Patricia 9, 117
Vermeulen, Anna 14, 245
Vigier Moreno, Francisco J. 20, 375
Vilaplana Prieto, Cristina 6, 63
Vinagre Laranjeira, Margarita 9, 129

X

Xavier, Antonio Carlos 12, 201

Z

Zanoni, Greta 9, 141

www.ingramcontent.com/pod-product-compliance
Lightning Source LLC
Chambersburg PA
CBHW021133230426
43667CB00005B/100